Ruth

Themes and Issues in Biblical Studies
Series Editors:
Diana V. Edelman, University of Oslo
Philippe Guillaume, University of Berne

The edited volumes in this series are intended to complement traditional verse-by-verse commentaries and study bibles and introduce readers to the main themes and issues associated with the books forming the Hebrew Bible and the New Testament. The field of biblical studies has been in flux over the past half-century. The questions asked of the text are changing and with that, new theoretical frameworks are being applied to the texts that render some of the traditional methods and their underlying presuppositions unhelpful.

Consensus positions are being challenged as long-standing controversies are also being revisited in light of newer developments and evidence. Readers will gain insight into the current state of affairs relating to a specific book and the latest ideas being proposed, making the series the go-to source for cutting edge research.

Published
Deuteronomy: Outside the Box
Edited by Diana V. Edelman and Philippe Guillaume

Ruth

Edited by Rhiannon Graybill
and Philippe Guillaume

SHEFFIELD UK   BRISTOL CT

Published by Equinox Publishing Ltd.

UK: Office 415, The Workstation, 15 Paternoster Row, Sheffield, South Yorkshire S1 2BX

USA: ISD, 70 Enterprise Drive, Bristol, CT 06010

www.equinoxpub.com

First published in book form 2025
The chapters of this volume were first published online by Equinox Publishing Ltd Chapters 2–6 published 2023. Chapters 7–11 published 2024. Preface and Chapters 1 and 12–14 published 2025.

© Rhiannon Graybill, Philippe Guillaume and contributors 2025

All rights reserved. No part of this publication may be reproduced or transmitted in any form or by any means, electronic or mechanical, including photocopying, recording or any information storage or retrieval system, without prior permission in writing from the publishers.

British Library Cataloguing-in-Publication Data

A catalogue record for this book is available from the British Library.

ISBN-13	978 1 80050 693 0	(hardback)
	978 1 80050 757 9	(paperback)
	978 1 80050 694 7	(ePDF)
	978 1 80050 717 3	(ePub)

Library of Congress Cataloging-in-Publication Data

Names: Graybill, Rhiannon, 1984- editor | Guillaume, Philippe, 1960- editor

Title: Ruth / edited by Rhiannon Graybill and Philippe Guillaume.
Description: Sheffield ; Bristol : Equinox, 2025. | Series: Themes and issues in biblical studies | Includes bibliographical references and index. | Summary: "The Book of Ruth is an all-time Bible favorite. This volume maps an uncompromising way forward between patriarchy and advocacy"-- Provided by publisher.
Identifiers: LCCN 2025011725 | ISBN 9781800506930 hardback | ISBN 9781800507579 paperback | ISBN 9781800506947 pdf | ISBN 9781800507173 epub
Subjects: LCSH: Bible. Ruth--Criticism, interpretation, etc.
Classification: LCC BS1315.52 .R88 2025 | DDC 222/.3506--dc23/eng/20250724
LC record available at https://lccn.loc.gov/2025011725

Typeset by Sparks – www.sparkspublishing.com

Contents

Preface: Tips on How to Use This Volume   vii
    Rhiannon Graybill and Philippe Guillaume

1. Ruth or Routh? Introduction to the Textual Analysis of the Book of Ruth   1
    Philippe Guillaume, Rhiannon Graybill and William Krisel

2. One Plus One Equals Three: The Economics of Land Shares According to Boaz   31
    Philippe Guillaume

3. The Torah in Ruth?   64
    Philippe Guillaume

4. Reading Ruth Canonically as the Central Panel of a Literary Triptych   84
    William Krisel

5. After the Idyll Ends: Ruth and the Uses of Disappointment   107
    Rhiannon Graybill

6. Obed, Son of Boaz, an Israelite: Should Ruth be Read through the Lens of Deuteronomy's Laws about Moabites?   126
    Jonathan Thambyrajah

7. Naomi and Ruth: A Tale of Two Wives?   140
    William Krisel

8. It's a Charming Story of Faithful Living, but …: Interpretive Tensions in the Book of Ruth   162
    Rebecca Lindsay

9. Wisdom in a Time of Prose: Form, Function, and the Book of Ruth   190
    Laura Quick

10.	Ruth and Moab: Abjection and Intimacy *Peter Sabo and Francis Landy*	208
11.	The Moral Content of Caring for Oneself (First) *Jennifer J. Williams*	231
12.	Who is the Central Character in the Book of Ruth? *Anthony H. Dekker and John T. Dekker*	254
13.	Is Ruth a Rapist? The Sexual Victimization of Boaz *Jennifer Lehmann*	274
14.	The Story of Ruth according to Peter Comestor *Sara Moscone*	291

Author Index	305
Biblical Index	309
Subject Index	314

Preface: Tips on How to Use This Volume

Rhiannon Graybill and Philippe Guillaume

Though a mere four chapters, the book of Ruth is a fascinating text. Ruth, the woman who gives her name to the book, is a compelling character, confronted by adversity at every turn and yet still, somehow, able to find a happy ending (or is it?). Naomi and Boaz, too, draw our interest, even as certain key details remain unclear. (Why does Naomi say nothing when Ruth pledges herself to her? Does Boaz wish to marry Ruth, or to marry her to a kinsman? What happens on the threshing floor?) The book pleases and delights first-time readers, even as it rewards careful study and rereading. At the same time, the book of Ruth is well suited to readings from a wide range of hermeneutical approaches: textual criticism, literary criticism, economic history, sociological analysis, feminist reading, queer reading, and postcolonial and decolonial approaches.

This Ruth volume belongs to the Themes and Issues in Biblical Studies series. The only changes between the e-versions and hardback and paperback versions are some added cross-references to other chapters in the collection when necessary, as well as indexes to facilitate the reassessment of the status quo of entrenched hypotheses that have become factoids and of ideas that have passed their "sell-by" date as to produce a line-by-line commentary. As is the case with this series, most of the chapters of the volume have been available as e-publications shortly following their completion: https://www.equinoxpub.com/home/themes-issues-biblical-studies/. Because of this rolling publishing model, the volume is not organized in thematic sections. Instead, the chapters are ordered according to the time they were completed and e-published, thus rewarding our authors with timely publication.

The book of Ruth is filled with movement across borders and to new homelands. We suggest the following itineraries to move through the present volume. The first itinerary (A) is organized thematically and divides the chapters into three groups. The second itinerary (B) shows how chapters can be read in pairs, which is especially useful for a weekly or biweekly class schedule. Both itineraries offer new perspectives on the book of Ruth.

Itinerary A

The first itinerary divides the chapters into three groups, focused on literary and thematic approaches (Group 1), historical, economic, and ethical matters (Group 2), and textual considerations (Group 3).

Group 1: Chapters 5, 8, 9, 10, 12 and 13

Chapter 10, "Ruth and Moab: Abjection and Intimacy" serves as a first approach to Ruth by offering a literary reading of the book as a whole. Here, Peter Sabo and Francis Landy draw out the intricate literary and poetic structure of the work. Next, in Chapter 12 Anthony H. Dekker and John T. Dekker use social network analysis to set forth the question that serves as the title, "Who is the Central Character in the Book of Ruth?". They demonstrate that the main character shifts in each chapter: Naomi in Ruth 1, Ruth in Ruth 2 and 3, and Boaz in Ruth 4.

With the three main protagonists in place, readers are ready to face the array of portrayals of the heroes of the tale to get beyond the traditional idyllic readings of the tale and uncover its ideological premises. Feminist readings have already denounced the way patriarchalism used the figures of Naomi, Ruth, and Boaz to bolster its social hegemony. In line with this approach, in Chapter 8 ("It's a Charming Story of Faithful Living, but…"), Rebecca Lindsay challenges bucolic assumptions about the book and calls on readers to notice the exploitative dynamics between characters that underlie a seemingly happy story. Chapter 5 continues the discussion with "After the Idyll Ends: Ruth and the Uses of Disappointment." Rhiannon Graybill draws on work on queer feeling and affect to argue for the importance of disappointment in reading the book of Ruth. Jennifer Lehmann goes even further by asking in Chapter 13, "Is Ruth a Rapist?".

Finally, Chapter 9, "Wisdom in a Time of Prose: Form, Function, and the Book of Ruth," takes up the question of genre, and of the book's relationship to the so-called "wisdom literature." Laura Quick argues that Ruth can be understood as a wisdom text – but one that destabilizes traditional wisdom tenets and complicates the genre.

Group 2: Chapters 2, 3, 6, 11, 14

The bargaining between Boaz and Almony Polony at the gate of Bethleem (Ruth 4:1–12) involves a web of economic matters – land tenure, marriage, dowries, inheritance – that are presupposed but never fully explained. Therefore, exegetes have long turned to legal passages from the Torah to explain away what seems to be taken for granted. In Chapter 14 ("The Story of Ruth according to Peter Comestor") Sara Moscone shows that this reading strategy goes back as far as the twelfth century CE if not earlier, as exemplified by Peter Comestor's *Historia Scholastica*, a biblical rewriting that unites biblical paraphrase and historical exegesis. Against this entrenched interpretative approach, Chapter 6 ("Obed, Son of Boaz, An Israelite") shows that the book of Ruth is read more clearly without imposing the framework of laws regulating intermarriage. Jonathan Thambyrajah demonstrates that Obed can clearly be identified as an Israelite rather than a Moabite like his mother.

Philippe Guillaume's two chapters gesture in the same direction. In Chapter 3 ("The Torah in Ruth?") he underlines two dangers of the common recourse to the so-called laws of land redemption (Lev 25), Levirate marriage (Deut 25, gleanings Lev 13; 23; Deut 24) and the inheritance of Zelophehad's daughters (Num 27; 36). Since the conditions stipulated in these legal texts do not fit the situations in which Ruth, Naomi, and Boaz find themselves, Chapter 2 ("One Plus One Equals Three") takes up Naomi's sale of Elimelech's field to place the matter of land shares and a widow's inheritance rights at the heart of the tale, which reveal Naomi and Boaz to be tricksters.

Far from reducing Ruth to a sordid tale of greed, in Chapter 11, "The Moral Content of Caring for Oneself (First)," Jennifer Williams reads the book of Ruth together with Michel Foucault's famous notion of "the care of the self," arguing that Ruth's actions are best understood through this framework.

Group 3: Chapters 4, 7, 1

Chapters 4, 7, and 1 constitute a third cluster focusing on the Greek translation of Ruth and its position in the Septuagint, where it follows Judges. William Krisel's Chapter 4, "Reading Ruth Canonically as the Central Panel of a Literary Triptych," addresses the placement of Ruth in the Christian Old Testament/Septuagint (between Judges and 1 Samuel) and the Hebrew Bible (in the *Ketuvim* or Writings). The Greek canon likely reflects an earlier version of the Hebrew canon. In Chapter 7 ("Naomi and Ruth: A Tale of Two Wives?") he analyzes the variants in Ruth 3 to recover clear traces of an earlier version of the tale that had Naomi seconding

Ruth on tricking Boaz on the threshing floor. This naturally leads to Chapter 1 ("Ruth or Routh?"), where the fundamentals of the scientific analysis of the different texts of Ruth from the Dead Sea scrolls, Hebrew and Greek traditions is taken up.

Itinerary B

Alternatively, some chapters may be used in pairs.

On genre, Chapters 4 and 9 oppose the place of Greek Ruth between Judges and Samuel and Hebrew Ruth as a wisdom text among the Writings.

Regarding personal interest, Chapter 2 reads Naomi and Boaz as tricksters, while Chapter 11 goes even further to justify their doings as "self-care." In both cases, the notion of sacrificial love is challenged?

Considering the "bed trick" on the threshing floor, the legitimate question of whether Ruth may be viewed as a rapist (Chapter 13) is deepened in Chapter 7 by introducing the role played by Naomi in the affair.

More technical and challenging, the discussions of the *ketiv-qeres* in Ruth 3:3–4 in Chapter 7 and Ruth 4:5 in Chapter 2 open new horizons for Ruth scholarship. First is the challenge of the often-assumed primacy of the Hebrew text over the Greek. Second is how readers resist what is actually written in the Hebrew text (the so-called *ketiv*) and develop suggestions about what should be read or heard instead. Third is how resistance to what is written in the supposedly more reliable Hebrew text becomes entrenched in a reading tradition that leads the majority of commentators to prefer what is *not* written (the so-called *qere*) against the first principle of textual criticism. How misleading "the consensus" can be!

After textual issues, intertextuality is covered by Chapters 3 (Torah), 6 (Obed) and 10 (Moab).

Examples of current critical approaches are found in Chapter 5 (queer reading) and Chapter 8 (post-colonial reading).

Finally, whereas Chapter 12 reveals the complexity of the tale in which each scene foregrounds a different character, Chapter 14 reveals that most of the questions that continue to challenge Ruth scholarship were already discussed in twelfth-century Western Europe.

In whatever way this volume is used, you can expect to be informed about key issues and themes in Ruth and know something of the history of debate, learn some novel solutions, and walk away feeling much better informed about past and present understandings of the significance of the book in its originating culture and its ongoing potential to influence contemporary culture.

About the Editors

Rhiannon Graybill is Marcus M. and Carole M. Weinstein & Gilbert M. and Fannie S. Rosenthal Chair of Jewish Studies at the University of Richmond, USA. She is the author of *Texts after Terror: Rape, Sexual Violence, and the Hebrew Prophets* (Oxford, 2021) and *Are We Not Men?: Unstable Masculinity in the Hebrew Prophets* (Oxford, 2016) and multiple articles on gender, sexuality, and biblical texts. She has also co-authored two books with John Kaltner and Steven L. McKenzie: *Jonah: A New Translation with Notes and Commentary* (Yale University Press, 2023) and *What Are They Saying about the Book of Jonah?* (Paulist Press, 2024). At present, Graybill is working on a new book about the female body in the Hebrew Bible.

Philippe Guillaume is Lecturer at the University of Berne. In 2024, he coedited with Diana Edelman *The Old Testament Hebrew Scriptures in Five Minutes* and *Deuteronomy: Outside the Box,* the inaugural volume of the Themes and Issues in Biblical Studies series, both at Equinox.

Chapter 1
Ruth or Routh? Introduction to the Textual Analysis of the Book of Ruth

Philippe Guillaume, Rhiannon Graybill and William Krisel

Abstract

This chapter discusses the numerous textual variants in Ruth attested by four Dead Sea scrolls, the Septuagint and the *ketiv-qere* notes in the Masoretic Hebrew text edited in the *Biblia Hebraica Stuttgartiensis* and now in the *Biblia Hebraica Quinta*. The aim is to warn that decisions regarding which reading is preferable reflect a venerable reading tradition that often stands at loggerheads with actual textual witnesses. The variants confirm the existence of alternative plots and author characterizations that modern translations of Ruth tend to erase.

Keywords: Dead Sea scrolls, Septuagint, *ketiv-qere*, Naomi, Boaz, textual criticism, BHS, BHQ, book of Ruth

Scholarly studies of the book of Ruth begin with an analysis of the story in Hebrew. The first step in this process is determining, as best as we can, what the original text actually said. This process is somewhat complicated, because multiple variants exist. These include the Hebrew Masoretic text (the standard starting point for Hebrew interpretation), the Dead Sea Scrolls (a collection of manuscripts discovered in the twentieth century, which include a slightly different Hebrew text of Ruth), and the Septuagint, the Greek translation of the Hebrew text undertaken during the Hellenistic period. Careful study reveals that the Septuagint is based on a Hebrew manuscript tradition very close to – but not identical to – the Masoretic text. For this reason, "it is methodologically sound to focus on the Greek text" (de Waard 1973, 500–501) as a key source for reconstructing the Hebrew original. Adding to the complexity, there are also variant readings preserved *within* the Masoretic text. Known as *ketiv-qere*, these are indications in the text that one version of a word is written (*ketiv*) but it should be read aloud as something else.

In the present moment, dwelling on the intricacies of Hebrew variants may feel quaint. After all, countless modern commentaries on the Bible are easily available in English and seem to promise to bypass the efforts of a minimal mastery of Hebrew and Greek. Modern commentators, however, are liable to the same temptations as ancient copyists and translators: personal preferences and reading tradition based on the number of manuscripts, while the renown granted to previous commentators can also function as a wet blanket, covering over minority views. Furthermore, the variants confirm the existence of alternative plots that modern translations of Ruth tend to erase. For all these reasons, it is worth beginning reading Ruth with a consideration of the text.

The approach we utilize here is known as "historico-critical exegesis" (exegesis simply means "interpretation.") Historico-critical exegesis seeks to recover the original – or at least the "more original" – form of a text (the original may lie beyond recovery, however hard we try). A basic insight of this process is that texts consist of multiple layers. Uncovering these layers and seeking the oldest is a process of diachronic interpretation, which can be contrasted with synchronic interpretation. The latter deals with the received text or the final form of the text. Scholars have developed a set of tools to help uncover the layers of a text and recover, as much as possible, an original.

This chapter provides basic guidance to the study of the textual versions of Ruth. Never before were there so many convenient tools to identify variants, thanks to the critical apparatus of the standard critical editions of the Masoretic text of the Hebrew Bible, first the *Biblia Hebraica Kittel* (BHK 1906–1937), then the revised *Biblia Hebraica Stuttgartensia* (BHS 1967–1998), and now the *Biblia Hebraica Quinta* (BHQ 2004 for the *Megillot*). Yet, their technical jargon and Latin sigla are daunting for anyone entering the field of Ruth studies.

A few additional comments on our method: we leave aside the information supplied by the Hebrew accents and the massora (marks added by the Masoretes) and abstain from giving precedence and preference to any particular reading. We believe that future advances depend on the ability of members of a larger audience to make up their own mind and not to grant final authority to the opinion expressed in the critical notes. The *BHQ* is a step forward compared to the *BHK* and *BHS*, as it adds comments in plain English on some of the notes of the critical apparatus (for Ruth see de Waard 2004, 51*–56*). These comments decipher the technical sigla used in the critical notes printed under the Hebrew text (de Waard 2004, 3–10) and justify the editor's opinion on the priority to be granted to the different readings. The scholarship of the learned editors is precious, but the editors inevitably remain interpreters as much as the ancient copyists and translators, the fruits of whose labors we enjoy today.

As an invitation to benefit from the available exegetical source, we present here a compendium of the existing variants in the three most crucial sources (Dead Sea scrolls, Septuagint and Masoretic text) followed by an analysis of the most significant variants (in our eyes). To avoid getting bogged down by a mass of details, non-specialists can skip sections 1–5 below and first consider the conclusions in section 6.

1. Qumran variants

The first set of variants we wish to discuss come from the Qumran texts or Dead Sea Scrolls (the two terms are used interchangeably). The earliest witnesses of Ruth come from two caves opposite Khirbet Qumran on the western shore of the Dead Sea. Table 1 lists the four Ruth fragments.

In addition to these fragments of three scrolls, MS 5441 from the privately held Schøyen collection in Norway has recently been published. It is a small leather fragment (5.7 × 4.1 cm) piece allegedly coming from Cave 4 and presented as 4Q(?)Ruth (Torleif 2016b). How it reached this collection is a well-guarded secret as it involves legal matters regarding antiquity trafficking. The scroll owner's version of the acquisition does not mention MS 5441 and repeatedly states the requests made by previous owners to remain anonymous (Schøyen 2016). The scholarly publication of such unprovenanced artifacts has become a major issue because it increases the commercial value of such objects and thus fosters the looting of archaeological sites through illegal excavations, antiquities trafficking, and the production of forgeries (Muscarella 2000).

Table 1: Ruth in the Dead Sea scrolls published in the series Discoveries in the Judean Desert (DJD)

Scroll	Publication	Contents	Plate	Approx. date	Variants
2Q16Ruth[a]	DJD III	2:13–3:2; 3:4–8; 4:3–4	XIV	50–0 BCE	none
2Q17Ruth[b]	DJD III	3:13–18	XV	50 BCE	3:14–15
4Q104Ruth[a]	DJD XVI	1:1–12	XXIV	50 BCE	1:2
4Q105Ruth[b]	DJD XVI	1:1–6, 12–15	XXIV	50 BCE–50 CE	1:3, 12

Furthermore, the contents of MS 5441 suggest that it is a forgery, despite the fact that the leather itself may be old (Torleif 2016a). The first complete word of Line 1 (מודע) reflects the *qere* of the MT of Ruth 2:1 (see below). Then, the first letters of line 2 are precisely the second part of the name of Naomi's husband "Elimelech" in the MT, while it is "Abimelech" in the LXX (Bonanno 2021). The first two letters of the name are missing. Any traces of the second letter, either the *lamed* of Elimelech or the *beth* of Abimelech, would have presented fresh evidence in favor of the MT or of the LXX, raising a sensation and calling for in-depth analysis of the leather and of the ink. Well acquainted with textual and legal issues, forgers today privilege less sensational discoveries that nevertheless find enough buyers. Hence, line 3 reflects a similar caution with the particle הנ against הואin the MT, a mere orthographic variant of little consequence.

The scholars who published the fragment play it safe by stating that "even small fragments in The Schøyen Collection and the American collections preserve textual variants suggested by the editors of *BHK* and *BHS*" as well as the "many 'hesitant hands,'" and the mix of "earlier and later scribal features… may cast doubt on the authenticity of a fragment" (Torleif 2016a, 53). Though the script is semiformal "but hesitant" and "exhibits some but not all of the late Herodian features," the specialist is confident enough to conclude that "MS 5441 was copied around the middle of the first century AD" (Langlois 2016, 107), despite having himself warned about the great uncertainty attached to dating on the basis of paleographic studies (Langlois 2016, 79).

These features cast enough doubts to justify the rejection of Schøyen MS 5441 from the list of Ruth witnesses from the Dead Sea scrolls. Scholars are often tempted to associate their names with the first publication of such artifacts, the argument being that the new information they present is too valuable to be lost for the scholarly community, thus justifying the role of private collectors who are naturally keen to have scholars contribute to the "demonstrable role of private collections in preserving our precious and shared human heritage in an uncertain world" (Schøyen Collection 2020).

As is the case with many Dead Sea scrolls, their fragmentary state limits the new evidence that can be gained from them (White Crawford 2024).

Thus 4Q(?)Ruth can be safely ignored, and the available evidence remains so far that used by the BHQ. The evidence provided by the Dead Sea Scrolls is summarized as follows:

> Sometimes, the Qumran evidence is so fragmentary that almost nothing can be concluded, e.g., in 2:23. Where it can be deciphered, it frequently supports M (1:14; 2:14; 2:20; 3:7). Occasionally, the Qumran

materials support versional evidence over against M, as 2QRuth[b] in 3:14, and, perhaps 4QRuth[a] in the case of 1:9. In some rare cases, a plus is found which is not shared by any witness, e.g., the reading שם of 2QRuth[b] in 3:15. (de Waard 2004, 5*)

The key issue is whether or not a case such as 2QRuth[b] in 3:15 should be ignored because it is not supported by any other witness. Does it deserve special attention precisely because it may potentially be the sole available hint to an alternative form of the Ruth story? We propose yes. Divergent texts were not necessarily available to the ancient Greek translators. If and when several were available, the translators could have selected the form they preferred. Or they could have chosen to "improve" the text according to their preference. All this suggests that given the century-long process of transmission and interpretation the story went through, even variants attested by a sole textual witness deserve attention.

Table 2 lists the cases when the DSS fragments are evoked in the critical apparatus of the *BHQ*. Only the cases where the reading is unclear (ש[ם] in 1:2; *two sons* in 1:12; מה in 3:16) or too fragmentary (1:15; 2:23) are ignored.

In addition to the technical term "*Vorlage*," a German term that designates the text used by translators, we use the following sigla:

- G = Greek text printed in the *Biblia Graeca Septuaginta* (Rahlfs 2006)
- M = the Hebrew Masoretic text printed in *BHS* (Elliger and Rudolph 1997) and *BHQ* (de Waard 2004)
- S = Syriac Bible or Peshitta (Lee 1826; 1979)
- T = Targum of Ruth (Beattie 1994; Levine 1973)
- V = Vulgate (Weber and Gryson 2007)

Table 3 doubles the eight cases considered significant in de Waard (2004, 5*), with eighteen cases where the DSS fragments deserve attention, despite their fragmentary state.

Table 2: Percentage of whole words preserved in Qumran Ruth scrolls

	Number of preserved whole words at Qumran	Total number of words in the relevant verses in M	Preserved whole words at Qumran
2Q16Ruth[a]	89	318	28%
2Q17Ruth[b]	15	98	15%
4Q104Ruth[a]	59	174	34%
4Q105Ruth[b]	14	151	9%

Table 3: Significant references to DSS scrolls in BHQ Ruth

Ruth	Manuscript	Interpretation
1:1a	4Q104Ruth[a]	= M "in the *days*" vs "in the judging" of the judges G
1:1b	4Q104Ruth[a-b]	= M some G V T "*two*" sons vs "sons" in some G S
1:2	4Q104Ruth[a]	They habited/settled (וישבו) vs "they were" M G T; "they delayed" V
1:5	4Q104Ruth[a]	= M V T vs G S where the sons die after Elimelech as in v. 3
1:9	4Q104Ruth[a]	V supports 4Q104's קולם reading of M's -קולן as an antiquated feminine dual
1:14	4Q105Ruth[b]	= M vs + "and she returned to her people" in the versions
2:14	2Q16Ruth[a]	ויצבט "he picked up" = M vs ויצבר "he piled up" followed by the versions
2:18	2Q16Ruth[a]	בשבעה "by her fill" vs משבעה M G "from her fill"
2:19	2Q16Ruth[a]	Blank space betweenהעשתה and שם, but large enough to fit the words in M
2:21a	2Q16Ruth[a]	= M "Ruth the Moabite" vs only "Ruth" G V S
2:21b	2Q16Ruth[a]	= M הנערים "young men" vs G παιδάριον "children" (neuter) and some G mss κορασίων "girls"
2:22	2Q16Ruth[a]	נערותו "his young women" vs M נערותיו "their young women"
2:23	2Q16Ruth[a]	ללוט? "to conceal, cover?" vs ללקט "to glean" M G S T
3:3	2Q16Ruth[a]	שמלתיך "garments" = *qere* V S T vs *ketiv* שמלתך "garment" G
3:7	2Q16Ruth[a]	= M OL V S וישת "and he drank" omitted in G
3:14	2Q17Ruth[b]	מרגלותיו "feet" = M *qere* and versions vs "foot or male organ?" M *ketiv*
3:14	2Q17Ruth[b]	= V S "she came" vs "the woman came" M and "a woman came" in G
3:15	2Q17Ruth[b]	+ שם "there" after "he measured" vs M G V T

2. LXX Variants

The second set of variants to consider involve differences between the Hebrew and the Septuagint (abbreviated LXX) Greek translation (Table 4). Bonanno (2024, 55–72) lists the differences G displays against M, leaving aside the complex matter of the different texts and families of texts of the Greek text, for which Quast (2006) is a crucial resource. Additions and omissions in the Greek against the Hebrew can result from the translation of a different form of Hebrew text (i.e., a different *Vorlage*), from errors of the translator, or from the translator's attempt to clarify a word or a passage that did not make sense or which sense was obvious enough but which the translator preferred to avoid. Given the closeness of the Greek text of Ruth, the translator did not "allow much room for exegetical embellishment" (Bons 2015, 124). Nevertheless, G presents some significant variants.

Table 4: Variants in the LXX

Ruth	Variants	Interpretation
1:2–4:9	Ἀβειμέλεχ ≠ אלמלך	G Abimelech vs M Elimelech
1:5–6	ἀνδρὸς αὐτῆς… υἱῶν αὐτῆς ≠ ילדיה ואישה	G her husband and her two sons vs M her two children and her husband
1:12	γενηθῆναί με ἀνδρὶ ≠ הייתי הלילה לאיש	G to be with a man vs M to be with a man *tonight*.
1:14	+ καὶ ἐπέστρεψεν εἰς τὸν λαὸν αὐτῆς	G adds "and she returned to her people"
1:20–21	ὁ ἱκανός ≠ שדי but ≈ ש די	G the Sufficient One vs M El Shaddai
1:22	Νωεμιν καὶ Ρουθ < נעמי ורות… עמה	G omits "with her"
2:2–3:18	θύγατερ ≠ בתי	G daughter vs M my daughter
2:5–6	νεᾶνις ≈ נערה	young woman
2:7	ἀγρός ≠ בית	G field vs M house
2:8	κορασίων μου ≈ נערתי	my girls = 2:22–23; 3:2
2:13	ἐγὼ ἔσομαι ὡς μία τῶν παιδισκῶν σου ≠ אני לא אהיה כאחת שפחתיך	G I shall be like one of your maidservants vs M I am *not* as one of your maidservants
2:14a	Ἤδη ὥρα ≈ לעת	It is already time
2:14b	ἐβούνισεν ≠ ויצבט	G Boos heaped vs M he picked up
2:16	βαστάξατε αὐτῇ καί γε παραβάλλοντες παραβαλεῖτε αὐτῇ ἐκ τῶν βεβουνισμένων > תשלו לה מן הצבתים	G adds "By all means carry for her, and even throw aside something for her from the bundles"
2:20	τῶν ἀγχιστευόντων ἡμᾶς ≠ מגאלנו	G our redeemers vs M our redeemer
3:3	σὺ δὲ λούσῃ > ורחצת	G you shall bathe vs M and bathe
3:7	καὶ ἔφαγεν < ויאכל וישת	G omits he drank
3:11	φυλὴ λαοῦ μου ≈ שער עמי	G *clan* of my people = M gate of his people
4:3	δέδοται ≈ מכרה	G given vs M traded
4:4	ἀγχιστεύεις ≠ יגאל	G legitimate heir vs M redeemer
4:5	καὶ αὐτὴ κτήσασθαί σε δεῖ ≠ קניתי	G it is necessary for you vs M I acquired
4:7	τοῦτο τὸ δικαίωμα > וזאת	G adds the statute in former times
4:8	Κτῆσαι σεαυτῷ τὴν ἀγχιστείαν μου > קנה לך	G adds my right of inheritance
4:11	ὁ λαὸς οἱ ἐν τῇ πύλῃ Μάτυρες. καὶ οἱ πρεσβύτεροι < העם… וזקנים עדים	in G only the people who were at the gate say "We are witnesses" and its the elders who bless Boaz's union with Ruth.

3. Other Witnesses

The so-called Peshitta in Christian Aramaic or Syriac is one of the earliest translations of the Bible after the LXX (Lee 1979). It provides an important number of "coincidences" with the Greek, though the translator did not use the Greek "in any consistent way" and "in many instances" the Syriac stands alone (de Waard 2004, 7*).

The Targum of Ruth is a translation in Aramaic. It preserves numerous editorial additions that thus prevent ascribing a single date to the entire work.

> Whatever the time of origin of T may have been, its underlying Hebrew text is clearly that which is known to us from M. It is further characterized by much additional material that makes it twice as long as M. The additional material can sometimes be characterized as explicit information (3:11, 14; 4:7) and sometimes as a midrash (1:9). (de Waard 2004, 7*)

A "midrash" is an early form of biblical commentary, but this has little implications for us because the Hebrew text underlying T are in all cases that of the *qeres* (see below).

4. *Ketiv-Qere* in the Masoretic Text

The technical term *ketiv-qere* is the abbreviation of the Hebrew phrase "*ketiv we lo qere* (written but not read)," which designates notes in the margins of the Hebrew text to indicate letters or words that the authors of such notes thought should be read differently from the way they are written (Gordis 1937). In other words, the Masoretic scribes faithfully recorded the text which they were copying and disclosed in their marginal notes the changes to the text which they were proposing. The MT is thus like a "critical edition" of the Bible that indicates variant readings of the text. However, the MT became the "received text" in rabbinic Judaism, which viewed the *ketiv* (the older version) as incorrect and the *qere* (the newer version) as correct. This bias in favor of the newer MT readings was taken over by translators of the Hebrew Bible into modern languages. In our view, the older *qere* version of the text "as written" serves as a valuable text critical tool that has too often been overlooked by modern commentators of Ruth.

In the BHS, the current scholarly edition of the Hebrew Bible, these notes are signaled by a small circle above the word, although *not all* such circles indicate a *ketiv-qere*. When they do, they refer to a note in the margin with a Hebrew *qoph* (ק) with the suggested reading written above or beside it. The *BHS* usually provides what the modern editor considers the preferable reading in a footnote.

It is important to remember that the vocalization indicated in the text, i.e., the *ketiv*, is that of the *qere*, i.e., the way the Rabbis considered the word should be read. For instance, Ruth 3:3 displays two *ketiv-qere*s. The first concerns the word שמלתך with the vowels indicating how it should be read. The BHS consonants indicate the relevant consonants above the letter ק in the margin as שמלתיך, i.e., with an additional *yod* to indicate that the singular "clothe" should be read as "clothes." The second *ketiv-qere* is found two words later for וירדתי. This time above the second ק one finds וירדת to indicate that the *ty-* ending of the *ketiv* must not be taken as a first singular person "I shall go down" but should be read as indicated by the vocalization under it as a *te-* ending, a second person singular feminine, "you shall go down," obviously a major difference, which we discuss below.

Another situation arises when the Rabbis wanted us to read a word that is totally absent in the manuscripts. Hence, instead of a matter of reading what is written differently, it is a case of reading what is not written at all. The relevant vowels are thus printed under a blank space standing for the consonants indicated by the *qere* in the margin. Thus, in the margin one needs to distinguish אלי among the various small Hebrew letters to figure out that the vowels under the blank space are meant to be those of the three consonants אלי, thus "to me".

Table 5: *ketiv-qere* in the BHS of Ruth

Ruth	*ketiv* and parallels	*qere* and parallels
1:8	יעשה Yhwh will deal kindly with you T	יעש May Yhwh deal kindly with you. G V S
2:1	מידע Boaz as acquaintance	מודע Boaz as *kinsman* G V S T
3:3	שמלתך Put on your cloak! G	שמלתיך Put on your *cloaks*! V S T 2Q16Rutha
3:3	וירדתי I will go down	וירדת You will go down G V S T
3:4	ושכבתי I will lie down	ושכבת You will lie down G V S T
3:5	everything you said ø G V	אלי everything you said *to me* S T
3:12	כי אם because if I were a redeemer	כי because I *am* a redeemer G V S T
3:14	מרגלתו his foot	מרגלותיו his *feet* G V S T 2Q17Ruthb
3:14	בטרום she got up before = 2Q17Ruthb	G V S T read) ובטרם no difference in meaning(
3:17	for he said V	אלי for he said *to me* G T
4:4	ואדע I will know G S	ואדעה I *may* know OL V T
4:5	קניתי I acquire	קניתה you acquire G V S T
4:6	לגאול I cannot redeem	לגאל I cannot acquire

In most cases, a footnote in BHS and BHQ helps to decipher the *ketiv-qere*, though using basic Latin terms that take some effort to become familiar with.

Table 5 shows that the number of issues rises as the plot thickens. In the first two chapters, the proposed readings are of little consequence, but ch. 3 presents alternatives regarding the amount of clothing, the involvement of Naomi on the threshing floor (see Chapter 7 in this volume), and Boaz's status as redeemer. In ch. 4, the divergences impact the nature of the transaction (see Chapter 2 in this volume). In most cases, the versions agree with the *qere*, which can hardly be a coincidence (see below).

5. Interpreting the Significant Variants

Ruth 1:1a

From the very beginning, the Hebrew and Greek diverge. The Hebrew MT begins "and it came to pass in the *days* of the judges' judging," while the Greek (G) reads "and it came to pass when the Judges judged." Is the absence of "in the days of" in G significant? In considering this question, one point of comparison is Judg 19:1 and 21:25, which also refer to "the days of the judges judging"; there, G does not omit "the days" found in M.

Why then is "the days" missing in Ruth 1:1a? One possibility is that the omission of "in the days of" in Ruth 1:1 merely reflects a stylistic difference between the translators of Judges and Ruth. A second possibility is that the phrase "the days of the Judges" points to what is commonly referred to as a specific *time period* of the Judges. Here, the canonical location of the book of Ruth may be relevant. In the Greek Bible (followed by most English translations), Ruth comes immediately after the book of Judges, suggesting a possible temporal connection. However, in the Hebrew Bible, Ruth is part of the Writings, and more specifically one of the five *Megillot* or "scrolls" (Ruth, Song of Songs, Ecclesiastes/Qoheleth, Lamentations, Esther). This Hebrew placement indicates that Ruth was not conceived from the beginning as the sequel to Judges.

G is in fact the sole textual witness to omit the word "days" against all the other witnesses, including 4Q104Ruth[a]. T (1:1) even identifies Boaz with the minor judge Ibzan of Bethlehem (Judg 12:9) to reinforce the connection between Judges and Ruth. Therefore, the evidence leads to the counterintuitive suggestion that G's phrase "In the judging of the judges" is the sole witness of an incipit (or opening) of Ruth that either precedes the invention of the period of the Judges or ignores it. Contrary to G, the Hebrew text begins in Ruth 1:1 with a double incipit: "It happened (*wayehiy*) in the days..." followed by "A famine happened (*wayehiy*)". This could suggest that an earlier (unattested) version in Hebrew began with "and it came to pass that there was a famine in the land..." and that the reference to the days of the judges' judging was added secondarily, in order to provide a very ancient setting to a much more recent tale. The linking of "and it came to pass that there was a famine in the land" and "in the days of" could be based on Gen 26:1, which contains both of these elements. Double incipits are also used in Judg 17:6-7, 18:1, and 19:1, in which the first phrase is "in those days, there was no king in Israel." Ruth 1:1 is similar. In all four, a phrase is added that situates the narrative in the time of the judges. This preliminary information is the clue of a later redactional addition intended to integrate what were once independent narratives into a framework that permitted them to be appended at the end of Judges and before Samuel.

Therefore, two options are opened. One, a time lag is postulated between the translation of Ruth from a Hebrew manuscript that knew of the "judging" of the Judges but ignored a specific period of the Judges designated as the "days" of the judges. The rendering of Elimelech as Abimelech in G (see Table 5) turns *Routh* into the sequel of *Kritai* – the title of the book of Judges in the Greek Bible. Option two postulates that Abimelech was the name of Naomi's husband in the Hebrew *Vorlage* used by the translators of *Routh*. If so, the change of the name of Naomi's husband from Abimelech to Elimelech was done by Hebrew scribes who sought to disconnect the story of Ruth from the "evil" days of the Judges, as is the case in the Hebrew canon, where Ruth is one of the *Megillot*.

Ruth 1b

Only some Greek manuscripts and S have "sons" instead of "two sons." Either the translators took the liberty to omit an element they perceived as redundant because the next verse mentions "two sons," or an unspecified number of sons underlines the fulness of Bethlehem and sharpens the contrast with Moab, from which Naomi came back empty (Ruth 1:20-21). Or, the *Vorlage* could have read "sons" with G, which would mean that G is a witness to an older version than MT. This position is supported by the story of Noah and the ark. The first reference to Noah's family is in Gen 7:7: "And Noah and his sons and his wife and his sons' wives with him came to the ark." It is only when names are introduced that a detail like a cardinal number is used: "...Noah came, and Shem and Ham and Japheth, Noah's sons, and Noah's wife and his son's three wives with them to the ark" (Gen 7:13). It is therefore better Hebrew narrative style to introduce characters first by their relationship status to the protagonist, and then to provide detailed information such as their names and their number in a later verse. Similarly, Ruth 1:3 ends with "and she was left with her two sons". But the next verse is closely linked: "They took Moabite wives, the name of the *first*, Orpah, and the name of the *second*, Ruth" (Ruth 1:4).

Ruth 1:2

With "they settled" in Moab rather than "they were" there, 4Q104Ruth[a] alone underlines the permanency of the migration of Elimelech's family. T interprets it as a guilty delay and states that the family served there as royal adjutants (Levine 1973, 17–18). De Waard (2004, 51*) prefers M and the other witnesses, but admits that a question mark is necessary. Indeed, an opposite tendency is equally possible, i.e., attempts to reduce Elimelech's guilt – but not the lethality of Moab – to exonerate Boaz from accepting a Moabite as wife. Given the antiquity of 4Q104Ruth[a], "they *remained* there" (NETS) is justified, except that it is *not* a rendering of the Greek verb ἦσαν that means "they were" as much as M's *wayihyo* (ויהיו). This shows that modern translators are as prone to interpretation as their ancient predecessors and that one cannot rely on translations alone to evaluate the weight of variant readings. MT uses the verb "to be" in the phrase, "and they came to the fields of Moab and they were there." This is a customary idiom that is usually translated in modern bibles as "remained there" (Exod 24:18; 34:28; Judg 17:4.12). G translates the verb literally as "and they were there." NETS interpretively renders the Greek "And they were there" as "And they remained there." Interestingly, 4Q104Ruth[a] updates the Hebrew idiom used in 1:2, which may have fallen into disuse, by replacing "and they were there" with "and they settled there."

Ruth 1:5

4Q104Ruth[a] with V and T emphasizes the death of the sons by reversing the logic of v. 4, presenting it as a greater or additional blow for Naomi beside the death of Elimelech. G contains two variants in relation to M. First, while M reads, "and the woman was left without her two sons and her husband," G reverses the order to read, "and the woman was left without her husband and her two sons." Second, M does not actually have "her two sons" as per NRSV and most English translations. The Hebrew text uses the noun *yeled* "child." The Greek translators considered that it was inappropriate to refer to adult married men as "children" and replaced it with "sons." The principle of *lectio difficilior* would suggest that M reflects the *Vorlage* on this point and that the Greek translators wanted to "improve" the text. M is supported by 4Q104Ruth[a], both in terms of the order of presenting the loss of the children and the husband and using the word for "children" rather than "sons."

Ruth 1:8

This verse is the first of a series of twelve *ketiv-qere* notes. The *ketiv* and T read, "The Lord *will deal* kindly with you" (יעשׂה indicative imperfect), while the *qere* and G have "*May* the Lord *deal* kindly with you" (יעשׂ and ποήσαι using the jussive/optative), only expressing a wish to insinuate doubt over the willingness of Yhwh to bless anyone in Moab. Thus, Ruth 1:9 may be read to mean "The Lord *will give* you security in the house of your husband" or as "*May* the Lord *give* you security in the house of your husband." One of the stylistic characteristics of the LXX is to systematically interpret all phrases that refer to what God will do using the jussive/optative. *Routh* follows this practice (see 1:8.9.17; 2:12; 3:10; 4:11.12.14). The reason is probably theological; human beings cannot affirm what God will do but can only pray to God to do something. Ruth 1:8 is one of the relatively rare examples of a Hebrew verb having a special jussive form that is different from the imperfect form. The *qere* in 1:8 may thus be interpreted in two ways. First, it transforms an intentional imperfect form in the *ketiv* into a jussive form to change the meaning of the verse. Second, it simply corrects a grammatical error in the *ketiv* but does not change the original meaning. The strongest argument in favor of the first interpretation is that the same Hebrew verb in 1:8 is also used in 1:17 in Ruth's well-known entreaty to Naomi, "Where you die, I will die, there will I be buried. The Lord *will do* thus and so to me, and more as well, if even death parts me from you!" In this verse the Masoretes do *not* correct the imperfect to read as a jussive. In contrast, G translates the last sentence using the jussive/optative: "*May* the Lord *do* thus and so to me and more..." This suggests that the Masoretes intended to change the meaning of 1:8 from the affirmative statement, "the Lord will deal kindly with you" to the entreaty form of a prayer, "may the Lord deal kindly with you." The strongest argument in favor of the second interpretation--that the Masoretes simply wanted to correct a grammatical error--is that the only other usage of the jussive form of the verb in question in MT is syntactically similar to Ruth 1:8. Second Sam 2:6 reads, "*May the Lord deal kindly* and faithfully *with you.*" This suggests that the purpose of the *qere* in Ruth 1:8 was to harmonize that verse with 2 Sam 2:6.

Ruth 1:9

V and T support 4Q104Ruth[a]'s קולם against MT's קוֹלָן (plural form *qolām*, "their voices") to read a an antiquated feminine dual form (*qolāim*), i.e., "their two voices". After ordering her daughters-in-law to return to Moab, Naomi wishes them well and then "she kissed them, and they lifted up their voices and they wept" (1:9). This verse closely resembles 1:14: "And they lifted up their voices and they wept again; and Orpah kissed her mother-in-law, but Ruth clung to her." Both of these verses raise the interpretive question as to exactly which of the three women "lifted up their voices and wept." The plural implies that all three women cried and wept, as they do again in v. 14. The dual implies that only Orpah and Ruth express grief when Naomi tells them that she wants to send them back to their mother's home. De Waard (2004, 51*) rejects the feminine dual as too speculative, though the trace of an old grammatical form in a first century BCE manuscript is a possibility. The implication is that Naomi did not weep in v. 9 because she was relieved to rid herself of daughters-in-law who would inevitably be an additional burden when she returns to Bethlehem (see Chapter 2 in this volume). That she weeps in v. 14 is then caused not by the departure of Orpah but by her failure to part with Ruth, too.

Ruth 1:12

The omission of this night (*halaylāh* הלילה) in G misses the drama of Naomi's declaration – "even if I were to be with a man this very night" or "even if I were to belong to a man this very night". This is the first of a series of omissions by the Greek translator deemed as "euphemisms" (de Waard 1973, 511–512; BHQ). The translator supposedly avoided what may have been perceived as offensive or indecent to the audience. Another motivation for the omission of the reference to the night in 1:12 could be to avoid what could be foreshadowing in the Hebrew original of the role played by Naomi in the seduction of Boaz in Ruth 3 (see below 3:3–5 and Chapters 7 and 13 in this volume).

Ruth 1:14

Against 4Q105Ruth[b] and M, the versions add "and she returned to her people" after Orpah kissed Naomi. Either the versions glossed their *Vorlage* or M abbreviated a longer text. Given M's agreement with 4Q105Ruth[b], de Waard (2004, 52*) is justified in favoring the first option.

Ruth 1:15–16

G reads M's ambiguous אלהיה (*'eloheyha*) as a plural "her (Orpah's) gods" but the no less ambiguous אלהיך (*'elohayik*) in the next verse as a singular that refers to Yhwh. The Hebrew word *'elohim* is a plural noun with an ambiguous meaning. It is used hundreds of times in MT to mean "God" (as in "you shall love Yhwh your God") and almost as many times to refer to the "gods" or "god" of neighboring countries. In 1:15, G translates *'elohim* as a plural noun (her gods) and in 1:16 as a singular (your God shall be my God). Historically, the implication that Moabites – contrary to Israelites – were polytheists is probably erroneous, but it enhances the radicality of Ruth's desire to accept Naomi's God as hers, which T paraphrases as a "demand to be converted" (Levine 1973, 22).

Ruth 1:20–21

G translates the divine name "Shaddai" by splitting it into two words, *še day* (ש די) as "The Powerful" (ὁ ἱκανός) or the "Sufficient One" (NETS), as is the case in some Greek manuscripts (Gen 17:1; 35:11; 43:4; 48:3; 49:25; Exod 6:3; Ezek 1:24; 10:5; Ps 68(67):15; 90(91):1; see Bertram 1958).

Ruth 1:22

G does not have "with her" (*'imāh* עמה) after the description of Naomi's return journey to Bethlehem. The omission may be intentional, possibly to take into account Naomi's silence when she acknowledges Ruth's declaration of intention to return to Bethlehem with Naomi (1:18), a silence broken only after they had arrived (2:2). But a later addition in M is also possible, in this case either to underline the contrast between Ruth and Orpah or simply to harmonize the verse with a similar phrase in 2:6.

At the end of ch. 1, the variants display two contradictory and yet complementary interpretative trends. On the one hand, they accentuate Moab's lethality following Deut 23:2. On the other hand, they stress the acceptability of Ruth despite her Moabite origins.

Ruth 2:1

The narrator describes Boaz as an acquaintance of Naomi's husband who is also a prominent rich man. But the Masoretes correct the *ketiv* מידע (*myd'* "acquaintance") to read מודע(*mwd'* possibly "kinsman") in the *qere*. From a stylistic perspective, this is an unusual change for the Masoretes to make as the *ketiv* is a relatively common word, being used to mean "acquaintance" or "friend" in 2 Kgs 10:11; Pss 31:12; 55:14; 88:9, 19; Job 19:14. There is nothing in any of these passages to suggest that a person's acquaintance is a close relative. The proposed change in the *qere* is to an extremely rare word used only two other times, in Ruth 3:2 and Prov 7:4. As both words (which are both participles functioning as nouns) are derived from the same Hebrew root meaning "to know," the derivative sense of "acquaintance" is more appealing at first glance. The typical way in Hebrew to refer to a kinsman is as a "brother." Indeed, the only real evidence for interpreting the *qere* reading to mean "kinsman" rather than "acquaintance" is based on the context of 3:2. In 3:1 Naomi explains the facts of life to Ruth and tells her that she needs to find some "security" (which readers would probably have understood to mean a rich husband) so that "it will be well with you." In the next verse, Naomi identifies Boaz as *mode'tānw,* a word only used one other time in Prov 7:4, it is not even clear that this word means "kinsman" rather than "acquaintance." In fact, it is later European commentators who basically invent the meaning of "kinsman" for this rare word. Their motivation is to create a logical link between Boaz's status as a close relative and his right of redemption that will become central to the plotline in Ruth 3 and 4. But in returning to the text-critical analysis of Ruth, the variants are not particularly helpful in supporting their scholarly hypothesis. In the final analysis, whether G is translating the *ketiv* or the *qere* in 2:1, it uses the same translation value in both 2:1 and 3:2 – Boaz is an acquaintance or friend but not necessarily a kinsman. In our view, the cases of 2:1 and 3:2 are examples of modern commentators trying to force a meaning on a rare word that suits their purpose of making the overall story more coherent than it is, in fact.

Ruth 2:2–3:18

In ch. 1 (1:1;12;13), Naomi addresses Ruth and Orpah as "my daughters" (*benotay* בנתי, which is accurately reflected in G as θυγατέρες μου, *thugateres mou*). However, a change occurs in chs. 2 and 3. Whereas in the Hebrew (2:2, 8; 2:22; 3:10–11, 16, 18), Naomi and Boaz address Ruth as "my daughter" (*byty* ביתי), the Greek drops the pronoun "my," and Ruth is addressed simply as "daughter" (θύγατερ). As the change between Ruth 1 and Ruth 2–3 is systematic in G, it may transmit a nuance not found in the Hebrew. Since the change occurs at the point at which Ruth disobeys her mother-in-law and insists on accompanying her to Bethlehem, Naomi's ceasing to call Ruth "my daughter" may be a subtle way for the Greek translators to emphasize that Naomi did not consider herself responsible for "her" daughter and that Ruth has to begin fending for herself. In the case of Boaz, it may have been inappropriate for a man to refer to a young woman as "his" daughter when she wasn't. In the Gospels, "daughter" (without the possessive pronoun) is used by men to refer to young women who are not related to them (Matt 9:22; Mark 5:34). But the important text-critical question is whether the Hebrew *Vorlage* from which the Greek translators worked included or omitted "my" before daughter in the seven instances in which it is present in the MT. While it is true that there are many passages in the Hebrew Bible, especially in the prophets, that refer to the "daughter of my people," we are unable to find any examples close to the case in G Ruth in which a specific young woman is addressed in direct dialog as "daughter" rather than "my daughter." For these reasons, we conclude that the G omission of the possessive pronoun "my" before daughter is an innovation of the G text, probably intended to reflect a then current practice in Greek of not describing another man's daughter as "my daughter."

Ruth 2:5–6

In these verses, both Boaz and his employee, a young man in charge of the reapers, refer to Ruth as a *na'arāh* (נערה) in M. This common word, often translated as "young woman," refers in Hebrew to post-pubescent girls who are not married. Ruth and the young women who work in Boaz's fields are all described this way throughout the Hebrew version of book, in 2:5, 6, 8, 22, 23; 3:2; 4:12. However, G uses varied vocabulary in these verses, ranging from *neanis* (νεᾶνις) in 2:5, to *pais* (παῖς) in 2:6, to *korasion* (κοράσιον) in 2:8, 22, 23; 3:2, to *paidiskē* (παιδίσκη) in 4:12 (see Bons 2002, 155; 2014, 219). In the LXX, νεᾶνις is used in passages that discuss young women of marriageable age who are, indeed, still virgins (Deut 22:19-29; 1 Kgs 1:1-4). It is possible that the use of this word in G 2:5 is intended to foreshadow the fact that the young woman Boaz encounters in his fields will later become his wife. However, when Boaz's employee responds to tell his master who Ruth is, he refers to her as a Moabite servant *child* (παῖς), a word that is used to refer to both boys and girls who work in domestic service for other families. Is Boaz's employee advising his boss that Ruth not only is a Moabite but also is a mere servant child and thus below his dignity as a potential wife or concubine?

Ruth 2:7

In explaining what a good worker Ruth is, Boaz's employee tells him in 2:7 that she came to the fields and has been working all day long, from morning until now. He then adds an additional quality that uses an unusual

Hebrew idiom: "resting but little in the house" (šibtāh habayit me'āṭ שבתה הבית מעט). As the word for "house" in Hebrew covers a broad semantic field, it is possible that it also referred to covered huts found in the fields where workers could sit down under a sun screen. Probably in an attempt to clarify the verse, G replaces "until now" with "until evening" and "in the house" with "in the field."

Ruth 2:8, 22–23; 3:2

As mentioned, G replaces na'arāh (נערה), young woman of marriageable age, with κοράσιον in 2:8.22.23; 3:2. In all four of these passages, Boaz, Naomi and the narrator use this term to describe the young women who work in Boaz's fields. While the Hebrew is ambiguous, G appears to be drawing a distinction between Ruth, who is a young woman of marriageable age, and the other young women who work in the fields who are servant girls.

Ruth 2:13

Ruth addresses Boaz to thank him for deigning to speak to "your servant girl (šifḥah) even though I am not one of your servant girls (šifḥot)." G reworks this verse rather substantially to read "...your servant girl δούλη (doulē), and here I am, I will be like one of your slave girls (παιδίσκη paidiskē)." Both Hebrew and Greek have rich and varied vocabularies to refer to female servants. The dividing line between a young woman who "serves" a man in his household and who sleeps with him in his bed as his concubine is hard to draw. For example, Jacob is described in Gen 30:43 as having grown very rich, owning female slaves (šifḥot/παιδίσκαι), male slaves, camels, and donkeys. But Rachel also gave Jacob "her slave-girl (šifḥah/παιδίσκη) Bilhah as concubine. Jacob went into her" (Gen 30:4). If the G variant is significant, it is because it replaces the double use of šifḥah in the same verse with two approximate synonyms and it has Ruth affirming (rather than negating) that she will become one of Boaz's slave girls. It is unlikely that these changes reflect a different *Vorlage* than the one underlying MT. Both versions are equally laden with sexual innuendo and play on the double role of female servants as both slave girls and concubines. Both use a change in vocabulary to signal the change in perception of Ruth from being a na'arāh in 2:5.6.8 to a šifḥah in 2:13. The anticipated denouement in both M and G is not the happy end of modern readings, but Ruth's transfer into Boaz's household – not necessarily a less happy end but with different implications for the status of Ruth and Naomi. The narrator presupposed his audience's understanding of the implications of the customs that are involved in the story: self-indenture, land tenure, widow inheritance, sexual access to slaves and servants and thus does not delve in the legal details of the different transactions involved. Interpreters logically turn to the Torah to decipher these customs but tend to confuse the customs described there as binding laws and to downplay the difference between the specific conditions required, for instance, for a levirate marriage, which clearly are not applicable to Boaz's union with Ruth (see Chapter 3 in this volume). As we progress in our discussion of the variants, we shall realize that the translator was well aware of these customs.

Ruth 2:16

The emphatic *šol tāšollu lah* (של תשלו לה) is rendered literally with the same emphatic form of the verb βαστάζω (βαστάζοντης βαστάξατε αὐτῇ) and then repeated with the verb παραβαλλλω (καί γε παραβάλλοντες παραβαλεῖτε αὐτῇ) to describe what is to be done to the *ṣebātym* (צבתים) rendered by G as βεβουνισμένων "heaps" (from βουνίζω) but "bundles" in NETS. In fact, M's *ṣebātym* is the sole occurrence where it would mean "sheaves" (HALOT 3,1000). The Hebrew writer seems to have coined it purposely to echo the semantic field of the root *šll* (שלל "to plunder") and evoke the notion of forceful removal. The Greek translator must have had good reasons to deviate so much from the Hebrew. We suggest that what Boaz requires from his reapers is exactly what would justify any owner of the harvest to dismiss workers who purposely drop ears for gleaners they seek to favor. Obviously, Boaz cannot be accused of dishonesty since the harvest is his. Was the translator dampening Boaz's extravagant generosity that seem far too foolish for a level-headed village notable who learned to control his passions and avoid *hubris*?

Ruth 2:20

G reads Boaz as one ~~out~~ of several potential redeemers (ἐκ τῶν ἀγχιστευόντων ἡμᾶς) where M has a singular *migo'elnw* (מגאלנו). Though odd because the prefix *min* as much as *ek* presupposes several redeemers, the singular should not be rejected out-of-hand as erroneous. The singular can express Naomi's claim that Boaz is the sole redeemer, which turns his affirmation to the contrary in 3:12 as merely rhetorical and the precedence he grants to Pelony Almony in 2:4 as a polite gesture rather than obedience to any sort of law or custom derived from the Torah.

Ruth 2:21a

2Q16Ruthª supports M with "Ruth the Moabite" against only "Ruth" in G V S, thus downplaying her foreignness in order to enhance her "conversion" and the Moabite origins of Obed and of David too (see Chapter 6 in this volume).

Ruth 2:21b

2Q16Ruthª supports M's "young men" (הנערים) against "girls" (κορασίων) in some G manuscripts that harmonize with the girls in v. 22.

Ruth 2:22

In addition to the difference between 2Q16Ruthª and M (girl/girls), NRSV's "it is better" is misleading in the absence of a *mem* to justify the comparison, though it seeks to explain the mention of young men in v. 21 and "young women" in v. 22, i.e., Boaz said to stick with the men, but Naomi said that it was preferable to stick with the women.

Ruth 2:23

As Ruth stayed with Boaz's reapers until the end of the wheat harvest, 2QRuthª may suggest that she did more than merely continue to glean. Though all the other witnesses have "gleaning" and that the meaning of *lwṭ* "to act in secret" is not obvious in the context of harvesting, Baillet (2005, 73) notes the traces of the *qoph* of ללקט, which was supposedly added in the interline above the defective *waw*, which allows him to correct ללוט to ללקוט. BHQ's designation of *llwṭ* ("to conceal, cover" from verb לוט) as a writing mistake with no mention of a correction above might be an implicit admission of the weakness of Baillet's claim.

Ruth 3:3–5

The three *ketiv-qere* notes in vv. 3–5 are the first of a series of eight in ch. 3, a rare concentration of *ketiv-qeres* combined with variants in the DSS and in Greek. Whereas M only has the imperative of verb "to bathe" in 3:3, G adds the pronoun "you" (*su*) and places it before the verb to indicate topical prominence (Fresch 2021, 89). NETS's "Now bathe!" loses much of the nuance. The verbs are in the converted perfect in Hebrew, not the imperative. G resisted the temptation to transform this set of converted perfects into the imperative in Greek. In Hebrew, the first equivalent of an imperative is the negation + imperfect "but do not make yourself known to the man" (3:3). Naomi is telling Ruth what the plan is: "you will bathe and clothe yourself and I will go down to the threshing floor". Naomi's first order to Ruth is to hide herself from sight until Boaz is drunk and sleepy.

The first *qere* in v. 3 first seems insignificant since its plural "your clothes" (*simlotayik* שמלתיך) is supported by the versions, excepted G that agrees with *ketiv*'s singular "your clothe" (*simlotek* שמלתך, τὸν ἱματισμόν σου). The *qere* seeks to "overdress" Ruth to make her a less likely candidate for sexual relations.

The next *qeres* suggest an answer as they correct Naomi's "I will go down (*weyāradtiy* וירדתי) and "I will lie down" (*wešākābtiy* ושכבתי) into "you will go down (*weyāradte* וירדת) and "you will lie down" (*wešākābte* ושכבת) beside Boaz (see Chapter 6 in this volume). The change implies an entirely different plot in which Naomi does more than instruct Ruth to meet Boaz on the threshing floor. She plans to go and lie there herself. The Rabbis rejected this scenario and instructed readers to tell a story in which Naomi conceives the plan but sends Ruth to accomplish it. What role would have Naomi played in the darkness of the winnowed grain can only be speculated. The text as it is written and the systematic corrections of the *qeres* are hard and fast evidence of the existence of an alternative version that was duly transmitted through the centuries and against which corrections were merely added as *qeres* in the margins of the Hebrew text. Before the addition of *qeres*, Rabbinical tradition confirms that the *ketivs* in 3:3 should be read as the first person singular and taken to represent the text as written. In a sixth century CE midrash on Ruth, the rabbis interpret Naomi's statement, "I will go down to the threshing floor (per the *ketiv*) to mean "My merit will go down to the threshing floor with you" (Ruth Rabbah 5). The medieval commentator Rashi (1040–1105 CE), follows Ruth Rabbah's interpretation of 3:3 in his commentary on the five *megillot* and adds the additional comment "and protect you from any mishap." What is important here is that these two important rabbinical sources understood the *ketiv* to be an intentional use of the first person singular and not a scribal error or example of archaic usage of the second person singular feminine. The rabbis explained away Naomi's presence on the threshing floor to mean that Naomi's virtue would accompany Ruth on her sexual adventure as a kind of talisman to protect her from sin.

Nevertheless, some readers today still perceive the "improved" version of the *qeres* as Naomi "pimping" Ruth (see Chapters 5 and 8 in this volume). That the bait was a Moabite used to prepare the line of the Davidic dynasty could have justified the dubious means to that aim, all the more so as it portrayed Naomi as a worthy descendant of a long line of tricksters à la Jacob/Israel. Nevertheless, trickster figures remain too ambiguous to assuage the desire to shield the two Israelite heroes – Boaz and Naomi – from any accusations regarding what appears as a trap to secure the favors of one of the most wealthy Bethlehemites.

In light of the three *qere*s of 3:3–5, the addition of the pronoun "you" (*su*) in the Greek in v. 3 reflects the same motivation. "Now *you* bathe!" isolates Naomi from the preparation of Ruth for her encounter alone with Boaz. Therefore, G retains M's singular "(piece of) clothing" because several items could have suggested that both women dressed up for the nightly outing.

If 2Q16Ruth[a] transmits an earlier form of the text than M, the *ketiv* is influenced by G with which it agrees on the singular "(piece of) clothing" that reduces the possibility to have Naomi dress up with Ruth. On the contrary, if 2Q16Ruth[a] transmits a secondary form of the text, the *qere*'s plural "clothes" followed by the other versions reflects a later stage in the textual history of Ruth when the corrected version with Ruth alone on the threshing floor was established enough to allow a further improvement with additional clothes to shield Ruth from any indecency. Given the lack of temporal anchor to establish the precedence, the improvement of the story was a long process that began already with the Greek translation if not earlier. Again, in both v. 3 and v. 4, G and *qere* agree.

The next *qere* adds the word אלי to "everything you said *to me* I will do," against G and *ketiv*. Had G agreed with the *qere*, the hypothesis that the change from "I" to "you" in vv. 3–4 went back to the Greek translator would have been bolstered, but it is not.

Ruth 3:7

G alone omits Boaz's drinking before he retires to the threshing floor, thus avoiding the suggestion that he acted under the influence of drunkenness. Or, 2Q16Ruth[a] and M followed by OL, V, and S added it to exculpate him from accepting to marry a Moabite, something that can be seen as contradicting the ban on the acceptance of any Moabites in the assembly of the Lord (Deut 23:3).

Ruth 3:11; 4:10

With *phulē* (φυλή) for "gate" (שער), the Greek translator chose a term that sounded similar to "door" (πύλη), which transposed the local flavor of the negotiations in ch. 4 on the broader tribal level and thus contributed much to the genealogical understanding of the proximity the term *goel* implies.

Ruth 3:12

The *qere* ignores the particle *'im* in the compound כי אם to indicate that Boaz is indeed a *go'el*, though the same expression is attested in the same confirmation effect of "indeed" in 2 Kgs 5:20 and Jer 51:14. Again, G and *qere* agree.

Ruth 3:14

A full discussion of this crucial verse is given in ch. 6 of this volume. The fact that the *qere* is supported by 2Q17Ruth[b] and the versions is not sufficient to justify reading the singular מרגלותו as a graphic error. As it stands, v. 14 begins with an odd "She laid his foot until morning" (*watiškab marglāto 'ad haboqer* ותשכב מרגלתו עד הבקר). Other variants in this verse, i.e., G's "a woman" (*gunē* γυνὴ) instead of M's "the woman" and no woman at all in 2Q17Ruth[b], V and S are enough to justify the suspicion that v. 14 is not simply the result of a graphic error and of a haplography (so de Waard 2004, 8). What happened after Boaz's promise is now unsaid, but the Greek translator strove to distance Ruth from Boaz by adding "the place" (*topos* τόπος) in v. 7, "that in front of his feet" (*ta pros* τὰ πρὸς) rendered as "the place at his feet" in NETS and simply "before his feet" in v. 14. The masculine subject "he went" (*wayabo'* ויבא) instead of the feminine "she went [to] the city" is a final clue to be added to the case in favor of major interventions in this verse. In this case again, G and *qere* agree.

Ruth 3:15

This verse marks the last variant attested by the Dea Sea Scroll, again 2Q17Ruth[b] reading שם "there" instead of שש "six" in M, G, V, and T or *lh* "for her" in S.

Ruth 3:17

As in 3:5, the *qere* adds אלי in "for he said *to me*". That the same plus is found in G and in T reflects the authority the Rabbis ascribed to the Greek translation that was completed centuries before the production of the *ketiv-qere*. Though pleonastic in a context where Ruth was supposed to be alone with Boaz, that it is *to Ruth* that Boaz spoke about the secret gift of barley further erases the presence of Naomi on the threshing floor. Therefore, this *qere* is yet another clue of the alternative plot that involved Naomi's presence at the threshing floor.

Ruth 4:1

Instead of anonymizing Mr So-and-So (*pelony almony*), G introduces him with a rare term that describes his function: the *agxisteutēs* (ἀγχιστευτὴς) "companion, friend," contrary to the term *agxisteus* (ἀγχιστεύς) "legitimate heir" Ruth use to describe Boaz on the threshing floor in 3:9 (see BDAG 2015, 23). Both terms derive from the verb ἐγγίζω "to approach," but the translator made a point of using a rare term to distinguish the ties between Boaz and Elimelech/Abimelech from the other biblical passages referring to "next-of-kin" in Lev 25, Num 36 and Deut 25 (see Chapter 3 in this volume).

Ruth 4:3

G renders M's מכרה (*mākrāh* confirmed by 2QRuth[a]) as δέδοται, a passive form of verb *didōmi* "to give" for Hebrew and Semitic *mkr* that expresses "trading" rather than merely selling. At stake is the process that makes it possible for Naomi to trade a land share she inherited from her husband and whether she intervenes as owner or usufructor (see Chapter 2 in this volume). Contrary to most modern commentators, G's notion of "giving" and further "to grant, assign, transmit" (BDAG 2015, 521) underline the fact that Naomi is *not* selling a field for which she would immediately receive an equivalent in silver.

Ruth 4:4

The next variant in G is simply the result of the need to avoid the somewhat difficult third person within Boaz's address when the narrative logic expects a second person "if you redeem, redeem, but if *he* does not redeem, let me know. The translator took the liberty to drop "he shall redeem" to obtain a smoother phrase "if he redeems, redeem! but if you do not redeem tell me". The *qere* that follows (ואדעה instead of ואדע) is only a matter of intensification of the action. Therefore, γνώσομαι corresponds as much to the *ketiv* as to the *qere*.

Ruth 4:5

With this verse we touch the heart of the transaction. The interpretation of the entire story hangs on whether or not the *qere*'s "you have (also) acquired" (קָנִיתָה,*qāniytāh*) is preferred to *ketiv* "I have (already) acquired" (קָנִיתִי,*qāniytiy*). The difference is discussed in Chapter 2 in this volume where, contrary to the majority of current studies, the *ketiv* is preferred because it corresponds to the narrative logic. On the contrary, the *qere* seems to reflect G's belabored "it is necessary for you to acquire her also" (καὶ αὐτὴ κτήσασθαί σε δεῖ), which suggests that the Rabbis who added the *qere* were influenced by G and corrected M accordingly (more on this issue below in section 6).

Ruth 4:7

G merely makes explicit what is implicit in the extremely condensed זאת, a pronominal feminine adjective meaning "this", as a "statute" (δικαίωμα). That the translator did not use the term "law" is significant and is at loggerheads with the common search of legal parallels in the Torah to interpret Ruth (see Chapter 3 in this volume).

Ruth 4:11

Though M distinguishes the elders from "all the people who were in the gate," both groups – people and elders – testify as witnesses and pronounce the good wishes over the union of Boaz with Ruth. G limits the function of witness to the people only, and reserves the statement of the good wishes to the elders; both are clues of different legal procedures in Palestine and in Hellenistic Egypt.

Ruth 4:12

Paidiskē (παιδίσκη) is used to render *naʿarah*, as in 2:13. Because in 4:10–11 Ruth is described as the woman who enters Boaz's house, Eberhard Bons claims that it "is highly unlikely that the text now implies that he is marrying a slave girl, as is the case in Gen 16:1ff.. where Hagar is also called παιδίσκη" (2002, 161). To counter this fact, which he finds unpalatable, Bons reverts to classical texts that use the term *paidiskē* for a young woman who is free, he but admits that this meaning is marginal in the Hellenistic period (Bons 2002, 161). What matters for the elders is that Ruth is young enough to bear a son for Elimelech or for Mahlon (contrary to Naomi, see 1:11-12), something that has no bearing on her status, servile or free. Just like Hagar, Ruth serves as surrogate mother for Naomi, which shields Obed from any issues regarding the servile status and foreignness of his biological mother (see Chapter 6 in this volume).

6. Implications for the Interpretation of Ruth

The above analysis may seem to give too much importance to minor textual variants. The aim is to bring forth the potential of a new approach that would resist the temptation to ignore out of hand variants that do not fit one's preconceived reading of the story. Apart from the variants that involve the use of close synonyms and merely transmit minor nuances, those variants discussed above offer clues for the existence of an alternative plot (mostly in 3:3–5), of different legal procedures (4:1–12), or of a desire to enhance the portrait of the protagonists of an earlier tale in which they were presented unashamedly as tricksters. The importance of the "politically correct" being nothing new, efforts were made to align the tricksters with Hellenistic moral ideals. Granting greater attention to the variants also yields significant returns regarding the history of the text.

6.1 *Qere* or *Ketiv*?

In general, *ketiv*s reflect an older form of the text than the *qere*s (Joüon and Muraoka 2008, 65). In Ruth, it is most likely so because the *lectio* or "reading" they transmit is clearly the most difficult one, and according to the basic principle of *lectio difficilior probabilior* ("the more difficult reading is the more likely"), the *ketiv*s should be given preference. Yet, few are the commentaries and studies that give precedence of the *ketiv*s, because the plot they presuppose differs so much from the story we know that taking them into account would introduce major changes, particularly to the portrayal of Naomi and Boaz. In short, if Naomi goes down to the threshing floor before or with Ruth, her role in the manipulation of Boaz is enhanced. If Boaz uses Ruth to block the customary transmission of Elimelech's share, he would appear as a willful participant in Naomi's scheme rather than a victim of the bed-trick on the threshing floor (see Chapter 13 in this volume). Though Naomi presents herself as the powerful victim of El-Shadday (1:20), the plot transmitted by the *ketiv*s is coherent, but it is easier to give in to the weight of textual evidence and point out that G follows the *qere*s.

6.2 When our Ruth is More Routh Than Hebrew Ruth

G renders most of the times the *qere*, except in three cases. The first, γνώριμος in 2:1, can reflect the *qere* as much as the *ketiv*, so this case is ambiguous. The other two clearly follow the *ketiv*, where the difference between the *ketiv* and the *qere* is minimal (a piece of clothing versus clothes in 3:3, to align with the garment in 3:15?) or where the *qere* produces a redundant reading ("Ruth said to her: 'Everything that you say *to me* I will do'" in 3:5). Therefore, the agreement between G and the *qere*s is too systematic not to raise questions as to their relationship.

Whether or not the small additions and omissions in G were the work of the translator or result from a differing *Vorlage* "remains open" (Bons 2015, 124). Yet, a possibility remains that the Rabbis were aware of the Greek translation and introduced *qere*s to align M accordingly. Either the Greek so permeated the reading tradition that the Hebrew text was read according to the modifications introduced by the Alexandrian translator, or G itself reflected the reading tradition that predated even the translation.

Understanding how the Greek translator dealt with the Hebrew reveals that current exegetical tradition is very similar to the Targum of Ruth. Apart from being in modern languages, commentaries are an "eclectic arrangement of diverse sources intended to address doctrinal problems, fill lacunae, illustrate abstractions, inspire faith, eulogize the *Torah*, and convey that the "book was written to show how great is the reward for those who perform deeds of loving-kindness (Ruth R. II.14)," thus having the "various didactic, polemical, and inspirational *midrashim* fused into a continuous narrative" (Levine 1973, v). In effect, we modern readers and interpreters are not so different from Josephus, who emphasized the obedience of Ruth towards Naomi (*Ant.* 5.318–37, especially 5.329).

Works Cited

Baillet, Maurice. 2005. "Textes des grottes 2Q, 3Q, 6Q, 7Q à 10Q." Pages 45–165 in *Les 'Petites Grottes' de Qumran*. Edited by Maurice Baillet, Jósef Tadeuz Milik and Roland de Vaux. 2005. Dead Sea Discoveries III. Oxford: Clarendon.

BDAG 2015 = *The Brill Dictionary of Ancient Greek*. Edited by Franco Montanari. Leiden: Brill

Beattie, Derek R. G. 1994. *The Targum of Ruth, Translated with Introduction, Apparatus, and Notes*. Edinburgh: T&T Clark.

Bertram, Georg. 1958. "'ΙΚΑΝΌΣ in den griechischen Übersetzungen des Ats als Wiedergabe von *schadday*." *Zeitschrift für die alttestamentliche Wissenschaft* 70: 20–31.

BHK 1906–1937 = *Biblia Hebraica Kittel*. Edited by Rudolf Kittel and Paul Kahle. Leipzig: J. C. Hinrichs.

BHQ 2004 = *Biblia Hebraica Quinta*. Edited by Jan de Waard, R. Altmann and Adriaan Schenker. Stuttgart: Deutsche Bibelgesellschaft.

BHS 1967–1998 = *Biblia Hebraica Stuttgartensia*. Edited by Karl Elliger and Wilhelm Rudolf. Stuttgart: Deutsche Bibelgesellschaft.

Bonanno, Beatrice. 2021. "Elimelech or Abimelech? A Study on the Textual Variant of the Name of Noemin's Husband in LXX-Ruth." *Biblische Zeitschrift* 65: 308–321.

–––––. 2024. *The Septuagint of Ruth. Translation Technique, Textual History, and Theological Issues*. Turnhout: Brepols.

Bons, Eberhard. 2002. "The Vocabulary of Servitude in the Septuagint of the Book of Ruth." *Journal for the Study of Judaism* 33: 153–163; reprint as Pages 241–249 in *Textkritik und Textgeschichte. Studien zur Septuaginta und zum hebräischen Alten Testament*. FAT 93. Edited by Eberhard Bons. Tübingen: Mohr Siebeck.

–––––. 2014. "Die Septuaginta-Version des Buches Rut." Pages 202–224 in *Textkritik und Textgeschichte. Studien zur Septuaginta und zum hebräischen Alten Testament* Forschungen zum Alten Testament 93. Edited by Eberhard Bons. Tübingen: Mohr Siebeck.

–––––. 2015. "Ruth." Pages 118–126 in *T&T Clark Companion to Septuagint*. Edited by James K. Aitken K. London: T&T Clark.

de Waard, Jan. 2004. "Ruth." Pages 3–10, *51–56 in *Megillot*. Edited by Jan de Waard, R. Altmann and Adriaan Schenker. Biblia Hebraica Quinta 18. Stuttgart: Deutsche Bibelgesellschaft.

–––––. 1973. "Translation Techniques Used by the Greek Translators of Ruth." *Biblica* 54: 499–515.

Elliger, Karl, and W. Rudolph. 1997. *Biblia Hebraica Stuttgartensia*. Stuttgart: Deutsche Bibelgesellschaft.

Fresch, Christopher J. 2021. "The Septuagint and Discourse Grammar." Pages 79–92 in *T&T Clark Handbook of Septuagint Research*. Edited by William A. Ross and W. Edward Glenny. London: T&T Clark.

Gordis, Robert. 1937. *The Biblical Text in the Making*. Ktav. 2nd edition 1971.

Joüon, Paul, and Takamitsu Muraoka. 2008. *A Grammar of Biblical Hebrew*. Rome: Pontifical Biblical Institute.

Langlois, Michael. 2016. "Paleographic Analysis of the Dead Sea Scrolls in The Schøyen Collection." Pages 79–128 in *Gleanings from the Caves: Dead Sea Scrolls and Artifacts from the Schøyen Collection*. Edited by Torleif Elgvin, Kipp Davis and Michael Langlois. London: Bloomsbury T&T Clark.

Lee, Samuel. 1979. *Vetus Testamentum Syriace*. London: United Bible Societies.

Levine, Etan. 1973. *The Aramaic Version of Ruth*. Rome: Biblical Institute.

Muscarella, Oscar White. 2000. *The Lie Became Great. The Forgery of Ancient Near Eastern Cultures. Studies in the Art and Archaeology of Antiquity*. Groningen: Styx.

Quast, Udo editor. 2006. *Ruth*. Septuaginta: Vetus Testamentum Graecum IV.3. Göttingen: Vandenhoeck & Ruprecht.

Rahlfs, Alfred. 2006. *Septuaginta*. Stuttgart: Deutsche Bibelgesellschaft.

Schøyen, Martin. 2016. Acquisition and Ownership History: A Personal Reflection." Pages 27–31 in *Gleanings from the Caves: Dead Sea Scrolls and Artifacts from the Schøyen Collection*. Edited by Torleif Elgvin, Kipp Davis and Michael Langlois. London: Bloomsbury T&T Clark.

Schøyen Collection. 2020. "Statement in Response to Recent Media Attacks on the Integrity of the Schøyen Collection." https://www.schoyencollection.com/news-items/statement-on-fake-news. Accessed October 24, 2024.

Torleif, Elgvin. 2016a. "MS 5441. 4Q(?)Ruth (Ruth 2.1–2)."Pages 243–246 in *Gleanings from the Caves: Dead Sea Scrolls and Artifacts from the Schøyen Collection*. Edited by Elgvin, D. Kipp Davis and Michael Langlois. London: Bloomsbury T&T Clark.

———. 2016b. "Texts and Artefacts from the Judean Desert in the Schøyen Collection: An Overview." Pages 51–60 in *Gleanings from the Caves: Dead Sea Scrolls and Artifacts from the Schøyen Collection*. Edited by Elgvin, D. Kipp Davis and Michael Langlois. London: Bloomsbury T&T Clark.

Weber, Robert and Roger Gryson. 2007. *Biblia sacra iuxta vulgatam versionem*. Stuttgart: Deutsche Bibelgesellschaft.

White Crawford, Sidnie. 2024. "What Do the Dead Sea Scrolls Reveal about the Biblical Text." Pages 172–175 in *The Old Testament Hebrew Scriptures in Five Minutes*. Edited by Philippe Guillaume and Diana Edelman. Sheffield: Equinox.

About the Authors

Philippe Guillaume is Lecturer at the University of Berne. In 2024, he coedited with Diana Edelman *The Old Testament Hebrew Scriptures in Five Minutes* and *Deuteronomy: Outside the Box*, the inaugural volume of the Themes and Issues in Biblical Studies series, both at Equinox.

Rhiannon Graybill is Marcus M. and Carole M. Weinstein & Gilbert M. and Fannie S. Rosenthal Chair of Jewish Studies at the University of Richmond, USA. She is the author of *Texts after Terror: Rape, Sexual Violence, and the Hebrew Prophets* (Oxford, 2021) and *Are We Not Men?: Unstable Masculinity in the Hebrew Prophets* (Oxford, 2016) and multiple articles on gender, sexuality, and biblical texts. She has also co-authored two books with John Kaltner and Steven L. McKenzie: *Jonah: A New Translation with Notes and Commentary* (Yale University Press, 2023) and *What Are They Saying about the Book of Jonah?* (Paulist Press, 2024). At present, Graybill is working on a new book about the female body in the Hebrew Bible.

William Krisel is a lecturer at Institut Catholique de Paris (Catholic University of Paris). His recent publications include *Judges 19-21 and the "Othering" of Benjamin: A Golah Polemic against the Autochthonous Inhabitants of the Land?* (Leiden: Brill, 2022); "Methodological Problems in Intertextual Analyses of Old Testament Texts: Genesis 19 and Judges 19 as a Case Study," *Scandinavian Journal of the Old Testament* 36:2 (2022); "Was the Levite's Concubine Unfaithful or Angry? A Proposed Solution to the Text Critical Problem in Judges 19:2," *Old Testament Essays* 33, 2 (2020).

CHAPTER 2
ONE PLUS ONE EQUALS THREE: THE ECONOMICS OF LAND SHARES ACCORDING TO BOAZ

Philippe Guillaume

Abstract

Focusing on Ruth 4, the present chapter favors the *ketib* readings (as long argued, e.g. by Sasson) and argues that it is as members of the Bethlehem village commune that Boaz and Pelony Almony discuss the acquisition of Elimelech's land share. As Elimelech's widow, Naomi has the customary right to trade her usufruct of that share against her own upkeep. That Boaz manages to obtain Ruth's usufruct of Mahlon's share too is a feat given Ruth's Moabite origins. But that Boaz forces Bethlehem to accept his acquisition of Chilion's share in addition to Elimelech's and Mahlon is beyond any customary procedure. It presents both Boaz and Naomi as tricksters, Ruth as Naomi's self-indentured slave and the Bethlehem commune as too happy to accept the trick in exchange of placing the burden of feeding the two widows upon Boaz's shoulder. Economics take precedence over benevolence.

Keywords: Book of Ruth, open-field tenure, *ketiv-qere*, widows rights, brotherhood, tricksters, land-shares, usufruct

The plot of the Ruth tale is straightforward. The narrator already supplies key information in the first verse of Chapter 2 that names Boaz as the man of the hour. Narrative tension builds as we learn how he and Naomi set about to achieve their purposes through mundane economic practices, which pack the last three chapters (Hubbard 1988, 165–67). The present contribution is dedicated to the analysis of such practices and appraises their moral concerns.

The story opens with the combination of two common enough disasters: a drought that forces a family to move away and the untimely death of the head of the family and both of his sons before they had time to sire a son. The story pushes these common misfortunes to the point where the common solutions to such disasters are excluded. The sequel of events is as follows:

- Elimelech dies while in Moab, leaving his wife Naomi without the benefits of the traditional support networks in Bethlehem, his home town.
- Elimelech and Naomi's two sons also die in Moab.
- Both sons die childless, even though they had "lifted" (taken) wives there.
- Fourth, Naomi is too old to sire another son to perpetuate Elimelech's line.
- The wives of Elimelech's sons, Orpah and Ruth, are not Bethlehemites, at least not Ruth, who is systematically designated "the Moabite."
- Since Naomi's obvious solution is to return to Bethlehem, she asks Orpah and Ruth to return to their mothers' homes, but Ruth refuses and clings to Naomi. Hence, instead of arriving in Bethlehem alone, Naomi returns encumbered with another woman who is equally bereaved of her husband but who, as a Moabite, probably has never set foot in Bethlehem before.

As in the initial chapters of the book of Job, the outcome is a total disaster from which the rest of the story must extricate its hero.

Though we would refer to Naomi, Orpah, and Ruth as "widows," the Hebrew term *'almanah* is never used in the tale. Ruth is designated the "wife of the dead one" (*'ešet ha-mmet,* 4:5). The story's plot weaves around the schemes Naomi and Ruth devise to avoid becoming widows, namely needing public relief (see Deut 14:29). To circumvent the undesirable status of widowhood, women trade their fertility, which is their most valuable asset on the marital market. Marriage is not an option for menopausal Naomi (1:11) but remains the only solution able to be envisioned for Orpah and Ruth (1:9). The problem is that, unlike Naomi who bore two sons, Orpah and Ruth have failed to prove their fertility while married. They may turn out to be sterile. Their ratings on the marriage market are thus much lower than when they first married.

Often praised as an act of devotion to Naomi and her god, Ruth's desire to cling to Naomi may well be more opportunistic than Orpah's choice to return to her mother's home (Brenner 1999, 159). In the event that such a home still exists, it is not necessarily able or willing to welcome a widowed daughter.

For Naomi, however, Ruth's wish to stay with her represents an additional burden (Rees 2015, 107), and she expresses no appreciation of Ruth's "Wherever you go I shall go..." (1:16–17) (which would become memorable). Naomi responds with utter silence all the way to Bethlehem, where she burst into wails over her own plight: "Do not call me Naomi, call me Bitter" (1:20). Yet, the uproar her return (*watāšob*, singular) stirs up in Bethlehem (1:19) is caused as much by Naomi's unfortunate circumstances as by the presence of a second woman, a foreign one who is neither a "virgin" nor a mother. How Naomi can turn these handicaps into assets provides the necessary tension for a good tale.

1. Elimelech's Field Share

Bitter-Naomi left Bethlehem full but returns empty (1:21): bereaved of her husband and sons and too old to give birth to another son. Despite her heartrending words, Bitter-Naomi is not destitute. She remains the wife of one who had been a local man. Naomi's origins are irrelevant. It is the fact that she married a man from Bethlehem that entitles her to at least one of the rights her late husband held in Bethlehem. This right is only specified in Chapter 4 as "the share of the field that [is/was] for our brother, for Elimelech" (*ḥelqat ha-śadeh 'ašer le'aḥinu le'elimelek*; 4:3).

To clarify the nature of Elimelech's land-ownership, several possibilities may be imagined on the basis of the recurring references to redeemers (2:20; 3:9–12; 4:3–16): (a) Elimelech sold his land or borrowed money for the journey and left his land in the hands of a creditor as security before his departure to Moab; (b) he did nothing, hoping to return and relying on the goodwill of neighbors; (c) he left his land in the hands of a relative to look after in his absence (Sasson 1978, 61; Jackson 2017, 113–16).

None of these scenarios, however, fits the data provided by the text. Possibility (a) is excluded because there are no hints of a previous sale and even less of a loan in which transfer of possession to a creditor served as security. To be able to sell Elimelech's land, Naomi would either have had to own it in partnership with her husband before they left for Moab, or she would have had to inherit it when Elimelech's estate was settled immediately upon her return to Bethlehem. Co-ownership is unlikely, however, since the share of the field is always designated as Elimelech's, never as Naomi's or Elimelech and Naomi's. The story revolves around the fate of Elimelech's estate, which needs to be settled when Naomi returns to Bethlehem.

Nor are neighbors mentioned to support possibility (b). In 2:1, the narrator introduces Boaz as an acquaintance of Elimelech's (*myodaʻ* or *modaʻ*), and in 2:20 Naomi refers to Boaz not as a neighbor but as "close to us" and one of multiple potential redeemers. Such closeness seems to favor the identification of redeemers with relatives. Much depends on the implications of the right of a *go'el*, a task commonly undertaken by referring to references in the Torah (e.g., Embry 2016). These approaches infer a knowledge of the Torah by both the writer and the audience and presume the writer would have felt compelled to formulate the denouement in accordance with the Torah.

It is possible to obviate such inferences by noting that in 4:3, Boaz does not refer to a field but to a *share* of the field, which is not owned by Elimelech but was *for* him. Moreover, Boaz does not refer to Elimelech as a friend, neighbor, or acquaintance of his, but as "our *brother*," in other words, a brother of both Boaz and the other potential redeemer, Pelony Almony (henceforth PA).

This "share of field for our brother Elimelech" integrates three precise legal statements that require some decoding for a modern readership unacquainted with ancient methods of land tenure.

1.1 A Field Share

The above three possibilities are all weak because they conceive of Elimelech's ownership in the modern sense of freehold and his share of land as a specified field or plot of land. A modern reader assumes Naomi was returning to Bethlehem to claim a property that still belonged to her husband. A field share, however, is not equivalent to a specified field.

A "share (*ḥelqah*) of the field" first appears in 2:3 in reference to Boaz's land, in which Ruth finds herself gleaning. In both instances, the Septuagint renders *ḥelqat ha-śadeh* as *meris tou agrou*, a "part, portion," or more precisely, a "share of field." In his retelling of the Ruth story in Book 5 of his *Judean Antiquities*, Josephus concurs. Twice he evokes land. In V.324, Boaz's land in which Ruth gleans is designated *chōrion* (χωρίον), rendered as "ground" (Thackeray 1978, 145) or "parcel" (Begg 2005, 81). Then, in V.333, Elimelech's land is designated *klērōn* (κλήρων), rendered as "heritage" (Thackeray 1978, 149; Begg 2005, 83). Greek *klērōn* is as much an inheritance as a piece of land assigned by lot. The notion of allotment – land distributed by drawing lots – is crucial for understanding the transaction at the gate. What Elimelech's share of land implies was probably quite transparent to the original audience, because it refers to a well-attested type of communal land tenure (Guillaume 2012, 28–55) that

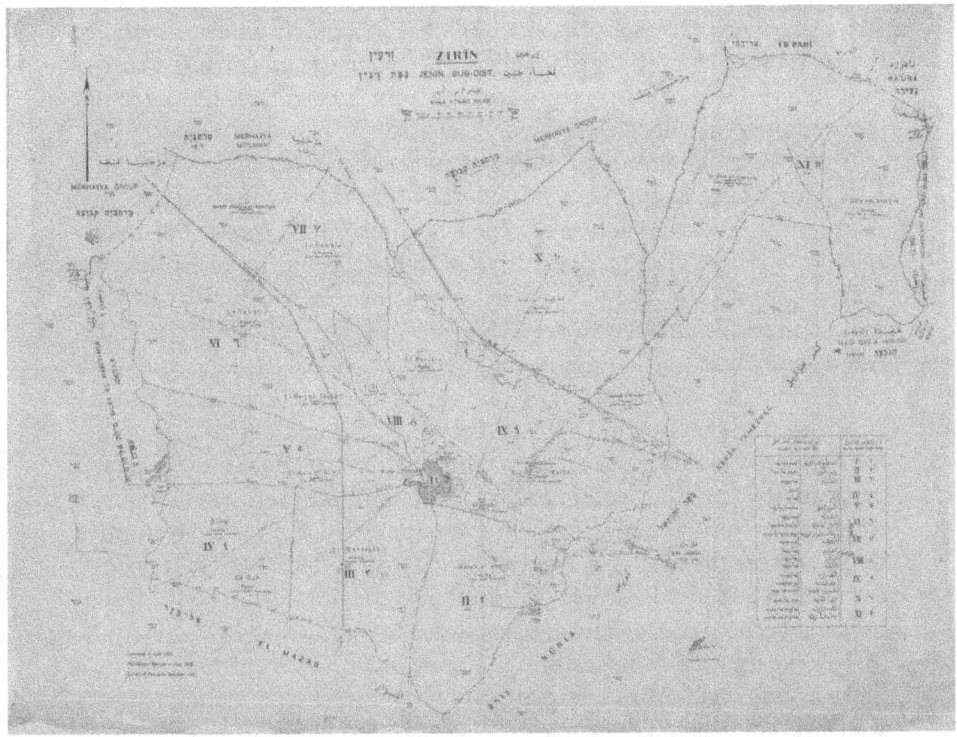

Figure 1: Map of Zerʻin, 1932, courtesy of Kibbutz Yizrael archives.

lasted until the twentieth century CE, as shown by the following example from Galilee (Figure 1).

The map identifies the sectors around Zerʻin – the name of the Palestinian village on the site of biblical Jezreel – available for dry cultivation such as *el waʻr, el muntār and ʻein el-Meita*. The surveyor designated these sectors "*mashaʻ*," that is, undivided arable land cultivated communally (see Guillaume 2012, 28–52). A second parenthesis adds "Dist[ributed] when necessary." The specificity of these areas becomes obvious when compared with the plots delimited with dotted lines on the eastern (right) side of the map. These plots are marked "Cult[ivated] Irr[igated]." Thanks to the clearing of the silt that had blocked it, the water from the *Spring of the Dead* (ʻAyn el-Meite) flowed again and allowed the Zerʻinis to grow prized summer crops like watermelons (Thomas Barnett *et al.*, forthcoming). Contrary to the area south of the spring, the irrigated parcels are not marked *mashaʻ* because they have a different function and a different status.

"When necessary," that is, when required by the needs of entitled members, the sectors under cultivation were further split into strips according to the number of shareholders. For the sake of equitability, the strips attributed to each shareholder were located in different parts of the sectors under cultivation to even out disparities and ensure that the best lots in term of solar exposure, gradient and soil quality were not granted in perpetuity to the same "brother."

This type of land tenure is now virtually extinct; hence, our difficulty today to be able to appreciate the details that the negotiation between Boaz and PA evokes. Contrary to gardens, arable land was so intimately related to shares that two verses after the first mention of Elimelech's field share ḥelqah is dropped and śadeh becomes the shorter way to refer to field shares (4:5). Nevertheless, "the share of the field" (ḥelqat ha-śadeh) refers to an immaterial right to the use of communal land.

The field (ha-śadeh) represents the belt of arable land used for the dry cultivation of grain within a kilometer or two around Bethlehem. In the well-attested practice of communal cultivation, the pool of arable land managed by the local commune was split into different sectors; some were under cultivation while others were fallowed and grazed to control weeds. Before the tractor revolutionized the so-called open-field system, the sectors under cultivation were split into strips according to the number of shareholders, usually adult males.

To keep up with demographic changes, strips were redistributed on a more or less regular basis according to the number of shareholders who were present to claim their share. This is why Jeremiah hastened to reach Anathoth in time to be included in the allotment of strips (Jer 37:12). Strips were attributed by drawing lots; the Hebrew and Greek terms *gôrāl* and *klēros* designate both the allocated strips (the "lots") and the means (stones, knucklebones, arrows...) used to randomize the allocation and avoid contestation by attributing the final decision to God.

Once the allotments were made, each member plowed, sowed, hoed and harvested the strips that were his for that given growing season – November to June for wheat and barley. During that period, the strips allocated to him were indeed his to use, and Boaz advises Ruth not to glean in another field (2:8). As the location of strips changed according to the fallowing and redistribution cycles, the limits of individual strips were indicated by flimsy landmarks meant to last only until the next redistribution and could, consequently, be easily moved to encroach on the neighbor's strip sown with the same plant at the same vegetative stage. Hence the warnings not to move or remove landmarks (Deut 19:14; Hos 5:10; Prov 22:28; 23:10).

1.2 A Share *for* Elimelech

In the biblical world, as in many parts of the world today, God is the owner of the land (Lev 25:23) through his vicar on earth. Farmers and home owners who cultivate or occupy parts of that land do not own it outright. They only possess the usufruct, namely, the right to enjoy the use and the advantages of another's property under agreed terms. Communal land was inalienable because usufructuaries were not freeholders. In Ruth 4:3, both the words "our brother" and "Elimelech" are preceded by a *lamed* (*le'aḥinu le'elimelech*). The share of field is not Elimelech's; it is *for* Elimelech. Yhwh owns the land. Elimelech was entitled to the usufruct of a share of Yhwh's land at Bethlehem. As one of the members of the Bethlehem assembly, Elimelech enjoyed a share in the land managed by this council. The clue to the existence of such an assembly is the fact that Boaz refers to Elimelech as "our brother" when he addresses PA (4:3).

1.3 *Our Brother* Elimelech

The fact that Boaz refers to Elimelech as "our brother" in his address to PA is easily missed due to the NRSV's rendering of the term *'aḥynw* as "our kinsman." The term "brother" was commonly used to refer to business partners in Ugarit (PRU IV 1956, 189 see 17.314) and in Mesopotamia, where the terms ŠEŠ and PAB are used for Akkadian *aḫu* to mean "colleague, partner" in craftsmanship contexts. In SAA 8 296, brothers built a storeroom (Hunger 1992, 296); in SAA 13 27 s.1, thirty-one brothers released someone from the locks of Aššur (also SAA 13 40 3, "Good health to my brother" in Oppenheimer and Reiner 1964, 202).

Beyond kinship ties, brotherly status could refer to membership of Neo-Hittite funerary associations (Woudhuizen 2019) and to business partnerships (Porten and Yardeni 1986–1999, 48–49). In the Hebrew Bible, half of the 49 occurrences of the term *aḥ* in Deuteronomy can refer to business partners rather than to siblings (Guillaume 2021, 316–21). There is no reason to exclude that dual meaning of brotherhood in Ruth, where Boaz is as much a brother as PA is. They hold equal rights to claim Elimelech's share. Both are designated *go'el*, "redeemer": Boaz in 2:20; 3:9, 12; and PA in 3:12; 4:1, 3, 6, 8. Both are potential redeemers because they are brothers, that is, members of the Bethlehem assembly to which Elimelech also belonged. This membership is the crux of the matter. Instead of presenting Boaz as kin, the narrator introduces Boaz as an acquaintance of Naomi's husband "for Naomi, [there was] an acquaintance (*meyuda'* or *muda'*) to her man" (2:1). Besides "acquaintance," the term *meyuda'* or *muda'* can be understood as "understanding." Whatever the nature of that "acquaintance" or "understanding" between Boaz and Elimelech, it differed from kinship ties because Naomi explains to Ruth that Boaz is "closer to us among our redeemers" (*qarob lanu mego'elnu* 2:20). Yet, readers tend to ignore the points made by the narrator and Naomi because Boaz warns Ruth that PA is a closer redeemer than he is (*go'el qarob mimmeny* 3:12) and in 4:4, Boaz asserts his position as next in line after PA. The equal status of Boaz and PA as brothers is ignored in favor of kinship, which supposedly establishes PA's precedence over Boaz. In fact, kinship only establishes the order in which Elimelech's share is offered. PA gets first choice for the acquisition of Elimelech's share because he is first in the line of kinship. Boaz gets second choice based on kinship.

Kinship is a matter of seemliness more than a legal obligation. Boaz has good reasons to insist on decorum, which will become clear below. Simply put, Boaz and PA are legally equals as members (brothers), but PA might be a closer cousin to Elimelech than Boaz, a fact Boaz is keen to underline (3:12; 4:4). Boaz was a closer acquaintance to Elimelech than PA, though Naomi never explains what makes Boaz closer than the other potential redeemer(s), just as Boaz never explains why PA is a closer redeemer than he himself is.

The failure to distinguish between partnership and kinship is a collateral effect of the failure to understand the difference between a field share and a land share. Peter Lau is certainly correct that the term "brother" denotes a male sibling sharing the same parent(s), but a "brother" is not necessarily "also a clansman from the wider kinship group" (Lau 2015, 20; same in Nu 2015, 65–68). Indeed, 2:1 states that Boaz belongs to Elimelech's family (*mišpaḥah*), but what qualifies him as *go'el* is not "the wider kinship group" but membership in the Bethlehem village community as well as Boaz's closer position as an acquaintance on the basis of business and other ties with Elimelech when he was alive.

To recapitulate, the "share of the field that was for our brother, for Elimelech" refers not to a specific plot of land around Bethlehem but to the share of communal land Elimelech was entitled to as a member of the Bethlehem village community that managed the arable land in partnership. It is as members of this community who have the closest kinship ties to Elimelech that Boaz and PA have the option to take over Elimelech's share from or on behalf of Naomi ahead of other male members of the village commune. The question now is the fate of a share when a shareholder leaves the village or dies.

2. Eligible Beneficiaries to Land Shares

The discussion between PA and Boaz at the gate (Chapter 4) is the denouement of the entire plot. It is crucial to understand what the transaction implies, what PA expected to acquire, why he eventually desists, and what Boaz's marriage to Ruth implies for all parties concerned.

As was the custom in open-field systems, the Ruth tale presupposes that Elimelech's share went back into the pool of communal land when he left for Moab but that his right to his share remained valid upon his return. Consequently, during the ten-year absence of Elimelech's family (1:4), his share and those of his adult sons would not have been taken into account when field strips were redistributed among the brothers who were physically present in Bethlehem. Elimelech and his sons having died in Moab, Naomi returns to claim her right to Elimelech's share of the communal land. There is no need to postulate, as Bernard Jackson does, that PA hoped "that Elimelekh and his family would never return, but, if they did so, that he would be able to claim merely to have been looking after the property in their interest" (2017, 113–16).

Jackson's scenario would be valid in a modern system of land tenure where communal land has been privatized and split into fixed parcels owned by individual farmers. The same applies to the hypotheses that "Elimelech would surely have disposed of all his holdings before leaving for Moab" (Gordis 1974, 256), or that Elimelech's "land abandoned for a decade was being harvested either by a family or neighbor" (Sasson 1978, 61).

Instead of selling a field that had remained fallow or had been cultivated by others while Elimelech's family was in Moab, Naomi trades (*mkr*) Elimelech's share of field. The verb *mkr* in 4:3 should be taken in the broad sense of "making a trade deal" or "making an exchange deal" – or, to use a current financial term, "asset swapping" – rather than "selling" in our modern understanding of that term. She trades, or in this case, leases the usufruct rights associated with her dead husband's share to someone who will support her and Ruth in return. Similarly, in 4:4–10, the verb *qnh* is better rendered as "to acquire" than "to buy." The deal involves the cashless exchange of non-fungible assets, not the purchase of a property.

2.1 Naomi's Right to Use Elimelech's Share

While communal land cannot be sold because it belongs to God, shareholders are free to lease their share to others. Though shareholders are adult males, no one contests Naomi's right to claim the share of her late husband. Her return conveniently occurs during the harvest (1:22) when stores are at their fullest and when gleaning is possible, affording time for a redistribution of land before the next plowing season to take into account the change in the number of shareholders present following her return.

Entitled as she is to claim the usufruct of Elimelech's estate, Naomi nevertheless faces a predicament. She has no sons to help her cultivate the share of their deceased father. Nor does she have the means to buy seed for the coming year. She also needs to feed herself and Ruth over the next twelve months before the next harvest. How will Naomi make the most of the assets at her disposal?

2.2 Pelony Almony and Boaz's Rights to Elimelech's Share

As two members of the group of owners of shares of Bethlehem's communal land, Boaz and PA have to decide which of them will acquire Elimelech's share, due their additional status of *go'el*. The tale ignores other shareholders and non-shareholders who may have been interested in renting Elimelech's share from Naomi. The other Bethlehemites are onlookers at the gate proceedings until they are asked to witness the list of Boaz's acquisitions (4:9).

When in 2:1, the narrator introduces Boaz as an acquaintance, he adds that he is also a prominent/wealthy man (*'yš gibbor ḥayil*). This status apparently is not shared by PA, who admits that acquiring Elimelech's share would damage his inheritance (4:6), even though he is the first *go'el* ahead of Boaz. As brothers, the two are equals, but socially or economically, PA appears to be inferior to Boaz. Prominence is the decisive factor, and Boaz praises Ruth for having rejected other matches, rich or poor (3:10). Hence, one must take Boaz's apparent deference to PA in regard to his priority over Elimelech's share with a pinch of salt.

2.3 Obed as Heir of Elimelech's Share

The discussion between PA and Boaz is spurred on by Naomi's decision to reactivate Elimelech's share so she can lease its usufruct rights to support herself and Ruth in the future. It is urgent to decide who will assume the unexpected burden of feeding the two women until the next harvest. Whoever cultivates Elimelech's share is to supply Naomi's food for the coming year.

Naomi is too old to bear another heir for the deceased Elimelech (Hubbard 1988, 51), and the Hagar solution (Gen 16) is impossible. Contrary to Abraham, Elimelech is dead, and Naomi owns no slave, even if Ruth has chosen to put herself entirely at Naomi's disposal (see §4). The solution will be Naomi's adoption of Obed to prevent Elimelech's share from being extinguished upon Naomi's death. The adoption will not physically deprive Ruth of her son but will secure the ownership of Elimelech's share even after Naomi's death.

The moment Ruth gives birth to Obed, the women attribute the birth to Yhwh's blessing of Naomi, whom he has not deprived (*šbt*, hiphil) of a redeemer (4:14). The redeemer is *not* Boaz; it is Obed, who redeems Elimelech's share through his adoption by Naomi. Though Naomi is deemed Obed's "nurse" (*'omenet* 4:16), in the next verse the women explicitly declare that "a son is born for Naomi" (*yulled ben lenā'omi*). Ties established by milk are stronger than blood ties (Chapman 2012), though even the milk here is symbolic.

But there is more. The blessing by which the entire citizenry of Bethlehem validates Boaz's acquisitions (4:11) anticipates that Ruth, like Rachel and Leah, is expected to bear more than a single son. While Elimelech's share is redeemed by the adoption of Obed, Mahlon's share remains without a legitimate heir.

3. The Small Script

PA's decision to let Boaz take Elimelech's share solves the matter of Naomi's upkeep. Nothing indicates, however, that the annuity against which she trades Elimelech's share would suffice to feed Ruth, too. Ruth's status in Bethlehem is more complicated than Naomi's because she is a Moabite. Yet, contrary to Naomi, Ruth enters Bethlehem not quite as empty-handed as Naomi. She is young enough to bear sons, though she has yet to prove her fertility as we hear nothing of children born from Ruth's marriage with Mahlon.

Marriage is the solution to secure Ruth's upkeep for as long as her marriage lasts. As the writer has already dropped heavy hints by stating that the strips in which Ruth finds herself gleaning are Boaz's (2:3), it is clear whom Ruth ought to marry. To build narrative tension, the plot relies instead on how Ruth's fate intersects with Naomi's fate and how Boaz will convince PA to drop his right of preemption over Elimelech's share, even though PA expresses his desire to redeem it.

Redemption involves recovering the use of a person or asset that was lost through foreclosure or to service an antichretic loan (Lev 25; see Guillaume 2012, 192-96; 2022a, 26; contrast with Adams 2014, 105 and 110). None of the cases considered in Leviticus 25 apply to Naomi or Ruth. Both are free of any encumbrance that would call for redemption. What is open for redemption is land shares.

As Naomi's right of use (usufruct) to Elimelech's share is recognized, does Ruth enjoy the same right to claim her late husband's share, since Mahlon son of Elimelech was a Bethlehemite too? The matter of the marginal *ketiv-qere* in 4:5 is discussed below (§5). For the moment, the text is taken as it stands because it makes sense as it is. In 4:5 Boaz explains to PA that the acquisition of Elimelech's share has no bearings on Ruth's fate:

> Boaz said: "in the day of your acquisition of the field from the hand of Naomi, but from with (*ume'et*) Ruth the Moabite wife of the dead I acquire/d (*ketiv*: *qanyty*) [the duty] to raise the name of the dead on his inheritance."

With these words, Boaz announces that he is about to marry Ruth, something the audience knows already. What neither the audience or PA realize is that this marriage impacts on the acquisition of Elimelech's share. In other words, Boaz circumscribes PA's choice as to whether or not to acquire Elimelech's share. For PA, the prospect of acquiring Elimelech's share without Ruth is not attractive and he withdraws, justifying his decision in v. 6 by stating that he cannot (*lo' 'ukal*) redeem "lest I destroy my inheritance" (*pen 'ašḥiyt 'et naḥalatiy*). The implication is that PA had considered Ruth as part of the package. The additional advantage of the *ketiv* is that it better renders justice to the awkward formulation "and/ but from" (ומאת, *ume'et*, see Zevit 2005, 599). It does not mean that the land is acquired from both Naomi and Ruth (against Lau 2011, 68). On the contrary, it distinguishes between two different actions, each one related to a different woman: the acquisition of Elimelech's land from Naomi and the perpetuation of Elimelech's name through Ruth, which is exactly what eventually happens when Obed is born.

Once Boaz informs him that Ruth is not part of the deal, PA desists from his initial desire to redeem Elimelech's share (4:6). This suggests that rather than a burden (as is the case with the *qere*), Ruth is the cherry on the cake, a cherry that Boaz deprives PA of.

What is less clear is the weight to be given to PA's claim that the acquisition of Elimelech's share without Ruth would destroy his inheritance. One would expect instead that acquiring the land share without Ruth would be *less* of a burden for PA and that he would thus be *more* willing to confirm his initial decision.

One way to overcome this inconsistency is to understand the danger to PA's inheritance as no more than a face-saving move when PA realizes that Boaz wants Elimelech's share in addition to Ruth. Though they are equals as brothers and Boaz grants PA priority of choice, PA bows down to Boaz because he is socially no match for Boaz. In this sense, the economics are only a polite excuse to desist, and the inheritance PA wishes to preserve is a decent relationship with Boaz, who would be aggrieved if PA insisted on a right to acquire Elimelech's share, a right Boaz grants him merely on the basis of kinship. The price of peace with Boaz is to give up Elimelech's share and Ruth. If so, Boaz merely pretends that PA is first in line and PA merely pretends that he cannot assume the burden of the upkeep of the two women. Politeness and keeping appearances intact are of course highly desirable, but they ought not be confused with legal obligations. The Ruth tale relies on custom, customary law even, but it would be precarious to draw legal obligations from such a tale.

Boaz's statements differ according to whom he addresses. To Ruth, Boaz warns that PA might stand in the way (3:12). To PA, he states that Ruth is not part of the deal (4:5). When negotiating contracts, such double language is not surprising. It is part of the game, as in the case with Ephron and Abraham at Machpelah (Gen 23; Sternberg 1991).

Boaz is portrayed as a ruthless bargainer, all the more so if PA would, in fact, have been able to assume the burden of taking care of both Naomi and Ruth. This does not lessen Boaz's generosity, but it adds an extra dimension to his portrait and to PA's, who might have been no less capable than Boaz but gives up what would have been a good deal for both in order to preserve the peace.

The moment PA removes his sandal to signify his decision, Boaz asks all present at the gate to witness that he has acquired "all that (is/was) for Elimelech and all that (is/was) for Chilion and Mahlon." Boaz foregrounds the land and bundles it into a neat package before officially announcing that he is marrying Ruth. After that, the narrative moves fast forwards to the happy end and the rest is history. Yet, it is worth stopping to examine the contents of Boaz's package.

Whatever else "all that [is] for Elimelech" (*kol 'ašer l'elimelek*) refers to, it includes the share of field, the preoccupying subject since the beginning of Chapter 4. Sonnet (2021, 146) takes the mention of Chilion and Mahlon as a clue that Elimelech had not yet split his land between his two sons. This, however, presupposes that Elimelech owned land rather than a share of land. As discussed above (§1), this is unlikely in an open-field system where shares of communal land were attributed to adult sons rather than split between them, so that, instead of receiving an amount of land that shrunk from one generation to the next in proportion to the number of heirs, the corresponding amount of communal land for each share is the same for all shareholders.

As long as arable land is freely available, as this was the case in the underpopulated ancient world, fluctuations in the number of entitled "brothers" was dealt with by simply adjusting the amount of available acreage of fallow land required. When necessary, more arable land would be cleared to ensure that the share each member received was sufficient for the subsistence of their dependants and the same for all.

As a rule of thumb, Renger (1987, 59) calculated the yearly consumption of an average family of five (Kalla 1996, 253) at 2,160 *sila* of barley (1 *sila* = 1 liter), some 400 liters of barley per person per year. Given the uncertainties over the comparative density of ancient wheat and barley, one can only trust that these 400 liters correspond very roughly to the 170 kgs of wheat included in the bare bones subsistence basket that includes 20 kgs of beans or lentils, 5 kgs of meat and 5 kgs of oil per person per year (Scheidel 2010, 434). In short, Boaz would have to disburse close to a ton (metric or imperial) of grain besides seeds and other expenses before hoping to recoup his expenses from the yield of the three shares.

The net result is that having managed to convince PA to give up Elimelech's share by removing Ruth from the deal offered by Naomi, Boaz takes for himself three shares when PA had been offered a single one, Elimelech's. Naomi trades her usufruct to that share against food as an annuity. What about the two additional shares?

3.1 Mahlon's Share as Ruth's Dowry

Though land shares are granted to sons and not to daughters, land is nevertheless tied to women as mothers. Since Naomi is entitled to claim Elimelech's share as his widow, in theory at least, Ruth should enjoy the same right. She is not merely "a Moabite widow among Israelites" (so, Sinnott 2020, 87), but, as much as Naomi, she was the wife of a local man and is, thus, entitled to claim any possession of her late husband, Mahlon. She was not a mere *ger*, if such a status applied to women. In contrast to Naomi, however, Ruth is still of marriageable age. Therefore, Ruth is entitled to the usufruct of Mahlon's share, a share that PA cannot claim because it goes to Ruth's next husband, Boaz himself. Mahlon's share serves as the dowry Ruth brings into her union with Boaz. PA may have hoped to secure Mahlon's share besides Elimelech's, but Boaz warns him that there is no way PA will get Mahlon's share.

Often misrepresented as a "bride price," the dowry was essentially the capital a daughter received from her father upon marriage, whereas sons had to wait for their father's death to inherit their share of the paternal estate. The dowry was often used by a husband, though his wife retained full ownership of it. The husband was obliged to hand it back to his wife should he repudiate her or to transmit it to her legitimate heirs if she died before her spouse (Stol 2016, 134–45; Benjamin 2017, 7).

Boaz's claim to Mahlon's share, a claim no one contests, means that, despite her Moabite origins, Ruth enjoys the same inheritance rights as Naomi since both had married members of the Bethlehem brotherhood. Even if Mahlon had left Bethlehem before coming of age and had thus never actually cultivated a share of field, as the son of a Bethlehem shareholder, Mahlon would have been entitled to claim one should he ever return, once an adult. Through his untimely death, Mahlon never did, but the fact that he married Ruth in Moab secures Ruth's right to the use of his share in Bethlehem, unless her Moabite origins are deemed a sufficient hurdle to prevent her from claiming the usufruct of Mahlon's share. In other words, death terminates birth rights, but rights acquired by marriage survive the death of the husband.

Bringing Mahlon's share into the discussion confirms the old view that the redemption of Elimelech's share has "nothing intrinsically to do with Ruth's remarriage" (Beattie 1978, 65; Sasson 1978). It also solves the disputed understanding of the particle *ky* in 3:9. Commonly rendered as "spread your wing over your handmaid *for* you are a redeemer," v. 3:9b is "largely responsible for the association of Ruth's request for marriage to Boaz's obligation as a *go'el*" (Sasson 1978, 53). The disentanglement of the redemption of the land from Ruth's marriage does not imply that no land is involved in Ruth's marriage. As argued here, the mention of Elimelech's share and the acquisition of everything that belonged to Elimelech and his two sons involves three shares (see below on Chilion's share). "Acquisition" is preferable to buying since no cash is exchanged. Ruth is not the object of a sale but is the person through whom Boaz acquires Mahlon's share (Sasson 1979, 108–51).

As Ruth's next spouse, Boaz has every interest in Mahlon's share of land, the produce of which he will use to feed Ruth. In the event of repudiation, Ruth would use Mahlon's share to convince another man to marry her as long as she remains in Bethlehem. Were her union with Boaz eventually to prove fertile, Mahlon's share would pass on to Ruth's son(s), namely, the one(s) born *after* Obed. In the so-called patriarchal world of the Hebrew Bible, women owned no land. Nor did men. Men were granted land shares when they came of age, as long as they resided in the village they were associated with through descent. Daughters were not entitled to land shares, but as mothers women secured land shares for their sons.

3.2 Chilion's Share as Interests for Boaz

While Boaz got Bethlehem to accept that Ruth was entitled to the usufruct of Mahlon's share, adding Chilion into the deal is another matter. Hubbard is a rare interpreter to note that "the extent of the purchase probably took the reader by surprise" (1988, 255) and to suspect that Boaz may have tricked PA. Indeed, Boaz made no mention of Chilion in 4:5 when he delineated the deal before PA, but he lists Chilion *before* Mahlon in the inventory of his acquisitions. Chilion was Elimelech's son as much as Mahlon, but, contrary to Mahlon's widow (Ruth), Orpah did not cling to Naomi. Boaz only marries Ruth, and no widow's right applies to Chilion's share of field because his widow did not turn up in Bethlehem to claim that share. Either "all that [is] for Chilion and Mahlon" includes goods and properties other than land shares, or the acquisition of Chilion's share by Boaz oversteps what should have legitimately reverted to him as acquirer of Elimelech's share and as Ruth's spouse.

Feminist readers suspect that Boaz was not as selfless as idyllic reading used to view him. Quoting Susan Niditch (2000, xviii) who listed Boaz among biblical tricksters, Kristin Saxegaard (2010, 163) declares Boaz a trickster who manages to make PA take off his sandal, though he is the "younger brother" and "win Ruth, avoid gossip, and even become the one whose name will be proclaimed in Bethlehem (4:11)."

The matter of land shares further clarifies why Boaz deserves the title of trickster. The trick Boaz plays on his Bethlehem associates is not that he is the "younger brother." Seniority may play a role, but all Bethlehem-born adult males enjoyed the same right to a share of the communal land they managed in partnership. Nor is the fact that Boaz wins Ruth the matter. The trick is the self-attribution of *three* shares – Elimelech's, Mahlon's and Chilion's – in exchange for the upkeep of only *two* widows. While PA was only offered one share, Boaz takes three shares for himself and no one at the gate objects, which does not exclude the possibility of behind-the-scenes gossip, given "the extent of the purchase" (Hubbard 1988, 255).

Boaz attributes to himself a leonine deal. Winner-takes-all Boaz acquires three shares, a trick that crowns the plot. In one daring move, Boaz solves the plight of the two widows and gains an extra share. Does the trick make Boaz a crook?

If "everything that belongs to Chilion" includes a share of field equivalent to Elimelech's and Mahlon's, what was the narrator up to in presenting his hero in a way that may be viewed as outrightly dishonest? Can the acquisition of that third share be justified from an economic point of view?

From the vantage point of the other shareholders, the return of Naomi and Ruth means an additional two mouths to feed for the coming year out of what has just been harvested. In the absence of pressure on the availability of land – the most likely scenario – three additional shares to be allotted in the upcoming redistribution of strips represent a much lighter burden for the other shareholders than the prospect of feeding Naomi and Ruth throughout the coming year. The Bethlehemite "brothers" can produce those strips to be allotted simply by reducing the fallowed surface of land. In the worst case, they would have to clear more land to account for these extra shares, were they not offset by the departure or death of other brothers. Therefore, all brothers may be relieved to see that Boaz is assuming the role expected from an *'ish gibbor ḥayil* (2:1). By acquiring Naomi's share and marrying Ruth, Boaz saves PA and his peers from the burden of having to feed those two unexpected extra mouths.

PA and the entire Bethlehem village commune accept the leonine deal because it saves them from assuming that burden collectively.

From Boaz's point of view, the grain Chilion's share might produce in the next harvest compensates the provision of immediate relief for Naomi and Ruth and covers the extra costs of cultivation of Elimelech and Mahlon's shares (plowing, seeding, harvesting, threshing and storage). In this sense, the produce Boaz hopes to collect from Chilion's share is the legitimate reward for the risk he assumes by investing capital and immobilizing it for an entire year. Instead of selling the surplus grain he has just harvested, Boaz has to store it to feed Naomi and Ruth and to use some of it as seed for the three additional land shares he secures. He might also have to hire plowing teams and certainly more harvesters (2:6-7). Worse, he might have to borrow grain in the coming November to sow these extra strips, which means greater indebtedness. Hence, despite the trickery involved to obtain it, Chilion's share is similar to the interest drawn from a loan. At this point, Bible readers will object that the Torah forbids charging interest on consumption loans. This requires a discussion of the matter of interest.

Interest-free loans are commonly interpreted as benevolence towards the poor (Levin 2014, 57), which is nonsense, since no one grants loans to impoverished people. Lending implies creditworthiness on the part of the borrower, in other words, the ability of the borrower to convince a lender that he will most likely be able to service his debt and reimburse the loan. Unless poverty means something other than destitution, what the "poor" need are alms, not loans. The spiritualization of poverty has blurred the crucial distinction between loans and alms (e.g. Levin 2001, 261).

The prohibition against charging interest in Deut 23:20 (English 19) reads, "You shall not charge interest on loans to another Israelite, interest on money, interest on provisions, interest on anything that is lent" (NRSV). This rendering is riddled with translational issues. First of all, "another Israelite" is, in Hebrew and Greek, "your brother" (*'aḥika, adelphos sou*). The notion of brotherhood is relevant to Ruth, where the negotiations between Boaz and PA occur between brothers before elders and the rest of the local population.

Second, to "charge interest" is, in the Hebrew of Deut 23:20, a "bite" (*nešek*). Deuteronomy ignores the other designation of interest attested in Lev 25:36, *tarbit*, which designates an increment received from a loan in the form of a gift or any other form as an amount added to the lent capital, either during the term of the loan or as a penalty after the term has expired. Hence, what Deuteronomy explicitly condemns is the "bite" on the principal, that is a portion that is excised from the principal by the lender at the time of the transfer of the silver (*kesep*) or food (*'okal*) to the borrower, though this deduction is omitted in the promissory note (Gamoran 1971, 132). Thus, if "A" agrees to lend "B" 100 but "A" only hands over 90 to "B," who is committed to pay "A" back 100, the deduction taken up front corresponds in reality to what would have been a rate of interest of 11.11 percent (and not 10 percent, because the borrower "B" has only had the use of 90 percent of the loan). This practice is well-attested as a means of circumventing the ban on interest-bearing loans in cultures that prohibit interest.

In short, Deuteronomy implicitly condones interest in the form of increase and explicitly condemns interest in the form of a discount on the capital actually lent. The focus is on the duplicity involved in recording a sum that is above what is actually disbursed, not on the practice of rewarding the risk taken by the lender. As no economy can function without credit, Deuteronomy's economic approach is too pragmatic to quench credit by proscribing the legitimate reward of risk (Guillaume 2022b). Therefore, Boaz behaves in accordance with Deuteronomy by securing a third share to compensate for the risks he takes in feeding both Naomi and Ruth (who, for all he knows, might be sterile) and by cultivating three additional shares that might not cover expenses if the next harvest proves to be a poor one. Compliance with Deuteronomy's approach to credit does not imply any reliance of the Ruth tale on the Torah, however (see Chapter 3 in this volume).

4. Ruth's Self-Indenture

The status Ruth obtains through marriage to Boaz is of interest for the present state of the research on Ruth, which has grown more suspicious of the previous tendency to view Boaz as a disinterested savior. Feminist exegesis challenges patriarchalism, supposedly a trait in Ruth, where Ruth's best choice is an older Boaz, whose modern counterparts are the so-called "sugar-daddies" (West and Haddad 2016, 145–46; see also Yee 2009, 133).

The benefits young women obtain from sugar-daddies are hardly acceptable to feminist sensibilities that view equality and economic independence as requirements for the liberation of women.

The Ruth tale, however, displays another, even less palatable aspect of dependence that involves women primarily, that is, the control Naomi obtained over Ruth when Ruth decided to cling (*dabqah*, 1:14) to her. Sin-lung Tong noted that Ruth had put herself under obligation to serve Naomi (2015, 41; already Sasson 1979, 124; and Brenner 1999, 158–62). Yet, the serving involved is quite similar to slavery, including sexual exploitation (Graybill 2021, 107–09).

The only mention of "love" in Ruth is Ruth's love towards Naomi (4:15), which, in light of the case of the servant who decides to enter into perpetual slavery in the household of the master he loves (Exod 21:6; Deut 15:16), is not necessarily a clue pointing to lesbianism (Krutzsch 2015, 204). Instead, it is a clue about self-indenture. The final part of Ruth's oath, "May Yhwh do thus and so to me, and more as well, if even death parts me from you," (1:17) implies more than devotion. These words have contractual force. They imply that from that moment on, Ruth places herself in perpetual slavery to Naomi, except that it is not formalized by the piercing of an ear (Deut 15:17).

Indeed, Ruth is never described as Naomi's slave, but she always acts with the permission of Naomi, except on the occasion when she takes the initiative to invite Boaz to spread his wing over her (3:9). When Boaz encounters Ruth for the first time among his harvesters, he does not ask his foreman, "Who is this young woman?" but "For whom" (*lemiy*) is she, that is, to whom does she belong? (2:5). This does not necessarily imply slavery, but it indicates that no such young woman is expected to roam freely without being sent there by a particular household, either as a salaried day laborer or to repay an antichretic loan. In all cases, economic implications are involved, and Boaz needs to know who sent Ruth in order to keep account of her salary or the number of work days to knock off the debtor's ledger.

Ruth ends her initial encounter with Boaz by thanking him for his kindness – literally "speaking to the heart of your servant" (*šifḥateka*) – although she is *not* one of his servants (2:13). These words express a desire to be attached to Boaz and underline at the same time her dependence to someone one, in other words, Naomi.

When they announce the birth of Obed to Naomi, the women of Bethlehem duly refer to Ruth as "your daughter-in-law, who loves you" (Ruth 4:15). This is a likely reference to the reason evoked as the motivation for self-indenture: "if he says to you 'I will not go out from you' because he loves you..." (Deut 15:16).

In exchange for Ruth's attachment to her, Naomi has the duty to find rest (*manowaḥ*, 3:1) for Ruth. As a newcomer in Bethlehem, Ruth has to prove her mettle, and her submissive dedication to Naomi gains her the respect of the entire Bethlehemite community (2:11). Boaz evokes Ruth's hard-gained reputation as decisive in his willingness to marry her (3:10). In Ruth and everywhere else, loving kindness is not built on thin air; it is maintained by concrete expressions of reciprocity. In Ruth's case, submission and hard work in the field are key to her acceptance by Bethlehem and the basis for Boaz's decision to risk marrying her despite her apparent failure to produce children for her previous husband.

5. The Early Reception of Ruth

Having deciphered the economics of land shares in the open-field system of land tenure presupposed in the Ruth story, it is time to turn to the major issue of the *ketiv-qere* in Ruth 4:5. This marginal note has generated two entirely different readings of Ruth. Almost everyone today follows the translators (from LXX to NRSV) and the majority of commentators (e.g. Hubbard 1988; Fischer 2001; Schipper 2016), who give precedence to the *qere* (קָנִיתָה, *qnyth* "you acquired") over against the *ketiv* (קניתי, *qnyty* "I acquired"). This "consensus" is the result of Edward Campbell's influential Anchor Bible Commentary on Ruth (1975) in which he dismissed Derek Beattie's arguments in favor of the *ketiv* (Beattie 1971; 1974). He stated simply that the *ketiv* "fails completely to accord with the language of 3:12–13 and is out of place with the whole thrust of the threshing floor and gate episodes" and "violates the internal consistency of the Ruth story" (Campbell 1975, 146, quoting Rowley 1952, 185 n. 1 and Rudolph 1962, 59). In Chapter 3 in this volume, I critically assess Campbell's argument and conclude in favor of the primacy of the *ketiv*.

Yet, Beattie (1971; 1974) was not alone in favoring the *ketiv*. Theodorus Vriezen (1948, 80–88) had preceded him and Jack Sasson (1978; 1979, 119–36; 1987, 326; 1989, 119–36), Kirsten Nielsen (1985, 209), Dana Fewell and David Gunn (1989), and André Lacocque (2004, 130) also read Ruth 4:5 with the *ketiv*, in which Boaz warns PA, who has just declared his willingness to acquire Elimelech's share of field, "I [Boaz] have [already] acquired (*qanyty*) Ruth."

Instead of the *ketiv*, the *qere* warns PA that alongside acquiring Elimelech's share, "you have acquired (*qanytah*) Ruth [too]." The *ketiv* decouples Ruth from the deal. The *qere* bundles her with Elimelech's field share. With the *ketiv*, Ruth is a prize that tops the deal of which Boaz deprives PA. The *ketiv* "provides an important logical requirement of the plot" (Fewell and Gunn 1989, 52). The news of Boaz's marriage confronts PA with "the possibility that there could be a male heir to Mahlon" (Fewell and Gunn 1989, 52). This is indeed new, as only a few hours earlier, Boaz agreed to the plan of Naomi and Ruth. On the contrary, the *qere* makes PA the only person at the gate ignorant of a seemingly fundamental obligation, while attempts at explaining the legal basis of the postulated *ge'ullah* marriage remain "tendentious in the extreme" (Fewell and Gunn 1989, 58). Since the *ketiv* makes sense as the follow-up to the threshing floor scene, why introduce a *qere* that turns the denouement upside down and turns Ruth into an encumbrance that convinces PA to desist?

5.1 The *Qere* as a Clue to Resistance

The *ketiv-qere* was introduced centuries after the initial stages of the production of Ruth. The *ketiv-qere* belongs to the early reception history of the Ruth tale and clearly reflects a long tradition of reading that resisted, consciously or not, the plain meaning of the Hebrew text. Flavius Josephus read Ruth through the lens of the *qere* - even if it was not yet noted in the margin of any actual manuscript. Josephus tied the exegesis of Ruth to the laws of the Pentateuch by having Boaz declare to PA "... if you wish to possess their fields, you must, according to the laws, marry [her]" (Ant. 5, 333; Begg 2005, 84). Whichever meaning of the term "law" Josephus used here (see Bay 2022), it simply follows the Alexandrian translators whose rendering relies on the *qere*:

> the day you acquire the field from the hand of Neomin and from Routh the Moabite, the wife of the deceased, it is necessary (δεῖ) for you to acquire her also in order to raise up the name of the deceased on his inheritance. (Ruth 4:5, NETS)

With δεῖ ("you must"), the translators introduced the notion of obligation, which is exactly what the so-called law of the levirate abstains from doing when it grants the right of the *levir* to refuse to impregnate the wife of the dead brother (Deut 25:7), despite the public shaming that such a refusal entails. In spite of his desire to follow the Hebrew text, Jerome's Latin version, the Vulgate, follows the Greek:

> ... quando emeris agrum de manu mulieris Ruth *quoque* Moabitidem quae uxor defuncti fuit *debes* accipere ut suscites nomen propinqui tui in hereditate sua.

> ... when you buy land from the hand of the woman Ruth, you must also take the Moabitess who was the wife of the deceased, so that you can raise up the name of your relative in his inheritance. (Ruth 4:5)

Jerome resolved the awkward "and/but from with" with *quoque* ("and even"), thus following the Alexandrian translators and Josephus, who set the reading tradition that eventually gave birth to the *qere*. By the fourth century CE, this tradition was so well established that Jerome reproduced the Greek δεῖ with the verb *debes* ("you are obliged") though there is no equivalent in the Hebrew.

Understanding the portion of field as Naomi's usufruct of Elimelech's share renders most references to "laws" irrelevant; the Jubilee (Lev 25) as much as Zelophehad's daughters (Num 27 and 36) and the levirate (Deut 25), as I argue in Chapter 3 in this volume. These intertextual references cloud the issue and have prevented readers from noticing the leonine deal Boaz attributed to himself.

Worse, it led to the view that both the field and Ruth are *bought* (e.g., Laffey and Leonard-Fleckman 2017, 131–33). Nevertheless, the suspicion that Naomi's order to sleep at the feet of Boaz involves sexual commerce was current in fifth-century CE Antioch, where Theodoret, in an effort to save Ruth's reputation, argued in his *Quaestiones in Ruth* that the aim was not that Ruth might "charge by the hour" (Mitchell 1999, 203).

The transmission of field shares rather than the buying of fields and women throws new light on the motivation for the introduction of the marginal *qere* in 4:5. The *qere*'s presentation of Ruth as an encumbrance only makes sense when her right to Mahlon's share is ignored. Postulating that Mahlon's share is included in whatever belonged to him and reckoning the usufruct of that share as Ruth's dowry is coherent with the *ketiv*, which enhances the position of Ruth as the cherry topping the cake Boaz shrewdly won over PA. Those responsible for the introduction of the *qere* must have been aware that Boaz's deal implied Ruth's right to the usufruct of Mahlon's share, something they objected to sufficiently to justify the introduction of the *qere*. Instead of securing a second share for Boaz, the *qere* turns Ruth into a dead weight, which enhances Boaz's generosity, all the more so when his acquisition of three shares is ignored. Blind to the three-share trick, readers only see Boaz's sacrificial selflessness and PA's miserliness. Yet, with the *qere*, Ruth 4 became the only biblical instance "where a man acquiring land also acquires a widow" (Laffey and Leonard-Fleckman 2017, 134) though it has long been recognized that PA had no social obligation to marry Ruth when he redeemed Elimelech's share (Green 1982, 58; Fewell and Gunn 1989, 50). From then on, the exegesis of Ruth got tied into knots, which in itself was a minor issue compared with the benefits gained from obscuring the plain meaning of the story.

5.2 Resistance to the Rights of Non-Natives

The book of Ruth is often adduced as a reaction to the xenophobic tendency expressed in Ezra-Nehemiah (i.e., Berlin 2010, 12–14; Ashkenazi and Frymer-Kensky 2011, xviii–xix; Jones 2016, 137–76). The welcome Ruth the Moabite receives in Bethlehem would be some kind of antidote to the issue of the divorce of foreign wives in Ezra 10.

This applies particularly to readings of Ruth in light of the *qere*, which ignores Ruth's right to Mahlon's share on the basis of her Moabite origins by making marriage with a local man Ruth's sole option. Without any rights to land, Ruth is the dead weight PA decides to avoid in order to preserve his inheritance, contrary to Boaz, whose generosity is enhanced to the point that it renders the three-share trick invisible to most interpreters. Ignoring Boaz's appropriation of "everything that belonged to Elimelech, Chilion and Mahlon" presents his marrying of Ruth as being against his own interests.

Placing the matter of the attribution of land shares center stage affords a peek into the world of the first Ruth writers. It is time to come up with a few suggestions regarding the reactions that eventually generated the *ketiv-qere*.

A first inference is that Ruth was written in a world where people like Boaz thought some traditional ways had to be adapted to seize new economic opportunities offered by a recent demand for barley and wheat. To respond adequately, wealthy individuals would have argued that local communes needed to increase the surface of arable land under their control. To do so, they should reduce the fallowing cycles, putting cleared land under the plow more often and/or clearing more land for dry cultivation. As this would require capital beyond the ability of local shareholders, the right to field shares should be extended to non-native residents and to non-resident natives.

Ruth the Moabite is a cypher for non-native residents and Orpha, Chilion's spouse, a cypher for non-resident natives. The way to integrate non-native residents is through marriage with native residents. The rights of native non-residents, in particular when they are no longer alive, like Chilion, would be far more difficult to justify unless the field shares to which they are entitled were added to those allotted to resident natives who, like Boaz, had the means to cultivate them. The fact that Jeremiah 32 details the procedure by which, though being confined in Jerusalem, Jeremiah acquired a field share from his cousin suggests that granting such shares to non-residents was not an entirely new process. Yet, it had not been felt problematic enough to spur a text challenging the custom of only granting shares to those physically present when lots were redistributed.

A second inference is a concern over escheat, that is, the reversion of land shares to the Crown or State in the absence of legal heirs. Whereas the rights of Elimelech and his sons to field shares would have been forfeited because of their permanent absence from Bethlehem, the deal between Naomi and Boaz secured these shares for the Bethlehem commune.

In the Ruth scenario, a ruler might have a legitimate claim to Chilion's share because neither Chilion's sons nor his widow claimed it. Hence, that ruler could grant Chilion's share to one of his courtiers, with the consequence of introducing non-natives into the pool of entitled shareholders. The number of non-natives would also grow when the usufructuary of Mahlon's share, Ruth, did not produce a son to secure his share. This is exactly the kind of situation that is avoided when Boaz, with the blessing of everyone in Bethlehem, grants himself the three shares that otherwise are liable to revert to the "Crown" (i.e. a local or overall ruler presenting himself as Yhwh's legitimate representative).

Whether the pressure came from non-natives who had the backing of a ruler or from local grandees like Boaz who sought to block the arrival of external claimants, the primary audience of the Ruth tale felt under pressure, and a scribe responded to the situation by writing a text that demonstrated how to block the arrival of non-natives and non-residents before resident natives found themselves a minority at home.

That Ruth was a Moabite did not matter as long as the land of the sons she bore to a Bethlehemite remained in the hands of the local community. In this context, one may suspect that PA might be a cypher for non-natives whose brotherly status cannot be challenged but who must be prevented from acquiring more field shares than those he already owns. The pressure grew to the point where the original call for the attribution of "orphaned" shares to locals led to a reading of Ruth 4:5 that was the exact opposite of what the original writer had intended (i.e. one that had been favorable to non-natives).

5.3 From Tricksters to Torah-Abiding Jews

The issue over the attribution of land shares was a crucial matter on the local scene. The Hellenistic scene generated broader issues related to inter-ethnic matters. In a world where nascent Judaism found itself competing with other ethnic, Jewish writers argued that Moses had preceded the Greeks in a number of inventions, such as laws, and that one of the characteristics of the Jewish ethnos was its high level of morality, equal if not superior to that of other ethnic. In this well-attested competition, the trickster lost much of its previous appeal. Figures like Jacob were best kept for internal consumption as the chutzpah that made them prevail over other tricksters was liable to backfire. In Alexandria, where Jews found themselves under pressure to be recognized as legitimate citizens, the Hebrew women's plunder of their Egyptian neighbors just before they escaped was best suppressed. Hence, contrary to the Samaritan Pentateuch that has Moses order both the men and women to plunder the Egyptians (Exod 3:22), the Masoretic text and the Septuagint have only the women do it, somewhat exonerating the men; this point is not noted by Joel Allen (2008, 27–28). Something similar seems to have occurred in Ruth with the Greek rendering that eventually led to the *ketiv-qere* in 4:5 (and possibly too in Naomi's "wife-swapping" plan in 3:3–4). Instead of the *ketiv* of 4:5 that presents how Naomi's ploy enabled Boaz to prevail over a potential redeemer, the *qere* turns the proceedings at the gate into a discussion about legal issues over which ink continues to be spilled (see Chapter 3 in this volume).

6. Sugar-Daddy Boaz and Conniving Naomi Today: Heroes or Villains?

Taking Elimelech's field as his share of communal land managed by the Bethlehem brotherhood in no way tarnishes the bucolic romance. What it challenges is the naive moralism of older interpretations, that is, the selfless dedication of the three main actors who only sought the interest of the others. The deal Boaz strikes with Naomi greatly improves their individual economic prospects. The two women enter the household of the most prominent man of the community. The risks each one takes are well rewarded, as any successful business venture should be. The gains they obtain are fully deserved. Even if the move of each actor is motivated solely by self-interest (see Chapter 11 in this volume), this in no way coats their actions with injustice. Today's readership finds this approach problematic, however.

Naomi believes she has a future to look forward to in Bethlehem (against De Villiers 2017, 40), i.e., by claiming her widow's right to Elimelech's usufruct. But she guesses that her future could be even brighter if she returned with one younger widow, but only one. The presence of Orpah besides Ruth would have annihilated the competitive advantage of the deal, since it would have involved feeding *three* widows in exchange for *three* shares. Orpah gone, Naomi can offer a far more advantageous bargain by using the attractive Ruth as bait for any man affluent enough to bear the cost of feeding two extra mouths right away. The moment Ruth voluntarily indentures herself to Naomi, Naomi plays the role of the conniving mother as well as that of the master who gives a wife to his Hebrew servant in the hope that the servant will opt for self-indenture when his time of service is reached because he loves his wife and children (Exod 21:5). Naomi gives Ruth to Boaz, who fathers a son for Naomi, who in turn serves as Obed's guardian.

Self-indenture may have been Ruth's sole avenue to solve her plight. It is a fact of life where options are in limited supply:

> Reality as it presents itself in the lives of individuals and communities, comes in the guise of "life in its emptiness," life in its brokenness. "Life in its fulness" requires an effort, and the key role players are individuals within such troubled situations who take initiative to heal and to make a difference. (de Villiers 2017, 35)

Ruth is the tale of three individuals who take initiatives to generate change. In the brokenness of her widowhood, Ruth decides to cling to Naomi. The fact that she embraces her fate transforms necessity into choice; a choice that enables God to "turn the need into a blessing" (Lindström 2019, 237). Even if she might have had no mother's house in Moab to return to, the fact that Ruth insists on following Naomi makes the difference between a victim and one who assumes the consequences of one's choice and pays the price to obtain the sought-after benefit. As Boaz admits, Ruth's youth and courage catch the eyes of younger men among whom she is free to pursue a spouse. Her compliance with Naomi's order to chase after Boaz is the consequence of her oath to die with and for Naomi. To have the choice of selling "her body to a man old enough to be her father" (Moyo 2016, 87), she first sells herself body and soul to Naomi, who trades her to Boaz in exchange for immediate relief.

However abhorrent sugar-daddies may be today, the young women who accept transactional sexual relations with older men are "not necessarily victims, but active agents in these relationships," as long as they deliver their part in the deal (West and Haddad 2016, 145–46). Hence, there is no reason to smear the beauty of the tale because it arose within a patriarchal society. Even today, some women find it more advantageous to marry an old patriarch than a younger man because greater wealth compensates for reduced virility, something that they might not necessarily consider as problematic.

Ruth is the tale of a deal involving three very unequal parties. Ruth contributes her youth, Boaz his status as brother, and Naomi Elimelech's share of land. The assets of Ruth and Boaz are acquired by birth, Naomi's by marriage. Any transaction, however, involves risks, which each party seeks to mitigate. Ruth compensates for her yet unproven fertility with labor. Boaz makes full use of his standing in the Bethlehem brotherhood to obtain Chilion's share to mitigate the risk of Ruth's yet unproven fertility. Naomi compensates for her old age with matchmaking.

Whatever happens on the threshing floor, Boaz does not rape Ruth (see Chapter 13 in this volume). On the contrary, the initiative is Ruth's. It is not out of charity that she obtains what she needs to survive from a compliant Boaz (against Moyo 2016, 88 n. 16). Though she vanishes the moment she gives birth to Obed, Ruth obtains more than immediate survival. Through the twelve occurrences of her name, she is the central character of the book (see Chapter 12 in this volume); it is the book of Ruth, not of Boaz, not of Naomi.

The story in no way challenges the rules of societies in which the preferred avenue for a woman's career comes through her relationship to men. Naomi and Boaz second the view that marriage is the better option; the question is the choice of the best husband. Yet, the story cuts short the self-pity Naomi expresses when she arrives at Bethlehem. Instead of teaching that women should accept their subjection to a patriarchal order, the tale praises resourcefulness, even if it involves behind-the-scene maneuvers and treading the fine line between customary expectations and shady ploys like the three-shares trick.

The temptation to read victims instead of heroes or survivors in Ruth arises from the tendency to focus on the individual and forget the communal, a bias that in Ruth's case leads exegetes to "treat society as nothing more than a collection of unrelated individuals who just happen to live together" (Kaminsky 1995, 188). Ruth presents a trio of conspiring schemers who manipulate the "system," much as Abraham does when he sells Sarah, Jacob when he outwits Laban, or Tamar, who forces Judah to deliver. In short, *chutzpah* pays. Readers are free to reject the moral of the tale, but this does not excuse them from figuring its dynamics, recognizing its literary beauty, and admitting that, at the end of the day, the need to survive outweighs legalities or even equity.

Conclusion

The present chapter identifies the issues that appear today as the source of much confusion in the exegesis of the short book of Ruth:

- the failure to understand the open-field system (shares in the use of a field rather than freehold ownership of a field)
- the otherwise legitimate denunciations of patriarchalism that view women as mere victims and renders today's readers oblivious to the crucial role women and widows played in the acquisition and transmission of field shares
- the divorce of ethics from economics, which has led readers to consider a good deal necessarily immoral and self-sacrifice as the only acceptable economic behavior for the benefit of the poor.

An economic approach recovers the centrality of brotherhood in Ruth. It is not as Elimelech's kin that Boaz is involved but as one member of the Bethlehem village commune that manages its arable land in partnership. Though Boaz presents himself as second-in-line to PA, as brothers they are equally entitled to take over Elimelech's share in exchange for Naomi's upkeep. Though PA eventually states that he cannot afford Ruth's upkeep in addition to that of Naomi, according to the *ketiv*, this cannot be the reason for his decision to desist. PA expected to marry Ruth in addition to taking care of Naomi, but he evokes economic reasons as an excuse once he realizes that Boaz had made a deal with Naomi behind his back. Though both the narrator and Naomi state outright that Boaz is the best candidate, readers take Boaz's words at face value when in fact his statements about PA's priority are part of the same rhetorical strategy and face-saving tactic as PA's excuse for desisting. PA preserves his dignity by pretending that he cannot afford Ruth after having stated that he could, while Boaz pretends that PA stands in the way and gets first choice in order to appear as the sole remaining candidate and also to be in a better position to force Bethlehem to accept the three-share trick. The statements made by parties involved in a delicate negotiation do not reflect their actual situation. The error is to ignore that Boaz and PA are engaged in a tug of economic war to win the deal offered by Naomi.

Viewing the transmission of land shares as the central issue reinforces the validity of the *ketiv* and underlines the secondary nature of the *qere*, the introduction of which succeeded in rendering the entire Ruth story unintelligible. The common appeals to Torah laws hardly help, though it was inevitable to refer to the Torah once Ruth became part and parcel of the biblical lore. As a sequel of the days of the Judges (see Chapter 3 in this volume), Boaz did not need to be a paragon of Torah observance any more than his great-grandson King David is in Samuel-Kings. Yet, the process of "canonization" has sharpened the exemplary nature of biblical figures, as models or as counter-models. The focus on Naomi and Boaz – the heroes of the first tale where they are smart tricksters – shifted towards Ruth and Boaz – paradigms of self-sacrificial behavior – while PA served as a villain and Naomi a victim. The enthusiastic blessings that follow the marriage of Boaz and the birth of Obed silence the issue of Ruth's Moabite origins when it is read in light of the prohibition to seek the welfare of any Ammonite and Moabite in Deut 23. Readers became oblivious also to the moral of the story, which claims that old and rich husbands are preferable to young ones, and to Ruth's quasi-servitude to Naomi, though it is crucial to her acceptance in a hostile environment.

The *qere* is the logical accomplishment of this process. Instead of the legitimate holder of the usufruct of Mahlon's share, which she brings as dowry into her second marriage, Ruth is an encumbrance, while Boaz's appropriation of Chilion's share becomes almost invisible, though economically it is acceptable as compensation for the risks taken. After the reading of Ruth by Josephus and even Jerome in light of the *qere*, the exegesis of Ruth found itself in the deep ruts dug by the Alexandrian translators.

The recovery of the economics involved in the story confirms the primacy of the *ketiv* and reveals the resistance expressed through the *qere*. Despite the vast availability of arable land in the ancient world, the acceptance of newcomers as shareholders was always considered a threat to the prerogatives of long-established locals, who would rather dispense with the benefit of young blood and continue managing their land between themselves.

In conclusion, an economic reading counterbalances the current interest in the sexual orientations and inclinations of Boaz, Ruth and Naomi. Business extends beyond the threshing floor scene (Krutzsch 2015, 203). The primary focus of the entire Ruth tale is economic. It is through smart deals that survival is ensured.

Works Cited

Adams, Samuel L. 2014. *Social and Economic Life in Second Temple Judea*. Louisville, KY: Westminster John Knox.

Allen, Joel S. 2008. *The Despoliation of Egypt in Pre-Rabbinic, Rabbinic, and Patristic Traditions*. Leiden: Brill 2008.

Bay, Carson. 2022. "Not 'Natural Law': [The] Law(s) of Nature ([ὁ/ον] νόμος/ νόμοι φύσεως) in Flavius Josephus." *Jewish Studies Internet Journal* 22: 1–41.

Beattie, Dereck R. G. 1971. "Kethibh and Qere in Ruth IV 5." *Vetus Testamentum* 21: 490–94.

-----. 1974. "The Book of Ruth as Evidence for Israelite Legal Practice." *Vetus Testamentum* 24: 251–67.

-----. 1978. "Redemption in Ruth, and Related Matters: A Response to Jack M. Sasson." *Journal for the Study of the Old Testament* 5,3: 65–68.

Begg, Christopher. 2005. *Judean Antiquities Books 5-7*. Leiden: Brill.

Benjamin, Don C. 2017. "The Land Rights of Women in Deuteronomy." *Biblical Theology Bulletin* 47: 3–15.

Berlin, Adele. 2010. "Legal Fiction: Levirate cum Land Redemption in Ruth." *Journal of Ancient Judaism* 1: 3–18.

Brenner, Athaliah. 1999. "Ruth as a Foreign Worker and the Politics of Exogamy." Pages 158–62 in *The Feminist Companion to the Bible, Second Series*. Edited by Athaliah Brenner. Sheffield: Sheffield Academic.

Campbell, Edward F. Jr. 1975. *Ruth: A New Translation with Introduction, Notes and Commentary*. Garden City: Doubleday.

Chapman, Cynthia R. 2012. "'Oh that You Were Like a Mother to Me, One Who Had Nursed at My Mother's Breasts'. Breast Milk as a Kinship-Forging Substance," *Journal of Hebrew Scriptures* 12 (2012), https://doi.org/10.5508/jhs.2012.v12.a7.

De Villiers, Gerda. 2017. "Economy: Taking Risks and Overstepping Boundaries in the Book of Ruth." Pages 35–50 in *Economic - Life in Its fullness*. Verbum et Ecclesia Supplement 1, 38(3), a1623. https://doi.org/10.4102/ve.v38i3.1623.

Embry, Brad. 2016. "Legalities in the Book of Ruth." *Journal for the Study of the Old Testament* 41.1: 31–44.

Eskenazi, Tamara C. and Tikva Frymer-Kensky. 2011. *The JPS Bible Commentary: Ruth*. Philadelphia: Jewish Publication Society.

Fewell, Danna Nolan and David M. Gunn. 1989. "Boaz, Pillar of Society: Measures of Worth in the Book of Ruth." *Journal for the Study of the Old Testament* 45: 45–59.

Fischer, Irmtraud. 2001. *Rut*. Freiburg: Herder.

Gamoran, Hillel. 1971. "The Biblical Law against Loans on Interest." *Journal of Near Eastern Studies* 30: 131–34.

Gordis, Robert. 1974. "Love, Marriage and Business in the Book of Ruth: A Chapter in Hebrew Customary Law." Pages 241–64 in *A Light in My Path. Old Testament Studies in Honor of Jacob M. Myers*. Edited by Howard N. Bream, Ralf D. Heim and Carey A. Moore. Philadelphia: Temple University Press.

Graybill, Rhiannon. 2021. *Texts after Terror: Rape, Sexual Violence and the Hebrew Bible*. New York. Oxford University Press.

Green, Barbara. 1982 "The Plot of the Biblical Story of Ruth," *Journal for the Study of the Old Testament* 23: 55–68.

Guillaume, Philippe. 2012. *Land, Credit and Crisis*. Sheffield: Equinox.

–––––. 2021. "Brothers in Deuteronomy: Zoom in on Lothar Perlitt's *Volk von Brüdern*." Pages 289–328 in *Deuteronomy in the Making: Studies in the Production of Debarim*. Edited by Diana Edelman, Benedetta Rossi, Kåre Berge and Philippe Guillaume. Berlin: de Gruyter.

–––––. 2022a. *The Economy of Deuteronomy's Core*. Sheffield: Equinox.

–––––. 2022b. "Pragmatism, Utopia and Dystopia in Deuteronomy." No pagination in *Deuteronomy: Outside the Box*. Edited by Diana Edelman and Philippe Guillaume. Themes and Issues in Biblical Studies 5. Sheffield: Equinox. Online: *Equinox eBooks Publishing, United Kingdom*. p. Oct 2023. ISBN 9781800503717. https://www.equinoxpub.com/home/view-chapter/?id=44611. Date accessed: 18 Jul 2023 doi: 10.1558/equinox.44611. Oct 2023.

Hubbard, Robert L. Jr. 1988. *The Book of Ruth*. Grand Rapids, MI: Eerdmans.

Hunger, Hermann. 1992. *Astrological Reports to Assyrian Kings*. State Archives of Assyria 8. Helsinki: Helsinki University Press.

Jackson, Bernard S. 2017. "Law and Narrative in the Book of Ruth: A Syntagmatic Reading." Pages 100–39 in *Judaism, Law and Literature*. Edited by Michael Baris and Vivian Laska. Liverpool: Deborah Charles Publications.

Jones, Edward Allen III. 2016. *Reading Ruth in the Restoration Period: A Call for Inclusion*. London: Bloomsbury.

Kalla, Gabor. 1996. "Das altbabylonische Wohnhaus und seine Struktur nach philologischen Quellen." Pages 247–56 in *Houses and Households in Ancient Mesopotamia*. Edited by Klaas R. Veenhof. Leiden and Istanbul: Peeters.

Kaminsky, Joel S. 1995. Corporate Responsibility in the Hebrew Bible. JSOTS 196. Sheffield Academic Press.

Krutzsch, Brett. 2015. "Un-Straightening Boaz in Ruth Scholarship." *Biblical Interpretation* 23/4–5: 541–52; reprinted Pages 197–204 in *The Bible, Gender and Sexuality*. Edited by Rhiannon Graybill and Lynn R. Huber. London: T&T Clark, 2021.

Lacocque, André. 2004. *Ruth*. Translated by K. C. Hanson. Minneapolis: Fortress.

Laffey, Alice L. and Mahri Leonard Fleckman. 2017. *Ruth* (Wisdom Commentary Series Book 8). Collegeville: Liturgical.

Lau, Peter H. W. 2011. *Identity and Ethics in the Book of Ruth: A Social Identity Approach*. Berlin: de Gruyter.

-----. 2015. "Another Postcolonial Reading of the Book of Ruth." Pages 15–34 in *Reading Ruth in Asia*. Edited by Jione Havea and Peter H. W. Lau. Atlanta: SBL.

Levin, Christoph. 2001. "The Poor in the Old Testament." *Religion and Theology* 8:3–4: 253–73.

-----. 2014. "Rereading Deuteronomy in the Persian and Hellenistic Periods: The Ethics of Brotherhood and the Care of the Poor." Pages 49–71 in *Deuteronomy - Kings as Emerging Authoritative Books: A Conversation*. Edited by Diana V. Edelman. Ancient Near Eastern Monographs 6. Atlanta: Society of Biblical Literature.

Linafelt, Tod and Timothy K. Beal. 1999. *Ruth and Esther*. Collegeville: Liturgical Press.

Lindström, Fredrik. 2019. "The Portrayal of Divine and Human in the Book of Ruth." Pages 224–47 In *God and Humans in the Hebrew Bible. A Festschrift for Lennart Boström on his 67th Birthday*. Edited by David Willgren. Sheffield: Sheffield Phoenix.

Mitchell, Margaret M. 1999. "Ruth at Antioch. An English Translation of Theodoret's 'Quaestiones in Ruth', with a Brief Commentary." Pages 195–214 in *Realia Dei. Essays in Archaeology and Biblical Interpretation in Honor of E.F. Campbell Jr. at his Retirement*. Edited by Prescott H. Williams, Jr. and Theodore Hiebert. Atlanta: Scholars.

Moyo, Fulata Lusungu. 2016. "'Traffic Violations': Hospitality, Foreignness and Exploitation: A Contextual Biblical Study of Ruth." *Journal of Feminist Studies in Religion* 32,2: 83–94.

Niditch, Susan. 2000. *A Prelude to Biblical Folklore: Underdogs and Tricksters*. 2nd edition. San Francisco. Harper & Row.

Nielsen, Kirsten. 1985. "Le Choix contre le droit dans le livre de Ruth. De l'aire de battage au tribunal." *Vetus Testamentum* 35: 201–12.

Nu, Roi. 2015. "A Reinterpretation of Levirate Marriage in Ruth 4:1–12 for Kachin Society." Pages 57–72 in *Reading Ruth in Asia*. Edited by Jione Havea and Peter H. W. Lau. Atlanta: SBL.

Oppenheimer, Leo and Erica Reiner, editors. 1964. *Chicago Assyrian Dictionary* vol. 1, A, Part 2. Chicago: Oriental Institute.

Porten, Bezalel and Ada Yardeni. 1986–1999. *Textbook of Aramaic Documents from Ancient Egypt.* 4 vols. Winona Lake: Eisenbrauns.

PRU 1956 = *Palais Royal d'Ugarit.* Vol. 4. Textes accadiens des archives sud (archives internationales). Mission de Ras Shamra 9. Edited by Jean Nougayrol. Paris: Imprimerie nationale.

Rees, Anthony. 2015. "The Boaz Solution: Reading Ruth in Light of Australian Asylum Seeker Discourse." Pages 99–110 in *Reading Ruth in Asia.* Edited by Jione Havea and Peter H. W. Lau. Atlanta: SBL.

Renger, Johannes. 1987. "Das Privateigentum an der Feldflur in der altbabylonischen Zeit." Pages 49–67 in *Das Grundeigentum in Mesopotamien.* Edited by Burchard Brentjes. Berlin: Akademie Verlag.

Rudolph, Wilhelm. 1962. *Das Buch Ruth, das Hohe Lied, die Klagelied.* Gütersloh: Mohn.

SAA = Cole, Steven W. and Peter Machinist (editors) with contributions by Simo Parpola. 1998. *Letters from Assyrian and Babylonian Priests to Kings Asarhaddon and Assurbanipal.* State Archives of Assyria 13. Helsinki: Helsinki University Press.

Sasson, Jack M. 1978. "The Issue of Ge'Ullah in Ruth." *Journal for the Study of the Old Testament* 5,3: 52–64.

-----. 1979. *Ruth. A New Translation with a Philological Commentary and a Formalist-Folklorist Interpretation.* Baltimore: Johns Hopkins University Press.

-----. 1987. "Ruth." Pages 321–28 in *The Literary Guide to the Bible.* Edited Robert Alter and Frank Kermode. Cambridge, MA: Harvard University Press.

-----. 1989. *Ruth. A New Translation with a Philological Commentary and a Formalist-Folklorist Interpretation.* Second corrected edition. Sheffield: JSOT Press.

Saxegaard, Kristin Moen. 2010. *Character Complexity in the Book of Ruth.* Tübingen: Mohr Siebeck.

Scheidel, Walter. 2010. "Real Wages in Early Economies: Evidence for Living Standards from 1800 BCE to 1300 CE." *Journal of the Economic and Social History of the Orient* 53,3: 425–62.

Schipper, Jeremy. 2016. *Ruth: A New Translation with Introduction and Commentary* (AB 7D), New Haven, CT: Yale University Press.

Sinnott, Alice M. 2020. *Ruth: An Earth Bible Commentary.* London: T.&T. Clark.

Sonnet, Jean-Pierre. 2021. *À l'ombre de ses ailes. Le livre de Ruth.* Brussels: Editions jésuites.

Sternberg, Meir. 1991. "Double Cave, Double Talk: the Indirections of Biblical Dialogue." Pages 28–57 in *Not in Heaven: Coherence and Complexity in Biblical Narrative.* Edited by Jason P. Rosenblatt and Joseph C. Sitterson, Jr. Bloomington: Indiana University Press.

Stol, Marten. 2016. *Women in the Ancient Near East.* Berlin: de Gruyter, 2016.

Thackeray, H. St. J. 1988. *Josephus, Jewish Antiquities, Books V–VIII.* Cambridge, MA: Harvard Universtity Press.

Thomas Barnett, Wendy, Norma Franklin, Philippe Guillaume and Jennie Ebeling. Forthcoming. "The Spring of Jezreel (יזרעאל): 'Ain el-Meiteh and the Village of Zir'in."

Tong, Sin-lung. 2015. "The Key to Successful Migration? Rereading Ruth's Confession (1:16–17) through the Eyes of Bhabha's Mimicry." Pages 35–46 in *Reading Ruth in Asia.* Edited by Jione Havea and Peter H. W. Lau. Atlanta: SBL.

Vriezen, Theodorus Christiaan. 1948. "Two Old Cruces." *Oudtestamentische Studiën* 5: 80–91.

West, Gerald O. and Beverley Haddad. 2016. "Boaz as 'Sugar Daddy': Rereading Ruth in the Context of HIV." *Journal of Theology for Southern Africa* 155: 137–56.

Woudhuizen, Fred C. 2019. "The Role of Brotherhoods in West-Luwian Religion (5th to 2nd Century BCE)." Pages 169–80 in *Economy of Religion in Anatolia: From the Early Second to the Middle of the First Millennium BCE.* Edited by Manfred Hutter and Sylvia Hutter-Braunsar. AOAT 467. Münster: Ugarit-Verlag.

Yee, Gale. 2009. "She Stood in Tears amid the Alien Corn." Pages 119–40 in *They Were All Together in One Place? Toward Minority Biblical Criticism.* Edited by Randall C. Bailey, Tat-siong Benny Liew, and Fernando F. Segovia. Leiden: Brill.

Zevit, Ziony. 2005. "Dating Ruth: Legal, Linguistic and Historical Observations." *Zeitschrift für die Alttestamentliche Wissenschaft* 117: 574–600.

About the Author

Philippe Guillaume is Lecturer at the University of Berne. In 2024, he coedited with Diana Edelman *The Old Testament Hebrew Scriptures in Five Minutes* and *Deuteronomy: Outside the Box,* the inaugural volume of the Themes and Issues in Biblical Studies series, both at Equinox.

Chapter 3
The Torah in Ruth?

Philippe Guillaume

Abstract

Ever since the Septuagint and Josephus, exegetes read the Ruth story in light of Torah-laws: levirate, redemption, gleaning, Zelophehad's daughters, ban of Moabites in the assembly. Uncovering the mismatch between the so-called laws of the Torah and their application in Ruth, this contribution underlines the necessity to distinguish the two versions of the story – the Hebrew and the Greek – as they follow entirely different scenarii, with the Greek one attempting to present Boaz as a law-abiding Jew, something foreign to the burden of the Hebrew version.

Keywords: Deuteronomy 25, Deuteronomy 23, levirate, Leviticus 25, redemption, gleaning, Numbers 25, Numbers 27, Numbers 36, Ruth

Forty years ago, Baruch Levine (1983, 95) noted that "For all its charm, the book of Ruth produces a certain *malaise*" because the many references to legal institutions it contains are difficult if not impossible to reconcile with other biblical and comparative sources. Despite the *malaise*, Ruth continues to be read in light of the Torah to explain the behavior of the protagonists. Gerda de Villiers (2018, 1, 4) writes that "Although the Torah is never mentioned directly, the narrative is certainly intensely aware of its contents" and that "although the book of Ruth is outside the Torah, the Torah is very much inside the book of Ruth."

De Villiers does concede that the book is "a fictional story of return" and not an "accurate depiction of legal practice, nor a midrash on Torah law per se" (2018, 11). Fiction affords plenty of liberty with reality, but if Ruth is not an accurate depiction of legal practice, are references to the

Torah at all necessary? For de Villiers, Ruth's vow parallels the Israelites' vow in the plains of Moab: it is a vow to obey the first command of the Torah (2018, 8). Other Torah motifs in Ruth would be leaving one's father and mother (Gen 2:24), the deaths of Er and Onan, an incident that "may vaguely resemble the Genesis narrative of Judah and Tamar," and gleaning manna and famine as allusions to the Exodus and Deuteronomy (De Villiers 2018, 6 and 9); none of them is a legal passage *per se*.

The clearest reference in Ruth to a legal procedure in the Torah is the sandal ritual performed at the gate of Bethlehem (Ruth 4:7-8), a ritual that recalls the sandal the widow pulls off the foot of the brother-in-law who refuses to impregnate her (Deut 25:9). Yet, even this ritual displays too many discrepancies with the way it is performed in Ruth to dispel the *malaise* that inevitably arises in the face of the lack of accuracy in the depiction of legal procedures and the vagueness of the allusions to the Torah. The sole explicit reference to the Pentateuch is the Tamar episode in Genesis 38 in Ruth 4:12. The closing genealogy in Ruth 4 refers to David, while Ruth 1:1 sets the story in the days of the Judges. Why, then, do we still read Ruth in light of the Torah?

1. Whence the Legal Readings of Ruth?

The notion that Ruth presupposes "laws" is found in Flavius Josephus's retelling of the Ruth story (ca. 37-100 CE). In his *Jewish Antiquities*, Josephus has Boaz warn the other redeemer "... if you wish to possess their fields, you must, according to the laws, marry [her]" (Ant. 5, 333 in Begg 2005, 84).

Here, Josephus agrees with the Alexandrian translators, whose rendering implies an obligation:

> ἐν ἡμέρᾳ τοῦ κτήσασθαί σε τὸν ἀγρὸν ἐκ χειρὸς Νωεμιν καὶ παρὰ Ρουθ τῆς Μωαβίτιδος γυναικὸς τοῦ τεθνηκότος, καὶ αὐτὴν κτήσασθαί σε δεῖ ὥστε ἀναστῆσαι τὸ ὄνομα τοῦ τεθνηκότος ἐπὶ τῆς κληρονομίας αὐτοῦ.

> the day you acquire the field from the hand of Neomin and from Ruth the Moabite, the wife of the deceased, *it is necessary for* (δεῖ) you to acquire *her also* in order to raise up the name of the deceased on his inheritance. (Ruth 4:5, New English Translation of the Septuagint)

Instead of "acquire," the alternative sense of the Greek verb κτάομαι (from which the form κτήσασθαί is derived), "to possess," helps move away from the notion of "acquisition" and "ownership." The redeemer who cultivates the field must, according to the Greek, also possess Ruth, in order to father a son. Both acts of possession have no implication on the ownership of the field and of Ruth. The novelty in the Greek is the introduction of the notion of obligation with δεῖ ("you must") that is not present in the consonantal Hebrew text (*ketiv*):[1]

> ויאמר בעז ביום קנותך השדה מיד נעמי ומאת רות המואביה אשת המת קניתי להקים שם המת על נחלתו

> Boaz said: "In the day of your acquiring of the field from the hand of Naomi, but from Ruth the Moabite the wife of the dead [one] I have acquired to raise the name of the dead over his inheritance." (Ruth 4:5)

The New Revised Standard Version's rendering follows the Greek but takes the acquisitions as final transfers of ownership, while the Hebrew plays here on the multiple meanings of the verb *qnh*, ranging from "to buy, acquire, transfer ownership, or appropriate" to the more figurative "possess, create, produce":

> Then Boaz said: "The day you acquire the field from the hand of Naomi, *you* are also acquiring Ruth the Moabite, the widow of the dead man, to maintain the dead man's name on his inheritance." (Ruth 4:5 NRSV)

The notion of obligation in the Greek text corresponds to the *qere* in the Hebrew, which suggests one read "you have acquired" (קניתה) instead of "I have acquired" (קניתי). The Greek rendering and the *qere* rely on the dual meaning of two of the three components of the form ומאת:

> the *waw* (ו) "and" or "but" that either links or opposes the two acquisitions (field and wife)

> the *mem* (מ) "from" that indicates the origin of the duty to raise the name of the deceased man (Mahlon)

> and *'et* (את) marking Ruth either as the object of Boaz's acquisition or with whom Mahlon's inheritance is to be preserved. את is used as "with" in 2:23, while עם "with" is used in 2:19.

The Greek translators and the Hebrew scribes who introduced the *qere* favored "and" for the *waw* and "*'et*" as marking Ruth as the object of the acquisition. The modern translator of the Septuagint went further by adding "also": "it is necessary for you to acquire her *also*."

Rather than translating the consonantal Hebrew, the English as much as the Greek produces a new text. A paraphrase of the consonantal Hebrew would name the deceased men whose possessions are involved and underline the opposition between the two acquisitions (taking the *waw*

---

1 *ketiv* (Aramaic for "witten") and *qere* ("read") are scribal notes dating back to the ninth–tenth centuries CE to indicate when a word is supposed to be read differently than it is actually written in the consonantal text of the Hebrew Bible.

as "but") and take Ruth not as the object of the acquisition but as the agent with whom the redeemer of the field could raise the name of the dead man:

> Boaz said: "The day you cultivate Elimelech's field for Naomi, be aware that I have already produced (קניתי) an heir for Mahlon through Ruth the Moabite, the wife of the late Mahlon." (Ruth 4:5 paraphrased)

With these words, Boaz announces to Bethlehem his marriage to Ruth. With these words, the narrator informs the audience aware of the previous scene that the marriage has, indeed, been consummated on the threshing floor. In both cases, the prospect of securing Elimelech's field from Naomi is thwarted because the field is, in effect, held in mortgage – the notion of "mortgage" having here its original sense of "dead pledge." In other words, the title to the field cannot be transferred because by marrying Boaz, Ruth now has a "debt" or moral obligation to perpetuate her late husband's family line, Mahlon. Bearing a son for Mahlon, she will have paid back her "debt" to his line and the moral "mortgage" will be lifted. Therefore, verse 5 evokes the late Mahlon twice because, despite his untimely death in Moab, he is the vital link between his father Elimelech and Boaz. As Obed is taken by Naomi as her own son, hence Elimelech's heir, Ruth will have to bear a second son to redeem Mahlon's share (see Chapter 2 in this volume).

The implication of the consonantal Hebrew text (*ketiv*) is that the union of Boaz and Ruth invalidates the permanent acquisition of Elimelech's share. Hence, the other redeemer desists *because* Boaz marries Ruth.

The Greek text and Josephus reads Ruth 4:5 through the lens of the *qere* – even if it was not yet noted in the margin of any actual manuscript the translators used. The implication of the *qere* is that the other redeemer desists because Boaz warns him that in addition to acquiring the field "you must acquire (קניתה)" Ruth too, as though he had been ignorant of such a crucial matter. In both cases Ruth is the encumbrance that convinces him to desist, but for different reasons. When Boaz states "I have acquired Ruth" (*ketiv*), the other desists because Ruth might give birth to a male heir who will prejudice the hold of any other redeemer over Elimelech's field (so Fewell and Gunn 1989, 52). When Boaz states "You have acquired Ruth" when you acquire the field (*qere*), Pelony desists because he *does not want* to marry Ruth. The outcome is the same, but the portrayal of the protagonists differs significantly.

With the *qere*, so-called Pelony Almony (see Sasson 2012), supposedly craves the field but rejects the burden of caring for Ruth. With the *ketiv*, he is willing to care for Naomi in exchange for cultivating Elimelech's field until he discovers that Boaz is marrying Ruth. He is a decent man who has been outsmarted, which enhances Boaz's standing and even more Naomi's, whose victory is all the more resounding that it was obtained without disparaging the opponent.

When Boaz states "I have acquired" (*ketiv*), the audience knows that Boaz has already promised to marry Ruth on the threshing floor. No such clear-cut situation avails with a Hebrew text read as "You have acquired." This *qere* conditions Ruth's marriage on the acquisition of the field, a condition that can only be supported by postulating an obligation, hence the rendering, "it is necessary (δεῖ) for you to acquire" in the Greek Bible.

The obligation need not rely on any particular law, unless "law" is taken as somewhat equivalent to the "law of nature," as is the case in *Jubilees* (Collins 2022, 14) and in the way in which Philo of Alexandria conceived of the Torah (Najman 1999). The purported obligation simply reflects the translator's desire to present the Alexandrian Jews of his days as moral people who take upon themselves to care for a widow when they cultivate the field of her late husband. With "you must, according to the laws, marry [her]," Josephus shared a similar desire when he wrote for a Roman readership, but he went a step further with the evocation of "laws" that supposedly made the acquisition of Elimelech's land dependent on marrying the wife of the deceased man. While Josephus's "laws" present the Jews as a law-abiding people, these "laws" remain a broad reference to the Torah rather than a reference to specific legal passages that inevitably occur in the minds of Ruth readers and translators versed in biblical culture. A review of the Torah passages that have been evoked by Ruth readers shows just how little light they cast on this delightful story, which suggests that the exegesis of Ruth may benefit from resisting the intertextual impulse.

2. Deuteronomy 25: Levirate Marriage

The Deuteronomic presentation of levirate applies under three conditions: after the death of a brother, if the brothers resided together at the time of death, and if the wife of the deceased had failed to produce an heir. Yet, these conditions do not constitute an obligation; the surviving brother remains free to decline, despite the social onus (Deut 25:5–10, see Guillaume 2021, 298–99; 2022). When addressing Pelony Almony, Boaz refers to Elimelech as "our brother" (Ruth 4:3). "Our brother" here does not necessarily imply that Boaz and Pelony Almony are siblings (see Chapter 2 in this volume), but even if they are siblings, nothing suggests that they resided together with Elimelech before he left for Moab. As it is the other redeemer rather than Ruth who takes off his sandal (4:7–8), we have no indication that whoever wrote Ruth 4:7–8 had ever read Deuteronomy 25 or intended to implement its commands (Gordis 1974, 248–52; Koosed

2011, 109). What would appear to be infringements of Torah requirements become what allows the "characters to go beyond the letter of the law in their interactions with one another" in Ruth (Koosed 2011, 110). Or, all the laws they observe need is to "be consistent with the narrative world in which the characters live. In that world reality, authority, convention and law are all ad hoc" (Wojcik 1985, 147).

Instead of a reference to a "law," the NRSV's translator cautiously rendered the initial words of Ruth 4:7 as "Now this [was the custom] in former times in Israel" (וזאת לפנים בישראל, *wezo't lepanym beyiśra'el*). The Hebrew, however, mentions neither custom nor law. Literally, the Hebrew simply states: "And this previously in Israel"), but Ruth scholars continue to conceive this custom as Deuteronomy's "law of levirate." This law would require Elimelech's brother, Pelony Almony or Boaz, to impregnate Naomi to father a son for Elimelech, overlooking the fact that Naomi is too old to conceive (1:12). Naomi's age prevents the levirate from palliating her predicament, even if a brother were to accept to play that role.

Why, then, does the redeemer remove his sandal (Ruth 4:8) when he tells Boaz to acquire Elimelech's right to a share of field? Is Pelony Almony consciously outsmarting the "law" by removing his sandal to block Naomi from spitting in his face? Why, moreover, does he not give his sandal to Boaz as he would be expected to do according to the purported custom stated in verse 7: "the one took off a sandal and gave (נתן, *natan*) it to the other"? The ancient translators were well aware of the problem and dealt with it in different ways (see Campbell 1975, 149–50). The Ruth tale is more than an inaccurate depiction of legal practice (De Villiers 2018, 11), because Pelony Almony is not even acting according to the custom the writer adduces. This further undermines the relevance of the "flexible interpretation of the Torah" (Lacocque 2004, 20–21) and the "playful engagement with legal traditions" (Adam 2018, 133). Why depict a legal practice inaccurately, when PA is not even acting according to custom?

Playing with the law is a dangerous game when the law is enforceable, requiring the punishment of offenders. It is possible that the writer meant to disparage the other redeemer by depicting him as a rather clumsy, law-abiding character. The scene would have gained much vividness by following the letter of the law and having Naomi spit in the face of Pelony Almony to ensure that his family be remembered as "the house of him whose sandal was removed" (Deut 25:10).

It is more effective to admit that the Ruth writer, assuming he knew Deuteronomy 25, did not view it as binding law. In fact, the Deuteronomic levirate law itself would seem to be a moderated version of a rigid custom since it grants the *levir* the liberty to refuse to take on his brother's widow despite the social onus such refusal entails. Hence, if "the author of Ruth recognized in the very detail of law a reflection of its lofty purposes" (Levine 1983, 98), Moses's lofty purpose was to free the Israelites from the inflexibility of the levirate custom. Were the Torah very much inside the book of Ruth, we could expect the redeemers there to exercise the liberty Moses granted them to refuse to take Ruth. On the contrary, the Ruth story displays two willing redeemers who are eager to fulfil the duty of the *levir*.

3. Leviticus 25: Rules for Redemption

Though they are commonly invoked in Ruth studies (e.g. Adams 2018, 132), the so-called "laws of redemption" in Leviticus 25 are hardly more relevant to the situation of Naomi than the levirate, despite the use of the term *go'el* and its cognates in both texts. Redemption involves recovering the use of a person or asset that its owner lost temporarily as the consequence of a lease or a loan secured with a pledge or other credit obligation (Hubbard 1988, 51; Guillaume 2022). None of the cases considered in Leviticus 25 apply to Naomi or Ruth. They were not pledged, and both are free of any encumbrance that would call for redemption. Instead, Elimelech's field share (4:3) is open for recovery. While away from Bethlehem, Elimelech did not use his land. The return of his widow brings to the fore Naomi's recovery of the use of Elimelech's land as well as Ruth's recovery of that of her late husband Mahlon, the son of Elimelch and Naomi. To maintain the alleged relevance of the Torah's rules for redemption, Robert L. Hubbard broadens the duties of the *go'el* to include the "aid of clan members, both the living who were perceived to be weak and vulnerable and the dead," that is, "far broader than the redemption acts taught in Lev 25 and those typical of the Levirate" (1988, 52). If so, references to the Torah are irrelevant.

4. Leviticus 19; 23; Deuteronomy 24: Rules on Gleaning

The so-called "law on gleaning" seems more promising, as it is a central theme in Ruth. Yet, as Fredrik Lindström notes (2019, 229), when she asks Boaz to be allowed to continue gleaning in his field, Ruth refers to herself as a *nokryah* (נכריה) "foreigner" (2:10) rather than a *ger*, the social category that grants gleaning rights in the Pentateuch (Lev 19:9–10; 23:22; Deut 24:19). Ruth may use a strategy of self-deprecation to generate pity and afford Boaz the liberty of treating her as a *ger* instead of claiming upfront a purported legal right to glean. Yet, Ruth is, in fact, more than a *ger*. The foreman sees her as a returnee (2:6). Even more significantly, Ruth is the wife of a deceased local man, Mahlon, the son of Elimelech; thus, she is no more a widow than Naomi in the Deuteronomic sense of a woman entitled to public support in the form of triennial tithes, gleanings and other rights (Deut 14:28–29; 24:17–21). For this reason, the Hebrew term "widow" (אלמנה, *almanah*) is never used in Ruth, and Naomi is not as destitute as her heart-rending words suggest when she reaches Bethlehem (1:20–21). No one contests her right to trade her usufruct of Elimelech's share, nor, eventually, Boaz's right to acquire Ruth's usufruct of Mahlon's share as well as Chilion's (see Chapter 2 in this volume). That Ruth should glean is the obvious thing to do at the time of the harvest. No law is required to do so, except the laws of nature that require finding food to survive. The central point is not that Ruth gleans but that she happens to glean in Boaz's lot.

5. Numbers 27 and 36: Zelophehad's Daughters

To bolster the validity of references to the Torah, Brad Embry turned to Numbers 27 and 36, arguing that the regulation regarding Zelophehad's daughters "resolves some of the longstanding curiosities" in Ruth (Embry 2016, 41). The study is based on the *qere* reading of Ruth 4:5, which indeed subjects the redemption of Elimelech's land to the requirement of marrying Ruth. Therefore, it is possible that the issue of the transmission of land rights to the daughters of men who died sonless influenced to some extent the process that culminated in the introduction of the *ketiv-qere*. The matter of the *qere* is discussed below (§7), but here the differences between the situation of Zelophehad's daughters and Naomi's are significant.

In the Ruth tale, Elimelech dies, as do his two sons. Elimelech's union with Naomi having been nevertheless fertile, the presence of surviving daughters could be postulated, placing them in a situation similar to Zelophehad's daughters. Embry, however, does not postulate that Elimelech sired any daughters. Instead, he postulates that Ruth inherited "land within Israelite society," which he considers could "hardly be a more explicit or significant expression of her inclusion in the community" (Embry 2016, 41). Rather than a purported landed inheritance, Ruth's supposed inclusion in the Bethlehemite community is the result of her marriage to a man who was a local. Nothing indicates that Ruth inherits land; all Naomi is able to do is to trade her usufruct of Elimelech's share. Being entitled to use the land share of her deceased husband does not mean that Naomi inherits the land. Right of use (usufruct) is granted to male members of the village commune and is passed on from father to sons (Lipiński 1976, 126). Hence, Naomi passes Elimelech's share on to Ruth's son, Obed, when she adopts him, even though Obed is the son of Ruth by Boaz. The adoption was an expediency because, had she not adopted Obed, Elimelech's share would, in line with customary practice, have reverted to the pool of Bethlehem's common land at the death of Naomi (see Chapter 2 in this volume).

The inheritance of Zelophehad's daughters would be relevant had Boaz sired no sons from previous marriages and Ruth only gave him daughters, which is the case with Zelophehad (Num 27:3). The birth of Obed and his adoption by Naomi solves the issue of the inheritance of Elimelech's land, thus rendering the inheritance of Zelophehad's daughters irrelevant.

The main issue in Numbers 36 is the impact of marriage on the fate of land. Zelophehad's daughters are forbidden to marry outside their father's tribe precisely because the land would otherwise pass on to the tribe of their husbands. The land the daughters brought into their marriage would be lost to Zelophehad's tribe because the land is passed on to the male line. Had Zelophehad's daughters actually owned their father's land – Embry (2016, 41) refers to fee simple (i.e., they had complete freedom to dispose of the land in whichever way they wanted during their lives) – that land might revert to Zelophehad's tribe. In the biblical world (as in Israel today still), however, arable land was not held in fee simple (Guillaume 2012, 17–53). Entitled adult males were granted land shares as long as they resided in their place of origin, while God, through his representative on earth, was the owner of the land (*allodium*). The share of those who moved away returned to the common pool but their right to a share of land remained valid when they returned.

In Ruth, tribal affiliation is not an issue. This is not to say that women play no role in the transmission of arable land. It is not as daughters (heirs) but as mothers (progenitors) that women intervene as the actual or potential bearers of the next male generation.

All in all, the relevance of the Zelophehad episode for the interpretation of Ruth is limited to the name of one of his daughters, Maḥalah (Num 26:33), the feminine form of Maḥlon, Ruth's late husband (Campbell 1975, 53). If and only if the similarity were intentional would the Ruth tale be critical of the transmission of land rights through daughters. Were the Torah chapters on Zelophehad's daughters very much in the book of Ruth, the writer of Ruth decided not to present his heroes to adhere to this Mosaic decree.

6. Numbers 25 and Deuteronomy 23: the Evil Moabites

The clear anti-Moabite bias displayed by the episode with Cozbi and the Moabite women in Numbers 25 (see Graybill 2024) and the ban on the entry of Ammonite and the Moabite males in the *qehal-Yhwh* in Deut 23:4(English 3) is the final Torah motif invoked by Ruth scholars (Braulik 1999, 8–11; Adam 2018, 133–37). In this case, however, there is no question that Bethlehem acts contrary to the Torah. The scribe who created Ruth supposedly opposed the Torah, or at least its rigorist reading in Ezra-Nehemiah.

The notion of a rigorist reading is based on the list of Ezra 9:1 that mentions the abominations of the *Moabites* along with the Canaanites, Hittites, Perizzites, Jebusites, Ammonites, Egyptians and Amorites, all accused of polluting Israel. The actual repudiation of foreign wives narrated in Ezra 10 lists the culprits who had married foreign women without stating their origins because the commandments Ezra quotes to justify the repudiation is broader than the ban of Deut 23:4 (English 3), which mentions neither marriage nor foreign wives. The clearest echo of Deuteronomy in Ezra is the absence of any mention of *Edomites* in the list of abominable nations in Ezra 9:1, along with Deut 23:8(English 7), which commands Israel not to abhor the Edomite. This is Ezra's sole concession to Deuteronomy, as Ezra 9:1 lists the Egyptians though Deut 23:8 (English 7) commands Israel not to abhor the Egyptian, either. The third-generation Egyptian is granted membership in the *qehal-Yhwh* not because he is a brother, as is the Edomite, but because Israel was a *ger* in Egypt. Ezra the scribe knew his Torah and avoided the Edomite in his abominations list but took the liberty to include the Egyptians. Nehemiah the governor is less punctilious and mentions Moabite women, after those from Ashdod and Ammon, whom some Jews had married (Neh 13:23).

The common claim that the Ruth tale opposes Ezra and Nehemiah is based on Ezra's subtle exegesis of Deuteronomy 23 and on Nehemiah's addition of Moabite wives beside those from Ashdod and Ammon, but it hardly supports the presence of Torah in Ruth. That Ezra and Nehemiah quote the Torah freely does not mean that the writer of Ruth did so, too. If he did, he opposed their reading of the Torah without building a case based on the Torah. To do so, Ruth the Moabite should have been Ruth the Edomite, whom the Israelites are told not to abhor. Hence, Jeremy Schipper sees "no reason why one must read Ruth against the backdrop of the condemnation of Judahite marriages with Moabites. One could just as easily read it as one of several examples of texts that discuss such marriages without a clear polemic against them" (2016, 40).

The gap between the Torah stipulations reviewed above and the way they are applied in Ruth is wide. To narrow the gap, scholars concede that Ruth is not the "work of an author whose main objective is rigorous adherence to the rules for Levirate marriage (Deut 25:5–10) or the Jubilee Year legislation (Leviticus 25)" (Adams 2018, 132); that Ruth merely demonstrates awareness of antecedent legal tradition (Levine 1983, 95–106); that the writer of Ruth considers the perpetuation of the family line "a matter of responsibility, not duty" (Lau 2011, 193); or that the characters in Ruth "illustrate how a post-exilic reader can behave in supraconventional ways" (Adam 2018, 136).

If Ruth displays flexible or playful interpretations of the Torah, or if its scribe did not seek to present a rigorous application of the law, is the Torah very much in Ruth? Much depends on which Ruth text version is read.

7. The Ketiv-Qere Complication

The *ketiv-qere* in Ruth 4:5 has already been presented in paragraph 1 above. It is necessary to return to it because it has generated two entirely different approaches to the reading of Ruth. Almost everyone today follows the translators (from LXX to NRSV) and the majority of commentators (for instance, Hubbard 1988; Bush 1996; Fischer 2001; Eskenazi and Frymer-Kensky 2011; Schipper 2016) in giving precedence to the *qere* (קָנִיתָה, *qnyth* "you acquired") over against the *ketiv* (קָנִיתִי, *qnyty* "I acquired"). Edward Campbell's influential Anchor Bible Commentary on Ruth (1975) dismissed Derek Beattie's arguments in favor of the *ketiv* (Beattie 1971; 1974) simply stating that the *ketiv* "fails completely to accord with the language of 3:12–13 and is out of place with the whole thrust of the threshing floor and gate episodes" and "violates the internal consistency of the Ruth story" (Campbell 1975, 146, quoting Rowley 1952, 185 n. 1 and Rudolph 1962, 59). Are those critiques valid?

Not all scholars have rejected the *ketiv*. After Theodorus Vriezen (1948, 80–88) and Beattie (1971; 1974), Jack Sasson (1978; 1979, 119–36; 1987, 326; 1989, 119–36), Kirsten Nielsen (1985, 209), Dana Fewell and David Gunn (1989), and André Lacocque (2004, 130) have read Ruth 4:5 with the *ketiv*. This list is probably not exhaustive. With the *ketiv,* Boaz announces "I [Boaz] have [already] acquired (*qanyty*) from [the share] with Ruth." Does this fail to accord with 3:12–13, as Campbell renders these verses?

[12]Now it is certainly true that I am a redeemer.

But there is also another redeemer

Nearer than I.

[13]Spend tonight (here), and in the morning

> If he will do the redeemer's part,
>
> Well and good, "let him redeem,"
>
> But if he does not want to do the redeemer's part,
>
> I will redeem you
>
> "As surely as Yahweh lived."
>
> Lie down until the morning. (Campbell 1975, 115)

Indeed, the pronoun "you" added to the verb "to redeem" (יגאלך "if he redeems *you*" and וגאלתיך "then I shall redeem *you*") in v. 13 gives the impression that the object of the redemption is Ruth and that redemption is accomplished by marrying her. Yet, Ruth's request to Boaz is not an explicit marriage offer. She asks Boaz to spread his wing over her because he is a redeemer (3:9). In light of the denouement, readers understand this wing-spreading invitation as a sexual and/or as a marriage request. As stated above (§3) the problem is that redemption does not concern Ruth, who is not affected by any legal impediment that would call for redemption. Ruth's problem is that her husband is dead, she is deprived of marital support until she can have Mahlon's field share reinstated by the communal brotherhood, she is a Moabite in Bethlehem, and though she twice presents herself as Boaz's servant (אמתך, *'amāteka*), she has no master upon whom she could rely for her upkeep after the harvesting season until her right of usufruct could be acted on.

At this point in the story, Boaz has not yet hired Ruth as one of his harvesters, which would have secured her some wages. He has only invited her to share in the meal of his reapers. Ruth urgently needs more lasting support. Naomi has promised to find a way to give her rest (3:1), signaling Boaz as the most likely provider of such rest (3:2). For all of Ruth's needs, the object of the negotiation at the gate between Boaz and the other redeemer is not Ruth. What Naomi offers is Elimelech's share of field, not Ruth.

If so, the accord between the *qere* and the language of 3:12–13 is not a better fit for "the whole thrust of the threshing floor and gate episodes" than the *ketiv*. The tension between the *ketiv* and 3:12–13 does support Campbell's claim that the *ketiv* "violates the internal consistency of the Ruth story." Reading 4:5 with the *ketiv* ascribes the double pronouns "you" in 3:13 to the narrator's art who, with "a certain amount of mystery" (Beattie 1971, 491), anticipates the denouement by correlating Ruth's marriage with Elimelech's land, precisely despite there being no legal obligation for the acquirer of the land to marry Ruth (McKane 1961, 38; Green 1982, 58; Fewell and Gunn 1989, 50). The *qere* ruins this rhetorical effect by postulating a purported legal obligation that the other redeemer was unaware of when he first agreed to redeem the land, which leads him to renounce his initial announcement when Boaz reminds him of this obligation. The levirate is then adduced to bolster the causal link between the land and the woman despite the major issues involved (see §2). From then on, the legal argument invoked to justify the obligation to marry Ruth runs into difficulties due to the ways the supposed legal obligation is observed. To escape the dilemma, levirate duty is pushed aside to make way for eroticism and the argument that Boaz was more interested in Ruth than in the land (Duncan 2000, 98).

The *ketiv* preserves the narrative tension by placing the two redeemers on the same level. Instead of presenting Pelony Almony as a miser who wants the land without the encumbrance of Ruth, Pelony is ready to assume his responsibilities and only desists when he learns that he cannot have Ruth because Boaz is marrying her. Or, had Pelony expected to acquire Naomi rather than Ruth when he agreed to acquire Elimelech's share (so Davies 1983, 233; Lau 2011, 74–80; Adams 2014, 54)? If so, he would have had even less reason to desist upon hearing that Boaz was marrying Ruth (Hubbard 1988, 59).

True, Boaz does not specify whose name he intends to raise, and for good reason. By simply stating that he is acquiring Ruth for himself to raise the name of the deceased (המת, *hammet*), Boaz leaves open the possibility that he will raise the name of more than a single man; hence, the three-share trick discussed in Chapter 2 in this volume.

Whether or not Pelony had expected to marry Naomi or Ruth makes little difference. He does not desist when he learns that he has to marry Ruth (so the *qere*); he desists when he realizes that Boaz is bent on acquiring Elimelech's share in addition to marrying Ruth. Pelony bows out before a socially superior Boaz, whose "opening speech is made in a tone of kindliness, reasonableness, even generosity" but then turns "solemn, almost threatening" (Beattie 1971, 492) as soon as PA declares his intention to redeem.

Whereas the *qere* degrades the portrayal of the other redeemer so as to use him as a foil for Boaz, the *ketiv* keeps him level with Boaz, who wins the deal, though not because his rival was supposedly incapable of figuring out the advantages that could be drawn from it. On the contrary, Pelony was willing to go ahead for the same reasons as Boaz. It was *not* in his interest to desist, but correctly interpreting Boaz's marriage announcement as the clue that he had been outwitted, he saves face by invoking the not-altogether spurious motif that going ahead with his initial decision would hurt his estate (נחלאה, *naḥalah* 4:6). Pelony was ready to redeem the land *and even* marry Ruth, but he was not ready to assume the cost of antagonizing Boaz, a wealthy, prominent local. Pelony thus preferred to pay the price of peace by letting Naomi complete the plan she concocted behind his back, as occurs in any good comedy.

The *qere* misses the game of nerves between the two Bethlehemite worthies and turns the other redeemer into an ignoramus unaware of the levirate when his problem is that Naomi had excluded him from the beginning by steering Ruth towards Boaz and using Ruth to get from Boaz a promise to intervene. Graced a peek into the threshing floor scene, readers are tricked into considering themselves omniscient until ch. 4, when they are at a loss to understand why the other desists, because not a word is said about behind-the-scene communications between Naomi and Boaz.

While the *qere* wallows in the ruts of dubious legalities, the *ketiv* shifts the matter away from any legal framework. Much more than "a matter of responsibility, not duty" (Lau 2011, 193), the deal between Naomi and Boaz is a matter of outsmarting a serious rival. Boaz did not acquire Ruth because he was expected to do so by some levirate custom or law but because he had given his word to Naomi through Ruth that he would do so despite the presence of a closer redeemer than him. It was a matter of honor, not of law; there was an obligation to honor one's promise, which is as binding as any written law, if not more so.

In addition, the *ketiv* avoids the issue arising from the *qere*, which implies that Ruth 4 is the only biblical instance "where a man acquiring land also acquires a widow" (Laffey and Leonard-Fleckman 2017, 134). Whereas the *qere* fosters intertextuality, it eventually gave birth to a unique case devoid of any biblical parallels.

Finally, the *ketiv* takes the form "and from with" (ומאת, *ume'et*, 4:5) into account. Instead of dismissing it as an error to be corrected by ignoring the *mem* as enclitic and *'et* as the marker of the accusative (see Schipper 2016, 165–66) to obtain "also Ruth... you acquire," with "from with," Boaz asserts Ruth's rights to the usufruct of Mahlon's share as much as Naomi's right to Elimelech's share, despite the fact that Ruth is *the* Moabite.

Though they introduced the notion of obligation in the Greek, the translators preserved Ruth's right to land in Bethlehem. Having Boaz warn the other redeemer that he would be acquiring the field "from the hand of Noemin *and from Ruth*" the LXX version states that there are two transferees of the field, Noemi and Ruth. The Massoretic punctuation in the *qere* version of 4:5 introduces the principal caesura (break; pause) in the verse after "from the hand of Naomi," the LXX reads the verse as if the break occurs after the words "wife of the deceased." Therefore, whether *'et* is taken as the marker of the accusative or as "with," the crucial matter is that Naomi's right to trade Elimelech's share implies Ruth's right to trade Mahlon's share. But there is more.

Ruth's right to Mahlon's share anticipates what turns out in v. 9 to be Chilion's share, too. The two verses dedicated to the sandal ritual conveniently delay the revelation of the list of Boaz's acquisition.

From (מִ, *min*) Ruth, Boaz acquires the land-share of Mahlon, Ruth's late husband. Since this implies that Ruth is granted equal rights with Naomi in regard to their shared status as wives of local men, despite Ruth's Moabite origins, *with* (אֵת, *'et*) Ruth means that Boaz claims the right to acquire Chilion's share alongside Mahlon's, though Orpah did not follow Naomi to Bethlehem. No law can justify this third share, except the laws of mathematics that render Chilion's share less visible and more acceptable when it represents a third of Boaz's acquisitions (alongside the shares of Elimelech and Mahlon) rather than half of his acquisitions, had Pelony acquired Elimelech's share and Boaz only those of Mahlon and Chilion. This is closer to trickery than to a slavish observance of any law, but it can be justified from an economic point of view (see Chapter 2 in this volume).

The sandal ritual is a red herring the cunning narrator used as a smoke screen to render the quantity of Boaz's acquisitions in vv. 9–10 almost invisible to readers, who miss the three-share trick Boaz has already announced in v. 5 with the weird form, "from with." Hubbard is a rare commentator to note that "the extent of the purchase probably took the [ancient] reader by surprise" (1988, 255). The Syriac and Old Latin translators were aware of the issue and curtailed the list by abstaining from translating some of it (see Schipper 2016, 196).

8. Marriage customs

While the *ketiv* should be taken seriously as reflecting the state of the tale before the Greek translations introduced the notion of obligation and laws, the sandal ritual may, indeed, echo Deut 25, confirming after all that the Torah is very much in Ruth – not to regulate behavior according to the law of the levirate but to trick readers into accepting Boaz as the hero, even a Torah-abiding one, when he is, in fact, an heir of tricky Jacob who outwitted tricky Laban and Rachel, who tricks her own father (Gen 29–31). For anyone wanting to maintain the Torah in Ruth, the law that is observed in the book is found in the mouth of Laban's daughters. To justify Jacob's manipulation of the reproduction of their father's sheep to his own benefit, Rachel and Leah delineate the implications of the law of ancient marriages:

> Is there still for us any share or inheritance in our father's house? Are we not reckoned foreigners by him, for he has traded us? He has eaten

(even) our silver! Therefore, all that God has withdrawn from our father is for us and for our sons. (Gen 31:14–16)

Their father's loss was their sons' gain; not their children's gain as modern renderings have it, but their sons'. Whereas Jacob provided fourteen years of free labor in exchange for Laban's daughters, Rachel and Leah argue that whatever Jacob pilfered from Laban is God's compensation for the dowry their father did not give them.

As is the case with Boaz's acquisitions – Ruth and three land shares – no actual silver is involved, except as the fourteen years of Jacob's labor Laban capitalized and against which he traded (מכר, *makar*) his daughters without giving them their share of inheritance as dowry. Naomi equally trades Elimelech's share (*makar*, 4:3) against the advance supply of whatever that share may produce in the upcoming year. Like Laban, Boaz *gives* Ruth no dowry. Unlike Laban, however, Boaz *ensures* a dowry for Ruth in the form of Mahlon's share, which he *secures* for her by marrying her. Had Ruth remained unmarried, Pelony could have cultivated Elimelech's share in exchange for feeding Naomi who in turn would have to feed Ruth as her servant or self-indentured slave (see Chapter 2 in this volume). Married again to another Bethlehemite, Ruth would find herself in the same position as Naomi in the event of Boaz's death. She would be able to trade Mahlon's share of field against her own upkeep.

Whereas Laban's daughters become foreigners to their father's family following their marriage, Ruth's second marriage and birthing of Obed re-integrates her into Elimelech's line. The moment Boaz promised to do all Ruth said or even ordered (taking the verb *'amar* in its more imperious sense than mere speaking), he was bound to his word and by public opinion, which recognized Ruth as a worthy woman on the basis of the faithfulness (*ḥesed*, חסד) she displayed towards Naomi. In this case, Boaz's promise to comply with Ruth's imperious demand was a faithful response to her loyalty (3:11) and a display of his own faithfulness, something Boaz deprived Pelony of. Such *ḥesed* is not self-sacrificial, though it "entails going beyond the boundaries of what is required" (Steinmetz 2016, 389). All parties benefit from it. Yet, neither Laban nor Jacob for that matter displayed any such *ḥesed*, involved as they were in a tit-for-tat economic contest. It is Elohim who transfers Laban's wealth to his daughter's sons (Gen 31:16) and whose ancestral images Rachel steals (31:30). And it is the same Elohim to whom Ruth devoted herself for life before crossing the Jordan and entering Yhwh's territory (Ruth 1:17).

Ruth's behavior is more in line with characters in the patriarchal narratives of Genesis than with what Moses expected from the Israelites in Exodus–Deuteronomy. Genesis and Ruth display women taking pivotal initiatives that may breach accepted customs (Nielsen 1985, 203), to the point that, more than Boaz, it is Ruth who "plays the man" (Purcell 2022).

Conclusion

The first requirement for anyone entering the well-plowed field of Ruth scholarship is to be clear about which Ruth will be discussed – the Ruth of the *ketiv* or the Ruth of the *qere*. It is legitimate to follow the venerable tradition established by the Greek text, as long as one is aware that the *ketiv* most likely represents an earlier version of Ruth, closer to how the tale was first conceived. The mention of the sandal in 4:7–8 may well be an addition alluding to Deuteronomy, though hardly meant to depict the protagonists as Torah-abiding figures. Therefore, the evocation of the Torah to clarify the plot of this delightful story is a paradoxical phenomenon, given the once obsessive tendency of the guild to search for the original text. The Ruth tale is a rare instance of a text with the explicit mark of an earlier form of the text – the *ketiv* – that has been rejected in favor of a late scribal interpretation – the *qere* – which overturns the meaning of the entire story.

Reading Ruth against the background of Leviticus, Numbers and Deuteronomy presupposes a knowledge of these laws on the part of the scribe who wrote Ruth and a willingness on his part to present the heroes as Torah-abiding, which they are not. Though the patriarchal narratives of the Torah abound in tricksters, the scribes who introduced the *ketiv-qere* in Ruth 4:5 portrayed Boaz as an expert in legalities in their own image. Designating the attitude of the writer of Ruth as "meta-legal" is a convenient cop-out from the misfit between the so-called laws of the Torah and their application in Ruth.

Fresh approaches to the exegesis of Ruth have much to gain from resisting the temptation to establish connections with the Torah. That the scribes who produced the *ketiv-qere* read Ruth in light of the Torah and that the *ketiv-qere* reflects centuries of readings attested by the Alexandrian translators followed by Josephus and even by Jerome does not mean that we should follow suit. There is more in the Bible than Moses and more to life than obedience to the Law. Being faithful to one's word (*ḥesed*) is the virtue that Ruth and Boaz illustrate and for which Jacob and Laban serve as counter-models. If the Torah is very much in Ruth, it is first of all in the stories of Genesis 29–31 that it is found most clearly.

Works Cited

Adams, Samuel L. 2018. "The Book of Ruth as Social Commentary in Early Judaism." Pages 127–39 in *Figures who Shape Scriptures, Scriptures that Shape Figures: Essays in Honour of Benjamin G. Wright III*. Edited by Géza G. Xeravits and Greg Schmidt Goering. Berlin: De Gruyter. https://doi.org/10.1515/9783110596373-008.

Beattie, Dereck R. G. 1971. "Kethibh and Qere in Ruth IV 5." *Vetus Testamentum* 21: 490–94.

-----. 1974. "The Book of Ruth as Evidence for Israelite Legal Practice." *Vetus Testamentum* 24: 251–67.

Begg, Christopher. 2005. *Judean Antiquities Books 5-7*. Leiden: Brill.

Braulik, Georg. 1999. "The Book of Ruth as Intra-Biblical Critique on the Deuteronomic Law." *Acta Theologica* 19:1–20.

Bush, Frederick W. 1996. *Ruth/Esther*. Word Bibical Commentary 9. Dallas: Word Books.

Campbell, Edward F. Jr. 1975. *Ruth: A New Translation with Introduction, Notes and Commentary*. Garden City: Doubleday.

Collins, John J. 2022. "The Torah in its Symbolic and Prescriptive Functions." *Hebrew Bible and Ancient Israel* 11: 3–18.

Davies, Eryl W. 1983. "Ruth IV 5 and the Duties of the *gō'ēl*." *Vetus Testamentum* 33: 231–34.

De Villiers, Gerda. 2018. "The Pentateuch and its Reception in the Book of Ruth: Constructing Israelite Identity." *Journal for Semitics* 27,1: 18 pages.

Duncan, Celena M. 2000. "The Book of Ruth: On Boundaries, Love and Truth." Pages 92–102 in *Take back the Word: A Queer Reading of the Bible*. Edited by Robert E. Goss and Mona West. Cleveland: Pilgrim.

Embry, Brad. 2016. "Legalities in the Book of Ruth." *Journal for the Study of the Old Testament* 41.1: 31–44.

Eskenazi, Tamara C. and Tikva Frymer-Kensky. 2011. *The JPS Bible Commentary: Ruth*. Philadelphia: Jewish Publication Society.

Fewell, Danna Nolan and David M. Gunn. 1989. "Boaz, Pillar of Society: Measures of Worth in the Book of Ruth." *Journal for the Study of the Old Testament* 45: 45–59.

Fischer, Irmtraud. 2001. *Rut*. Freiburg: Herder.

Gordis, Robert. 1974. "Love, Marriage and Business in the Book of Ruth: A Chapter in Hebrew Customary Law." Pages 241–64 in *A Light in My Path. Old Testament Studies in Honor of Jacob M. Myers*. Edited by Howard N. Bream, Ralf D. Heim and Carey A. Moore. Philadelphia: Temple University Press.

Graybill, Rhiannon. 2024. "'Long Since Murdered': Cozbi, The Kreutzer Sonata, and the Limits of Narrating Sexual Violence." Pages 29–47 in *Narrating Rape: Shifting Perspectives in (Biblical) Literature and Popular*

Culture. Edited by Juliana M. Claassens, Rhiannon Graybill and Christl Maier.

Green, Barbara. 1982 "The Plot of the Biblical Story of Ruth," *Journal for the Study of the Old Testament* 23: 55–68.

Guillaume, Philippe. 2012. *Land, Credit and Crisis*. Sheffield: Equinox.

-----. 2021. "Brothers in Deuteronomy: Zoom in on Lothar Perlitt's Volk von Brüdern." Pages 289–328 in *Deuteronomy in the Making: Studies in the Production of Debarim*. Edited by Diana Edelman, Benedetta Rossi, Kåre Berge and Philippe Guillaume. Berlin: de Gruyter.

-----. 2023. "Basic Tools to Figure out the Economy of Deuteronomy 12–26." No pagination in *Deuteronomy: Outside the Box*. Edited by Diana Edelman and Philippe Guillaume. Themes and Issues in Biblical Studies 5. Sheffield: Equinox. Online. Equinox eBooks Publishing, United Kingkdom. p. Oct 2023. ISBN 9781800503717. https://www.equinoxpub.com/home/view-chapter/?id=44278. Date accessed: 18 Jul 2023 doi: 10.1558/equinox.44278. Oct 2023

Hubbard, Robert L. Jr. 1988. *The Book of Ruth*. Grand Rapids, MI: Eerdmans.

Koosed, Jennifer L. 2011. *Gleaning Ruth. A Biblical Heroine and Her Afterlives*. Columbia: South Carolina University Press.

Lacocque, André. 2004. *Ruth*. Translated by K. C. Hanson. Minneapolis: Fortress.

Laffey, Alice L. and Mahri Leonard-Fleckman. 2017 *Ruth* (Wisdom Commentary 8). Collegeville: Liturgical.

Lau, Peter H. W. 2011. *Identity and Ethics in the Book of Ruth: A Social Identity Approach*. Berlin: de Gruyter.

Levine, Baruch A. 1983. "Legal Themes in the Book of Ruth." Pages 95–106 in *The Quest For the Kingdom of God: Studies in Honor of George E. Mendenhall*. Edited by Herbert Bardwell Huffmon, Frank A Spina and Alberto Ravinell Whitney Green. Winona Lake: Eisenbrauns.

Lipiński, Edouard. 1976. "Le mariage de Ruth." *Vetus Testamentum* 26: 125–27.

Lindström, Fredrik. 2019. "The Portrayal of Divine and Human in the Book of Ruth." Pages 224–47 In *God and Humans in the Hebrew Bible. A Festschrift for Lennart Boström on his 67th Birthday*. Sheffield: Sheffield Phoenix.

McKane, William. 1961. "Ruth and Boaz." *Transactions of the Glasgow Oriental Society* 19: 29–40.

Najman, Hindy. 1999. "The Law of Nature and the Authority of Mosaic Law." *The Studia Philonica Annual* 11: 55–73.

Nielsen, Kirsten. 1985. "Le choix contre le droit dans le livre de Ruth. De l'aire de battage au tribunal." *Vetus Testamentum* 35: 201–12.

Purcell, Richard Anthony. 2022. "Playing the Man in the Book of Ruth: Reshaping the Masculine Ideal." *Biblical Interpretation* 30: 486–508.

Rowley, Harold H. 1952. "The Marriage of Ruth." Pages 163–86 in *The Servant of the Lord and Other Essays on the Old Testament*. Edited by H. H. Rowley. London: Lutterworth.

Rudolph, Wilhelm. 1962. *Das Buch Ruth, das Hohe Lied, die Klagelied.* Gütersloh: Mohn.
Sasson, Jack M. 1978. "The Issue of Ge'Ullah in Ruth." *Journal for the Study of the Old Testament* 5,3: 52–64.
-----. 1979. *Ruth. A New Translation with a Philological Commentary and a Formalist-Folklorist Interpretation.* Baltimore: Johns Hopkins University Press.
-----. 1987. "Ruth." Pages 28–321 in *The Literary Guide to the Bible.* Edited Robert Alter and Frank Kermode. Cambridge, MA: Harvard University Press.
-----. 1989. *Ruth. A New Translation with a Philological Commentary and a Formalist-Folklorist Interpretation.* Second corrected edition. Sheffield: JSOT Press.
-----. 2012. "Farewell to 'Mr So and So' (Ruth 4.1)?" Pages 251–56 in *Making a Difference. Essays on the Bible and Judaism in Honor of Tamara Cohn Eskenazi.* Edited by David J.A. Clines, Kent Harold Richards and Jacob L. Wright. Sheffield: Phoenix.
Schipper, Jeremy. 2016. *Ruth: A New Translation with Introduction and Commentary* (AB 7D), New Haven, CT: Yale University Press.
Steinmetz, Devora. 2016. "Interpretation and Enactment: The Yerushalmi Story of Elisha ben Abuyah and the Book of Ruth." *Association for Jewish Studies Review* 40: 359–92.
Vriezen, Theodorus Christiaan. 1948. "Two Old Cruces." *Oudtestamentische Studiën* 5: 80–91.
Wojcik, Jan. 1985. "Improvising Rules in the Book of Ruth." *Publications of the Modern Language Association of America* 100: 145–53.

About the Author

Philippe Guillaume is Lecturer at the University of Berne. In 2024, he coedited with Diana Edelman *The Old Testament Hebrew Scriptures in Five Minutes* and *Deuteronomy: Outside the Box,* the inaugural volume of the Themes and Issues in Biblical Studies series, both at Equinox.

CHAPTER 4
READING RUTH CANONICALLY AS THE CENTRAL PANEL OF A LITERARY TRIPTYCH

William Krisel

Abstract

The Book of Ruth has its place in very different canonical positions in the Christian Old Testament and the Hebrew Bible. Following the Septuagint, Ruth is located between Judges and 1 Samuel in the Christian canon. In the Hebrew canon, Ruth can be found among the Ketuvim (Writings) either between Proverbs and Song of Songs or between Song of Songs and Lamentations, depending on the rabbinical tradition this is followed. This chapter argues that there are a sufficient number of structural, semantic and literary connections between Ruth and the concluding chapters of Judges and the opening chapters of Samuel to indicate that Ruth may have been written as a response to those texts, thereby forming the central panel of a literary triptych. This literary evidence increases the likelihood that the Greek canon reflects an earlier version of the Hebrew canon. Early Christian and Jewish sources, especially Jerome and the Bava Batra tractate of the Babylonian Talmud, support the proposition that Ruth originally had its place between Judges and Samuel and was moved to the Ketuvim (Writings) sometime after the third century CE.

Keywords: Ruth, Judges 19-21, 1 Samuel 1-7, Hebrew canon, Greek canon, history of the canon, Jerome, Bava Batra, canonical interpretation

To the great relief of readers and scholars alike, the book of Ruth is one of the shortest books in the Bible. Its brevity encourages the reader to read it like a modern novella and to search for the meaning of the story of Naomi, Ruth and Boaz within the four corners of its short text. Although the Hebrew Bible (HB) is replete with dozens of discrete narratives that, like Ruth, are based on a plotline that has its own beginning, middle and end, these stories are typically embedded in longer narrative cycles that encourage readers, both ancient and modern, to read the text within a broader narrative framework. In contrast, Ruth has the canonical status of a separate book in both the HB and Christian Old Testament (OT), which tends to isolate it from the books that precede and follow it. In the oldest extant complete manuscript of the HB, Codex Leningradensis dated to the first decade of the eleventh century ce, Ruth, a narrative, follows Proverbs, a book of sayings, and precedes Song of Songs, a book of poetry; this mix of genres further deprives Ruth of narrative context. The literary context of Ruth is very different in the Greek canon. There, the book follows Judges and precedes Samuel. As one narrative in a long sequence of possibly related narratives, the Greek canon permits Ruth to be read in a broader literary context. It will be argued in this chapter that (i) there are structural, semantic and literary grounds that suggest that Ruth has a close literary connection with the concluding chapters of Judges and opening chapters of Samuel, and (ii) there are historical reasons that support the position that Ruth originally had its place between these two books in the Hebrew canon and was moved to the Ketuvim (Writings) sometime after the third century CE. These two propositions will be explored below.

A. The Literary Place of Ruth in the Broad Canonical Context between Judges 13 and 1 Samuel 1–7

A continuous reading of the final received versions of the books of Judges through Samuel in the MT and LXX suggests that there is an important thematic caesura in the narrative framework between Judges 13–16 (the Samson story) and 1 Samuel 1–7 (the Samuel story). Although Samson and Samuel have very different personalities and their life trajectories follow different paths, there are a number of structural and thematic parallels that appear to link Judges 13–16 with 1 Sam 1–7, as if the Samuel narrative may have originally followed directly after the Samson narrative in an early version of the so-called Deuteronomistic History (Römer and de Pury 2000, 102–103; Kratz 2005, 196; Müller 2013, 211–219). The links between the two narratives include the following.

Similar Incipits

The incipits that introduce the Samson and Samuel narratives are semantically similar. The words shared in common by both incipits are indicated in italics.

> *And it came to pass that there was a certain man from* Zorah, of the family of Dan, *and his name was* Manoah. His wife was infertile and had *borne no children* (Judg 13:2; except as otherwise indicated, all translations from Hebrew and Greek in this chapter are my own).

> *And it came to pass that there was a certain man from* Ramathaim-zophim from the hill country of Ephraim, *and his name was* Elkanah the son of Jeroham, the son of Elihu, the son of Tohu, the son of Zuph, an Ephraimite. And he had two wives: the name of one was Hannah and the name of the other was Peninnah; and Peninnah *had borne children*, but Hannah had not. (1 Sam 1:1-2)

Importantly, these are the only two narratives in the HB that begin with the words, "And it came to pass that there was a certain man."

Similar Narrative Roles for Samson and Samuel

Samson and Samuel are both born to infertile mothers who conceive with divine assistance (Judg 13:2; 1 Sam 1:19). Both Samson and Samuel are "consecrated" from birth to Yhwh "and no razor shall go up on his head" (Judg 13:5a; 1 Sam 1:11). While Samson is destined to "begin to deliver Israel from the hands of the Philistines" (Judg 13:5), it is Samuel who will succeed in defeating the Philistines: "And the hand of Yhwh was against the Philistines all the days of Samuel" (1 Sam 7:13). At the end of both narratives, the protagonists are referred to as "judges"; Samson "judged Israel 20 years in the days of the Philistines" (Judg 15:20) and "Samuel judged Israel all the days of his life" (1 Sam 7:15).

However, this narrative arc spanning the Samson and Samuel stories is interrupted by a seemingly heterogenous set of narratives comprising Judges 17–18 and Judges 19–21 in the MT, and Judges 17–18, Judges 19–21 and Ruth in the LXX. Most scholars agree that these three narratives were composed by different authors at different times. Yet, there is no consensus on either the absolute or relative dating of each text. I argue below that the "author" of Ruth was familiar with a version of the texts known to us as Judges 19–21 and 1 Samuel 1–7, and intended the story of Ruth, Naomi and Boaz to be read as a "response" to both of these narratives.

Understanding the "Gap Texts" between the Samson and Samuel Stories

While most modern commentators assume that the Samuel story followed directly after the Samson story in the so-called Deuteronomistic History and treat Judges 17–18 and 19–21 as later additions to the book of Judges (Römer and de Pury 1996, 102–03; Kratz 2005, 196; *contra* Müller 2013, 211–19), others have taken the position that Ruth formed a third part of the "gap" texts that were added between the Samson and Samuel stories. Edward F. Campbell, Jr argues that Ruth and Judges 19–21 share a number of semantic correspondences that "taken together may suggest a relationship between the two stories" (Campbell 1975, 35). Tod Linafelt (1999) expands Campbell's analysis to identify similar semantic links between Ruth and 1 Samuel. Linafelt considers that his and Campbell's observations have far-reaching consequences:

> This has opened up the possibility that Ruth was not moved to its position [in the Greek canon] between Judges and 1 Samuel because it seemed to fit there, but that it has a more intrinsic connection with those two books. In fact, it becomes possible to speculate that the book of Ruth was written as and intended to be a connector between these two books. (Linafelt 1999, xviii)

Timothy J. Stone (2013; 2015) has revisited the question of Ruth's original place in the Hebrew canon and concludes that "it may have been the author's intent to have Ruth added to the Former Prophets in this exact position [between Judges and 1 Samuel]" (Stone 2015, 181). The arguments advanced by Campbell, Linafelt and Stone will be discussed below.

Campbell's suggestion that there may be a relationship between Judges 19–21 and Ruth is based on the identification of a small handful of semantic similarities between the two texts. These include the observations that (i) the negative particle *'al* is used as an independent negative in Judg 19:23 and Ruth 1:13 and (ii) the verb *naśa'* (נשׂא "to lift up") is used to mean "to marry" in Judg 21:23 and Ruth 1:4. In relation to the first example of semantic correspondence, Campbell acknowledges that there are at least four other occurrences in the HB of the use of the negative particle *'al* as an independent negative. The relatively wide distribution of this grammatical usage (Gen 19:18; Judg 19:23; Ruth 1:4; 2 Sam 13:16; 2 Kgs 3:13; 4:16), which involves the use of a single word, weakens the methodological value of treating it as an indication of the literary dependence of one text on another. In relation to the use of verb "to lift up" to mean "to marry," Campbell states that Judg 21:23 and Ruth 1:4 represent "the only other preexilic use of the idiom" (Campbell 1975, 35). This reasoning is circular; Campbell assumes as a given that these two texts should be dated prior to the exile and then concludes that they alone contain an otherwise unattested lexical expression. The verb "to lift up" is used to mean "to marry" in seven other verses in the books of Ezra–Nehemiah and Chronicles. It is methodologically more parsimonious to interpret this usage in Judges 19–21 and Ruth as a clue to the late date of composition of these two texts (or of important parts thereof).

Linafelt argues that similar structural and semantic correspondences link Ruth and Samuel. He advances two principal arguments in favor of this position. First, Ruth ends with a genealogy of the "generations of Perez" that ends with David (Ruth 4:18–22). Linafelt notes that because genealogies are always used to open (rather than to close) biblical narratives, "the ending of Ruth actually functions to open out to another story. And the most natural story to follow a genealogical list that leads to the name of David would be the story of David's succession to the throne, told in the books of Samuel" (Linafelt, 1999, xx; for a similar position see, Ziegler 2015, 18–20). The problem, of course, is that Ruth is actually followed by the *Samuel* story rather than the David story, which begins sixteen chapters later.

Stephen Dempster raises another, broader, objection to Linafelt's position. According to Dempster, "The announcement of [David's] future birth would be an unprecedented occurrence in the sequence Genesis to Kings" because these texts do not refer to important characters by name until the stories of their births are actually recounted (Dempster 2015, 109). Dempster concludes that the Davidic genealogy at the end of Ruth functions better as a "suitable segue into the Psalter – David's book" (Dempster 2015, 110). This point is discussed further in Section C below.

Linafelt's second argument in favor of a redactional link between Ruth and the books that follow it in the Greek canon is that Ruth has a chiastic literary structure that mirrors that of 2 Sam 5:13–8:18. Leaving aside the merits of Linafelt's structural comparison of these two texts, it can be questioned whether the argument serves as proof that Ruth must have been composed to follow Judges and precede 1 Samuel. Linafelt's position can be interpreted more narrowly to mean that Ruth was written later than a key narrative in 2 Samuel and that the former shows literary dependence on the latter. In my view, this does not demonstrate that Ruth was actually written to serve as a transitional text to 1 Samuel.

Stone's extensive work on the canonical history of Ruth (2013; 2015) integrates the observations of Campbell and Linafelt into a broader theoretical perspective, positing that almost all of the books of the HB contain "catchwords" or "catchphrases" in their concluding verses that are repeated in the opening verses of the next book. These links were stitched into the "seams" between books by successive generations of redactors to create a "canonical or compilational poetics" that give the entire canon a "purposeful shape" (Stone 2015, 179). In relation to Ruth, Stone argues that there is a catchphrase that links Judges 21 to Ruth 1 and another that links Ruth 4 to 1 Samuel 1. However, Stone's analysis is complicated by the fact that he also argues that there is a catchphrase in Judges 21 that links Judges directly to 1 Samuel and a catchphrase in Proverbs 31 that links Proverbs to Ruth. Stone takes the position that these multiple links indicate that Ruth was originally introduced into an already existing compilation of the Former Prophets that followed a Judges–Samuel sequence and was then moved to an early compilation of the Ketuvim that followed a Proverbs–Ruth sequence.

Stone's catchword that links Judges 21 to Ruth 1 is the same one noted by Campbell and Linafelt, i.e., the verb "to lift up" to mean "to marry" in Judg 21:23 and Ruth 1:4. Stone argues that this catchword was added to one or the other text in order to link Judges and Ruth at their seam. Stone believes that this shared verbal form is not coincidental for two reasons. First, "It is vital to note that it is not the *mere presence* of these connections at any point in adjacent books but the *location of these connections at the very edges of the book* that renders them compilationally significant" (Stone 2015, 181; emphasis in the original). Second, because the more common use of the verb *laqaḥ* (לקח "to take") to mean "to marry" appears elsewhere in Judg 19:1; 21:22; Ruth 4:13, the best explanation for the change to the use of the verb "to lift up" is that it was intended to function "as canonical 'glue' to connect the beginning of Ruth to the end of Judges" (Stone 2015, 181). It can be noted that the importance of the catchword Stone has identified as the "canonical glue" linking Judges 21 and Ruth 1 was not noted by the Greek translators of the LXX. The two Hebrew verbs used to signify marriage in these passages are all translated with the Greek verb *lambanó* (λαμβάνω).

Stone's argument raises methodological problems. To prove that the use of the verb "to lift up" for "to marry" is intended to function as canonical "glue," it is necessary to consider other possible explanations of the phenomenon and to demonstrate why they are less convincing than the new interpretation being proposed. In my view, Stone overlooks a number of other explanations for why the verb "to lift up" is used in Judg 21:23 and Ruth 1:4. One such explanation is that it is highly likely that both Judges 21 and Ruth are composite texts; i.e., their final versions include numerous elements added by redactors working over several generations. I have demonstrated elsewhere that Judg 21:22 (where the verb "to take" is used) is a late interpolation that interrupts a pericope from an earlier stratum running from 21:17–23* where "to lift up" is used (Krisel 2022, 381–82; 389–90). In this case, the use of different verbs signifying "to marry" simply reflects the vocabulary of two different "authors," both working during the Persian period. In the case of Ruth, it is possible that significant parts of chs. 1 and 4 were written by different authors who used different vocabulary. I am not aware of any recent scholarship proposing a thorough diachronic analysis of Ruth; this is a question that remains to be addressed in Ruth studies.

Stone identifies a single catchphrase that links Ruth with 1 Samuel. In his view, Ruth 4:15 ("He [Obed] will be for you a restorer of life and a sustainer in your old age, for your daughter-in-law who loves you gave birth to him [and] she is *better to you* than seven *sons*") was intended to link the book of Ruth to the books of Samuel because in 1 Sam 1:8, Elkanah asks Hannah, "Am I not *better to you* than ten *sons?*" The parallelism between these two verses is less obvious in the LXX, where Ruth is compared to seven *sons* (υἱούς) while Elkanah compares himself to ten *children* (τέκνα). As Stone insists so strongly on the importance of identifying semantic connections found "at the very edges of the book," it is curious that the sole semantic link between Ruth and Samuel would be located eight verses before the end of Ruth and eight verses into 1 Samuel. Stone's identification of the older link between Judges 19–21 and Samuel, the use of the toponym "Shiloh" in Judg 21:19–21 and 1 Sam 1:3–6, lies closer to the seam between these two books and is therefore more convincing when applying Stone's own criteria.

I agree with Campbell, Linafelt and Stone that the Ruth writer was familiar with a version of the texts known to us as Judges 19–21 and 1 Samuel 1–7 and probably intended the novella about Ruth, Naomi and Boaz to be read as a "response" to both of these narratives. However, as a methodological corrective to the weaknesses of relying on semantic and structural parallels discussed above, I take the position that there are several well-developed *thematic* similarities between the three narratives that rise above the level of mere coincidence or the reuse of what Robert Alter calls "type scenes" (Alter 1981, 47–62).

B. Reading Judges 19–21, Ruth, and 1 Samuel 1–7 as a Literary Triptych

At first glance, these three narratives appear to share very little in common. Judges 19–21 is a long and often incoherent story of gang rape, civil war, tribal animosity and reconciliation. Ruth is a well-crafted novella focused on three well-developed characters that reads like a love story with an ethical twist. 1 Sam 1–7 is a complex set of interlocking stories involving the infertile Hannah, the good boy Samuel, the evil priest Eli, and a war story between Israelites and Philistines revolving around the capture and recovery of the "ark of God." However, there are a number of thematic and structural elements that are common to all three of these narratives, which suggest that the author of one may have been familiar with the other two texts.

One of the important thematic threads that run through Judges 19–21, Ruth and 1 Samuel 1–7 is a concern over two different but interrelated problems: first, the problem posed by widows and widowers who want to remarry; second, the problem of preserving the names of men who die without surviving offspring. This section discusses the treatment of these twin issues first in Ruth, and then in the narratives that precede and follow Ruth in the Greek canon. It is worth noting in passing that while widows represented a well-recognized social category in ancient Israel (Steinberg 2004), there is no specific word in Hebrew that denotes widowers and their status is not generally discussed in the HB. Judges 19–21 is thus a rare text in which male widowhood is a key issue.

Widows, Remarriage and Preserving Inheritance in Ruth

Ruth is a young widow without children. While young virgins may have been prized as ideal wives in the ancient world, it appears that marriage between men and young widows was not stigmatized. Among other biblical figures, David married two such widows, Abigail, "the widow of Nabal" and Bathsheba, the "widow of Uriah, the Hittite." The threshold problem confronted by Ruth in the narrative is therefore to find a new husband. Indeed, Naomi encourages Ruth to return to the house of her mother in Moab "to find security in the house of her [next] husband" (Ruth 1:9). While Naomi's advice to her daughter-in-law was no doubt wise and would have been anticipated by readers, the narrative introduces a complication in the plotline that challenges the reader's expectations: Ruth does not want to remain in Moab but wishes to return to Judah with her mother-in-law. The young widow justifies her decision with the lofty statement, "For wherever you go, I will go; wherever you lodge, I will lodge; your people are my people, and your God, my God" (Ruth 1:16). However, it is not immediately clear to the reader why Ruth's noble decision to remain loyal to her mother-in-law will diminish her chances of finding a second husband after she returns to Bethlehem. Is it because she is a Moabite by birth and Judeans are unlikely to want to marry a "foreign woman"? This explanation would make sense to ancient readers steeped in the anti-intermarriage polemics of Ezra and Nehemiah (Ezra 9–10 and Nehemiah 13). Is it because the reader expects that Naomi will be returning to her own parent's household in Bethlehem and Ruth's arrival may be unwelcome? Is there really no hope that Ruth might find an important man in Bethlehem to marry as Abigail and Bathsheba did?

Indeed, immediately following her return to Bethlehem, Ruth sets out to the neighboring fields to glean barley. As a poor and hungry widow, she had the right to walk through the fields at harvest time to pick grain left behind by the harvesters. But it would be entirely reasonable for the reader to think that Ruth may also have gone gleaning in the hopes of finding a husband. The text supports this aspect of Ruth's motivation. In seeking Naomi's permission to leave the house – the text does not tell the reader whether the two women are lodging with Naomi's family, Elimelech's family, or are in fact homeless – Ruth asks "Please let me go to the field and glean among the ears of grain in the footsteps of *some man* who may look upon me with favor" (Ruth 2:2). And this is exactly what happens. The narrator promptly informs the reader that "chance (*mikreh*) led her to a plot of land belonging to Boaz who was of Elimelech's family" (Ruth 2:3b).

As this is a story about a widow's search for a new husband, and "chance" has brought Ruth to glean in fields owned by Boaz, the reader can anticipate that the story will have a happy ending and that Ruth will marry Boaz and bear his children. To make a long love story short, the narrator confirms towards the end of the story that "Boaz took Ruth, and she became his wife, and he went in to her. And Yhwh gave her conception, and she gave birth to a son" (Ruth 4:13). In one of the postscripts to the narrative, the reader is given the child's complete genealogy. He is indeed the son of Boaz and he will become the father of Jesse and the grandfather of David (Ruth 4:21–22).

Between Ruth's chance meeting with Boaz in the fields and the birth of their son, the narrative introduces a complicated and meandering tale that presents (or re-presents) Ruth's relationship with Boaz as a kind of "levirate" marriage in which the widow's closest willing kin "buys" the widow in order to provide her deceased former husband with proxy progeny. As stated by Boaz, "Moreover, I have acquired Ruth the Moabitess, the widow of Mahlon, to be my wife in order to raise up the name of the deceased on his inheritance, so that the name of the deceased may not be cut off from his brothers or from the gates of his place; you are witnesses today" (Ruth 4:10).

The final version of the book of Ruth in both its MT and LXX versions thus interweaves two stories that respond to different problems; first, finding a new husband for a young widow; second, preserving the "name" of a deceased man who dies without surviving children. The literary ingenuity of the narrative is that a form of levirate marriage between Ruth and her deceased husband's closest willing kin is presented as the solution to both problems. Ruth is a young woman who seeks to remarry and have children of her own as well as a vehicle to assure that her deceased husband's name is not "cut off from his brothers or from the gates of his place." Boaz is a respected local dignitary who is attracted to a young and attractive woman who will give him children as well as a pious observer of the ancient custom of marrying a widow in order to preserve another man's inheritance to the possible detriment of his own. It is possible that the theme of levirate marriage was introduced into the text by a later redactor in order to transform a lusty love story into a pious moral lesson. However, as discussed in the following section, the twinned motifs of finding a second spouse for a widow or widower and preserving the name and inheritance of a man who dies without surviving children is in fact the theme of Judges 19–21, the narrative that precedes Ruth in the Greek canon.

Widowers, Remarriage and Preserving Inheritance in Judges 19–21

This narrative is long and meandering and includes a number of digressions and subplots. The dramatic thrust that drives the narrative can be summarized as follows. Men of the tribe of Benjamin gang rape and murder a married woman. A pan-Israelite assembly demands that Benjamin delivers the criminals for trial and punishment. The men of Benjamin refuse. Acting collectively, the sons of Israel go to war with one of their own, the tribe of Benjamin. The civil war is bloody and hundreds of thousands die on both sides. In the end, Israel is victorious, having killed all Benjaminite men, women and children, save a small remnant of 600 men who flee to the desert seeking refuge. However, Israel's victory raises a problem. As the 600 surviving Benjaminites are widowers without surviving children, Israel must find wives for them so that "a tribe will not be blotted out from among Israel" (Judg 21:17b).

The reader expects that this problem will be solved by the sons of Israel giving 600 daughters of their own in marriage to the surviving Benjaminites. However, the narrator explains at the outset of the story in Judges 21 that "the men of Israel had sworn at Mizpah, saying: A man from among us will not give his daughter to Benjamin as wife" (Judg 21:1a). The text does not provide the reader with any explanation for this oath; it appears in the narrative as if out of nowhere. Was it sworn in a burst of anger against Benjamin at the outset of the civil war? Is the oath sworn by the men of Israel in Judges 21 intended to echo the oath that Nehemiah made the Jews swear in relation to the Ashdodites, Ammonites and Moabites, "You shall not give your daughters to their sons or take any of their daughters for your sons or for yourselves" (Neh 13:25)? On this reading, the sons of Israel are "othering" the sons of Benjamin by assimilating them to the status of Moabites and other foreigners with whom marriage is forbidden (Krisel 2022, 384–87, 404). Whatever the reason, the reader is left to understand that once an oath is sworn, it must be honored.

The sons of Israel come up with a plan for finding wives for Benjamin. They send 12,000 soldiers to Yabesh-Gilead, a trans-Jordanian town, which had not answered the call to join in the civil war against Benjamin. The mission is to slaughter all the men, women and children of the town with the exception of the "virgin girls who have not known a man, in relation to the bed of a male" (Judg 21:12a). The slaughter completed, the sons of Israel "proclaim peace" to the 600 surviving Benjaminites and give them the captured girls of Yabesh-Gilead to take as wives. Although the problem of finding wives for Benjamin appears to be solved, the narrative introduces a surprising twist: "they had not found enough for them" (Judg 21:14b). In fact, only 400 virgin girls had been captured, leaving 200 Benjaminites without brides.

The plan for finding 200 more brides involves the Benjaminite survivors going to Shiloh at the time of an annual festival and hiding in the vineyards waiting for girls to come out dancing. The sons of Israel command them to "seize for yourselves, each man his woman, from among the daughters of Shiloh" (Judg 21:20). They do so and return to the land of Benjamin with their wives. This bizarre story has a "happy" ending for the 600 surviving Benjaminites and their new wives: "And they went. And they returned to their inheritance. And they rebuilt the cities. And they dwelled in them" (Judg 21:23b).

Although the context in which the motif of "finding a husband for Ruth" is developed is very different from that of "finding wives for Benjamin," there are semantic parallels that unite them. The sons of Israel are moved to find wives for Benjamin "so that a tribe will not be blotted out (ימחה yimmāḥeh) from among Israel" (Judg 21:17b). The closest parallel to this concept of being "blotted out from among Israel" can be found in the presentation of the levirate laws in Deuteronomy 25:5–10: "And it shall be that the first-born whom she bears shall assume the name of his dead brother, so that his name will not be blotted out (yimmāḥeh) from among Israel" (Deut 25:6). Boaz's reason for marrying Ruth uses similar language: "so that "the name of the deceased [Mahlon] will not be cut off (יכרת yikkāret) from among his brothers" (Ruth 4:10). Both statements draw the reader's attention to the levirate laws without quoting directly from Deut 25:5–10. A possible intertext for both Judg 21:17b and Ruth 4:10 may be Psalm 109 which links the "cutting off" of surviving heirs with the "blotting out" of a name. The psalmist curses his oppressor with the imprecation, "May his posterity be cut off (yikkāret); may their names be blotted out (yimmāḥ) in the next generation" (Ps 109:13).

Childless Women, Inheritance and Preservation of Name in 1 Samuel 1–7

To be sure, the motif of finding a spouse for childless widows and widowers appears to be absent in 1 Samuel 1–7. The principal female character, Hannah, is a married woman who is unable to conceive, "because Yhwh had shut up her womb" (1 Sam 1:6). This problem is solved, as in many biblical narratives, by a divine intervention. Hannah vows that if Yhwh "gives" her a son, she will "give him to Yhwh all the days of his life" to serve as a cultic attendant at the sanctuary of Shiloh (1 Sam 1:11). The reader can reasonably wonder whether Hannah has struck a bad bargain. Because she has to give back to God the son that he had given her, Hannah will find herself once again in the position of being a childless wife in a polygamous marriage. The narrative hints at Hannah's reluctance to give up her only child. When her husband wants to bring the baby Samuel to the priest Eli to serve in the sanctuary, Hannah resists. She tells Elkanah that she will not give up her child "until he has been weaned. Then I shall bring him and present him before Yhwh and he will stay there forever" (1 Sam 1:22).

Hannah remains faithful to her vow and brings young Samuel to the sanctuary and is only able to visit him once a year during the annual pilgrimage to Shiloh, possibly the same annual festival where the Benjaminite survivors found wives in Judges 21. This infertile woman who has been blessed by God with a son finds herself in the same position as at the outset of the narrative, a childless woman in a polygamous marriage. However, the narrative includes a short digression in which the reader learns that Hannah later gives birth to three more sons and two daughters. This is presented as the fulfillment of Eli's blessing of Elkanah, "May Yhwh grant you seed from this woman in exchange for the one which she has made over to Yhwh" (1 Sam 2:20). Depending on the context, "seed" (זרע zera') can refer figuratively to a specific child fathered by a man or to his descendants over many generations. In the context of Elkanah's polygamous marriage to two women, it is reasonable to interpret the reference to the man's "seed from this woman" to mean the descendants or heirs of Elkanah and Hannah over many generations. The word "seed" is used only once in Ruth and with the same meaning. When Boaz publicly states his willingness to marry Ruth, the people at the gate and the elders proclaim in unison "And may your house be like the house of Perez whom Tamar bore to Judah, from the seed that Yhwh will give you from this young woman" (Ruth 4:12). The parallelism between this verse and 1 Sam 2:20 is reinforced by the fact that both statements start with a jussive verb ("May your house be..." and "May Yhwh grant you...").

Although the miraculous birth of Samuel is given great emphasis in the Samuel story, it is echoed in miniature in the birth scene in Ruth: "So Boaz took Ruth, and she became his wife, and he went in to her. And *Yhwh gave her conception, and she gave birth to a son*" (Ruth 4:13). As birth scenes in the HB are usually structured to follow a common semantic pattern, the intrusion of Yhwh in the birth of a child to Ruth, who is described as a "young woman" (נאה *na'arah*), seems curious. In the six other birth scenes that follow a man who "goes in to" a woman (Gen 29:23; 30:4; 38:2; 38:18; Judg 16:1; 2 Sam 12:24), there is no mention of a divine role in conception that follows. It is possible that the author of Ruth (or a later redactor) is intentionally modeling Ruth's birth of Obed on Hannah's birth of Samuel: "Elkanah knew his wife Hannah and *Yhwh remembered her* [...] and *Hannah conceived and gave birth to a son*" (1 Sam 1:19–20a).

According to Jones (2016, 97), divine intervention in pregnancy only occurs in the HB in stories about *infertile* women. Unlike Hannah, the text does not state that Ruth is infertile, though she had not become pregnant during her marriage to Chilion. Boaz may thus be concerned that she may in fact be infertile and unable to bear him children, an essential part of his bargain to acquire Ruth's inheritance rights. It is thus possible that the text is portraying Ruth as both a childless widow, thereby bringing her into literary relationship with the childless widowers in Judges 21, and a barren woman, thereby bringing her into literary relationship with Hannah's miraculous birth of Samuel in 1 Samuel 1.

The motif of heirs and inheritance, which is central in Judges 21 and Ruth, and is hinted at in the digression in 1 Samuel 2:18–21 concerning the birth of descendants of Elkanah and Hannah to replace the child given to Yhwh, is more fully developed in the Samuel narrative in the subplot concerning the evil sons of the priest Eli. Eli has two sons, Hophni and Phineas, who abuse their priestly functions and do evil. Yhwh decides to punish the two young men and their father who had failed to discipline them in the performance of their duties. Yhwh first communicates his plans to Eli through the mouth of a "man of God who came to Eli." The punishment is twofold; the death of the two young men as well as a curse on the "house" of Eli, i.e., on his descendants over the generations to come: "A time is coming when I will sever (gādaʻtî גדעתי) your strength (zroʻakā זרעך) and the strength of your father's house, and there shall be no elder in your house" (1 Sam 2:31). This verse has parallels in both Judges 19–21 and Ruth.

The verb "to sever" is also used in Judges 21 to refer to the childless widowers of Benjamin. The sons of Israel say, "One tribe from among Israel has been severed today. What shall we do for them, for those who remain, for wives?" (Judg 21:6b–7a).

The noun zro'ā (זרע, literally "arm" or "shoulder"), refers figuratively to a person's strength or power. However, the spelling and pronunciation of the word is so close to that of "seed, descendants" (zera' זרע) that it can be suspected that the Samuel narrative is engaging in word play. Indeed, the LXX translates 1 Sam 2:31 as if the text read zera' rather than zro'ā: "Behold, the days come when I will destroy your seed and the seed of your father's house." It is possible to read the community's blessing of Boaz in Ruth 4:12 ("And may your house be like the house of Perez whom Tamar bore to Judah, from the seed that Yhwh will give you from this young woman") as an intertextual reference to Yhwh's curse on Eli in 1 Sam 2:31 ("A time is coming when I will sever your strength/seed and the strength/seed of your father's house, and there shall be no elder in your house").

The curse on Eli's house continues with the words, "And this will be the sign to you which shall come concerning your two sons, Hophni and Phinehas: on the same day both of them shall die" (1 Sam 2:34). Later in the Samuel narrative, Eli's two sons are in fact killed (1 Sam 4:11). When Eli hears the news of their death, "he fell backward off the seat of honor beside the gate, broke his neck and died; for he was an old man and heavy" (1 Sam 4:18). When Eli's pregnant daughter-in-law heard the news that both Eli and her husband Phinehas had died, she miscarried and, although her child survived, the mother died in childbirth (1 Sam 4:19–22). Although she is a minor character in the Samuel narrative, the striking down of a "daughter-in-law" in childbirth contrasts with the raising up of a "daughter-in-law" in Ruth. The word "daughter-in-law" (kallāh כלה) is actually quite rare in the HB. The only women described as daughters-in-law in the HB are Sarah (Gen 11:31), Tamar (Gen 38:11.16.24; 1 Chron 2:4), Ruth (Ruth 1:22; 2:20.22; 4:15.19) and Phinehas' unnamed widow (1 Sam 4:19).

The conclusion at this stage is that Judg 19–21, Ruth and 1 Sam 1–7, three narratives that follow each other in the Greek canon, focus on a double set of problems: first, the problem posed by widows and widowers who want to remarry; second, the problem of preserving the names of men who die without surviving offspring. As the narrative development of this theme is different in the three texts, the literary relationship is not obvious at first glance. In Judg 19–21, the twin problems are posed in relation to 600 men who have lost their wives and children in war. The sons of Israel ask the question, "What shall we do for them, for those who remain, for wives?" (Judg 21:7a; 21:16b). This concern for the status of a widower who no longer has any feasible remarriage options is intertwined with the concern that if the 600 surviving Benjaminites die without descendants, an entire tribe will be "blotted out from among Israel" (Judg 21:17b). In Ruth, the twin problems are developed separately and then joined in the conclusion. Ruth 1–3 addresses the problem of finding a new husband for the widowed Ruth. Ruth 4 raises the concern over how to prevent "the name of the deceased [Mahlon]" from being "cut off from among his brothers" (Ruth 4:10). In 1 Samuel 1–7, the twin problems are reversed. Hannah is not a widow but she is infertile. Her problem is solved by Yhwh giving her the miraculous birth of a son, Samuel. However, this happy event serves as a foil to create another problem: in "giving" Samuel to Yhwh to serve as a cultic attendant, Hannah again finds herself without children in a polygamous marriage. The priest Eli solves this problem when he blesses Hannah's husband Elimelech, "May Yhwh grant you descendants from this woman in exchange for the one which she has made over to Yhwh" (1 Sam 2:20). The blessing is fulfilled and Hannah later gives birth another five times, giving Elimelech many descendants through her. Eli's blessing has a parallel in the community's blessing on Boaz "May your house be like the house of Perez whom Tamar bore to Judah, from the descendants who Yhwh will give you from this young woman" (Ruth 4:12).

The thematic links between Judges 19–21, Ruth and 1 Samuel 1–7 identified above suggest that these narratives have a genetic relationship and are not simply independent compositions that coincidentally share certain elements in common. However, the compositional history of the three texts is not obvious. One way to untangle the genealogical relationship between them is to start with the question, "Why Moab?" Why do Elimelech and Naomi leave Bethlehem during a famine to "sojourn" in Moab (a place with even less rainfall) rather than anywhere else? One likely answer is that Moabites are the quintessential "other" or foreigner (נכרי *nokri*) in the HB. According to both Deut 23:4 and Neh 13:1, "They and their descendants are forever forbidden entry into the congregation of Yhwh" (Deut 23:4). Nehemiah returns to the otherness of the Moabites in Neh 13:25 when he commands the Golah community "You shall not give your daughters to their sons, nor take of their daughters for your sons or for yourselves" (Neh 13:25). These are the "foreign wives" from whom Ezra orders the Golah to separate in Ezra 10. In contrast, Ruth the Moabite, a "foreign wife," is portrayed as a heroic woman who marries Boaz, an upstanding Judean man. Victor H. Matthews (2004, 209) contends that Ruth is "raising a religious argument against the enforcement of endogmatic [sic] marriage practices by Ezra and Nehemiah in the fifth century BCE." It is also possible that Ruth's positively-valanced mixed marriage is more specifically intended to be a literary response to Judges 21.

As discussed, the entire narrative problem of finding wives for widowed Benjaminites is triggered by the oath that the sons of Israel had sworn "A man from among us will not give his daughter to Benjamin as wife" (Judg 21:1; cf. 21:7.18). This vocabulary directly echoes that of Nehemiah's order in Neh 13:25. Rather than reading Ruth as a broadbrush response to the anti-mixed marriage polemic in Ezra–Nehemiah, the fact that Ruth follows Judges 21 in the Greek canon suggests that Ruth is in fact a specific response to the position being taken in Judges. While Judges 21 takes a fellow Israelite tribe and excludes them by "othering" them as if they were Moabites, it can be argued that Ruth takes a born Moabite and integrates her into Israel as a heroic woman and ancestor of David. To be sure, the anti-mixed marriage polemic in Ezra–Nehemiah underlies both Judges 19–21 and Ruth. However, the numerous links between these two texts makes it more likely that the literary purpose of Ruth is to respond in a direct way to the theme of finding wives for Benjamin as developed in Judges 21.

A simple (over-simplistic?) solution to the compositional relationship between Judges 19–21, Ruth and 1 Samuel 1–7 is to assume that the Samuel story is the oldest, having originally been the narrative that followed the Samson story. Judges 21 takes over the theme of preserving the name of men who would otherwise die without surviving children from 1 Samuel 1–2 and introduces the problem of excluding Benjamin from Israel into the mix. Ruth is then crafted as a response to Judges 19–21 and takes over from Judges 21 the twinned themes of finding spouses for widows as well as preserving the name of a man who dies without surviving children from being "blotted out" or "cut off." But as the central panel in a triptych, Ruth also shares thematic and semantic elements with 1 Samuel 1–7. Notwithstanding the likely complex redactional history of all three narratives, readers of the final versions of the texts, with one following the other as in the Greek canon, gain heuristic benefit from reading them as a triptych.

C. Ruth's Itinerant Place in the Hebrew Canon

The place of Ruth in the canon is very different in the Christian and Jewish canons that are recognized as authoritative today. Catholic, Orthodox and Protestant churches agree that Ruth follows Judges and precedes Samuel in the second of the four parts of the Christian OT called the "Historical Books." All currents of contemporary Judaism follow a tripartite division of the HB (Torah, Nevi'im or Prophets, and Ketuvim or Writings). They concur that Ruth follows Song of Songs and precedes Lamentations among the Writings. While the antiquity of Ruth's place in the order of the Christian canon is well attested, the situation in the Hebrew canon is more complex. The history of the place of Ruth in the Christian and

Hebrew canons will be briefly summarized below (for a more detailed discussion, see Krisel, 2021).

The Place of Ruth in the History of the Christian Canon

The earliest source to discuss the canonical order of Ruth is Melito, a second-century CE bishop of Sardis. In his Ecclesiastical History, Eusebius quotes from a letter of Melito in which the bishop states that he had traveled to the "east" where he "learned accurately the books of the Old Testament" (Eusebius, Hist. eccl. 4.26, 12–14). Melito lists Ruth as following Judges and preceding 1 Reigns (1 Samuel). All surviving third- and fourth-century Christian sources agree on this Judges–Ruth–Samuel sequence. The only disagreement among early sources over the canonical place of Ruth relates to whether Ruth should be counted as a separate book (as is the case in the LXX and all later Christian versions of the OT) or was a continuation of Judges, with Ruth 1:1 following on the same page directly after Judg 21:25. As this disagreement does not directly impact the question of whether Ruth followed Judges and preceded Samuel, it is not discussed in this chapter.

The Place of Ruth in the History of the Hebrew Canon

The earliest sources to discuss the place of Ruth in the Hebrew Canon are the early Christian theologian and translator, Jerome and the authors of a tractate in the Babylonian Talmud called Bava Batra. These two sources are roughly contemporaneous; Jerome wrote towards the end of the fourth century and the relevant portions of Bava Batra have been dated between the second half of the third century and the end of the fifth century (Lightstone 2002, 178). Both sources provide valuable information on the canonical status of Ruth but both have been, in my opinion, misread or "overread" by both Christian and Jewish scholars. Jerome is usually interpreted as standing for the proposition that Jewish rabbis of Jerome's time placed Ruth among the second part of the HB, the Prophets, after Judges and before Samuel. Bava Batra is usually understood as confirming that Ruth formed part of the Writings, as its first book (which would mean after Malachi, the last book of the Prophets), followed by Psalms. Later on, rabbinical authorities moved Ruth again to its current place in the HB between Song of Songs and Lamentations.

A close reading of both Jerome and Bava Batra yields a more nuanced conclusion – that these two early sources confirm that there was a divergence of views among early rabbis with some holding that Ruth formed part of the Prophets, coming after Judges and before Samuel, and others holding that Ruth is the first book of the Writings followed by Psalms. The difference between the two sources is that they disagree as to which position represented the "majority" view and which the "minority" view. Jerome argues that Ruth's position as part of the Prophets was the majority view and Bava Batra contends that Ruth's position as part of the Writings was the majority view. Importantly, however, they both agree that there was a recognized minority position among certain rabbinical authorities. It is the existence of this minority voice that is often overlooked by scholars in their readings of Jerome and Bava Batra.

Jerome on Ruth

Jerome was a Christian theologian who embarked on the mammoth project of preparing a new translation of the Bible into Latin. In the case of the OT, Jerome believed that the Latin version should be a translation of a Hebrew text rather than of the Greek LXX. He spent fifteen years on this project (390–405 ce) and traveled to Jerusalem and Bethlehem to study Hebrew with Jewish rabbis and to use their biblical scrolls as the basis of his Latin translation. It is therefore reasonable to consider Jerome's canon list to be a reliable witness of one version of the Hebrew canon used by Jews during the fourth century. Jerome refers to the tripartite division of the Hebrew canon and lists the contents of each division in his prologue (known as the Prologus Galeatus) to his commentary on Samuel and Kings, which is generally dated to c. 393 (Gallagher and Meade 2017, 198). Jerome states that the Hebrew canon included both Ruth and Lamentations among the Prophets, with Ruth following Judges and Lamentations following Jeremiah. Importantly, however, he goes on to say, "Some (nonnulli) include Ruth and Kinoth (Lamentations) among the Hagiographa (Writings)." I interpret Jerome to mean that there was a divergence of view among rabbis of his day on the canonical order of Ruth; a majority thought that Ruth followed Judges and preceded Samuel in the Prophets while a minority held that Ruth was a separate book included among the Writings.

Bava Batra on Ruth

The Bava Batra tractate in the Babylonian Talmud is customarily cited as the earliest Jewish authority for the proposition that Ruth is a separate book forming part of the Writings (Lim 2013, 35; Gallagher and Meade 2017, 65–69). In the relevant portion, folios 14b–15a, the tractate mentions Ruth in three authoritative statements (called baraitot; the plural of baraita) followed by rabbinical debate. The first baraita states, "Our sages taught: The order of the Nevi'im (Prophets) is Joshua, and Judges, Samuel and Kings, Jeremiah and Ezekiel, Isaiah and the Twelve (minor Prophets)." The second states, "The order of the Writings [is] Ruth and the Book of Psalms, and Job and Proverbs; Ecclesiastes, Song of Songs, and Lamentations; Daniel and the Scroll of Esther. Ezra and Chronicles." The third states, "And who wrote [the books of the Bible]? Moses wrote his own book, and the portion of Balaam, and Job. Joshua wrote his own book and the [last] eight verses in the Torah. Samuel wrote his own book, Judges, and Ruth. [...]. Jeremiah wrote his own book, and the book of Kings and Lamentations [...]."

Making Sense of *Bava Batra*

These baraitot can be understood as proposing two different canonical systems of ordering. The system proposed by the third baraita groups biblical books by authors. Thus, Judges, Ruth and Samuel are grouped together because their authorship is ascribed to the prophet Samuel, and Jeremiah is grouped with Lamentations because they are believed to have been authored by the prophet Jeremiah. This order closely resembles the late fourth-century Hebrew canon described by Jerome in which Ruth follows Judges and Lamentations follows Jeremiah. In contrast, the first and second baraitot use a somewhat bewildering canonical logic which merits further examination.

The system proposed in these two baraitot is based on scroll length; that is, the books are ordered in ascending or descending order according to the length of the individual scrolls on which they were written.

The three major prophets are listed in the first baraita as Jeremiah, Ezekiel and Isaiah rather than as Isaiah, Jeremiah and Ezekiel as attested by Sirach (Sir 48:20; 49:7–9), by all early Christian sources, and by Codex Aleppo and Codex Leningradensis. The curious order proposed by the first baraita can be understood as listing the books in descending order of scroll length, i.e., Jeremiah (33,002 words), followed by Ezekiel (29,918 words), followed by Isaiah (25,608 words), followed by the Book of Twelve (21,837 words).

The second baraita orders the Writings according to a double logic of scroll length. First, Psalms through Song of Songs are listed in descending order of size, except that Ruth is placed before Psalms and Lamentations is listed after Song of Songs. Then, the remaining Writings follow a logic of ascending order of size, with Daniel being the shortest scroll and Chronicles the longest. However, this order is broken by Esther which is intercalated between Daniel and Ezra–Nehemiah. Table 1 presents the order of the Prophets and Writings according to scroll size as proposed

Table 1: *The canonical order in* Bava Batra *according to number of words*

Latter Prophets in descending order	First Writings in descending order (except Ruth)	Second Writings in ascending order (except Esther)
Jeremiah (33,002)	*Ruth (2,039)*	Daniel (9,001)
Ezekiel (29,918)	Psalms (30,147)	*Esther (4,932)*
Isaiah (25,608)	Job (12,674)	Ezra-Nehemiah (14,112)
Twelve (21,837)	Proverbs (9,921)	Chronicles (38,013)
	Ecclesiastes (4,537)	
	Song of Songs (2,020)	
	Lamentations (2,324)	

in the first two baraitot, with the three books that deviate from the scroll size order indicated in italics.

I propose that the three books that break the ordering of the Writings based on scroll length – Ruth, Lamentations and Esther – were added to an earlier list of the Writings in which they were not present. In this case, Ruth and Lamentations originally belonged to the Prophets, as Jerome explicitly states was the case in the Hebrew canon of his day and as the third baraita implicitly views as an acceptable alternative order of the Prophets. Ruth and Lamentations were later moved to the Writings, while the case of Esther is more complicated and probably relates to its disputed status as a canonical book. This issue is beyond the purview of this chapter.

The notion that a collection of scrolls might be ordered according to their size makes sense in a scroll (rather than codex) culture where a large number of scrolls of different sizes needed to be stored in a library room in an organized manner. Ordering scrolls by size facilitates the retrieval of a specific scroll without having to open the scroll to read the first words. This concern over scroll size is supported by the rabbinical discussion that follows the first baraita of Bava Batra in which Rabbi Jonathan took the position that because the prophet Hosea wrote before Isaiah, his book should be listed as the first of the Latter Prophets rather than included in the Book of Twelve. Another rabbi then responded, "[Were it written separately,] since it is small it would be lost." According to the same logic, the short scrolls of Ruth and Lamentations were moved to the Writings, a collection that includes a number of small scrolls, so that they "would not be lost" among the longer scrolls of the Prophets.

The fact that Ruth and Lamentations (and Esther) are the only three books that break the strict ordering of the Writings in Bava Batra according to descending and then ascending scroll size further supports the hypothesis that they are late additions to an already established order of the Writings. If this hypothesis is correct, it means that the

Judges–Ruth–Samuel sequence of the Greek canon reflects an earlier version of the Hebrew canon than the one found in Jewish medieval and later manuscripts of the HB.

D. Perspectives for Further Research

The analysis of Judges 19–21, Ruth and 1 Samuel 1–7 proposed in this chapter follows a synchronic approach; i.e., reading the texts according to their final versions in the MT and LXX. The conclusions reached could be impacted when the three texts are analyzed diachronically; i.e., with a view to identifying the various redactional strata that underlie each text. While Judges 19–21 and 1 Samuel 1–7 have been the subject of diachronic analyses, I am not aware of any recent scholars who have attempted to reconstruct the redaction history of Ruth. Such a study would be a valuable contribution to Ruth studies.

Linafelt's position that the Davidic genealogy at the end of Ruth should be interpreted as an appropriate introduction to the story of David in the book of Samuel has been criticized because Ruth is actually followed by the story of Samuel. However, in the Chronicler's version of Samuel-Kings, the events described in 1 Samuel 1–2 Samuel 4 are completely absent, except for the brief description of the death of Saul in 1 Chronicles 10. Following Linafelt, it is possible that Ruth was intended as an introduction to a version of Samuel that more closely resembles 1 Chronicles 11–21 than the MT and LXX versions of Samuel. This possibility would lend support to Graeme Auld's hypothesis that both Samuel-Kings and Chronicles are redacted versions of a shorter common source that may have begun with the anointing of David as king (Auld 2021).

The notion advanced in this chapter that ordering books by scroll length makes good sense in a pre-codex world should be explored cross-culturally. As scrolls were widely used in other literate societies across the globe, there may be evidence of how these cultures organized their libraries to facilitate the identification and retrieval of specific scrolls in the collection.

Works Cited

Alter, Robert. 1981. *The Art of Biblical Narrative*. New York: Basic Books.
Auld, Graeme. 2021. "Deuteronomy and the Older Royal Narrative: Some Core Questions." Pages 219–42 in *Deuteronomy in the Making. Studies in the Production of Debarim*. Edited by Diana Edelman, Benedetta Rossi, Kåre Berge and Philippe Guillaume. Berlin: de Gruyter.

Campbell, Edward F. 1975. *Ruth: A New Translation with Introduction, Notes and Commentary*. Garden City: Doubleday.

Dempster, Stephen. 2015. "A Wandering Moabite: Ruth – A Book in Search of a Canonical Home." Pages 87–118 in *The Shape of the Writings*. Edited by Julius Steinberg and Timothy J. Stone. Winona Lake: Eisenbrauns.

Gallagher, Edmon L. and John D. Meade. 2017. *The Biblical Canon Lists from Early Christianity*. Texts and Analysis. Oxford: Oxford University Press.

Jones, Edward A. 2016. *Reading Ruth in the Restoration Period: A Call for Inclusion*. London: Bloomsbury.

Kratz, Reinhard G. 2005. *The Composition of the Narrative Books of the Old Testament*. London: T&T Clark International.

Krisel, William. 2021. "The Place of Ruth in the Hebrew Canon: A New Hypothesis." *Estudios Bíblicos* 79,1: 63–76.

-----. 2022. *Judges 19–21 and the "Othering" of Benjamin: A Golah Polemic against the Autochthonous Inhabitants of the Land?* Leiden: Brill.

Lightstone, Jack N. 2002. "The Rabbi's Tale: The Canon of the Hebrew Bible and the Early Rabbinic Guild." Pages 163–81 in *The Canon Debate*. Edited by Lee M. McDonald and James A. Sanders. Peabody: Henrickson.

Lim, Timothy H. 2013. *The Formation of the Jewish Canon*. New Haven: Yale University Press.

Linafelt, Tod. 1999. *Ruth*. Collegeville: The Liturgical Press.

Matthews, Victor H. 2004. *Judges and Ruth*. Cambridge: Cambridge University Press.

Müller, Reinhard. 2013. "1 Samuel 1 as the Opening Chapter of the Deuteronomistic History?" Pages 207–24 in *Is Samuel among the Deuteronomists? Current Views on the Place of Samuel in a Deuteronomistic History*. Edited by Cynthia Edenburg and Juha Pakkala. Atlanta: Society of Biblical Literature.

Steinberg, Naomi A. 2004. "Romancing the Widow: The Economic Distinctions between the 'almanâ, the 'iššâ-'almanâ and the 'ešet-hammet." Pages 327–46 in *God's Word for Our World. Volume I: Biblical Studies in Honor of Simon John de Vries*. Edited by J. Harold Ellens, Deborah L. Ellens, Rolf P. Knierim and Isaac Kalimi. Journal for the Study of the Old Testament Supplement Series 388. Volume 2. New York and London: T&T Clark International.

Römer, Thomas and Albert de Pury. 2000. "Deuteronomistic Historiography (HD): History of Research and Debated Issues." Pages 24–141 in *Israel Constructs its History: Deuteronomistic History in Recent Research*. Edited by Albert de Pury, Thomas Römer and Jean Daniel Macchi. Journal for the Study of the Old Testament Supplements 306. Sheffield: Sheffield Academic.

Stone, Timothy J. 2013. *The Compilational History of the Megilloth: Canon, Contoured Intertextuality and Meaning in the Writings*. FAT 2/59. Tübingen: Mohr Siebeck.

-----. 2015. "The Search for Order: The Compilational History of Ruth." Pages 175–85 in *The Shape of the Writings*. Edited by Julius Steinberg and Timothy J. Stone. Winona Lake: Eisenbrauns.

Ziegler, Yael 2015. *Ruth: From Alienation to Monarchy*. Maggid Studies in Tanakh; Stone Edition. Jerusalem: Koren Publishers.

About the Author

William Krisel is a lecturer at Institut Catholique de Paris (Catholic University of Paris). His recent publications include *Judges 19-21 and the "Othering" of Benjamin: A Golah Polemic against the Autochthonous Inhabitants of the Land?* (Leiden: Brill, 2022); "Methodological Problems in Intertextual Analyses of Old Testament Texts: Genesis 19 and Judges 19 as a Case Study," *Scandinavian Journal of the Old Testament* 36:2 (2022); "Was the Levite's Concubine Unfaithful or Angry? A Proposed Solution to the Text Critical Problem in Judges 19:2," *Old Testament Essays* 33, 2 (2020).

Chapter 5
After the Idyll Ends:
Ruth and the Uses of Disappointment

Rhiannon Graybill

Abstract

The book of Ruth is often considered to be a happy story. It is also celebrated as a happy text for feminist and queer biblical interpretation. However, Ruth is also frequently disappointing, as the book complicates or fails to meet our expectations of a positive female relationship of friendship, solidarity, or love. This chapter argues for the importance of disappointment in reading Ruth. Drawing on work on queer feeling and affect, it charts four forms of disappointment: unhappy objects, cruel optimism, queer failure, and "no fun." Each of these modalities of disappointment is associated with the work of a specific queer theorist: unhappy objects hail from Sara Ahmed's queer and feminist critique of happiness; cruel optimism originates with Lauren Berlant; queer failure is most closely associated with Jack Halberstam's The Queer Art of Failure, and no fun is a framework borrowed from Bo Ruberg's work on queerness and video games. Separately and together, they offer new ways of understanding disappointment in Ruth, suggesting that unhappy, uncomfortable, and unpleasant feeling can be useful, liberating, or even worldmaking.

Keywords: queer, affect, failure, cruel optimism, happiness, Ruth

The book of Ruth is often considered to be a happy story. Though it begins with famine and death, it hardly lingers there. Instead, Ruth's is a story of devotion, of hard work, of "women working out their own salvation" and "women transforming culture" (Trible 1978, 196). These women, of course, are Ruth and her mother-in-law Naomi, whose bond forms the core of the book. The book's four chapters chart Ruth's devotion to Naomi, Ruth's work gleaning in Boaz's fields, and Naomi's plans to capture Boaz's attention, using her daughter-in-law. The story quickly moves toward a classic happy ending: a marriage and a baby.

In addition to its felicitous plot, the book of Ruth is also a happy text for many interpreters. For many feminists, Ruth offers a story of female solidarity and companionship in the face of hardship. The Hebrew Bible is filled with misogyny, patriarchy, and Very Bad Things happening to women; women are usually mothers, daughters, or dead. Against this backdrop, the book of Ruth seems a welcome respite. Here, the men die without fanfare, while the women's actions, emotions, and relationship to the Israelite God are foregrounded. Unsurprisingly, the book and its female characters have a rich history in feminist interpretation (e.g. Trible 1978, 166–90; Shemesh 2013; Masenya 1998, 82–85; Powell 2018). The book of Ruth is similarly a "happy" text for lesbian (Alpert 1994), bisexual (Duncan 2000), and queer interpreters (West 2019). It contains one of the clearest statements of same sex love – and indeed of any sort of love – in the biblical text. Ruth's words of devotion to Naomi are widely used in marriage and commitment ceremonies (Alpert 1994, 91–92). And for readers and interpreters seeking LGBTQ representation in the text, Ruth and Naomi are a marquis couple – and unlike David and Jonathan, their relationship does not end with death, but rather a home, a child, and a secure future.

But happiness is not all we find in Ruth. Equally important, I will argue, is *disappointment*, which circulates both in the text and in its history of interpretation. The narrative is filled with disappointments, in the form of sadness, confusion, frustration, and failure. The ending of Ruth, often lauded as a happy ending, can equally be read as a disappointing one: Ruth is exploited for her labor and erased from her own story (Yee 2009). This is one form of hermeneutic disappointment: the supposed happy ending is no longer so happy (Graybill 2020). The feeling of disappointment becomes especially acute when we center feminist and/or queer reading positions: a story about female empowerment, or a story about love between women, has revealed itself to be a story about exploitation, once again.

Disappointment often leads to cynicism, either toward the text or toward the feminist and queer methods that have led to this impasse. I propose, instead, embracing disappointment as part of a queer practice of reading Ruth. I will argue that the book of Ruth is, in important ways, a *disappointing text*. I intend this description in several ways: the book of Ruth disappoints its readers, especially readers with feminist and queer commitments. But it is also, for all its appearances of a "happy ending," a story filled with disappointment. Disappointment thus functions both within the literary world of the text and as in its interpretation. Drawing on work on queer feeling and affect, I will chart four forms of disappointment: unhappy objects, cruel optimism, queer failure, and "no fun." Each of these modalities of disappointment is associated with the work of a specific queer theorist: *unhappy objects* hail from Sara Ahmed's queer and feminist critique of happiness; *cruel optimism* originates with Lauren Berlant; *queer failure* is most closely associated with Jack Halberstam's *The Queer Art of Failure*, and *no fun* is a framework borrowed from Bo Ruberg's work on queerness and video games (Ahmed 2010; Berlant 2011; Halberstam 2011; Ruberg 2019). Separately and together, they offer new ways of understanding disappointment in Ruth.

While a reading centered on disappointment may seem, well, *disappointing*, I will argue that this reading practice also opens queer space, both in the narrative and in the space of reception. Disappointment can even be part of a practice of queer worldmaking. As feminists, queer interpreters, and readers committed to liberation, disappointment may be the best possible thing to happen to us.

1. "The Loveliest Little Epic and Idyllic Whole," Or, Isn't Ruth a Happy Story?

In identifying Ruth as a disappointing text, I am breaking with a lengthy history of interpretation that treats the book as a happy story, or at least a story with a happy ending. But I am hardly the first interpreter to make this break (see Fewell and Gunn 1988). Not all feminists are so sanguine in their judgments of Ruth: often, a closer examination reveals hints of gendered oppression. There is also a well-established body of critique, much of it written from intersectional perspectives emphasizing ethnicity, post/coloniality, and social class, that argues that Ruth's story is fundamentally a story about exploitation. Gale Yee, for example, has argued that Ruth is stereotyped as a "model minority" and "perpetual foreigner" who is exploited for her labor and eventually erased from the text (Yee 2009, 128–32). Athalya Brenner has described her as an exploited migrant worker (Brenner 2010). Fulata Lusungu Moyo (2016) explores the threat of sexual violence and sexual trafficking in the narrative. Even readers who do not go so far as to describe Naomi as a pimp or labor trafficker emphasize the way that Ruth is asked to sacrifice her own happiness and identity in the service of her mother-in-law and husband. Masenya (1998) is more positive on the relationship between mother-in-law and daughter-in-law.

Adding to the ickiness is the way the story is used in religious communities: Ruth's subordination to Naomi is used to justify the subordination of daughters-in-law in the space of the family (Sakenfeld 2002, 170). And Ruth Preser raises the question of Ruth's own desires: "How can we perform a feminist and queer reading of Ruth's absent narrative, a tale of arguable rape, of trafficking in human organs, of seducing a wealthy man in order to survive, in order to belong? What if she did not want a child? What if she did not want to be a mother?" (Preser 2017, 58).

Especially to readers seeking happiness, liberation, or a bit of both in the book of Ruth, these critiques are troubling. They are also convincing. My own previous work on Ruth was inspired by the very mixed feelings I experienced reading the book and the bodies of feminist and queer scholarship attending to it (Graybill 2020). I felt torn between empowering and uplifting readings, which presented Ruth and Naomi as friends or lovers, and readings that stressed Ruth's exploitation at Naomi's hands. Trying to balance these two perspectives, I found myself returning again and again to Jione Havea's observation that exploitation and love are by no means mutually exclusive (Havea 2015, 124). And I turned to queer theorist Heather Love's work on "backward feeling" as a way of naming and processing my ambivalent mess of feelings toward the text (Love 2007). Ruth, I have suggested, is a book filled with backward feeling. "Backward feeling" and the related formulation, "feeling backward," name a complicated, melancholic feeling toward the past – a loss of what maybe never was. "Backward feeling" also invokes the embarrassment that our own feelings can create for us: I may be reluctant to admit that I wanted a text (Ruth) to be something it wasn't (a heartwarming love story). In the case of queer and feminist reading, the book of Ruth becomes a potent site for backward feeling precisely because our strong desires to find love, eroticism, and/or solidarity between Ruth and Naomi cannot, ultimately, be squared with the objections that postcolonial, Marxist, and similar readings raise.

Here I turn from backward feeling in general to a related feeling, that of disappointment. Specifically, the book of Ruth is disappointing because of all the ways it fails to live up to our feminist and/or queer expectations. It's not the straightforward story of liberation we hoped for. But this is not the only way disappointment comes into play in reading Ruth. Even a strictly literary reading uninterested in questions of gender, sexuality, feminism, or queerness may well leave us questioning the happiness of this "happy" text. Instead, unhappiness and disappointment seem to be everywhere:

- It is disappointing that Naomi, Elimelech, and their children flee famine in Israel, only to find famine in Moab (1:1–6).
- It is disappointing that three of the four named characters die in the first five verses (1:3, 5).

- It is disappointing that Ruth speaks some of the most beautiful words of devotion ever written to Naomi – and Naomi's only response is silence (1:16–18).
- It is disappointing that Naomi, deeply bitter about her suffering, cannot even persuade her friends to take her seriously and call her "Bitter" (1:20–21).
- It is disappointing that Naomi shows no special care toward Ruth, and only seems to truly take special interest when she is noticed by Boaz.
- It is disappointing that we don't really know what happened on the threshing floor, or why it makes Ruth a "woman of valor" (3:7–8, 11. On the ambiguity of translating *eshet hayyil* Goh 2015).
- It is disappointing that we don't know if Ruth understood the implications of Naomi's plan – did she understand just what Naomi was suggesting, and did she wish to go along with it, if so? Halton (2012, 35), for example, suggests that Naomi's plan is clearly sexual in nature, but Ruth's enactment deviates from it.
- It is disappointing that Ruth's relationship with Naomi, foregrounded in chapter 1, fades in chapter 4. This is especially disappointing for queer interpretations.
- It is disappointing that Ruth's status as a "model minority" (Yee 2009) Moabite does nothing to alter the overwhelming anti-Moabite orientation of the biblical text (see as well Chapter 6 in this volume).
- It is disappointing that Ruth's assimilation into Israelite society may really be a narrative justifying (and sexualizing) collaboration with a dominant imperial power (Donaldson 1999, 136–41).
- It is disappointing that Ruth herself fades away in the second half of 4, and her name disappears completely after 4:13.
- It is disappointing that the genealogy at the book's end exclusively describes men begetting men. It's not just Ruth who disappears, but women entirely (4:18–21).
- It is disappointing that Ruth is only four chapters. All too soon, we come to the end of the story, and the end of the only book of the Bible that focuses on relationships between women – this is all we have, and now it's over.

Of course, not all of these moments of disappointment are experienced by all readers or experienced equally strongly. For readers seeking a straight love story, it's reassuring when Ruth's bond with Naomi fades into the background. Few readers express much sorrow over the fates of Mahlon and Chilion, whose very names signal their coming demises. My point is not that everything in Ruth is disappointing, but rather that disappointment circulates around the text.

The poet Goethe famously described the book as "the loveliest little epic and idyllic whole ... that has been passed on to us" (Goethe 1986, 129, trans. and quoted in Fischer 2007, 140). As Irmtraud Fischer notes, "the ghost of [this] idea" has long "haunted" scholarly approaches to the book of Ruth (2007, 140). Hauntings, we might note, often involve disappointments or other unsettled business. Instead of attempting an exorcism on Ruth scholarship by insisting the book is unlovely, unidyllic, or without literary cohesion or merit, I want to take seriously disappointment as a path into the text. And so, in the sections that follow, I will explore four modalities of disappointment as a way of reading Ruth. Instead of downplaying or explaining away these moments of confusion, infelicity, or disappointment, I want to embrace them, and embrace reading Ruth as a *disappointing text*. As I have already indicated, I intend this term in multiple senses: disappointment (of multiple varieties) is present in the text, and the text itself is an object of disappointment (again, of multiple varieties). I use the terms "disappointment" and "disappointing" loosely; this is intentional (see also Graybill 2021, 10–12).

2. Unhappy Objects

My analysis of unhappy objects in the book of Ruth is informed by feminist and queer theorist Sara Ahmed and especially her book *The Promise of Happiness* (2010). I have already written elsewhere about Ahmed and unhappiness in Ruth; I summarize those arguments here and expand upon them to set the groundwork for the other three new modalities of disappointment that follow (Graybill 2020, 313–15).

In *The Promise of Happiness*, Ahmed explores the way happiness becomes attached to certain objects (this term is used loosely – a happy object can be a thing, a person, an idea, a way of being in the world). Happiness is not essential, a priori, or a necessary consequence of something being "good"; instead, it circulates and becomes associated with, particular things. Ahmed also switches the directionality we typically use when associating happiness and goodness: it is not that good things make us happy, but rather that we determine that happy things are good (Ahmed 2010, 13). In the Hebrew Bible, for example, Joseph's garment (Gen 37) and the plant that pleases Jonah (Jon 4:6–11) are straightforward examples of "happy objects" that become good because they cause happiness (Graybill 2019). Another example is the creation story in Genesis 1, where, except on the second day, God is pleased by each stage of creation and then identifies it as good or very good (Gen 1:4, 10, 12, 18, 21, 25, 31): happiness precedes and produces goodness.

As with happiness, so too with unhappiness, which attaches itself to certain objects. When we resist or refuse dominant happiness scripts – when we choose an unhappy object or trajectory over a happy one, or when we simply refuse to find an accepted happy object to be *happy*, we risk becoming "affect aliens" (Ahmed 2010, 49). Here, again recall Jonah and his refusal to accept God's command to be happy (Graybill 2019, 96–97,105). This theoretical framework also helps us understand the relationship between unhappiness and queerness: to be queer is to be oriented toward unhappy objects, rather than "happy" ones (heterosexuality, heterosexual marriage, procreation). At the same time, Ahmed (2010, 88–90) observes that the framework of unhappy stories is one way of giving voice to queer stories: there is a lengthy tradition in English-language literature and film of telling queer stories, as long as they have an unhappy ending.

All of this applies to Ruth in several ways. First, Ruth's extreme devotion to Naomi, expressed in her speech in 1:16–17, is from this perspective equal parts unhappy and queer. Ruth's vow – "Where you go, I will go; where you lodge, I will lodge; your people shall be my people, and your God my God. Where you die, I will die; there will I be buried" – certainly sounds "queer," in the way the word is often used to describe same sex desire. And unsurprisingly, it is often interpreted in this way (Alpert 1994, 91–94). Ruth's words are also potentially quite unhappy. First, there is no reason to believe that the vow will bring her happiness. "Wherever you go, I will go, wherever you lodge, I will lodge…" is unhappy because it represents a refusal of culturally endorsed happiness scripts – here, heterosexual marriage. Following the death of her sons, Naomi urges her daughters-in-law to return "to the house of your mother" (1:8) rather than remain with her. The instruction to return home carries with it an implicit promise of future heterosexual matrimony: when Ruth and Orpah wish to stay, Naomi stresses her lack of sons/future husbands for the two to marry (1:11–12). Orpah eventually accepts the command to happiness and returns home. Ruth, instead, clings (literally and figuratively) to her mother-in-law, who represents an unhappy object (1:15–17). Her refusal to leave Naomi is also queer, as Ahmed uses the term: Ruth orients herself *queerly*, toward a queer object. In insisting she will stay with Naomi, she not only pledges loyalty; she also demands what Ahmed (2010, 195) calls "the freedom to be unhappy."

Unhappy objects function in Ruth in other ways as well. When Boaz encounters Ruth, first in the field, then on the threshing floor, then at last acquiring her in marriage, she is arguably an unhappy object for him. After all, Ruth, as the text never lets us forget, is not an Israelite but a Moabite. Furthermore, Ruth comes encumbered with Naomi (the reverse is equally true!); the two cannot or will not be separated. While Celena

M. Duncan views the ending as a "happy bisexual family," we might also note the question of Ruth's lagging affections (Duncan 2000, 101). Her orientation toward Naomi must be adjusted, or at least accommodated, for the "happy ending" to occur. That Ruth herself seems to vanish in the final verses of the book – after 4:13 she is no longer mentioned by name, even when her child is born – seems to suggest that this is incompletely or inadequately accomplished. A trace of Ruth's prior "unhappy" orientation lingers; therefore, she must be elided, her child associated with Naomi and, with an eye to futurity, with David.

What I have described as the interpretive disappointment of reading Ruth can also be described with the framework of happy and unhappy objects. From the perspective of interpretive happiness, the book of Ruth is ambivalent. As I have already discussed, Ruth is traditionally viewed as an idyllic short story with a happy ending. The book also has a substantial history as a happy object for feminist and queer interpreters. The problem comes when Ruth is no longer a happy object for such interpretive projects. This does not mean that we cannot find queerness in the text, or friendship, or female collaboration. But it does mean we must put pressure on the easy assumption that the characters of Ruth and Naomi, or the book as a whole, are "good." I do not intend to adjudicate these points here, only to mention that if the book of Ruth becomes problematic from the perspective of an easy liberationist feminist or queer reading, then it has also become, in Ahmed's terms, an "unhappy object" for feminist and queer interpreters (Graybill 2020, 315).

3. Cruel Optimism

This discussion of unhappy objects segues to the second framework for theorizing disappointment, Lauren Berlant's notion of "cruel optimism." Queer optimism describes attachments that work against our own interests: Berlant explains,

> A relation of cruel optimism exists when something you desire is actually an obstacle to your flourishing. It might involve food, or a kind of love; it might be a fantasy of the good life, or a political project. It might rest on something simpler, too, like a new habit that promises to induce in you an improved way of being. These kinds of optimistic relation are not inherently cruel. They become cruel only when the object that draws your attachment actively impedes the aim that brought you to it initially. (Berlant 2011, 1)

Berlant's examples include romantic love, practices of self-improvement (diet, exercise, "wellness"), social mobility, and even the political itself.

We approach these objects with optimism and the hope of improvement; instead, they betray us. As such, they are "cruel."

While Berlant's focus in *Cruel Optimism* is on neoliberalism and the contemporary political moment, the notion of "cruel optimism" is not limited to this framework. It speaks, instead, to a wide range of attachments – including those in and around Ruth. The book itself opens with an episode of cruel optimism. Elimelech and Naomi flee to Moab with their two sons, hoping that it will provide them with a better life than the famine they leave in Israel. But this optimism proves cruel: all three men die; hunger comes to Moab; Naomi is grief-stricken and bereft. Even her speech reflects her suffering, as she addresses her daughters-in-law as male. Naomi's grammatical confusion may reflect trauma as she addresses her daughters-in-law in the masculine form in 1:8–9 and again in 1:11–13. Drawing on Robert Alter's observation that a character's first speech in the text often defines that character, Andrew R. Davis suggests that Naomi's grammatical infelicity telegraphs her distress. A few verses later, she will describe herself as "bitter" (1:20) – but "we need not wait for this self-description, because already in this first address the unevenness of her speech suggests her distraught state" (Davis 2013, 500). Or, it may open a space of queer possibility, as in a more optimistic reading set forth by Gil Rosenberg (2015, 594–96). Charting a middle path between trauma and queerness, I want to raise the possibility that Naomi's peculiar use of the masculine form is itself a lingering sign of cruel optimism, a trace of the attachment to her sons and the (re)productive future they represented even after their passing. This attachment, its cruelty now revealed, produces disturbances in her speech.

Ruth's attachment to Naomi also presents a striking instance of cruel optimism. In pledging herself to Naomi, Ruth provides no reasons, only devotion unto death and burial. But the very structure of the promise is optimistic, if we follow Berlant and "describe optimism as the force that moves you out of yourself and into the world in order to bring closer the satisfying something that you cannot generate on your own but sense in the wake of a person, a way of life, an object, project, concept, or scene" (Berlant 2011, 2). This is precisely what Ruth's words do: they move her out of her own world, and into Naomi's. In making her pledge, she desires to satisfy "something that [she] cannot generate on [her] own," but rather senses in or with Naomi. The attachment is not just optimistic; it is also cruel. This plays out in several ways. Naomi's silence in response to Ruth's vow (1:18) can be read as a (non)answer of striking cruelty. This effect is only amplified when we consider the next words Naomi speaks, which announce her bitterness:

Do not call me Naomi [Pleasant],

> call me Mara [bitter],
> for the Almighty has acted very bitterly toward me.
> I went away full,
> but Yahweh has brought me back empty;
> why call me Naomi
> when Yahweh has testified against me,
> and the Almighty has done evil to me? (1:20–21)

As a response to a declaration of fidelity, this is heart-wrenching in its non-acknowledgment. Ruth's optimism is cruel in other ways as well. Accompanying Naomi to Israel, she finds hard work in the fields gleaning, followed by Naomi's plan to entrap or seduce Boaz: a plan in which Ruth takes all the risk, while Naomi gains (all?) the reward. Ruth is an immigrant, who leaves her home but is never welcomed in her new country (Brenner 2010, 163; Rees 2018; Cottrill 2021, 93–94). She faces labor exploitation, and perhaps sexual exploitation as well – either pimped out by Naomi or simply subjected to the sexual violence that many immigrants and agricultural workers experience (Moyo 2016).

It is even possible to read the ending of the book – Boaz's marriage to Ruth and the birth of Obed, David's great-grandfather – as the ultimate cruelty. Yee sets this argument forth forcefully, though she does not use the specific language of "cruel optimism":

> Ruth's foreignness is the linchpin in the economics of the text. It sets her apart from those characters who do not work in the book but who appropriate her labor and her body … The insidious economic picture that surfaces in the book of Ruth is that the Israelites – in the persons of Naomi and Boaz – are those who do not work, who exploit and live off the surplus labor of the foreign Other. Naomi assimilates into the world of Israelite men, the landowners who possess the means of production, while the foreign female worker, Ruth, vanishes when her body is exhausted. (Yee 2009, 134)

Ruth's attachment to Naomi has come at the expense of her happiness, her labor, and even her body. The cruel optimism of migration is actualized in the biblical text.

Cruel optimism also offers another way of describing our attachments to reading Ruth, which I have previously introduced with reference to Ahmed's work. Here, I want to comment briefly on the cruel optimism of reading based on identification. If we look to the biblical texts to find ourselves, or to find a world that welcomes us, we are likely to be disappointed. The biblical text is many things and contains many things; it is not, however, a work of contemporary liberal pluralism (see Brintnall 2013, 52–53). And yet it is precisely because of the way the Bible is leveraged in so many homophobic polemics, and used to justify injustice, that it is so tempting to turn to the text to find tolerance. Ruth, Boaz, and Naomi as a queer or bisexual family is a comforting image, especially when the biblical texts are so often used against such families (Duncan 2000; West 2019). Ruth and Naomi working together to outsmart patriarchy is an inspiring bit of narrative girl-power when we find ourselves ground down by patriarchy and misogyny. These readings, to be clear, can be life-giving. But the text can also become an object of cruel optimism when we seek to force it into something it is not, to domesticate it and ignore the ickiness and horror that accompany the grace and play. Or, to return to the framework of disappointment: it can be disappointing when the Bible isn't what we want it, *know it*, to be.

4. Queer Failure

A third way to approach disappointment in and around Ruth is through the framework of queer failure. Just as Ahmed's work on happy and unhappy objects asks us to rethink *happiness* and Berlant's critique pushes back on the benevolence of *optimism,* so too does queer theorist Jack Halberstam ask us to rethink *failure* and the negativity associated with it. Instead of dismissing failure as lamentable or tragic, Halberstam takes failure both seriously and playfully. Failure, which Halberstam associates with James C. Scott's "weapons of the weak," is not necessarily negative. It is, instead, its own way of being, one that takes seriously (but also playfully) silliness, stupidity, forgetfulness, disappointment, and all the other unhappy and unserious affects that make us human. As Halberstam writes,

> To live is to fail, to bungle, to disappoint, and ultimately to die; rather than searching for ways around death and disappointment, the queer art of failure involves the acceptance of the finite, the embrace of the absurd, the silly, and the hopelessly goofy. Rather than resisting endings and limits, let us instead revel in and cleave to all of our own inevitable fantastic failures. (Halberstam 2011, 187)

Failure is also linked to queerness, in complex and important ways. While there is no necessary link between particular sexual practices or subjectivities and specific politics, including a politics of failing, "failure is located within that range of political affects that we call *queer*"; it likewise bears a special relation to queerness and queer ways of being the world (Halberstam 2011, 89). And the language of a "queer art of failure" gives us a vocabulary to describe "the social and symbolic systems that tether queerness to loss and failure," which "cannot be wished away" (Halberstam 2011, 98).

Halberstam's readings mostly center on contemporary cultural artifacts, with a particular focus on animated children's films (especially those produced by Pixar). But *The Queer Art of Failure* can apply, as well, to biblical texts, including the Acts of Thecla (Daniel-Hughes 2022) and Ruth. After all, Ruth is a biblical book in which failure circulates in many ways. Naomi and Elimelech leave Israel seeking a better life – and fail. Orpah and Ruth seek to stay with their mother-in-law – Orpah fails. Naomi demands a new name – but her request fails to be acknowledged. Ruth catches Boaz's eye but may well fail at doing what she is instructed to do on the threshing floor. The ambiguity of both the instructions and the events that follow leave this possibility open: does Naomi instruct one thing and Ruth do another? (Halton 2012, 35). The "bed trick" (see Chapters 7 and 13 in this volume); another framework for reading the events of chapter 3, represents another kind of failure, at traditional sex, matrimony, and gender roles (see also Black 1991, 20, 34). Peloni Almoni, Naomi's kinsman and Boaz's rival, fails to marry Ruth and acquire Mahlon and Chilion's land. Ruth marries an Israelite and yet, nevertheless, fails to shed her Moabite identity. The women of Bethlehem celebrate the birth of the child Obed, but fail to identify Ruth, instead naming Naomi (4:17). Read in this way, the book of Ruth becomes a sequence of errors and failures.

I propose reading these events as queer failures, in Halberstam's mode. Consider, for example, the scene of the threshing floor, which is rich with innuendo: Ruth prepares her body with washing and ointments; she surprises the intoxicated Boaz while he is sleeping; feet are uncovered, and Ruth spends the night but sneaks away unseen before morning. The intertextual echoes of the "bed trick" in Genesis 19, 29 and 37 underscore the sexual implications (Black 1991). The text does not, however, seem erotic, but rather something closer to comedic (Aschkenasy 2006, 34, 40–41). As a scheme to gain security for Ruth and Naomi, the plan succeeds, even as it fails at romance, and perhaps even at seduction – it is unclear whether actual sex occurs (Christina 2007). Absurd, silly, goofy, sexually unsuccessful – there is a queer art of failure at play here.

Ruth herself may be a queer failure in another way as well. In theorizing forms of queer failure, Halberstam turns to masochism, calling for a more robust interrogation of how masochism offers a way of thinking about "the relationship between self and other, self and technology, self and power" (Halberstam 2011, 135). What if we take seriously Ruth as a masochistic figure? After all, Ruth gives up everything to be with Naomi and to follow her – only to be given away by Naomi, to Boaz. As the narrative moves forward, Ruth becomes less and less agential; following the events of the threshing floor (which are Naomi's idea), she ceases taking initiative at all. The ending of chapter 4 can even be read as the climax of

Ruth's masochistic erasure, as she seems cut out of the narrative entirely (Halberstam 2011, 135–43). Masochism as a practice of queer failure offers a way to analyze Ruth's passivity and even erasure, without merely reducing her to the status of victim or acted-upon object.

Failure can also be a failure of memory. This, in turn, leads to an alternative way of interpreting Ruth's ending and the apparent forgetting of the book's protagonist in its final scene. The attribution of Obed's maternity to Naomi and the failure to mention Ruth in the final genealogy are often interpreted as nefarious signs of a dominant power erasing the labor of a foreign woman (Yee 2009). But there are other ways of reading this scene of forgetting. One of the principles of engagement Halberstam sets forth at the beginning of *The Queer Art of Failure* is "*suspect memorialization*" (Halberstam 2011, 14). This is because practices of memory simultaneously perform and conceal ideological labor. Invoking Toni Morrison's *Beloved*, Saidiya Hartman's *Lose Your Mother*, and Avery F. Gordon's *Ghostly Matters*, Halberstam notes that "memorialization has a tendency to tidy up disorderly histories," while "memory is itself a disciplinary mechanism that Foucault calls 'a ritual of power'" (Halberstam 2011, 15). Commemoration is always in the service of a political ideology: we see this in the erasure of Ruth from the final genealogy, and in Yee's correct analysis that this is a class and ethnically motivated act of compelled forgetting. What Halberstam's analysis adds here is this: the answer to this dilemma is not simply to add Ruth back in. All practices of memory are marked; remembering Ruth is no solution. This reading of the forgetting in chapter 4 also connects back to chapter 1, where Orpah "forgets" her mother-in-law by leaving her, while Ruth remains/remembers. The memorializing of Ruth that the book undertakes (though not in its final scene) is an act of remembering Ruth that forgets Orpah, as feminist critics have shown. But also: it may be better for Orpah to be forgotten, in that those doing the remembering are violent oppressors. To be forgotten is to be outside this script (see Donaldson 1999).

5. No Fun

Another intriguing application of Halberstam's "queer failure" – and the final modality of disappointment I want to consider here – is Bo Ruberg's work on "no fun" video gaming, which opens onto "no fun" as a world-making practice. Taking on the widely held assumption that gaming should be fun, Ruberg questions why so many gamers play games that are annoying, disappointing, emotionally painful, or difficult or impossible to win. It is not enough, Ruberg suggests, to dismiss these activities as attempts at fun, or to argue that losing and failing are simply ways of preparing for winning (and thus having fun). Instead, they urge us to take seriously *no fun* as an intentional and meaningful gaming choice. Drawing on Halberstam's work on queer failure, they argue for "no fun" gaming as queer experience, and one meaningfully analyzed in conversation with queer and affect theory.

While much of Ruberg's concern is with sketching a taxonomy of "no fun" games, on a broader level, their work is concerned with "no fun" as a form of play and a category of experience. Thus, "Turning attention to the seemingly unpleasant allows us to uncover underexplored modes of experience, both as players and queer subjects in the world" (Ruberg 2019, 181–82). Attending to no fun also means paying new attention to embodiment and feeling. Ruberg continues,

> No fun is also a call back to our bodies, a call to feel what players are not supposed to want to feel, a call to resist the normative thinking that dictates that the only games that matter are games that are "good" in the most traditional sense, and that the only players who matter are the ones who have fun playing them. In this way, no fun is also a challenge: a challenge to the status quo and a challenge to ourselves. Let us play boredom. Let us play anger. Let us play what hurts. Let us play in ways that are just as different and just as queer as we are as players. And let us take that hurt, modeled by the embodiment of gameplay, and carry it with us, driving us to find other playful, powerful, and overlooked sites of counter-affective potential in our lives both on-screen and off. (Ruberg 2019, 182)

No fun thus reminds us of what we have otherwise forgotten, our lived experience in living, feeling bodies. And this can include feeling disappointed.

The book of Ruth is not a video game; Ruth, Naomi, and Boaz are not playable characters. Still, I find Ruberg's call for "no fun" a valuable mode of reading this biblical text. Surrounded by misogyny, homophobia, and structures of exclusion – in the text, in the scholarly field, and in the world – feminist and queer biblical interpretation often approaches the text through a relation of identification. We read Ruth and identify with her. Consider Alpert's practice of "find[ing] hints of existences of women like ourselves" or Celena M. Duncan's bisexual identification with Ruth's relationships with Naomi and Boaz. Consider Phyllis Trible's struggle to carve out space for feminism in biblical studies and space for the Bible in feminism – and how her resolution to that struggle involves identifying with the book of Ruth (Trible 1978, 166–99; Duncan 2000). Consider how Yee's 2009 critique of empowering readings of Ruth is grounded in her own experiences of racism and alienation as a contemporary Chinese American (so, too, is Ruth dismissed as a "model minority" and "perpetual foreigner"). All of these interpretations, I would suggest, are ways of "playing" Ruth in reading the text. Ruberg's theory gives us language to discuss the possibility that play is not necessarily *fun* and that "no fun" is also important and meaningful. We can take seriously how we feel – including the disappointment we feel when the book of Ruth isn't the happy feminist and/or queer object we hoped for – without dismissing the body or giving up on the idea of interpretation as a practice of play.

"No fun" also gives space for negativity in interpretive play. Ruberg writes, "The traditional and often myopic focus on fun forecloses a rich array of difficult or "negative" emotions that can in fact shape a game's message as much as (if not more than) its content and mechanics" (Ruberg 2019, 165). So too with Ruth, a book that is shaped by its disappointing contours, as much as by its happy ones. It may be "no fun" to end with Ruth's erasure, or to take seriously that Ruth may be trafficked, or to consider that Ruth may in fact have sexually assaulted Boaz (see Chapter 13 in this volume). But these perspectives add to the book's and to its lasting hold on our interpretive imaginations.

6. The Uses of Disappointment: Affect, Attention, and Worldbuilding

An interpretation that takes feeling seriously, that attends to the body, and that engages in play (without reducing play to "fun") – this is a mode of interpretation engaged in affective worldbuilding. Like other affects and feelings, disappointment opens space for new ways of being in and with texts. This brings us to the question of affect theory and perhaps, to more familiar ground for biblical scholars. Long marginalized, ignored, or reviled, *feeling* has become a part of academic biblical studies. Affect theory explores both how affect works in texts and how texts affect (and are affected by) readers themselves (see Kotrosits 2016; Black and Koosed 2019). One key insight of this approach is that feeling is not secondary. Instead, the ways texts make us feel – and the ways those feelings make their way in, surreptitiously or otherwise, to our scholarship – is not incidental but essential. In an analysis of affect and violence in Judges, Amy Cottrill suggests that attending to affect is valuable because it "enables biblical exegetes to consider the role of the reader's embodied experience as a tool for textual interpretation" (Cottrill 2021, 431). In particular, Cottrill is interested in violence and in what reading violence does to us as readers: "how that bodily, affective response to violence creates interpretive possibilities for the text" (Cottrill 2021, 431).

Cottrill's attention to affect as an entry point into interpretation resonates with Ruberg's attention to the body and to bodily affect in moments of "no fun." And it echoes Maia Kotrosits' invitation to affect as a way of thinking about loss. Kotrosits writes,

> Attending to affect does – or, at least, can do – many things, but one of its most profound contributions is that it can help us move [the] subtext of loss to the foreground by privileging and giving a conceptual language for those potent and hazy experiences that are most basic and endemic to our living. Every theory, every story, may well have loss (or injury or fear or desire...) in it; talking about affect might help us better entertain those experiences in all their terrifying and unwieldy force, even to the point of being lost to them. For all that we've lost, though, attending to affect might be able to give us, if we can stand it, closer contact with the world in all its gravel, in all its polychromatic forms of vitality, movement, and sensation. (Kotrosits 2016, 47–48)

As an approach to biblical texts, this helps us see how stories work. It invites us to lose ourselves in them. It holds space for our own feelings and bodies as interpreters. And it makes possible a reanalysis of *disappointment* as a potent form of worldmaking.

In the case of Ruth, disappointment as a framework brings together the world within the text with our responses to it. As Cottrill suggests, it raises the possibility of "embodied experience as a tool for biblical interpretation." Ruth is disappointed. Naomi is disappointed. The feminists are disappointed. The queer interpreters are disappointed. *I am disappointed.* Disappointment cuts across these fields of difference. It also opens a space of possibility.

We see this in the work of each of the theorists considered here. For Ahmed, pushing back against scripts of happiness and unhappiness is part of a larger project of finding space for other ways of being, including forms of identity, kinship, and being in the larger world. For Berlant, naming and identifying cruel optimism is a first step toward diagnosing an oppressive structure and false promise. Halberstam transforms "queer failure" from a judgment to a space of possibility, again opening alternate ways of being. And Ruberg finds multiple forms of value – including pleasure and play – in what is "no fun."

So, too, the book of Ruth. The text is no simple happy little idyll. It is filled with disappointments, many of which never resolve satisfactorily. Naomi's theological complaint is never sufficiently addressed (Linafelt 2010, 128). And it is disappointing to us, in its failure to "do" a single thing or hold a single meaning. But it is here the possibility lies. In the case of Ruth, attending to the affect of disappointment helps us connect with the text "in all its gravel" and "polychromatic forms," to borrow

Kotrosits' phrases. Disappointment can even build a world. Unhappiness is everything.

Works Cited

Ahmed, Sara. 2010. *The Promise of Happiness*. Durham, NC: Duke University Press.

Alpert, Rebecca. 1994. "Finding Our Past: A Lesbian Interpretation of the Book of Ruth." Pages 91–96 in *Reading Ruth: Contemporary Women Reclaim a Sacred Story*. Edited by Judith A. Kates and Gail Twersky Reimer. New York: Ballantine.

Aschkenasy, Nehama. 2006. "The Book of Ruth as Comedy: Classical and Modern Perspectives." Pages 31–46 in *Scrolls of Love: Ruth and the Song of Songs*. Edited by Peter S. Hawkins and Lesleigh Cushing Stahlberg. New York: Fordham University Press.

Berlant, Lauren. 2011. *Cruel Optimism*. Durham, NC: Duke University Press.

Black, Fiona C. and Jennifer L. Koosed, eds. 2019. *Reading with Feeling: Affect Theory and the Bible*. Atlanta: Society of Biblical Literature.

Black, James. 1991. "Ruth in the Dark: Folktale, Law and Creative Ambiguity in the Old Testament." *Literature and Theology* 5 (1): 20–36.

Brenner, Athalya. 2010. "From Ruth to the 'Global Woman': Social and Legal Aspects." *Interpretation* 64 (2): 162–68.

Brintnall, Kent L. 2013. "Queer Studies and Religio." *Critical Research on Religion* 1: 51–61.

Cottrill, Amy. 2021. *Uncovering Violence: Reading Biblical Narratives as an Ethical Project*. Louisville: Westminster John Knox.

Christina, Greta. 2007. "Are We Having Sex Now or What?" Pages 3–8 in *Sex Matters: The Sexuality and Society Reader*. Edited by Mindy Stombler. Boston: Pearson.

Daniel-Hughes, Carly. 2022. "The Apostle of Failure: Queer Refusal, the Corinthian Letters, and Paul's Unflattering Characterization in the Acts of Thecla." *Biblical Interpretation* online advance publication (September 19, 2022): 1–23, https://doi.org/10.1163/15685152-20221688.

Davis, Andrew R. 2013. "The Literary Effect of Gender Discord in the Book of Ruth." *Journal of Biblical Literature* 132: 495–513.

Donaldson, Laura E. 1999. "The Sign of Orpah: Reading Ruth through Native Eyes." Pages 130–44 in *A Feminist Companion to Ruth and Esther*. Edited by Athalya Brenner. Sheffield: Sheffield Academic Press, 1999.

Duncan, Celena M. 2000. "The Book of Ruth: On Boundaries, Love, and Truth." Pages 92–102 in *Take Back the Word: A Queer Reading of the Bible*. Edited by Robert E. Goss and Mona West. Cleveland, OH: Pilgrim.

Fewell, Danna Nolan and David M. Gunn. 1988. "'A Son Is Born to Naomi!': Literary Allusions and Interpretation in the Book of Ruth." *Journal for the Study of the Old Testament* 13 (n. 40): 99–108.

Fischer, Irmtraud. 2007. "The Book of Ruth as Exegetical Literature." *European Judaism* 40 (2): 140–49, https://doi.org/10.3167/ej.2007.400213.

Goethe, Johann Wolfgang von. 1986. *Noten und Abhandlungen zu besserem Verständnis des west-östlichen Divans*. Edited by Hans-J. Weitz, Frankfurt: Insel.

Goh, Elaine Wei-Fun. 2015. "An Intertextual Reading of Ruth and Proverbs 31:10–31, with a Chinese Woman's Perspective." Pages 73–87 in *Reading Ruth in Asia*. Edited by Jione Havea and Peter H. W. Lau. Atlanta: Society of Biblical Literature.

Graybill, Rhiannon. 2019. "Prophecy and the Problem of Happiness: The Case of Jonah." Pages 95–112 in *Reading with Feeling: Affect Theory and the Bible*. Edited by Fiona C. Black and Jennifer L. Koosed. Atlanta: Society of Biblical Literature.

–––––. 2020. "'Even unto This Bitter Loving': Unhappiness and Backward Feelings in the Book of Ruth." *Biblical Interpretation* 29 (2020): 308–31, https://doi.org/10.1163/15685152-00284P11.

–––––. 2021. *Texts after Terror: Rape, Sexual Violence, and the Hebrew Bible*. New York: Oxford University Press.

Halberstam, Jack. 2011. *The Queer Art of Failure*. Durham, NC: Duke University Press.

Havea, Jione. 2015. "Stirring Naomi: Another Gleaning at the Edges of Ruth 1." Pages 111–24 in *Reading Ruth in Asia*. Edited by Jione Havea and Peter H. W. Lau. Atlanta: Society of Biblical Literature.

Halton, Charles. 2012. "An Indecent Proposal: The Theological Core of the Book of Ruth." *Scandinavian Journal of the Old Testament* 26 (1): 30–43.

Kotrosits, Maia. 2016. "How Things Feel: Biblical Studies, Affect Theory, and the (Im)Personal." *Brill Research Perspectives in Biblical Interpretation* 1 (1): 1–53, https://doi.org/10.1163/24057657-12340001.

Linafelt, Tod. 2010. "Narrative and Poetic Art in the Book of Ruth." *Interpretation* 64 (2): 117–29.

Love, Heather. 2007. *Feeling Backward: Loss and the Politics of Queer History*. Cambridge MA: Harvard University Press.

Masenya, Madipoane J. 1998. "'Ngwetši'(Bride): The Naomi-Ruth Story from an African-South African Woman's Perspective." *Journal of Feminist Studies in Religion* 14: 81–90.

Moyo, Fulata Lusungu. 2016. "'Traffic Violations': Hospitality, Foreignness, and Exploitation: A Contextual Biblical Study of Ruth." *Journal of Feminist Studies in Religion* 32: 83–94.

Powell, Stephanie Day. 2018. *Narrative Desire and the Book of Ruth*. LHB/OTS 662. London: T&T Clark.

Preser, Ruth. 2017. "Things I Learned from the Book of Ruth: Diasporic Readings of Queer Conversions." Pages 47–65 in *De/Constituting Wholes: Towards Partiality Without Parts*. Vienna: Turia + Kant.

Rees, Anthony. 2018. "The Boaz Solution: Reading Ruth in Light of Australian Asylum Seeker Discourse." Pages 39–60 in *The Five Scrolls*. Edited by Athalya Brenner-Idan, Gale A. Yee, and Archie C. C. Lee. London: T&T Clark.

Rosenberg, Gil. 2015. "New Authorities, New Readings." *Biblical Interpretation* 23 (4–5): 574–600.

Ruberg, Jo. 2019. *Video Games Have Always Been Queer*. New York: New York University Press.

Sakenfeld, Katharine Doob. 2002. "At the Threshing Floor: Sex, Reader Response, and a Hermeneutic of Survival." *Old Testament Essays* 15 (1): 164–78.

Shemesh, Yael. 2013. "The Stories of Women in a Men's World: The Books of Ruth, Esther, and Judith in Feminist Interpretations." Pages 258–62 in *Feminist Interpretation of the Hebrew Bible in Retrospect. I. Biblical Books*. Edited by Susanne Scholz. Sheffield: Sheffield Phoenix.

Trible, Phyllis. 1978. *God and the Rhetoric of Sexuality*. Philadelphia: Fortress.

West, Mona. 2019. "The Book of Ruth: An Example of Procreative Strategies for Queers." Pages 51–60 in *Our Families, Our Values*. Edited by Robert E. Gross and Amy Adams Squire Strongheart. New York: Routledge.

Yee, Gale E. 2009. "'She Stood in Tears Amid the Alien Corn': Ruth, the Perpetual Foreigner and Model Minority." Pages 119–40 in *They Were All Together in One Place? Toward Minority Biblical Criticism*. Edited by Randall C. Bailey, Tat-siong Benny Liew, and Fernando F. Segovia. Atlanta: Society of Biblical Literature.

About the Author

Rhiannon Graybill is Marcus M. and Carole M. Weinstein & Gilbert M. and Fannie S. Rosenthal Chair of Jewish Studies at the University of Richmond, USA. She is the author of *Texts after Terror: Rape, Sexual Violence, and the Hebrew Prophets* (Oxford, 2021) and *Are We Not Men?: Unstable Masculinity in the Hebrew Prophets* (Oxford, 2016) and multiple articles on gender, sexuality, and biblical texts. She has also co-authored two books with John Kaltner and Steven L. McKenzie: *Jonah: A New Translation with Notes and Commentary* (Yale University Press, 2023) and *What Are They Saying about the Book of Jonah?* (Paulist Press, 2024). At present, Graybill is working on a new book about the female body in the Hebrew Bible.

Chapter 6
Obed, Son of Boaz, an Israelite: Should Ruth be Read through the Lens of Deuteronomy's Laws about Moabites?

Jonathan Thambyrajah

Abstract

Many interpretations of the book of Ruth turn on questions of the ethnicity of Ruth. Implicit is the idea that the book of Ruth needs to be read through the lens of Deut 7:1–6 and 23:4–7, laws that regulate intermarriage and membership of the "assembly of Israel." However, after these laws from Deuteronomy are rid of the intellectual baggage of the intermarriage crisis in Ezra and Nehemiah and the story of Solomon's wives in 1 Kings 11, they do not apply to the situation described by the book of Ruth. The book of Ruth is read more clearly without imposing the framework of these laws. Rather, identification of Obed as an Israelite is entirely what should be expected, despite Ruth's Moabite ethnicity, according to the primordialist assumptions of the book of Ruth (in line with many other texts from the Hebrew Bible).

Keywords: Ruth, Obed, ethnicity, primordialism, constructivism, Deuteronomy, marriage

The idea that Obed is an Israelite is uncontested. Even so, the tendency of scholarship has been to read the book of Ruth through the interpretative lenses of Deut 7:1–6 and 23:4–7 [English, 23:3–6], laws that are understood to prohibit marriage with Moabites and exclude them and their descendants from the assembly (Block 2015, 45–46; Fentress-Williams 2012, 129; Hawk 2015, 27; Matthews 2004, 212). Therefore, it is surprising that Obed's status as an Israelite is so uncontested (e.g. Eskenazi and Frymer-Kensky

2011, xxiii) – according to this kind of approach, Obed *should* be excluded from Israel, precisely because of his Moabite ancestry/identity.

The issue of Obed's ethnicity is related to the issue of David's Moabite ancestry. Scholars have frequently found the idea that David had a Moabite ancestor problematic, based on their view that the laws from Deuteronomy prohibit either marriage with Moabites or the membership of their children in Israelite society (Linafelt 1999, 79; Matthews 2004, 209; Morocho 2021). Furthermore, some scholars even suggest that Ruth's marriage to Mahlon was never fully legitimate on the basis of Deuteronomy (Block 2015, 72; Fentress-Williams 2012, 40) or that his death was punishment for marrying a Moabite (Block 2015, 73). Similarly, for other scholars, the drama of Ruth's ethnicity and the supposed problem of her marrying Boaz is what drives the story (Gerleman 1965, 7; Hawk 2015, 20, 33; Köhlmoos 2009, xiv).

However, the realization that Obed is an Israelite should offer a point of hesitation for these approaches. If the book of Ruth is to be read in light of Deuteronomy, then Obed should not be considered an Israelite. There may be ways of trying to accommodate this fact and maintain the relevance of Deuteronomic laws, but I will suggest that greater clarity can be achieved by removing the Deuteronomic lens entirely. Instead, the apparent puzzle of Obed's ethnicity can be more clearly understood by carefully distinguishing between how modern readers tend to think about ethnicity and the assumptions about ethnicity that appear to undergird the book of Ruth.

1. The Puzzle of Obed's Israelite Ethnicity

One popular solution to the perceived dissonance between Obed and Ruth's ethnicity is to assume that Ruth herself has "become" an Israelite (Glover 2009). Treating Ruth as an Israelite rather than a Moabite seems to explain why Obed is an Israelite. It also exculpates Boaz from the law against marrying (as is supposed) Moabites (Deut 7:1–6; see 1 Kgs 11:1–8; Ezra 9:1–2). At first glance, this solution might be satisfying. However, even if Ruth does "become" an Israelite, it would not, in fact, solve the apparent problem: according to a rigid application of Deut 7 and 23 to the book of Ruth, Obed and David must still be excluded, because they would both still be within ten generations of a Moabite.

Another possible solution is to suggest that the book of Ruth is a deliberate polemic against Deuteronomic law (Adams 2018; Braulik 1999) or an invitation to interpret it flexibly (Wojcik 1985). According to this view, the book of Ruth *intends* to contradict the laws in Deuteronomy. However, there is little evidence within Ruth itself of a polemical attitude towards these laws, or even of sufficient knowledge of the book of Deuteronomy as we know it (see Schipper 2016, 38–40). I will suggest that the apparent contradiction is only the result of the overinterpretation of the Deuteronomic laws (especially under the influence of Ezra-Nehemiah). Rather than being the basis of a polemic, Ruth's marriage and Obed's Israelite status have very little to do with the laws found in Deuteronomy.

Another attempt to explain why Obed and David, the descendants of Moabites, could be included in Israel claims that the law was overruled by God's sovereign prerogative (Morocho 2021). Yet, if this is the case, one wonders why neither Boaz nor any of the Bethlehemites seem to betray any awareness of such a monumental event. If God is overruling the law, it seems that Boaz and the Bethlehemites were not told. Nevertheless, they (and the reader) arrive at the conclusion that Obed's inclusion is correct, without needing any intervention from God.

In fact, the reason that readers of the text of Ruth intuit that Obed is not a Moabite is because the rhetoric of the text works very hard to ensure that he is perceived as an Israelite. He is described as the son of Naomi (4:17) and the son of Boaz (4:21). He is also inscribed into two genealogies: The first connects him forward to David, the king of Israel (4:17); The second places him within the Judahite lineage of David through Perez (4:18–22). The reader has to work very hard to come away with an impression other than that Obed is an Israelite, because the text highlights his Israelite ancestry to the exclusion of his Moabite ancestry.

However, if Obed is an Israelite (according to the book of Ruth) and seemingly fully acceptable in the assembly, something must give way: either it is wrong to read the story of Ruth in light of Deut 23 and 7, or the way the anti-Moabite laws are typically read needs to be modified – or both.

2. Ethnic Assumptions in Deuteronomy 23 and its Application to Ruth

Deuteronomy 23:4–9 [English, 23:3–8] requires that no Moabite or Ammonite enter the assembly of the LORD, but that the third generation of Egyptians or Edomites may be admitted. The prohibition on Moabites and Ammonites is "eternal" (עַד־עוֹלָם); the reference to "even the tenth generation" (גַּם דּוֹר עֲשִׂירִי), rather than permitting the eleventh generation, merely serves to reinforce that even after ten generations the prohibition still stands (Christensen 1997, 536). So, in fact, even if Obed or David were in the eleventh generation, the idea that Ruth becomes an Israelite would solve nothing.

Although intermarriage is not discussed by this text (Brett 2010, 33; Southwood 2012, 142), it is nevertheless implicated in the discussion of the offspring of Moabites. Certainly, intermarriage with Moabites is not prohibited by this text. Still, the laws described by Deut 23 would in practice have consequences for an intermarried couple, or more accurately, for their children.

The ethnic rhetoric of Deut 23 operates on the assumption that having a Moabite ancestor excludes one from true Israelite identity: that is, the son of a Moabite is also a Moabite, regardless of any other consideration. The very concept of a "generation" (דּוֹר) of Moabites connects ethnicity with ancestry, and to an extreme extent: one Moabite ancestor, *even after ten generations*, is sufficient to classify someone as a Moabite, according to Deut 23.

This must be hyperbole. Even if one were to suggest that careful genealogies existed for every Israelite, all except the elite would be incapable of reading them (Rollston 2010). Most Israelites cannot have known whether any given individual had a Moabite ancestor at the distance of ten generations. In reality, therefore, the readers of texts like Deuteronomy may have accepted people as properly Israelite – even if they had foreign ancestry – because it is unrealistic to assume that such knowledge was readily apparent or easily accessible.

On the other hand, one must still understand the rhetorical point of this text: no Moabites, no children of Moabites, not ever. Moreover, if one wishes to read Ruth using Deut 23 as an interpretative lens, one is forced to accept the rhetoric and ethnic classification that Deuteronomy puts forward. Despite the hyperbole, the underlying assumptions of Deut 23 are still clear enough: that ethnicity is determined by ancestry. Therefore, reading Deut 23 alongside Ruth creates a dissonance: Deuteronomy 23 *seems* to assume that Obed would be a Moabite, to be excluded from the assembly of Israel. However, the rhetoric of Ruth 4 seems to affirm that Obed is fully Israelite.

3. The Inapplicability of Deuteronomy 7 to Ruth

3.1 Deuteronomy 7:1–6

Deuteronomy 7:1–6, however, is different. Although Deut 7:1–6 does not mention Moabites, the idea that it somehow applies to the book of Ruth is, nevertheless quite popular with some authors (Block 2015, 46; Eskenazi and Frymer-Kensky 2011, xi; Hawk 2015, 23). I will suggest that this way of reading Ruth is mistaken, by showing that it is based not in the laws in Deuteronomy themselves, but rather in reinterpretations of those laws in 1 Kgs 11 and Ezra-Nehemiah.

The facility with which modern readers of Ruth blur the lines between Deut 23 and Deut 7 perhaps derives in part from the assumption that there is no significance to which nations are listed in each text. However, this misunderstands the different context and purpose of each set of laws.

Deuteronomy 23:4-9 [English, 3-8] is concerned with how Israel interacts with its neighbors. Therefore, it deals specifically with those nations: Moab, Ammon, Edom, and Egypt. Deuteronomy 7:1-6 is only concerned with the nations that are to be displaced by the conquest: Hittites, Girgashites, and so on. The prohibition on marriage (and other treaties; see Craigie 1976, 177-78) has one singular goal: to ensure that the Israelites fully expel these nations. As it is written, Deut 7:1-6 does not countenance the possibility that interactions with these nations would continue to be an issue beyond the conquest. Some other texts do (Judg 2:1-5). However, both Deut 7:1-6 and Judg 2:1-5 are only interested in the nations that inhabit the land that Israel was to conquer. It is very questionable whether this kind of law should ever have been read in connection with Ruth, since Ruth is a Moabite from one of the neighboring nations rather than one of the nations that was to be conquered.

3.2 Deuteronomy 7 in 1 Kings 11

Despite the fact that Deut 7:1-4 in itself clearly does not apply to Moabites, two texts that refer to this idea do extend the applicability of the law to Moabites. It is under the (unwarranted) influence of these texts that scholars bring Deut 7 to bear on Ruth. The first of these, 1 Kgs 11, refers to Solomon's wives, and the second, Ezra 9, to the intermarriage crisis related in Ezra and Nehemiah. First Kings 11 does not refer to a situation of conquest, such as is imagined by Deut 7. Nevertheless, it does seem that 1 Kgs 11 is attempting to cite a previous command: "from which the LORD had said, 'do not associate with them nor let them associate with you; surely they will turn your hearts after other gods'" (1 Kgs 11:2). Deuteronomy 7:1-4 seems a plausible candidate (Brueggemann 2000, 143). Yet, 1 Kgs 11 is not a straightforward application of the law, but rather a reapplication: according to the literary setting of 1 Kgs 11 in Solomon's reign, the context which Deut 7:1-4 was addressing in the period of "the conquest" has long passed and now the law is being reimagined in order to apply it to a *different* context.

First Kings 11 picks up one particular aspect of Deut 7:1-6, namely the idea that intermarriage may lead people to serve "other gods" (Deut 7:4//1 Kgs 11:2, 4-8). However, whereas in Deut 7 the concern was that

Israelites would be led astray by allowing the Canaanites to persist among them, 1 Kgs 11 is concerned with an entirely different situation: a king who brings neighboring princesses into his household. Thus, the nations mentioned in 1 Kgs 11 are the Moabites, Ammonites, Edomites, Sidonians, and Hittites (i.e. neighboring nations) – a list that resembles Deut 23 much more than it resembles Deut 7. First Kings 11 seeks to establish the sinfulness of Solomon's actions by understanding them in light of a general principle derived from Deut 7:1-6: intermarriage with peoples that follow other gods can lead to idolatry. However, the context of the conquest is removed.

3.3 Deuteronomy 7 in Ezra 9

Similarly, Ezra 9 is not a straightforward reading of Deut 7 but a reimagining of it (see also Chapter 3 in this volume; Milgrom 2000, 1585). Thus, Ezra-Nehemiah omits mention of the risk of intermarriage causing apostasy that is so characteristic of the Deuteronomic law (Conczorowski 2011, 104) – though perhaps this motive is supposed to be understood implicitly (see Fensham 1982, 125). Further, in the context of the Achaemenid setting of Ezra and Nehemiah, the distinction between displaced Canaanite and neighbor has become meaningless: all are subjects of the Persians. Thus, Ezra 9:1 refers to a combination of former neighbors and Canaanites: the Canaanites, the Hittites, the Perizzites, the Jebusites, the Ammonites, the Moabites, the Egyptians, and the Amorites. Ezra 9–10 combines the prohibition of intermarriage with the Canaanites (Deut 7:3) with the exclusion of neighbors from the assembly (Deut 23:4-9 [3-8]). Thus, not only are the marriages dissolved, but the children are sent away from the assembly (Ezra 10:3). Ezra is concerned with idolatry through intermarriage (e.g. 9:14) and the (cultic?) impurity of the assembly through intermarriage (e.g. 9:2).

It might be possible to conceive of the restoration in Ezra and Nehemiah as a re-conquest, such that perhaps, Deut 7 would be made applicable once more to the situation. However, that is not the reasoning that is employed in Ezra 9:13-14. Although the original conquest is mentioned (9:11), Ezra's assumption (rightly or wrongly) is that the prohibition on intermarriage applies universally (9:14), because of the dangers of idolatry and cultic impurity. In the context of Ezra 9, this prohibition is applied to both kinds of foreigner (neighbor and inhabitant of Canaan), but this is a specific interpretative tactic made in the context of the books of Ezra and Nehemiah that does not obviously apply to Ruth.

3.4 Deuteronomy 7 in Ruth?

The idea that Deut 7 could be interpreted as a ban on marriage with Moabites does not derive from Deut 7 itself but from the reinterpretations of the law in 1 Kgs 11 and Ezra 9. These reinterpretations are not necessarily invalid – there is no reason why Ezra and the narratorial voice of 1 Kgs 11 should not try to derive more general principles about the law from the specific case described in Deut 7. Both attempts at reinterpretation follow a similar route: ethnic nomenclature (Canaanite, Moabite, etc.) becomes a proxy for the worship of foreign gods. It is the worship of foreign gods that these texts are concerned with prohibiting, rather than intermarriage with other ethnicities per se.

What is invalid, however, is to retroject the reinterpretations found in 1 Kgs 11 and Ezra 9 onto Deut 7:1–5. Deuteronomy 7 itself does not prohibit marriage with Moabites. It is doubly invalid, then, to introduce the prohibition on marriage with Moabites to Ruth on the pretense that it is derived from Deut 7.

Some authors think that Ezra 9–10 lies in the background of Ruth and that the issue of intermarriage in Ruth is a response to the crisis in Ezra and Nehemiah (Köhlmoos 2009, xiv–xvi, 70–71; de Villiers 2016). These books depict a crisis arising after the return of Judeans to Jerusalem and the province of Yehud from Babylonian exile. Although it is interesting to read Ruth alongside Ezra and Nehemiah, there is, in fact, little in the book of Ruth itself that suggests any familiarity with the situation as it is described in Ezra and Nehemiah. The way they frame the question of intermarriage is entirely a question of consulting, interpreting, and applying the "words of the God of Israel" and the book of the law (Ezra 9:1–4; Neh 10:28–30; 13:1–3). In Ruth, however, there is no such book of the law, and the characters certainly encounter no "words of God." If law is present, it is only in legal customs rather than precise citations of a written text (see also Chapter 3 in this volume). Even if one accepts the premise that Ruth is directed at the same intermarriage crisis that is described in Ezra and Nehemiah, it is certainly not engaging in the same kind of exegesis of the book of the law found in Ezra and Nehemiah and does not appear to engage with the legal arguments raised there. Therefore, it stretches the imagination to suggest that in this scenario, the book of Ruth blindly accepted the particular interpretation of Deut 7 and 23 that is put forward by Ezra the scribe in Ezra and Nehemiah.

When Deut 7:1–4 is relieved of the reinterpretative baggage of 1 Kgs 11 and Ezra 9, there is no reason to see any conflict between it and the events of Ruth. Ruth is set "in the days when the judges ruled" (Ruth 1:1). According to this setting, the book of Ruth begins with the assumption that the conquest is over, whereas Deut 7:1–4 only pertains to the nations that were to be conquered. Moreover, Moabites like Ruth are legitimate neighbors rather than a target of the conquest. Thus, Deut 7:1–4 poses no problem for a marriage between Boaz and Ruth, because marriage with neighboring nations like the Moabites was never forbidden in these four verses. Since Ruth is (or has become) a Yahwist, such a marriage is particularly unproblematic; she will not turn Obed to the worship of other gods. The habit of reading Deut 7 and 23 together as an interpretative lens for Ruth is mistaken, because Deut 7:1–4 contains no prohibition that is relevant to the situation described in Ruth.

4. Obed the Israelite and Ruth the Moabite: Ethnic Rhetoric in Ruth (and Beyond)

Whereas Deut 7:1–4 has been shown to be completely inapplicable to the message or interpretation of Ruth, Deut 23:4–9 remains seemingly relevant to some and challenges a modern reader's understanding of why Obed is fully accepted as an insider by the Bethlehemite community. In this section, I will suggest that this dissonance results from a clash between a modern, Western understanding of ethnicity and how this ancient text perceives ethnic groups and classifications.

First, we must admit that the text does assume that ethnic categories exist, because it labels characters as Moabite (Ruth 1:4, 1:22, 2:2, etc.) or Bethlehemite and Ephrathite (Ruth 1:1, 2). However, it is crucial to pay attention to how the text assigns these categories, which differs from how modern Western readers might assign them. For example, according to ethnic rhetoric of the text, Ruth's Moabite ethnicity persists to the end of the book (Thambyrajah 2021): even Boaz, at the moment when he announces his marriage to Ruth, insists on naming her a Moabite (4:10), and the women compare her to other foreign women: Rachel, Leah, and Tamar (4:11–12). After this point, Ruth disappears from the story. As we have seen, however, Obed's ethnicity is unambiguously placed in the category "Israelite" by this text's rhetoric. If Ruth is read in light of the assumptions of Deut 23, dissonance seems to appear: Obed should not receive such ready acceptance. Whatever the rhetoric of the text, he is the son of a Moabite mother and has Moabite grandparents.

However, Ruth and Deut 23 are not as far apart as it might initially appear. The fact that Ruth's Moabite ethnicity persists, despite her full assimilation to Bethlehemite society, implies that the book of Ruth is operating on "primordialist" assumptions (Thambyrajah 2021). Primordialism is a way of looking at ethnicity that assumes that ethnicity is determined by ancestry and is not subject to change (Chandra 2012, 136). The idea is closely related to the notion of "essentialism," or that ethnicity is a fundamental, immutable characteristic of humans. However, the reality of the situation is rarely so simple; in fact, it can be observed that individuals do cross boundaries and "change" their ethnic identity (Chandra 2012, esp. 139–40), when viewed from the perspective of modern (Western) constructivist theory. According to this view, ethnic identity is something that people construct based on multiple social factors.

Nevertheless, "ethnic actors" (and even supposedly modern scholars) frequently operate on primordialist assumptions (Brubaker 2004; Coakley 2018; Gil-White 1999; Maxwell 2020). Thus, there can be a mismatch in perceptions of ethnic identity between constructivist scholars and the primordialist communities they study, since the two operate on different presumptions about how a child's ethnicity is determined. For a society operating on primordialist assumptions, when a child is born to parents of different ethnic identities, there can only be three possibilities: the child derives its ethnicity from the mother alone, the father alone, or it is a combination of both. However, I will suggest that it is the case of the father's ethnicity determining the child's that best explains the situation in Ruth.

It has been observed that some primordialist societies compute ethnic status according to the ethnicity of the child's father (Gil-White 1999; 2002). For example, Gil-White studied a Mongol ethnic group, the Torguuds, and found that a child who has a Kazakh father and a Mongol mother will be perceived as Kazakh by almost all Torguuds, *even if* that child is raised according to Mongol customs and language and never meets a Kazakh other than the father (Gil-White 1999). While a person external to that society (say, a Westerner) might claim that the Torguuds are wrong and that the child has a claim to Mongol identity, both the Westerner and the Torguud are classifying the child on the basis of their own worldview. Each is canvassing their worldview, rhetorically, according to their presuppositions about ethnicity.

The rhetoric of Ruth argues that Ruth is a Moabite, despite her integration into Bethlehemite society, but Boaz and Obed are Israelites. Thus, the ethnic rhetoric of this text is that a child's ethnicity is determined by the father's ethnicity, just as in the case of the Torguuds. In fact, this assumption is frequently made in other texts of the Hebrew Bible. Joseph's children are counted as Israelites, despite their Egyptian mother – they are even counted as if they were sons of Jacob (Gen 48:5). Moses's children participate in the exodus, apparently as Israelites, despite their Midianite mother and upbringing (Exod 18:1–4), whereas Jethro the Midianite is sent away (Exod 18:27). They are even counted as priests in some texts (Judg 18:30, 1 Chr 23:14). There is no implication that Absalom is not an Israelite, despite his mother being a foreign princess (2 Sam 3:3). Nor is

Rehoboam excluded as king of Judah and a genuine Davidide because of his Ammonite mother (1 Kgs 14:21).

A close look at the Hebrew text of Deut 23:4-7 [English, 23:3-6] agrees with Israelite ethnicity being traced through males. It prohibits the (male) Moabite (מוֹאָבִי) from entering the assembly (23:4 [English, 23:3]) and the generations that come from him. Deuteronomy 23:2-9 [1-8], which describes the restrictions for entering the assembly, is very male-oriented, with a focus on male genitalia in 23:2 [23:1] and a use of the grammatical masculine throughout the eight verses. It is not entirely unreasonable to assume that the question of Moabite women, and whether *their* children are considered Israelites, is simply not in view here. The Mishnah seems to have arrived at a similar interpretation using entirely different logic (m. Yebam. 8:3), perhaps out of a need to harmonize the text. However, it is not an unreasonable reading of Deut 23:2-9 [1-8].

There is no need to appeal to Deut 23 specifically as a necessary lens through which to read the book of Ruth. The way the rhetoric classifies ethnicity in the book fits with the practices attested in the texts comprising the Hebrew Bible collection in general: Obed is an Israelite because his father Boaz is an Israelite, regardless of Ruth's ethnicity. If Boaz acts as a levir (however, see Eskenazi and Frymer-Kensky 2011, xxxii–xxxviii), then Obed's father is considered to be either Mahlon or Elimelech, and the same logic applies, since they too are Israelites. If Obed's ethnicity is determined in this way by his father not his mother, then David's ethnic status was never in doubt: he is no more a Moabite by ancestry than he is a Canaanite, due to Tamar's Canaanite ethnicity (Gen 38:2), or an Aramaean due to Leah's Aramaean ethnicity (Gen 28:1-5).

For modern readers of Ruth who are familiar with how "Jewishness" is determined today, the fact that Obed is counted fully as an Israelite in the book of Ruth may be particularly surprising. Jewish religious and ethnic identity has come to be primarily defined based on the mother's status, not the father's. Aspects of this matrilineal approach can be found as an underlying assumption in opinions recorded in early Rabbinic literature (e.g. m. Bik. 1:4-5; m. Qidd. 3:12-13; m. Yeb. 7:5). In the Rabbinic literature cited here, the question of Jewish identity incorporates elements of religious identity as well as elements of ancestry, and so the issue of the status of converts and their children becomes central to the discussion. The possibility of conversion demonstrates that by this stage, the question of Jewish identity was not solely about ancestry. Thus, by the Rabbinic period questions of ethnicity were not always viewed through a strictly primordialist lens. Nevertheless, patrilineality was still an important factor in Rabbinic thought, for example for the children of priests and Levites (m. Qidd. 3:12; see Exod 28:1).

5. Conclusion: Reading Ruth without the Specter of Prohibited Intermarriage

Obed is an Israelite, as his father was, and Ruth is a Moabite, as her father was. While this may confuse modern readers of Ruth, it is entirely consistent with primordialist assumptions about ethnicity that are common in biblical texts and beyond. Recognizing the logic that the text uses to classify the ethnicity of its major characters clarifies that the book of Ruth was never about whether or not David's Moabite ancestry was at all problematic for the dynasty. The perceived problems are only the result of incorrectly forcing the story to conform to a modern framework of ethnic identities.

Ruth, as a story, operates on common-sense principles of ethnic identity within a patrilineal, primordialist framework. Even in the modern world, people may not know the ethnic affiliation of all of their ancestors beyond a couple of generations. Similarly, determining someone's ethnicity in Ruth can only work on the scale of a few generations at most. Nevertheless, the primordialist understanding of ethnicity that is displayed in the book allows for these calculations to be made: every person's ethnic identity (based on all their patrilineal ancestors) can be computed based only on the knowledge of the ethnic identity of their father. This is how, despite modern intuitions, the book of Ruth does not hesitate to present Ruth as a Moabite, but Obed as an Israelite.

Doubtless, Ruth must still be read in light of anti-Moabite sentiment: Ruth is still an outsider in Bethlehem. However, it is a mistake to read that anti-Moabite sentiment stringently through the lens of the laws of Deut 7 and 23. Deuteronomy 7 is inapplicable; its association with Moabites belongs strictly to reinterpretations of the law in Kings, Ezra, and Nehemiah. Deuteronomy 23 belongs to the same basic primordialist worldview as the book of Ruth, and both assume a degree of anti-Moabite sentiment. If it is correct that Deut 23 is only concerned with the children of male Moabites, then it too is inapplicable to the situation described in Ruth.

One cannot speculate on the nature of the relationship between Ruth and Deuteronomy based solely on the laws about Moabites. The issue of Ruth's use of Deuteronomy is multi-dimensional, touching on many different areas of legal practice. However, for this particular issue, neither Deut 7:1–6 nor Deut 23:4–9 necessarily contain any regulations that are relevant to the situation as it is understood in the book of Ruth. At most, any disagreement turns on a rather arcane distinction about how ethnicity is determined. In this light, the book of Ruth is not attempting to critique the Deuteronomic laws. Both Ruth and Deuteronomy seem to operate on a similar set of assumptions about how ethnicity works.

However, Deuteronomy is largely irrelevant to this aspect of the book of Ruth.

It would be imprudent to generalize too much about all ancient Israelites and their view on ethnicity, based only on the book of Ruth. Of course, individuals and specific texts may attest a variety of approaches to ethnicity. Nevertheless, Ruth does stand as an example of the kind of beliefs about ethnicity that, as we have seen, are assumed in a number of biblical texts. The people who produced the book of Ruth and these other texts take a primordialist worldview for granted. Therefore, it seems probable that this was a widespread view at many stages of Israelite history.

Despite the best efforts of scholars to turn Ruth into a polemic against Deuteronomic exclusivism, it is best read as an irenic story, praising the virtuous character of David's ancestors. Rather than attempting to read Ruth as a corrective to Deuteronomy (or Ezra and Nehemiah), the challenge for interpreters is to figure out what the book of Ruth means on its own terms. It is an example that demonstrates the need for caution when using other books of the Hebrew Bible as a way to lay the foundations of all interpretation.

Nevertheless, the book of Ruth is still a book about the inclusion of outsiders. However, that inclusion is not achieved by militating against the law. Rather, Ruth is folded into the society by the ordinary means of marriage and family relationships. Far from being illegal and the cause of her husband's death, Ruth's marriage draws her into the Yahwist fold and is the single most effective tool in achieving her inclusion (and that of her son, Obed).

Works Cited

Adams, Samuel. 2018. "The Book of Ruth as Social Commentary in Early Judaism." Pages 127–39 in *Figures who Shape Scriptures, Scriptures that Shape Figures: Essays in Honour of Benjamin G. Wright III*. Edited by Géza G. Xeravits and Greg Schmidt Goering. Berlin: de Gruyter.

Block, Daniel. 2015. *Ruth: The King is Coming*. Zondervan Exegetical Commentary on the Old Testament. Grand Rapids: Zondervan.

Braulik, Georg. 1999. "The Book of Ruth as Intra-Biblical Critique on the Deuteronomic Law." *Acta Theologica* 19:1–20.

Brett, Mark. 2010. "National Identity as Commentary and as Metacommentary." Pages 29–40 in *Historiography and Identity (Re)formulation in Second Temple Historiographical Literature*. Edited by Louis Jonker. New York: T&T Clark.

Brubaker, Rogers. 2004. *Ethnicity Without Groups*. Cambridge MA: Harvard University Press.

Brueggemann, Walter. 2000. *1 & 2 Kings*. Smyth & Helwys Bible Commentary. Macon: Smyth & Helwys.

Chandra, Kanchan. 2012. "How Ethnic Identities Change." Pages 132–78 in *Constructivist Theories of Ethnic Politics*. Edited by Kanchan Chandra. Oxford: Oxford University Press.

Christensen, Duane. 1997. *Deuteronomy 1–21:9*. Word Biblical Commentary 6A. Grand Rapids: Zondervan.

Coakley, John. 2018. "'Primordialism' in Nationalism Studies: Theory or Ideology?" *Nations and Nationalism* 24: 327–47.

Conczorowski, Benedikt. 2012. "All the same as Ezra? Conceptual Differences between the Texts on Intermarriage in Genesis, Deuteronomy 7 and Ezra." Pages 89–108 in *Mixed Marriages Intermarriage and Group Identity in the Second Temple Period*. Edited by Christian Frevel. Library of the Hebrew Bible/Old Testament Studies. New York: T&T Clark.

Craigie, Peter. 1976. *The Book of Deuteronomy*. New International Commentary on the Old Testament. Grand Rapids: Eerdmans.

Eskenazi, Tamara and Tikva Frymer-Kensky. 2011. *Ruth: The Traditional Hebrew Text with the New JPS Translation*. Philadelphia: JPS.

Fensham, F. Charles. 1982. *The Books of Ezra and Nehemiah*. New International Commentary on the Old Testament. Grand Rapids: Eerdmans.

Fentress-Willliams, Judy. 2012. *Ruth*. Nashville: Abingdon.

Gerleman, Gillis. 1965. *Ruth; Das Hohelied*. BKAT 18. Neukirchen-Vluyn: Neukirchener Verlag.

Gil-White, Francisco José. 1999. "How Thick is Blood? The Plot Thickens… if Ethnic Actors are Primordialists, what Remains of the Circumstantialist/Primordialist Controversy?" *Ethnic and Racial Studies* 22: 789–820.

Gil-White, Francisco José. 2002. "The Evolutionary Psychology of Ethnicity." PhD dissertation, University of California, Los Angeles.

Glover, Neil. 2009. "Your People, My People: An Exploration of Ethnicity in Ruth." *Journal for the Study of the Old Testament* 33: 293–313.

Hawk, L. Daniel. 2015. *Ruth*. AOTC 7B. Nottingham: Apollos.

Köhlmoos, Melanie. 2009. *Ruth*. Das Alte Testament Deutsch. Göttingen: Vandenhoeck & Ruprecht.

Linafelt, Tod. 1999. "Ruth" in *Ruth; Esther*. By Tod Linafelt and Timothy Beal. Berit Olam. Collegeville: Liturgical.

Matthews, Victor. 2004. *Judges and Ruth*. New Cambridge Bible Commentary. Cambridge: Cambridge University Press.

Maxwell, Alexander. 2020. "Primordialism for Scholars Who Ought to Know Better: Anthony D. Smith's Critique of Modernization Theory." *Nationalities Papers* 48: 826–42.

Milgrom, Jacob. 2000. *Leviticus 17–22: A New Translation with Introduction and Commentary*. Anchor Bible 3A. London: Doubleday.

Morocho, Milton. 2021. "David a Moabite? An Analysis of Deuteronomy 23:3–6 and the Book of Ruth, and the Theological Implications of David's Lineage." PhD dissertation, Baptist Theological Seminary.

Rollston, Christopher. 2010. *Writing and Literacy in the World of Ancient Israel: Epigraphic Evidence from the Iron Age.* SBL: Archaeology and Biblical Studies 11. Atlanta: SBL.

Schipper, Jeremy. 2016. *Ruth: A New Translation with Introduction and Commentary.* Anchor Bible 7D. New Haven: Yale University Press.

Southwood, Katherine. 2012. *Ethnicity and the Mixed Marriage Crisis in Ezra 9-10: An Anthropological Approach.* Oxford Theological Monographs. Oxford: Oxford University Press.

Thambyrajah, Jonathan. 2021. "Israelite or Moabite? Ethnicity in the Book of Ruth." *Journal for the Study of the Old Testament* 46: 44–63.

Villiers, Gerda de. 2016. "The Book of Ruth in the Time of the Judges and Ruth, the Moabitess." *Verbum et Ecclesia* 37: 1–6.

Wojcik, Jan. 1985. "Improvising Rules in the Book of Ruth." *Publications of the Modern Language Association of America* 100: 145–53.

About the Author

Jonathan Thambyrajah is the Lecturer in Biblical Studies at the Broken Bay Institute – The Australian Institute of Theological Education (BBI-TAITE), and also lectures in Biblical Studies and Hebrew at the University of Sydney. As well as the topic of ethnicity in the Hebrew Bible, his research focuses on biblical languages, translations, and literature in the cross-cultural context of the Second Temple period and its aftermath (particularly Esther). He is also interested in how early translations of biblical books reflect the exegesis and interpretation of early Jewish and Christian communities.

Chapter 7
Naomi and Ruth: A Tale of Two Wives?

William Krisel

Abstract

It is always tempting to imagine that a single author sat down one day with quill, ink, and scroll in hand to compose the wonderful story that has been transmitted to posterity in the form of the Book of Ruth. However, it is far more likely that Ruth began like other biblical narratives as a very short text, possibly based on an oral tradition, that was then expanded and developed and reworked by later generations of scribes. This chapter will examine the textual and contextual traces that point to the existence of a sexier and less pious original version of the story in which Naomi goes down with Ruth to the threshing floor to surprise Boaz after he has fallen into a drunken sleep. Naomi tricks Boaz into sleeping with both women and then marrying them and fathering their sons. This older version of the narrative was significantly rewritten and overwritten by redactors to erase all references to Boaz's relationship with Naomi and to transform the story into a bucolic idyll about the pious, generous, and monogamous Boaz, the contented widow Naomi happy to live out her days as a surrogate grandmother, and the proverbial woman of excellence and ancestress of David, Ruth.

Keywords: Ruth, Naomi, Boaz, Obed, threshing floor, compositional history of Ruth, sexual euphemisms, levirate

The received text of Ruth, in both its Hebrew and Greek versions, portrays Boaz as a generous and kind man who comes to the rescue of both Naomi and Ruth, but in very different ways. In the case of Naomi, Boaz purchases her property interest in an agricultural field, thereby giving her a degree of financial security. In the case of Ruth, Boaz marries the young woman and fathers her son. However, there are textual and contextual reasons to suspect that an earlier version of the narrative told a very different story in which Naomi plots to have Boaz impregnate both her and Ruth, Boaz marries both women and has children with both of them. The textual traces of this "backstory" were carefully erased by successive generations of scribal redactors who modified the earlier text in order to portray Boaz as a pious monogamous man, Naomi as a contented widow happy to live out her days as a surrogate grandmother, and Ruth as a proverbial woman of excellence and ancestress of King David. This chapter examines the sparse evidence in the text that escaped later redactors' censorship, which points to the existence of a sexier and less pious original version of the story. The textual and contextual evidence will be presented first, followed by a more technical discussion of other commentators' attempts to downplay and obscure the textual problems in Ruth in their defense of the internal coherence of the final version of the text.

1. Textual and Contextual Problems in Ruth

The MT of Ruth contains an unusually high number of *qere-ketiv* scribal corrections, in which the Masoretic scribes recopied a particular word as it appeared in the older manuscript on which they were working (called the *ketiv* or "as written") but added a note in the margin of the new manuscript correcting the *ketiv* with another word which they thought was more appropriate (called the *qere* or "as read"). Although many of these textual changes in Ruth can be explained as spelling corrections, others change the meaning of the word in a significant way. These difficult cases of scribal correction in the MT merit close examination.

1.1 The Threshing Floor Episode (Ruth 3:1–15)

The "threshing floor episode" contains two *qere-ketiv* notes in 3:3 and in 3:4, which significantly alter the meaning of the narrative:

And *I* [Naomi] will go down to the threshing floor. (3:3 *ketiv*)

And *you* [Ruth] will go down to the threshing floor. (3:3 *qere*)

And you [Ruth] will come and you will uncover his feet and *I* [Naomi] will lie down. (3:4 *ketiv*)

And you [Ruth] will come and you will uncover his feet and *you* will lie down. (3:4 *qere*).

As the *ketiv* version of 3:3–4 is contextually inconsistent with the narrative as a whole in the final version of the text, most modern commentators either ignore the *ketiv* entirely in their interpretation of the threshing floor episode (e.g. Gray 1967; Bush 1996; Linafelt 1999; Matthews 2004) or dismiss the *ketiv* as an "archaic" Hebrew grammatical form with the same meaning as the *qere* (e.g. Campbell 1975, 120; Sasson 1979, 68; Block 2015, 165; Ziegler 2015, 292). Because these dismissals of the clear meaning of the *ketiv* in standard Biblical Hebrew as a first person singular verbal conjugation are unconvincing (see detailed discussion below), this section proposes a new reading of the threshing floor scene in Ruth 3:1–15 based on the *ketiv* version of the text.

The orders that Naomi gives to Ruth in 3:3–4 according to the *ketiv* version of the text read as follows, (all translations from the Hebrew Bible [hereafter, the "HB"] are mine unless otherwise indicated):

> ³And you will bathe. And you will anoint yourself [with perfume]. And you will put on your [best] clothes. And *I will go down* to the threshing floor; do not make yourself known to the man until he has finished eating and drinking. ⁴And it will come to pass when he lies down, that you will take note of the place where he sleeps. And you will come and uncover his feet [i.e. his genitals]. And *I will lie down*. And it will be he who will tell you what to do.

In the *ketiv*, Naomi, like Lot's daughters and Judah's daughter-in-law Tamar, is quite the trickster (for a discussion of the role of the "trickster" in biblical narratives, see Niditch 1987). Naomi's plan is that both she and Ruth will go down to the threshing floor and conceal themselves in a dark corner. Once Boaz has finished his supper and becomes drunk, Ruth will approach him shortly after nightfall and begin to undress him to expose his genitals (see discussion of the rare word customarily translated as "his feet" below). Boaz will be seduced by the smell of Ruth's young, perfumed skin, but it will in fact be Naomi who will then approach and lie down next to him to have sexual intercourse. Once the act is completed, and Boaz has fallen into a deep sleep, Naomi will slip away and Ruth will take her place by Boaz's side, presumably to have sex with him later in the night. With this ingenious plan, both women will have a chance of becoming pregnant by Boaz.

Indeed, when Boaz awakens suddenly at midnight (possibly because the alcohol had begun to wear off), he is surprised to find a woman lying with him. His first reaction is to ask "Who are you?" (3:9), as if he suspects that he has been tricked. Boaz's question is the same as the one Isaac asked of Esau, "Who are you?," when it was becoming clear to Isaac that Jacob had tricked him (Gen 27:32). This intertextual allusion to Jacob's tricking his father is reinforced by the fact that both Isaac and

Boaz respond physically to the tricksters' deceit in the same way: both of them began "to tremble" (חרד ḥrd Gen 27:33; Ruth 3:8). According to the narrator, Boaz was trembling because he found *a woman* (אשה *'išah*) lying next to him (3:8). The narrative stresses the age difference between Boaz and Ruth. Boaz calls her a "girl" (נערה *na'arāh*, 2:5.6) and even my "daughter" (2:8; 3:10-11) but never a "woman." Was Boaz trembling because he sensed that the person with whom he had drunken sex earlier in the evening was an adult woman and not the sweet-smelling young Ruth now lying by his side?

According to the *qere*, the person lying with Boaz identifies herself as "I am Ruth your maid." Is this Naomi pretending to be Ruth, as Jacob pretended to be his brother Esau? Or is it Ruth who has now taken the place of her mother-in-law in bed after Naomi had sex with Boaz and quickly slipped away while he was in his drunken stupor? Whether the speaker is Naomi or Ruth, she asks Boaz "to spread your wing (כנפך *knāpekā*) over your maid for you are a redeemer" (3:9). The noun "wing" has at least three related meanings in Biblical Hebrew; first, the "wing" of a bird, insect, seraph, cherub, or other flying creature or the "fin" of a marine creature, second, the "hem" or "edge" of a garment, and third, a euphemism for the male genitals. Most commentators translate the word in 3:9 in relation to the second meaning (e.g. "spread your cloak" (NRSV); "spread your covering" (NASV); "spread the skirt of your cloak" (NJB); "spread your robe" (TNK)). However, when used in relation to clothing in the HB, כנף refers only to the hem or edge and is usually followed by the words "of your garment" (e.g. Num 15:38; Deut 22:12; 1 Sam 15:27; 24:5.12(2x); Hag 2:12; *contra*, e.g. Ezek 16:8). As this is not the case in 3:9, it is more likely that "wing" is being used as a euphemism for Boaz's genitals (see Chapter 13 in this volume). This interpretation is reinforced by the fact that Ruth has already exposed his genitals in 3:7. Not only is the word for Boaz's "cloak" absent in the text of 3:9, but Ruth is speaking to him in a state of undress!

The sexual innuendo in 3:9 is obscured in the final version of the narrative by Boaz's pious statement in 2:12, "May Yhwh reward your work. And may your wages be full from Yhwh, the God of Israel, under whose *wings you have come* to seek refuge." It is possible that a later redactor added 2:12 to the narrative in order to orient the reader's understanding of 3:9 away from sex and marriage and towards protection and refuge, as if Boaz were God and not a man.

Boaz responds directly to the woman's request to "spread your wing over your maid":

> And now it is true I am a redeemer; however, there is a redeemer closer than I. Stay this night. And it will come to pass in the morning that if

he redeems you, good. But if he does not wish to redeem you, then I myself will redeem you, as Yhwh lives. Lie down [or sleep] until the morning. (3:12–13)

The question of what "redeemer" means in the context of Ruth 3 will be discussed in the following section. What is important for now is that Boaz seems to be giving chaste advice to the woman he found lying by his side in bed: "Stay this night. [...] Sleep (שכב *škb*) until the morning." However, the narrator's description of what actually happened contains an important difference: "And she lay (ותשכב; *watiškab*) beside his feet [his genitals] until morning" (3:14). Why does the narrator shift from Boaz's invitation that the woman "spend the night" and "sleep until the morning" to "she lay beside his feet [his genitals] until morning?" A likely interpretation is that the couple in fact had sex until dawn. The text plays with the ambiguity of the verb שכב (*škb*), which can mean either "to sleep" or "to lie," with a sexual euphemism for his genitals.

The narrator then adds that Ruth "rose before one could recognize another. For he had said 'Let it not be known that *the* woman came to the threshing floor'" (3:14). Boaz's reference to the "woman" is curious. As Boaz is speaking to Ruth, why doesn't he say, "Let it not be known that *you* came to the threshing floor?" Why does Boaz refer to his female visitor in the third person as "*the woman*"? The LXX corrects the logic of Boaz's statement to refer to "*a* woman (γυνὴ *gune*)." In addition, if Boaz is indeed referring to Ruth, why would he call a girl of her age "a woman" or "the woman" rather than a "girl" or a "maid" or even "my daughter"? The word "woman" preceded by the definite article appears only two other times in the book of Ruth, in 1:5 where it refers to Naomi and in 4:11 where, as argued below, it also refers to Naomi. Is Boaz warning Ruth in 3:14 not to tell anyone that *Naomi* (the woman) had also come down to the threshing floor and had sexual intercourse with Boaz earlier in the evening? Is this the sexual liaison that he wants to keep private and confidential?

The threshing floor scene reaches formal closure in 3:15 with the narrator's statement, "And he came (בוא *boʾ*) into the city." Although the gender of the pronoun is clearly masculine, many commentators translate the text as if it read, "And *she* came into the city" (e.g. NASV, NJB, TNK) because the following scene in 3:16–18, which is a dialogue between Ruth and Naomi in which Boaz is absent, begins with "And she came (בוא) to her mother-in-law." In my view, 3:16 should be read as it is written, "And *he* came into the city" (*pace* NRSV, TOB). In addition, the repetition of the verb בוא (to come; to enter) in two successive phrases is suspect and open to the suggestion that an earlier version of Ruth 3 ended with "And he came into the city," which leads seamlessly to 4:1: "And Boaz went up to the gate and he sat down there." The possibility should be considered that the intervening material in 3:16-18 was added by a later redactor to bolster Boaz's portrayal as a kind and generous man.

1.2 The Shifting Meaning of "Redeemer" between Ruth 3 and Ruth 4

It will be argued below that in Ruth 2-3, the concept of "redeemer" applies solely to a man who marries the childless widow of a close relative in order that the deceased family member's name may be preserved. As Boaz was a close relative of both Naomi's deceased husband Elimelech and of Ruth's deceased husband Mahlon, his customary duty to marry a childless widow and father her children could in theory apply to both Naomi and Ruth. In Boaz's reply to Ruth's (or was it Naomi's?) request on the threshing floor that Boaz marry her, Boaz states:

> [12]And now it is true I am a redeemer; however, there is a redeemer closer than I. [13] Stay this night. And it will come to pass in the morning that if he redeems *you*, good. But if he does not wish to redeem *you*, then I myself will redeem *you*, as Yhwh lives. Lie down [or sleep] until the morning." (3:12-13)

In this passage, the person who will be "redeemed" in the morning is the woman who requested that Boaz marry her. This link between redemption and marriage is supported by the very words of Ruth's (or Naomi's) request in 3:9 that Boaz "spread his wing over his maid." The speaker justifies her request with the prepositional phrase that immediately follows, "for you are *a redeemer*." The connection between redemption and marriage seems abundantly clear.

As discussed in Chapter 3 in this volume, the notion in Ruth 3 that Boaz has a customary obligation to marry Naomi and/or Ruth is *not* a direct application of the so-called "levirate" marriage provisions of Deut 25:5-7. First, the levirate marriage provisions only apply if *brothers dwell together* and one of them marries but then dies childless. Second, the provisions are not obligatory on the brothers. Third, Deut 25:5-7 does not contain any vocabulary relating to "to redeem," "redeemer" or "redemption." Fourth, the provisions do not address the question of priority of obligation to marry the widow, whether among a decedent's several brothers or more remote kinsmen. However, like the Ruth narrative, the story of Tamar and Judah is also based on the premise that a close relative is expected to marry a childless widow and father her child even though none of the levirate marriage provisions are satisfied in that text. In my view, the remarriage of childless widows should be viewed as a traditional literary *topos* in biblical narratives rather than as examples of the legal application of the Deuteronomic levirate marriage provisions.

Interestingly however, the autonomy of the childless widow literary *topos* did not prevent biblical authors from making intertextual allusions to the levirate marriage provisions of Deut 25:5–7. In the story of Tamar and Judah, Judah asks his son, Onan, to "*go into* the wife of your brother. *And you will perform your duty by her as a brother*" (Gen 38:8). As the verb translated as "perform your duty by her as a brother" (יבם *ybm*) is used only in Deut 25:5–7 and the story of Tamar and Judah, it is likely that Gen 38:8 is an intertextual allusion to Deut 25:5 which states, "her brother-in-law *will go into* her. And he will take her as his wife. *And he will perform his duty by her as a brother*." Similarly, Boaz's statement in 3:13, "*But if he does not wish to* redeem you, then I myself will redeem you" also contains an intertextual link to Deut 25:7: "*But if the man does not wish to* take his brother's wife..." These are the only two occurrences of the phrase, "But if he does not wish (ואם לא יחפץ *w'im lo 'yaḥpoṣ*)" in the HB. This allusion suggests that the infinitive construct phrase "to redeem you" in 3:13 is intended to be understood by the reader as having a meaning similar to the infinitive construct phrase, "to take his brother's wife (לקחת את יבמתו; *lāqat 'et yebimtô*)" in Deut 25:7.

Boaz's status as a "redeemer" undergoes transformation in the narrative as the story advances. The narrator's first description of Boaz's relationship status occurs in 2:1 (following the *ketiv*): "And Naomi's husband had an acquaintance, a worthy man, of Elimelech's family. And his name was Boaz." The word מידע *myd'*) is a passive (*Pu'al*) participle of the verb "to know" (ידע *yd'*) and is used elsewhere in the HB to mean an "acquaintance" or a "friend" (2 Kgs 10:11; Pss 31:12; 55:14; 88:9.19; Job 19:14). There is nothing in these passages to suggest that a person's acquaintance is a close relative. To the contrary, the acquaintance is paralleled with a "neighbor" in Ps 31:12; with a "person of my own rank" and a "companion" in Ps 55:14; and with "lover" and "companion" in Ps 88:19.

Tellingly, the word מידע in 2:1 is corrected with a *qere* to read מוֹדָע (*môda'*), a passive (*Hof'al*) participle of the verb "to know." Literally, the word refers to someone "who has been made known," but its contextual meaning is obscure because it occurs only three times in the HB: here in the *qere* of 2:1, in 3:2 ("And now, is not Boaz our *môda'* ?") and Prov 7:4 ("Say to wisdom, 'You are my sister,' And call understanding a *môda'* "). Many translations assume that the word מוֹדָע should be interpreted in these three passages to mean "kinsman" (e.g. NASV, NJB, NRSV, TNK, TOB). These three occurrences are a thin basis on which to claim with certainty that the word means "kinsman" rather than "acquaintance."

The Greek translators rendered the rare word מודע with γνώριμος (*gnōrimos*), an equally rare Greek noun, meaning "friend" or "companion" in the *qere* of Ruth 2:1; 3:2; Prov 7:4, and in 2 Sam 3:8. This last occurrence provides a helpful key to understanding the meaning of the rare word מוֹדָע. In David's speech to Abner in 2 Sam 3:8, he says, "Today I show kindness to the house of Saul your father, to his brothers and to his מֵרֵעֵהוּ (*mere'ehu*)." The noun מֵרֵעַ (*mere'a*) occurs ten times in the HB and is usually translated to mean "friend" or "companion" depending on the context (NASV, NJB, NRSV, TNK, TOB). Thus, the Greek translators understood מוֹדָע in 3:2 as having the same meaning as מרע ("friend" as in 2 Sam 3:8) rather than as "kinsman" as hypothesized by modern commentators.

Why did the Masoretes correct the relatively common word of the *ketiv* in 2:1 (מְיֻדָּע *meyudā'* "acquaintance") to read מוֹדָע (*môda'*) in the *qere*, a rare word with an obscure meaning? One possibility is that the textual change formed part of a gradual redactional process which transformed the portrayal of Boaz from an "acquaintance" of Elimelech in 2:1, to a "kinsman" of Elimelech in 3:2, and thus to a "redeemer" of his widow in 3:9.

Ruth 4 makes massive use of the verb "to redeem" and related cognates, "redeemer" and "redemption." However, these lexemes are used to refer to Boaz's act of acquiring Elimelech's field, not to his marriage to Ruth. The notion of a "redeemer" as a man who marries the childless widow of a close relative as expressed in Ruth 3 is transformed and "overwritten" in Ruth 4 to mean something entirely different. In my view, all or a significant part of Ruth 4:1–10 was added by a later redactor to shift the reader's attention away from the redemption by marriage theme – and its related sexual connotations – in Ruth 3 to the redemption by land acquisition theme in Ruth 4.

The late redactional quality of 4:1–10 is reinforced by the fact that Naomi's ownership of "the strip of the field that belonged to our brother Elimelech" – that forms the thematic groundwork for Boaz's real estate transaction – is completely unknown to the reader until Boaz discloses this important bit of information to Peloni Almoni in 4:3. Indeed, Naomi's status as a land owner (or at least entitled to the usufruct of her late husband's share; see Chapter 2 in this volume) contradicts everything the reader knows about the woman through the end of Ruth 3, where Naomi is portrayed as a penniless widow without surviving sons who encourages her daughter-in-law to glean in the fields to keep the two of them from dying of starvation. The abrupt shift in Naomi's life story in 4:3 from a poor widow to the possessor of a strip of field adjoining the property of her late husband's wealthy "brother" Boaz strongly suggests that much of Ruth 4 was added to the narrative when it was decided to shift the meaning of a redeemer from a man who marries a childless widow of a close relative to a man who purchases real estate (or pays off the mortgage on property) owned by one of his brothers/associates. This change has the effect of obscuring the acts of sexual intercourse between Boaz and Naomi and Boaz and Ruth that took place on the threshing floor. As a "redeemer," Boaz's relationship with Naomi becomes commercial and not sexual or marital.

1.3 The Blessings of Boaz's Marriages (Ruth 4:11-12, 14-15)

Boaz's negotiations with Peloni Almoni reach closure in 4:9-10 with Boaz's announcement to the assembled elders and all the people that they are witnesses to his acquisition from Naomi of all the property that belonged to Elimelech, Mahlon, and Chilion and to his acquisition of Ruth "to be my wife." The elders respond with a double blessing in 4:11-12 that merits close examination:

> ¹¹May Yhwh make the *woman* who is coming into your house like Rachel and Leah, the two of whom built the house of Israel. Become wealthy in Ephrathah. Proclaim a name in Bethlehem. ¹²And may your house be like the house of Perez whom Tamar bore to Judah, from the seed [offspring] which Yhwh shall give you by this *girl*.

The elders' collective response deals only with Boaz's marriage(s) and ignores the important property transaction he has just concluded with Naomi. This suggests that 4:11-12 may have formed part of the earlier version of Ruth before the insertion of 4:1-10. When read in the context of 4:10 in which Boaz marries only one woman, the reader of the final version of the narrative is encouraged to read the elders' double blessing as relating to the marriage of Boaz and *Ruth*. However, the double blessing can be understood in a different way when read in the context of the threshing floor scene in which Boaz was seduced by both Naomi and Ruth. The first blessing in 4:11 refers to *the woman* (האשה *ha'išāh*) who is coming into your house." The second blessing in 4:12 refers to the offspring that Boaz will father "by this *girl* (הנערה *hanna'ărah*)." The possibility should be considered that the first blessing relates to Naomi and the second to Ruth. This hypothesis is supported by the following arguments.

In the first blessing, the elders draw a comparison between Boaz's marriage and that of Jacob's marriages to Rachel and Leah. Although the understanding of these two wives of Jacob as being women "who built the house of Israel" has a biblical ring, in fact it has no basis in the HB. Leah and Rachel are never referred to together after Gen 33:7, except in Ruth 4:11. If positive comparisons to Rachel and Leah are not a customary biblical trope, why did the author of Ruth decide to mention them in 4:11? One possible answer is that both Boaz and Jacob were tricked into marrying two women. Laban tricked Jacob into marrying Leah in the first place and then tricked him into working another seven years to marry Rachel. Boaz is tricked by Naomi into marrying both her and Ruth. The deceit of both Laban and Naomi involves the specific *topos* of the trickster surreptitiously substituting one woman for another (Leah for Rachel and Naomi for Ruth) with the deception rendered plausible because sexual intercourse occurred in the dark and under the influence of alcohol (see Gen 29:21–25).

In the second blessing, the elders state their hope that the future "house" of Boaz "will be like the house of Perez." The expression "house of Perez" is unique (a *hapax*) in the HB. Judah's son Perez is not a notable figure, being mentioned only in genealogies in Genesis, Numbers, and Chronicles, and in two returnee lists in Nehemiah that identify families as belonging to the "sons of Perez." If Perez is a minor character in the HB, why are the future offspring of Boaz compared to the "house of Perez?" One answer is that the elders compare Ruth to Tamar because Tamar also tricked a man into marrying her and fathering her son Perez. If so, the births of both Obed and Perez share something in common; they are both the result of women's trickery.

The elders' blessings of Boaz's marriage(s) in 4:11–12 is followed by the narrator's factual notice in 4:13: "And Boaz took Ruth. And she became his wife. And he went into her. And Yhwh gave her conception. And she gave birth to a son." This verse seems out of place at this point in the narrative, which suggests that it may have been moved from elsewhere in the text to its current position between 4:12 and 4:14. This position will be defended in section 1.4 below.

When 4:14–15 is read as the direct continuation of 4:11–12, it becomes clear that the double set of matrimonial blessings pronounced collectively by the "elders" form a diptych with a parallel set of blessings spoken collectively the same day by the "women."

> [14]And the women said to Naomi, "Blessed is Yhwh who has not left you without a redeemer today. And may his name be proclaimed in Israel. [15a]And he will be for you a restorer of life who will secure your old age. [15b]For your daughter-in-law, who loves you, gave birth to him and is better to you than seven sons."

While the first of the elders' blessings ambiguously referred to "the woman who is coming into your house," the women make it abundantly clear that they are referring to Naomi rather than to Ruth. Naomi is blessed because Yhwh has finally granted her a "redeemer." Is Naomi's redeemer her new husband Boaz or Ruth's newborn child? Consistent with the understanding of the word "redeemer" in Ruth 3 as referring generally to a man who marries the childless widow of a deceased relative, and specifically to Boaz, the common sense understanding of 4:14 is that the women are referring to *Boaz* as Naomi's redeemer rather than to an infant who is 20 years away from being able to "secure [Naomi's] old age" (4:15a).

The women's second blessing, "And may his name be proclaimed in Israel," provides support for the hypothesis that the women are referring to Boaz (rather than Obed) as Naomi's redeemer. When the women's collective speech in 4:14-15 is read in parallel with the elders' speech in 4:12-13, the blessing, "And may his name be proclaimed in Israel" (4:14), can be interpreted as the women's response to the men's blessing of Boaz, "Become wealthy in Ephrathah. Proclaim a name in Bethlehem" (4:11). Indeed, the women seem to be engaged in a "bidding war" with the men. When the elders say, "Proclaim a name in *Bethlehem*," the women up the ante and respond, "May his name be proclaimed in *Israel*."

In my view, the men's blessings in 4:11-12 and the women's blessings in 4:14-15 follow the same structural pattern. First, the men bless Naomi (the woman who is coming into your house). Second, the men bless Boaz (Become wealthy... Proclaim a name). Third, the men bless Ruth (the seed Yhwh will give you by this girl). The women's speech follows the same pattern. First, the women bless Naomi (Blessed is Yhwh who has not left you without a redeemer today). Second, the women bless Boaz (May his name be proclaimed in Israel). Third, the women bless Ruth ([For] your daughter-in-law who loves you gave birth to him [a son]).

It is the final version of the women's third blessing in 4:15b that orients the reader to understand that Naomi's redeemer is Ruth's yet unnamed son. The key grammatical elements that are used to reach this result are (i) to link the second and third blessings with the particle *kî* (כִּי, for or because) and (ii) to affix a pronominal suffix to the key verb in the phrase to read "she gave birth to *him*" (יְלָדַתּוּ *yelādatu*). Although women are constantly giving birth to children in the HB, the verbal form יְלָדַתּוּ is a *hapax*. In contrast, the phrase "she gave birth to *a son* (וַתֵּלֶד בֵּן *wateled ben*)" occurs dozens of times in the HB, including in 4:13. Although speculative, it is possible that an earlier version of 4:15b read, "*And* your daughter-in-law who loves you gave birth to *a son*."

1.4 Textual and Contextual Problems in Ruth 4:13

As discussed above, the parallel blessings of Boaz's marriage(s) by the men and women of Bethlehem in 4:11-12,14-15 are interrupted by the narrator's factual notice in 4:13: "And Boaz took Ruth. And she became his wife. And he went into her. And Yhwh gave her conception. And she gave birth to a son." This verse seems out of place at this point in the narrative, which suggests that it may have been moved from elsewhere in the text to its current position between 4:12 and 4:14. This hypothesis is supported by five arguments.

First, the narrator's statement in 4:13 recounts events that took place over no less than nine months: marriage, sexual intercourse, conception, and the birth of a child. This telescoping of time and journalistic reporting of events is typical of factual notices in the HB, which typically occur in summary lists of events not recounted in the narrative genre, and in the concluding "happy ending" phrase of a narrative. However, 4:13 does not function as a literary closure to 4:1-12. To the contrary, the action rebounds in 4:14-16 with a speech collectively spoken by the women of Bethlehem that begins, "And the women said to Naomi..."

Second, between Naomi's statement to Ruth in 3:18 ("Wait, my daughter, until you know how the matter turns out; for the man will not rest until he has settled it *today*") and Boaz's public announcement in 4:9 ("You are witnesses *today* that I have bought from the hand of Naomi all that belonged to Elimelech and all that belonged to Chilion and Mahlon"), all of the action in the narrative takes place in a *single day*. In their first blessing of Naomi in 4:14, the women of Bethlehem say, "Blessed is Yhwh who has not left you without a redeemer *today*." The women's blessings in 4:14-16 may thus have been intended to mirror the men's blessings in 4:11-12, with both collective speeches occurring on the same day, one in response to the other.

Third, in the final version of the text Boaz waits to have intercourse with his bride until after the elders had become "witnesses" to his public announcement of his intention to marry Ruth and until the elders had blessed the event. This sequence of events suggests that 4:9-13 is describing a marriage *ceremony* like the one in Tobit 7:1-17. While rabbinic literature contains ample discussion of how marriages are to be formalized, the HB is silent on the subject. The final version of the text thus introduces the concept of a formal wedding ceremony followed by the sexual consummation of the marriage which is unknown in any other biblical narrative.

Fourth, the language of the notice in 4:13 is unusually long: "And Boaz took Ruth. And she became his wife. And he went into her. And Yhwh gave her conception. And she gave birth to a son." This statement consists of five short *wayyiqtol* phrases that follow each other sequentially. The reader reasonably assumes that the pronouns "she" and "her" all refer to Ruth. However, there are reasons to suspect that these phrases actually referred to two different women in the earliest version of the narrative. The first two phrases form a set and perfectly mirror the narrator's description of Isaac's marriage to Rebecca: "And he took Rebecca. And she became his wife" (Gen 24:67). The use of the verb "to be" as in "she became his wife" is also used in relation to three of David's marriages, in 1 Sam 25:42–43 and 2 Sam 11:27. However, the common expression, "and he went into her" does not follow "and she became his wife" in any of these cases as it does in Ruth 4:13. This suggests that "And he went into her. And Yhwh gave her conception and she gave birth to a son" may have applied to someone other than Ruth in an earlier version of the narrative.

Fifth, the sequence, "and he went into her. And she conceived. And she gave birth to a son" is a relatively common trope in the HB (e.g. Gen 30:4–5; 38:2–3; 1 Chr 7:23). The distinctive feature of Ruth 4:13 is that the woman's conception is said to have required divine intervention. According to Jones (2016, 97), divine intervention in pregnancy only occurs in the HB in stories about *infertile* women (e.g. Gen 21:1; 25:21; 29:31; 30:17; 1 Sam 1:19). This raises the question of which woman with whom Boaz had intercourse on the threshing floor would have needed divine intervention in order to become pregnant? Ruth is still a young woman of childbearing age; however, Naomi is older and has already stated that she is probably no longer capable of having children (1:11–12).

I propose that the phrase "And he went into her. And Yhwh gave her conception" refers to *Naomi* and may have appeared in the earlier version of the text after the phrase in 3:7 "And she lay down" just before Boaz awakens suddenly at midnight in 3:8 and discovers that "the woman was lying beside his feet." The phrase, "And Boaz took Ruth. And she became his wife" may have originally preceded the phrase in 3:14, "And she [Ruth] lay beside his feet until morning."

1.6. Textual and Contextual Problems in 4:16–22

The women's blessings in 4:14–15 are followed in the final version of the text by the "naming" episode in which the child supposedly born to Ruth is given the name Obed. However, this naming scene is unlike any other in the HB. The final version of the text reads, "And the neighbors gave him a name, saying, 'A son was born to Naomi.' And they named him Obed. He is the father of Jesse, the father of David" (4:17). As the only child fathered by Boaz in the final version is the son of Ruth, the phrase, "A son was born to Naomi" is rather curious. It has spawned a cottage industry among commentators who elaborate complex interpretations that revolve around Naomi "adopting" her surrogate "grandchild" Obed as her foster son. These interpretations are based on the premise that while the child born to Ruth has Boaz as his biological father, his "legal" father is actually Mahlon, Ruth's deceased husband and Naomi's son. On this assumption, Naomi becomes the "legal" (but not biological) grandmother of Obed. However, in 4:18–21, the narrator concludes the story with the statement that *Boaz* is the father of Obed, Obed of Jesse, and Jesse of David. This verse is an interpretative *crux* for most commentators. The final version of the text thus leaves readers with a problem that is triply confusing. Is Obed's mother Ruth or Naomi? Is Obed's father Boaz or Mahlon? Is David's great-grandfather Boaz or Mahlon?

My proposal for resolving the triple conundrum is to take the phrases "A son was born to Naomi" and "Boaz is the father of Obed" at face value and to posit that in an earlier version of the narrative, Boaz had sex with both Naomi and Ruth on the threshing floor, thus making them his two wives, each of whom bore him sons. One was raised by his mother Ruth and the other by his mother Naomi. The issue of Mahlon's absence from the concluding genealogy in 4:18–21 disappears when Boaz's redeemer status as developed in the narrative is understood *not* to be an application of the levirate provisions of Deut 25:5–7. Just as Perez is reckoned in biblical genealogies to be the son of *Judah* and not Er (Num 26:20; 1 Chron 2:3), so Obed is listed in 4:21–22 as being the son of *Boaz* and not Mahlon.

2. Technical Discussion of the Textual Problems in Ruth 3

This section addresses in detail the scholarly debate concerning the two principal textual problems in Ruth 3; first, the *qere-ketiv* problem in 3:3–4, and second, the meaning of the extremely rare word, מרגלות (*mrglot*) used in 3:4,7,8,14, which is customarily translated as "feet" (e.g. NASV, NJB, NRSV, TNK, TOB).

2.1 *Qere-Ketiv* Problem in 3:3–4

As discussed, the Masoretes made several changes to the text of Ruth that have substantially altered the meaning of the story. In 3:3–4, two verbs in the first person ("*I* will go down" and "*I* will lie down" in the *ketiv* are changed to the second person singular feminine ("*you* will go down" and "*you* will lie down") in the *qere*. A similar change occurs in 4:5, where the first person singular in the *ketiv* ("I have acquired") is changed to the second person singular *masculine* in the *qere* ("You have acquired"). The most parsimonious explanation of this phenomenon – the one proposed in this chapter for 3:3–4 (see also Chapters 1 and 2) for 4:5 – is that the *ketiv* reflects an older version of the text which the Masoretes elected to modify in the *qere*, probably because they thought that their changes made the story more coherent. However, an alternative explanation for the *qere-ketiv* problem in 3:3–4 was proposed over 100 years ago and has been followed by most modern commentators without discussion. This section will revisit this venerable but questionable hypothesis to identify its strengths and weaknesses.

One of the leading Hebrew philologists of the late nineteenth century, Emil Friedrich Kautzsch (1841-1910), proposed that the *ketiv* in 3:3-4 represents an archaic version of the second person singular feminine (GKC 1910, §44h; see also §90n). According to this hypothesis, the *qere* is understood to be a simple correction of an archaic verbal form into standard Biblical Hebrew that does not change the meaning of the verse. Kautzch's position was followed by a second influential early twentieth century Hebrew philologist, Paul Joüon (1947, §42f.). The thrust of the argument of Kautzch and Joüon is that Biblical Hebrew is a Semitic language that evolved from the same archaic language system that also produced Aramaic and Arabic, among other languages. As the second person singular feminine verbal conjugation in the perfect tense has an ending in *tiy* in Aramaic and in *ti* in Arabic, the *ketiv* in 3:3-4, in which the verbs also have an ending in *tiy*, thus represent archaic verbal forms that the Masoretes changed to the standard Biblical Hebrew verbal conjugation with an ending in *tᵉ*. The fact that the same archaic ending in *tiy* is used in standard Biblical Hebrew for the first person singular thus becomes an unfortunate and confusing coincidence. In Aramaic and Arabic this confusion does not arise, because the first person singular has a different ending.

What takes Kautzch's position out of the realm of the purely speculative is the fact that there are a number of other occurrences of Masoretic corrections of a first person singular in the *ketiv* to a second person singular feminine in the *qere*. As listed by Jacob M. Myers, there are 20 examples of what can be called the "*tiy-tᵉ* shift": Jer 2:33; 3:4,5; 4:19; 22:23(×2); 31:21; 46:11; 51:13; Ezek 16:13,18,22,31(×2), 43(×2),47,50,51; Ruth 3:3,4 (Myers 1955, 11). However, three of the examples Myers cites in Jeremiah (22:23[×2]; 51:13) are actually *participles* with a pronominal suffix ending in *tiy*. As the first person singular pronominal suffix for participles in standard Biblical Hebrew does *not* end in *tiy*, these three verses are not actually examples of a *ketiv* in the first person singular being corrected in the *qere* to a second person feminine singular. At first glance, Kautzch's position seems compelling because it assumes that the *qere-ketiv* change in Ruth 3:3-4 is simply another example of the same phenomenon that occurs in Jeremiah and Ezekiel. In my view, this position is an oversimplification of a complex problem.

First, the incidence of the "*tiy-tᵉ* shift" is both relatively rare and highly concentrated. Although it occurs 17 times (by my count) in the HB, it is limited to five chapters in Jeremiah, one chapter in Ezekiel and one chapter in Ruth. If in fact the *tiy-tᵉ* shift reflects an archaic form of

Biblical Hebrew as argued (or assumed) by most commentators, why does the shift occur in these five chapters and nowhere else in the HB?

Second, Ezek 16:59 contains a *qere-ketiv* showing a correction in the *opposite direction*. Where the *qere* has "*you* will do," the *ketiv* corrects this to "*I* will do." While this is usually interpreted as the correction of a scribal mistake, the changes in the other direction from the first person to the second person feminine are explained as the use of an archaic verbal form. Might some (or all) of the examples of the *tiy-t^e* shift in Ezek 16 also reflect the correction of simple scribal errors?

Third, although feminine verbal forms are considerably less common than masculine verbal forms in the HB, one of the characteristics of both Ezek 16 and Ruth 3 is that both chapters are about female characters and, thus, contain a significant number of feminine verbal forms. In both chapters, the text intersperses the so-called archaic feminine verbal forms ending in *tiy* with standard Biblical Hebrew forms ending in *t^e*. If, in fact, the *tiy-t^e* shift reflects an archaic form of Biblical Hebrew, why does the text of a single chapter shift back and forth from the archaic form to standard Biblical Hebrew?

Fourth, in the case of Ruth, and Ruth alone, rabbinical tradition affirms that the *ketiv* in 3:3 should be read as the first person singular and taken to represent the text as written. In a sixth-century CE midrash on Ruth, the rabbis interpret Naomi's statement, "I will go down to the threshing floor" (per the *ketiv*) to mean "*My merit* will go down to the threshing floor *with you*" (Ruth Rabbah 5). The medieval French commentator Rashi (1040–1105) follows *Ruth Rabbah*'s interpretation of 3:3 in his commentary on the five *megillot* and adds the additional comment "*and protect you from any mishap*." What is important for our purposes is that these two important rabbinical sources understood the *ketiv* to be an intentional use of the first person singular and not a scribal error or example of archaic usage of the second person singular feminine. The rabbis explained (or explained away) Naomi's presence on the threshing floor to mean that Naomi's virtue would accompany Ruth on her sexual adventure as a kind of talisman to protect her from sin.

Fifth, the existence of the *qere-ketiv* in 4:5 (see Chapters 1 and 2 in this volume) supports my position that the author intended to say exactly what is written in standard Biblical Hebrew in the *ketiv* version of 3:3–4. In 4:5, the *ketiv*, "I have acquired" is changed in the *qere* to "you have acquired" (or as most modern commentators translate with little justification, "you will also acquire"). The change here is from a verb ending in *tiy* (the first person singular) to a verb ending in *ah* (the second person singular *masculine*). The *ketiv* in 4:5 cannot possibly be argued to be an "archaic" form having the same meaning as the *qere*. In my opinion, the

Masoretic corrections in 3:3–4 and 4:5 were intended to change the *meaning* of the story for the reasons presented earlier in this chapter.

The above analysis suggests that while the use of the first person singular in Jer 2; 3; 4; 31 and 46 and Ezek 16 may be best explained as rare archaic forms of the second person singular feminine, the evidence indicates that the verbs ending in *tiy* in Ruth *ketiv* 3:3–4 and 4:5 are written in standard Biblical Hebrew and should be understood as first person singular verbs. The *qere* thus represents a change in the meaning of the story rather than a simple correction of a scribal error or updating of an archaic form. The question that needs to be addressed is *why* scribal editors would have changed an earlier version of the text as reflected in the *ketiv* to read something very different? I am only aware of one other author who has addressed this issue. Brian P. Irwin (2008) shares the view presented in this chapter that the verbs in *ketiv* 3:3–4 were written in standard Biblical Hebrew and were thus intended to be understood as first person singular verbs. However, Irwin takes the position that three versions of the text in 3:3–4 can be hypothesized. In the oldest, the verbs were in the second person implying that it was Ruth who was lying beside Boaz's feet (as reflected in the *qere*). A later generation of scribes changed the second person verbs to first person verbs (as reflected in the *ketiv*). The final Masoretic version of the text changed the verbal forms back to what they were in the oldest version (as reflected in the *qere*). The purpose of the hypothesized intermediate version of the text (which Irwin does not date) was "to minimize the role of Ruth – a goal that is achieved if Naomi replaces Ruth in the sexually charged atmosphere of the threshing floor." Irwin argues that the role of Ruth needed to be minimized because "[t]he incorporation of a Moabite woman into the nation of Israel, let alone into the line of David, would have struck many Israelites as nothing less than scandalous" (Irwin 2008, 336; see also Chapter 6 in this volume). By making the final textual change, "the Masoretes reintroduced the original reading of the text and restored Ruth to her full place in the history of Israel" (Irwin 2008, 338).

Irwin's position is unconvincing for three reasons. First, while the MT itself confirms that the *ketiv* is older than the *qere*, the existence of a textual version older than the *ketiv*, that happened to be identical to the *qere*, is purely speculative. Second, if Ruth's status as a Moabite needed to be "minimized" for theological purposes, why were the scribal changes in the hypothesized intermediate version limited to just 3:3–4? The glorification of Ruth, the Moabite, runs through the entire book of Ruth from the beginning to the end. Third, it is not clear how Naomi's presence along with Ruth at the threshing floor functions to "minimize the role of Ruth" in the intermediate version. To the contrary, it serves to introduce

Naomi into a sexually charged episode from which Irwin argues she was absent in the earlier version.

For the reasons set out in the first part of this chapter, I propose to read the "uncensored" *ketiv* in 3:3-4 as part of an earlier version of the book of Ruth in which Naomi put a plan into play in which Boaz would surreptitiously sleep with both Naomi and Ruth and father sons by both women. For theological reasons probably linked to the tradition that Boaz's child was David's grandfather, the sexually charged tale of Boaz's sleeping with both Naomi and Ruth during the same evening, marrying both of them and fathering two sons needed to be cleaned up. The *qere* version of 3:3-4, together with the introduction of the motif of Boaz purchasing Naomi's interest in an agricultural field and other additions to the text in Ruth 4, served to whitewash the older, bawdier text into a pious paeon to the moral virtues of Boaz, Naomi, and Ruth.

2.3 The Meaning of מרגלות (*mrglot* "feet"?) in 3:4,7,8,14

The form מַרְגְּלֹתָיו (*margelotāyw*) is used four times in Ruth 3 and its meaning is critical to understanding the threshing floor scene. As this rare word is used only one other time in the HB, in Dan 10:6, its meaning is not clear. Most modern bibles translate the word in 3:4 and 3:7 as "his feet" and in 3:8 and 3:14 as "at his feet" (NASV, NRSV, TNK, TOB). However, these translations are questionable, since the word for "his feet" that is used dozens of times in the HB is רַגְלָיו (*raglāyw*). What is clear is that the lexeme is based on the noun (רֶגֶל *regel*, foot), to which the prefix *ma* and the suffix *ot* have been added. This morphological construction resembles the noun מְרַאֲשֹׁות (*mera'ašot*), which is based on the noun "head" preceded by the prefix *ma* and followed by the suffix *ot*. As this word is used ten times, and always as an adverb, its meaning is clear: "by, at, near or beside a person's head." For example, "Saul lay sleeping inside the circle of the camp, with his spear stuck in the ground *beside his head*" (1 Sam 26:7).

Three preliminary conclusions can be drawn from these 10 usages of מְרַאֲשֹׁות; first, the prefix *ma*- indicates the place or area (*localis*) where the head is found (Sasson 1979, 69). Second, because this type of noun of place or location is never preceded by a preposition like "by, at, near, or beside," such a preposition seems to be implied in the word itself. Third, this type of noun always takes the *-ot* suffix that is typical of plural nouns with feminine endings, even when added to a noun such as "head," which would otherwise take a masculine plural masculine suffix or "feet," which would otherwise take a common dual suffix. As people only have one head, it is clear that מְרַאֲשֹׁות should be translated as "beside his head" rather than "beside his heads."

By extension from the meaning of מְרַאֲשׁוֹת, it can be concluded that the rare word מַרְגְּלוֹת used in 3:4,7,8,14 signifies the place of the foot (and not necessarily the "feet" as customarily translated) preceded by an implied preposition like "by, at, near or beside." Ruth 3:8 and 3:14 may thus be translated literally as "behold, a woman was lying *beside the place/area of his foot/feet*" and "she lay *beside the place/area of his foot/feet* until dawn."

The meaning in 3:4,7 is more problematic. Here, the word מַרְגְּלוֹת functions as the direct object of the *pi'el* verb גלה (*glh*, to uncover; to expose). As discussed above, the notion that the prefix *ma-* includes an implicit preposition such as "beside" and signifies the place or location of the body part in question, has been lost. In these two verses, the word מַרְגְּלֹתָיו appears to have the same meaning as רַגְלוֹ(*raglô*, his foot) or רַגְלָיו (*raglāyw*, his feet). The verb that "his foot" complements is the same in both 3:4 and 3:7: גלה in the *pi'el* (to uncover/expose). When used in the *pi'el*, the verb "to uncover/expose" is almost always followed by a direct object that relates to a euphemism for the sexual anatomy; e.g. nakedness, wing, harlotry, leg. For example, "The man who lies (שכב) with his father's wife has *uncovered his father's nakedness* (ערוה)" (Lev 20:11) and "Cursed is he who lies (שכב) with his father's wife, because he has *uncovered his father's wing* (כנף)" (Deut 27:20). When read in the light of these passages, Ruth 3:8,14 take on a clearer light. In both of these verses, after uncovering Boaz's foot/feet, the woman "lies [down] (שכב)" in the man's bed. Just as "uncovering his nakedness" and "uncovering his wing" are clearly euphemisms for exposing a man's genitals, so too is "uncovering Boaz's foot/feet."

It is generally recognized that "foot" is one of the standard euphemisms for male and female genitalia in the HB. The BDB dictionary lists the following examples: for male genitals, Judg 3:24; 1 Sam 24:3; 2 Kgs 18:27; Isa 7:20; 36:12; for female genitals, Deut 28:57; Ezek 16:25. To this list I would add Isa 6:2 ("Above him stood seraphim, each one with six wings: two to cover its face, two to cover its feet and two for flying") on the grounds that if these seraphim are intended to be modest supernatural beings, they probably were covering a part of their bodies other than their feet! If the foot is such a well-established euphemism for genitalia, the question arises why Ruth 3 uses the rare noun מרגלות, which is based on the word for foot, rather than the word "feet" itself? In my view, the noun מרגלות functions in 3:4,7,8,14 as a *double* euphemism; while רַגְלָיו ("his feet") would have been quickly interpreted by readers as a euphemism for Boaz's genitals, the use of the rare word מַרְגְּלֹתָיו adds an additional layer of obfuscation. Although speculative, it is possible that the earlier version in fact used רַגְלָיו and that the later, more pious version of the story introduced the word מַרְגְּלֹתָיו.

3. Conclusion: "Redeeming" the Tricksters

Who wrote the book of Ruth? It is always tempting to imagine that a single author sat down one day with quill, ink, and scroll in hand to compose the wonderful story that has been transmitted to posterity in the form of the text of Ruth as preserved in the MT. However, this version of the compositional history of Ruth is highly improbable. Like other biblical narratives, it is far more likely that Ruth began as a very short text, possibly based on an oral tradition, that was then expanded and developed and reworked by later generations of scribes. The scholarly process of reconstructing the various layers or strata that underlie the final version of a biblical text is generally called "redaction criticism" or "*Redaktionsgeschichte.*"

Ruth contains a number of clues that indicate that the text has undergone significant editorial revision. First, the presence of *qere-ketiv* notes in the MT confirm that the Masoretic scribes worked from older scrolls containing the *ketiv* version, which they then modified. Second, the theme of Naomi's ownership of an interest in an agricultural field, introduced into the plot for the first time in 4:3, contradicts the portrait of Naomi as a penniless widow without surviving family members. This suggests that the plot digression concerning Boaz's purchase of property from Naomi in 4:1–10 is an addition to the earlier version of the text. Third, the meaning of Boaz's status as a "redeemer" undergoes a shift in the narrative, from that of a man who marries a childless widow of a close relative in Ruth 2–3 to a man who purchases real estate owned by one of his brothers/associates in Ruth 4. Fourth, the story of the birth and naming of Boaz's son Obed contains a number of textual fractures and literary contradictions that have led many commentators to suspect that in an earlier version of the text, Boaz fathered two sons, one by Naomi and the other by Ruth (e.g. Sasson 1979, 157–78). Fifth, the numerous sexual innuendos that lie just below the surface of the final version of the text may indicate that themes relating to sex and sexuality were, in fact, much closer to the surface in the earlier version.

A formal reconstruction of the various textual strata that underlie the final version of Ruth is beyond the scope of this chapter. Instead, I have attempted to work from the sparse evidence in the text that survived later redactors' rewriting and overwriting of the narrative to identify the broad outlines of what was probably a sexier and less pious original earlier version of the story. Starting with the *qere-ketiv* notes in the MT, I have attempted to demonstrate that Ruth 3 originally told an engaging and suspenseful tale of Naomi's plot to have Boaz impregnate both her and Ruth on a dark night, far from the prying eyes of neighbors, after Boaz had fallen asleep drunk on the threshing floor. This older version of the narrative was significantly rewritten and overwritten by redactors to erase all references to Boaz's relationship with Naomi and the child she bore.

Once the redactors decided that Boaz had only one wife, Ruth, and one son, Obed (see Chapter 6 in this volume), the narrative needed to be substantially rewritten to promote the character, Ruth and to demote the character, Naomi. While Ruth was a Moabite, Naomi was a trickster. Ruth trumped Naomi in the final version, and the tricky story was theologically redeemed into a bucolic idyll about the pious, generous, and monogamous Boaz, the contented widow Naomi happy to live out her days as a surrogate grandmother, and the proverbial woman of excellence and ancestress of David, Ruth.

Works Cited

Block, Daniel I. 2015. *Ruth: The King is Coming.* Grand Rapids, MI: Zondervan.
Bush, Frederic W. 1996. *Ruth, Esther.* Word Bible Commentary. Dallas: Word Books.
Campbell, Edward F. 1975. *Ruth: A New Translation with Introduction, Notes and Commentary.* Garden City: Doubleday.
GKC. 1910. *Gesenius' Hebrew Grammar.* Edited by Emil Kautzsch. Translated by Arthur E. Cowley. 2nd ed. Oxford: Clarendon.
Gray, John. 1967. *Joshua, Judges and Ruth.* London: Thomas Nelson and Sons.
Irwin, Brian P. 2008. "Removing Ruth: *Tiqqune Sopherim* in Ruth 4.3–4?" *JSOT* 32, 3: 331–8.
Jones, Edward A. 2016. *Reading Ruth in the Restoration Period: A Call for Inclusion.* London: Bloomsbury.
Joüon, Paul. 1947. *A Grammar of Biblical Hebrew.* Translated and revised by T. Muraoka. 2 vols. Rome: Pontifical Biblical Institute.
Linafelt, Tod. 1999. *Ruth.* Collegeville: Liturgical Press.
Matthews, Victor H. 2004. *Judges and Ruth.* Cambridge: Cambridge University Press.
Myers, Jacob M. 1955. *The Linguistic and Literary Form of the Book of Ruth.* Leiden: E. J. Brill.
Niditch, Susan. 1987. *Underdogs and Tricksters: A Prelude to Biblical Folklore.* San Francisco: Harper & Row.
Sasson, Jack M. 1979. *Ruth.* Baltimore: Johns Hopkins University Press.
Ziegler, Yael 2015. *Ruth: From Alienation to Monarchy.* Maggid Studies in Tanakh; Stone Edition. Jerusalem: Koren Publishers.

About the Author

William Krisel is a lecturer at Institut Catholique de Paris (Catholic University of Paris). His recent publications include *Judges 19–21 and the "Othering" of Benjamin: A Golah Polemic against the Autochthonous Inhabitants of the Land?* (Leiden: Brill, 2022); "Methodological Problems in Intertextual Analyses of Old Testament Texts: Genesis 19 and Judges 19 as a Case Study," *Scandinavian Journal of the Old Testament* 36:2 (2022); "Was the Levite's Concubine Unfaithful or Angry? A Proposed Solution to the Text Critical Problem in Judges 19:2," *Old Testament Essays* 33, 2 (2020).

Chapter 8
It's a Charming Story of Faithful Living, but …:
Interpretive Tensions in the Book of Ruth

Rebecca Lindsay

Abstract

The book of Ruth is often read as a story that celebrates family, acceptance, and loyal lovingkindness. However, recent interpretations problematize the characterization of this narrative as idyllic, pointing to its troubling themes and the potentially exploitative dynamics between its characters. I argue that interpretations which highlight the charming and positive aspects of this narrative by turning away from its ambiguity and mess work to domesticate the story. Such interpretations train readers of Ruth, and other biblical stories, to frame out uncomfortable tensions of power and difference in the story world. Drawing on Sara Ahmed's observation that learning to notice what we are taught not to notice is "a form of political labor," I argue that learning to recognize these interpretive tensions can uncover similar tensions at work within diverse contemporary interpretive contexts. Through the uncomfortable work of turning towards what has previously been framed out of interpretations of Ruth, I explore how the narrative might become a conversation partner in noticing and naming entanglements of the idyllic and the exploitative.

Keywords: Ruth, settler colonialism, Bible in Australia

1. Introduction

The book of Ruth is celebrated within many interpretive traditions. Feminist readings, for example, celebrate this text, given its strong female characters, portrayal of women's agency, and female voice (van Dijk-Hemmes 1993; Caspi and Havrelock 1996; Fischer 1999). Queer readings also claim this text, given Ruth's vow of allegiance to her mother-in-law, Naomi, and the disruption the pair offer to heteronormative constructions of family (Alpert 1994; Powell 2018; West 2022, 2019). The incorporation of the often negatively stereotyped Moabite into a Bethlehemite family has likewise been hailed as an example of welcome and inclusion. These positive readings of the book can be understood as liberative theological contributions for communities that have experienced marginalization. Furthermore, the narrative continues to find life in communities of faith, read at Jewish Shavuot and in Christian marriage liturgies. Commentaries on Ruth often begin by noting its acceptance as a charming story of friendship, daring, and God's providence: idyll and delight (e.g. Bush 1996, 1–2; Block 2015, 29; Eskenazi and Frymer-Kensky 2011, xv–xiii; Koosed 2011, 1; Linafelt 1999, xiii; Sakenfeld 1999, 9).

The portrayal of the Ruth narrative as simply positive, however, has long been problematized. Idyllic readings fail to hold the complexity of the narrative, turning away from ambiguity, exploitation, and violence within the text to highlight its beauty. The book of Ruth *is* idyll and delight but ... it is not *simply* idyll and delight. The book's setting is suggestive of violence, the suggestion of cultural assimilation is troubling, and there are exploitative dynamics between its characters. How can these diverse interpretive elements of the narrative be held together, those that delight readers and those that uncover exploitation? What happens when interpretations of Ruth are not either/or, but are allowed to remain in the mess? To respond to these questions, I turn to the work of Sara Ahmed.

Ahmed (2017, 31) likens noticing systems of sexism and racism with a feminist consciousness to turning on a switch. The existence of an "on" switch highlights the default position as *not* noticing sexism, racism, and other marginalization. Adopting a second metaphor, Ahmed (2017, 32) argues that this default position highlights a process of screening out discomfort as we learn to turn away from experiences and ideologies that call patriarchal white social norms into question. Ahmed observes the foundational violence of this turning away:

> What do we learn not to notice? We learn not to notice some suffering, such that if the suffering of those deemed strangers appears, then it does so dimly, only at the edges of our consciousness ... We are learning

to screen out what gets in the way of our occupation of space. (Ahmed, 2017, 32)

Learning to not-pay-attention to the circumstances that enable racism and/or sexism means not being required to acknowledge racism and/or sexism as problematic. When we learn to recognize someone as a stranger, as a body out-of-place that we need not attend to, we are learning that their experience need not affect us, screening out "not only their suffering but their very existence" (Ahmed 2017, 32). Ahmed contends, however, that "if we have been taught to turn away, we have to learn to turn toward" (2017, 31). She argues that moving the switch to "on" and learning to notice is a particular kind of work such that "if a world can be what we learn not to notice, noticing becomes a form of political labor" (2017, 32).

While Ahmed's argument pertains to living a feminist and anti-racist life amidst patriarchal and racist norms, I suggest that it is also useful for biblical interpretation. Traditional interpretation is already a turning away, as what is assumed to be traditional tends to be aligned with readings that are formed within a "Western" worldview that claims a universalizing perspective (Kwok 2021, 2; Lim 2019, 54–56). Such interpretive framings can be both methodological and theological. Traditional interpretation includes the historical-critical methods that often sit underneath other interpretive lenses, including contextual readings. While historical-critical methods are often presented as "objective," they are contextually bound up with enlightenment European epistemologies. Even interpretation that seeks to attend to particularities of context can inadvertently be embedded in Western frameworks, perpetuating a Western universalism (Lim 2019, 3; Havea 2011). Much Ruth scholarship, for example, continues to be influenced by the form-critical work of Herman Gunkel, who categorized the narrative as an "idyll" (see Bush 1996, 33–47). This label restricts engagement with the book, turning away from what does not fit within it, to which I will return below.

Interpretation that reads biblical texts in theologically traditional ways can also perpetuate Western universalism. This happens by failing to critique (Western, often Christian) assumptions about what "good" living might be and in assuming that biblical texts will characterize God and human characters in positive and morally unambiguous ways. Such interpretation teaches readers to bracket out ambiguity or "not-niceness," particularly when these interpretations are for communities whose religious faith is embedded in these texts. While historical-critical scholarship and theological commentary can be in tension with each other, both are grounded in universalizing, Western epistemologies tending towards unified interpretation that avoids ambiguity. With Ahmed, then, we might ask what we learn to notice in traditional interpretations of biblical stories and what we learn to screen out. The political labor of such noticing addresses the kinds of stories the biblical texts are "allowed" to tell (with the hanging question of "by whom") and whether readers can remain in spaces of tension and ambiguity without needing to smooth over interpretations toward a happy or theologically "correct" conclusion.

In this chapter, I attend to interpretive tension by inhabiting the unsettled space of three "buts" within the Ruth narrative. I do this with the help of Ahmed's suggestion that I might learn to turn my attention toward what I have previously been taught to turn away from. The three "buts" that shape my learning are: (1) the interpretive tension between the narrative setting as idyllic and violent, (2) the interpretive tension between relationships of loyal lovingkindness and exploitation, and (3) the interpretive tension between Ruth's welcome into Israel and the erasure of her identity. That is, Ruth is a book with a charming and peaceful setting, but ... it contains violent elements throughout. This is a book about welcome and acceptance, but ... Ruth's presence in Bethlehem sits uncomfortably alongside her Moabite identity. This is a book about family and loyal lovingkindness, but ... the characters do not always act altruistically, with exploitative behavior seen in such examples as Naomi's manipulation of her daughter-in-law to entrap Boaz. Rather than turning away from these tensions, I intentionally turn toward them, even as such movement causes me discomfort in highlighting troubling themes and exploitative behavior within this biblical text.

Attending to these three tensions opens up interpretive possibilities for the book of Ruth, an interesting end in itself. I argue, however, that this is not an exercise simply in theory. Rather, there are corollaries between turning away from tension or turning toward it in biblical interpretation and this same process of turning away and toward in the shaping of lived social narratives. The smoothing over of tensions in biblical interpretation mirrors the desire for settled and comfortable understandings of social location. Learning to see biblical texts differently can contribute to shifting social perspective (and vice-versa). This is important, given that biblical interpretation takes place in social settings where power is distributed unevenly, where some bodies move more easily, and some voices are more likely to be heard, as demonstrated in minoritized biblical criticism (Bailey, Liew, and Segovia 2009; Liew and Segovia 2022). Turning toward interpretive tension helps to elucidate these imbalances and requires readers to confront issues they may find challenging within the text, but also within their lived context. Learning to embrace tensions instead of avoiding them is not a compartmentalized task but one that spills over into all of life. In the next section, I will develop what I mean by this in relation to my location within the settler colonial context of the lands now called Australia before exploring Ruth's three "buts."

2. (Settler) Social Location and Reading Ruth

In introducing Ahmed and her argument I have been writing in the first person plural. This writing itself is a screening out. In using "we" I assume commonalities with Ahmed as she theorizes, and I assume commonalities with you as you read. As a white, cisgender, straight, Christian, middle-class woman living in Australia, I conflate much in joining myself into such a "we." The creation of a stable and unified "we" in settler colonial space often erases Indigenous and other minoritized perspectives for the sake of dominant and dominating "settler common sense" (Rifkin 2013). In the process of learning to turn toward what I have been taught to turn away from, I become more aware of the limits of my knowing. I write suspicious of a sweeping first person plural and yet yearning for the creation of communities of solidarity, action, and care formed differently than through colonization.

Settler colonial space, including the lands now called Australia (Prentis 2021, 19), is invented, a fiction transformed into common-sense reality (Arthur 1999; Bell 2014, 14; Moreton-Robinson 2015, xiii; Rifkin 2013, 322–23). Within settler colonies, colonizers create belonging through Indigenous dispossession (Moreton-Robinson 2015, 3), primarily claiming and occupying land, rather than exploiting the labor of Indigenous peoples (Wolfe 1999, 1–2; Veracini 2022, 75). In Australia, the fiction is *terra nullius*, a legal concept stating that land colonized by the British was empty of inhabitants, a blank slate ready to be created and populated (Behrendt 2010a, 2010b). The lie of this fiction, the turning away if you like, is that the land was not empty. It was (is) in relationship with Aboriginal and Torres Strait Islander peoples whose sovereign care of it sustained the place that enticed British colonizers (Pascoe 2014). Ongoing structures of colonization enable Settler bodies greater freedom than Indigenous bodies. These lived colonial structures of (Western, liberal democratic) government, (English) language, and (extractive) understandings of land as property sit in tension with Indigenous counter-stories of connection with place as Indigenous presence pulls against Settler movements toward Indigenous dispossession and erasure.

I use the terms Indigenous and Settler to describe people within settler colonial space. The capital "I" used in Indigenous indicates respect for Aboriginal and Torres Strait Islander peoples, the first peoples of the Australian continent. This capitalization also occurs within other settler colonial locations, such as Canada, for identity markers including

Indigenous, Aboriginal, or First Nations. In adopting a capitalized "Settler" to name colonial descendants in Australia, I follow Emma Battell Lowman and Adam Barker (2015, 15) who name "Settler" as an identity "that connects a group of people with common practices" living on lands claimed as sovereign by Indigenous peoples. Indigenous and Settler are relational identities, brought into being (and tension) through processes and patterns of settler colonization (see Bell 2014, 5–11).

Biblical interpretation is foundational to the creation of settler colonial societies, with "biblical texts often used as colonial instruments of power, exploited with pre-emptive and self-interested strategies of reading" (Brett 2009, 31). The Bible is used to underwrite concepts such as the doctrine of discovery, European international law from the fifteenth and sixteenth centuries that enabled European nations to claim the lands they "discovered" (Miller et al. 2010), and *terra nullius*. These concepts were deployed by Christian European nations to exert control over land in other places, displacing and dehumanizing the peoples who lived there. At the time of Australia's colonization, for example, biblical texts were used to authorize colonial power (Brett 2009, 31). Biblical influence is seen in the use of motifs such as exodus, exile, and promised land to describe and justify "settlement" within Australia and other settler colonies such as the United States (Brett and Wolfe 2020; Curthoys 1999; Pattel-Gray 2023). There is increasing engagement with settler colonialism in and through the field of biblical studies, from both Indigenous and Settler perspectives (for example, Anderson 2019; Donaldson 1999; Griffin 2021; Paulson and Brett 2013; Pitkänen 2017), often focusing on the ways colonizing nations used conquest texts to justify their colonization of other peoples' lands (see Graybill 2023; Havrelock 2020; Hawk 2012; Warrior 1989).

Returning to Ahmed's language, I ask in relation to both biblical texts and to my Australian context, what I have been taught to turn away from, and what I might I learn to turn toward? The context of my living makes me both curious and nervous about how biblical texts are interpreted, whose interpretations from where are identified as normative, and what tensions are smoothed over in this process. I am confronted by the observation of Bidjara theologian Anne Pattel-Gray (2023, 248) that in Australia, "the Bible was used to justify racism, oppression, and the subjugation of First Nations people," through racist interpretive practices. This causes me to ask what interpretive tensions my settler common sense brackets out and what difference this makes both to my reading of the Bible and to the setting in which I read. If biblical interpretation has contributed to colonization in Australia, is it possible for it to be part of movements towards a decolonial something else?

Settler colonial societies are structured such that Settler occupation of Indigenous lands becomes normalized and "common sense" in everyday living (Rifkin 2013, 323, 337). This includes a discomfort with ambiguity, preferring a binary logic that classifies everything into what it is and what it is not (Bauman 1993). Mark Rifkin argues that attending to how these assumptions are sustained is part of the process of disrupting them, such that

> becoming conscious of the everyday enactment of settlement involves relinquishing the notion of an autonomous, extra-political selfhood existing in a place apart, instead opening onto a recognition not only of enduring Native presence within contemporary political economy but of the effaced history of imperial superintendence and displacement that provides the continuing condition of possibility for the sense of settler escape into the wilderness. (Rifkin 2013, 336)

As noted earlier, Ahmed likens learning to notice sexism and racism as turning on a switch. Once turned on, it is difficult to turn off again. The process of turning on the switch, though, is complicated, as it involves unlearning and relearning. When Ahmed writes of learning to turn toward what we have been taught to turn away from, I see this as part of the process of turning on the switch, learning to notice assumed settler common sense. This requires stepping into discomfort and ambiguity, into the place of interpretive tension.

I enter into interpretive tensions by creating further tension. I read contrapuntally, adopting the strategy of Edward Said (Said 1993). By placing my settler colonial context alongside the narrative of Ruth, I look for what I have previously framed out, as texts not usually read together sit in juxtaposition. I lean into Ahmed's observation, that what I have been taught to turn away from I might also turn toward. The texts I place alongside Ruth are written by Indigenous writers from these lands now called Australia. I explore the tension between charm and violence by reading the book's setting in the time of the judges (Ruth 1:1) and Naomi's bitterness (vv. 13, 20–21) alongside Munanjahli and South Sea Islander scholar Chelsea Watego's critique of hope (Watego 2021, 185–218). I enter the tension between love and exploitation by reading the scenes in Boaz's field (2:2–17) and on the threshing floor (3:1–14) with *Shadow Lines*, the biography Marda Marda author Stephen Kinnane writes of his grandparents' lives. Finally, I enter the tension of welcome and assimilation by considering Ruth's characterization as Moabite and/or Israelite alongside conflicting characterizations of Settler and Indigenous identity in the shipwreck story of Eliza Fraser, as retold by Euayelai and Gamillaroi scholar Larissa Behrendt (2016). Reading in this way draws connections between interpretive tensions in Ruth and the political labor required of Settlers in the Australian context.

In engaging the book of Ruth in conversation with settler colonialism, I do not identify particular characters as "Indigenous" or "Settler" (for a reading that maps ancient Israelite populations onto settler colonial frameworks, see Pitkänen 2017). Ruth and Naomi could both be understood as Indigenous and/or as migrants from differing standpoints. The book's setting in the time of the judges also suggests the possibility that Naomi and Boaz might be understood as relatively recent Settlers in the land. Alongside of this, if a postexilic dating is assumed, then further layers of (un)belonging emerge, in the complicated relationship between returnees from exile, the people of the land, and the land itself. Ultimately, I find it more helpful to use the ambiguity of relationships within the story to enable discussion about power and identity in contemporary settler colonial settings.

3. The First "But": Charmingly Violent

Interpretations of Ruth often highlight the text as "a lovely loophole of peace between wars" (Ostriker 2002, 344). The book's stated setting in the time of the judges (Ruth 1:1) locates it as a calm breath amidst the increasingly violent trajectory of the book of Judges. The end of Judges 19–21 is overtly violent as social order falls apart when each person does what is right in their own eyes (Judg 21:25). In contrast to Judges, the book of Ruth highlights the voices of women, with the speech of female characters including Naomi (Ruth 1:8–9, 11–13, 20–21; 2:2, 20, 22; 3:1–4, 16, 18), Ruth (1:10, 16–17; 2:1, 10, 13, 19, 21; 3:5, 9, 17), and the Bethlehemite women (1:19; 4:14–15, 17) countering the silence of women in the final chapters of Judges, including the Levite's concubine (Judg 19:1–30), the women of Jabesh-Gilead (21:8–14), and the daughters of Shiloh (21:19–23) (see Matheny 2022, 1–6, 243). The prominence of women's voices in the book of Ruth is worth celebrating (e.g. in Bledstein 1993; Caspi and Havrelock 1996, 55; Meyers 1993; van Dijk-Hemmes 1993) … but not at the expense of minimizing the violence found at each point of the narrative's unfolding.

There are multiple examples of violence sitting underneath the action of the narrative. No food in the house of bread (Bethlehem) suggests that something is not quite right (Ruth 1:1), and famine brings connotations, in the worldview of the text, of judgment brought about by God. Elimelech's escape to Moab raises suspicion about his character and motives, given Moab's incestuous origins (Gen 19:30–38) and ambiguous reputation within other biblical stories, as a sometime enemy of Israel

(Num 22:1-4; Judg 3:12-30; 2 Sam 8:2) which is also described as a place of refuge (Deut 2:29; 1 Sam 22:3-4). The verb used to describe Mahlon and Chilion's taking of wives, furthermore, *nsʾ* (Ruth 1:4), is the same verb used to describe the forcible snatching of women from Shiloh as kidnapped wives for Benjaminite men (Judg 21:23), perhaps suggesting that these are not peaceful unions. The death of Naomi's three men is a jolt to her wellbeing, leaving her bereft (*šʾr*) and distant from home (Ruth 1:3, 5).

As the story continues, a violent underlay emerges (see Cottrill 2021, 93-118). These signs of violence are overlooked when interpreters overlay characteristics of the faithful lovingkindness that is seen as a theme of the narrative. As Naomi sets off from Moab, it is in the faithful company of her daughters-in-law (v. 6). She is praised for her interest in the security of their futures (vv. 8-9), yet her words highlight displacements and precarity. Ruth's vow to remain with Naomi (16-17) is celebrated as "extravagant" (Linafelt 1999, 15) and radically counter-cultural (Trible 1978, 172-73), despite Naomi's ambivalent response (v. 18). Once Ruth and Naomi are in Bethlehem (v. 22), Boaz's field appears to become a safe-haven where Ruth can glean unencumbered (2:8-23) and become incorporated into the Bethlehemite community (Chapman 2023). Yet there is language that suggests violence in Bethlehem's fields for a woman, particularly a foreign one (vv. 9, 15, 22) (see Brenner 2010; Shepherd 2018).

When Naomi reveals her plan for Ruth to approach a sleeping Boaz (3:1-4), it is celebrated by some interpreters as a kindness in securing a husband and family for her daughter-in-law (Block 2015, 165-73; Olyan 2021, 83). Despite sexually charged language on the threshing floor (vv. 6-15), many interpreters present Ruth's encounter with Boaz as a romantic and chaste scene of the older man's almost fatherly care for the younger woman (Bush 1996, 165; Campbell 1975, 138), with Block (2015) dedicating his commentary to "*all the Boazes in history and in our time who accept their role as 'the wings of God' and offer refuge to the poor and marginalized.*" Yet the plan is based on using Ruth's body to entrap Boaz, with the possibility of sexual violence seen in Boaz's desire for secrecy (v. 14) and intertextual allusion to the story of Tamar and Judah (Gen 38). As Boaz meets with men at the city gates (Ruth 4:1-12), he is praised for bringing resolution to Naomi and Ruth's precarity, in marriage to Ruth and redemption of Naomi's field (Bush 1996, 126; Lau 2010, 261-62; Ostriker 2002, 356). Yet his generosity also arouses suspicion (Havea 2021, 132), his treatment of the nearer redeemer involves deception, and the scene presents Ruth as an object to be possessed, akin to a field (v. 5). As the story closes, the chorus of women names Ruth as better than seven sons for Naomi (v. 15) followed by her cooption into a genealogy of men (vv. 18-22). Ruth is finally celebrated, not for her own actions as by the women of Bethlehem (4:15), but for whom she births, as the great-grandmother of David (vv. 17, 21) and, eventually, ancestress of Jesus (Matt 1:5).

Identifying *Ruth* as charming impacts linguistic choices made by translators, as assumption of a peaceful setting frames out the possibility of violence. David Shepherd, for example, traces the linguistic choices made in English language translations of Ruth 2:9 and 2:22, regarding the comments of first Boaz (v. 9) and then Naomi (v. 22) to Ruth about the potential way the young male workers may treat her in the fields. Observing the influence of Gunkel's classification of the book as an idyll, Shepherd notes a tendency of English translations to use generic terms such as "touch" or "bother" for the Hebrew terms *ngʿ* and *pgʿ*, obscuring the likelihood that these terms are referring to a violent, potentially sexually violent, harassment (Shepherd 2001). Turning away from the possibility of violence in the fields conceals the precarity of Ruth's situation as a foreign woman gleaning in Bethlehem. Such interpretation fails to explore violence against women because it does not acknowledge this threat exists. It also misses evidence of neglect and unbalanced power in the relationship between Naomi and Ruth, a relationship to which I will return in the following section.

The minimization of violence in language describing Ruth's situation in the fields of Bethlehem mirrors similar processes in interpretive communities, such as in the commonly used language of "peaceful settlement" rather than "invasion" to describe the arrival of British colonizers in Australia. Such language obscures ongoing processes of colonization that displace Indigenous sovereignty to avoid discomfort for Settlers. Watego critiques the violent erasure of Indigenous presence and identity in Australia, as Settlers frame invasion out of their perspective (2021, 190–91). Indigenous erasure, she argues, is seen in Settler ignorance of Indigenous presence where they live and "is rendered irrelevant to them, precisely because of its relevance to them" (Watego 2021, 191). Returning to the book of Ruth, the desire to make the story "nice" turns away from language in the text that highlights violence associated with the fields. Alongside this, behaviors in the text that interpreters might find confronting are minimized, concurrently rendering the text ineffectual in discussion about ugly or violent elements that exist within interpretive communities (see Cottrill 2021, 20–24).

Watego's critique of the supposed peace of settler colonial space is particularly sharp regarding hope (2021, 189–218). Noting the long-term systemic injustice experienced by Indigenous peoples in Australia, she rejects hope as a useful concept, arguing that belief that "one sweet day, in one sweet move, race will be overcome" enables the continuation of colonial structures while providing a false sense of respite for Indigenous peoples (2021, 189, 194–98). In contrast, Watego advocates a nihilism that celebrates Indigenous living "not to sing of hope, but to speak to exhaustion and disappointment" (2021, 204). She identifies hope as a turning away from the harm of colonization on Indigenous bodies, "waiting for a good future while we live in a permanent hell" (2021, 197). Turning instead toward living "another day in the colony," she argues that for Indigenous people, "accepting the truth of the limitations of this place offers us far more promise than hope ever has" such that "the strategy for living in this place is found ... in the ugly truths told in the songs of the marginalized" (2021, 206–8). Watego recounts the "indignation, outrage, and patronizing concern" with which Settlers meet her rejection of hope as "irresponsible," affronted as she punctures Settler assumptions that Australia is a "good" place (2021, 197). I find resonance of Naomi's fierce grief and anger in Watego's confrontation. Naomi does not act as might be expected but refuses to be placated by hope. She rails against God, confronts the women of Bethlehem, and ignores Ruth.

Naomi's grief at the death of her family and her displacement from home is evident. Traditionally this grief is used as a plot set-up to highlight the providence of God (Block 2015, 109–11; Bush 1996, 45). Naomi does not hold back in her attribution of blame to God either in conversation with her daughters-in-law or with the women of Bethlehem. In seeking to turn Ruth and Orpah away from her on the road, Naomi states that her bitter experience derives from God (1:13). When the Bethlehemite women buzz over her return, she rejects their welcome and along with it the name Naomi, with its sweet and pleasant connotations (vv. 19–20). She names herself Mara, "bitter," to match the harsh experience of leaving Bethlehem full of family and returning empty, again attributing this depletion to God (v. 21). The violence minimized when Naomi's grief is overlooked is that of circumstance, out of her control, that shatters any sense that she is content. To minimize Naomi's grief is to discount her perspective and explain away her circumstances.

There is an interpretive tension held in Naomi's grief which, on the one hand, highlights her honesty and, on the other, seeks to move her quickly from anger to a posture of praise. Naomi can be likened to other Hebrew Bible characters who complain against God, particularly Job. Her grief-fueled accusations, however, have also been portrayed as illogical, confused, or uncomprehending by interpreters who posit that God's actions *must* be just, even if that justice is "mysterious" (Bush 1996, 86; Hubbard Jr. 1988, 14; Taute and Potgieter 2020, 2). Daniel Block, for example, characterizes Naomi's bitterness as "less than ideal" (2015, 51). He critiques her understanding of God as lacking in maturity and orthodoxy as she blames God for her circumstances (2015, 90–91, 99–105). Block's minimization of Naomi's agency protects God's character as faithful and just. Naomi's bitterness is seen as a teaching tool that will demonstrate these very characteristics of God. This requires turning away from the essence of Naomi's accusation, along with the possibility that hers might be an appropriate response to deep loss.

Neglect of Naomi's grief also points to the disregard of older women that is often found within Western cultures, a disregard that intensifies for Indigenous women and women of color (see Westwood 2023). Older women recount experiences of invisibility as they are overlooked, an experience which aligns with much commentary on the character of Naomi. Most obviously, the narrative is named for Ruth, despite Naomi being the woman who first centers (1:3) and then directs the plot (v. 6) and in whose name Obed is celebrated at its denouement (4:17). Yet commentary often sidelines the story of Naomi to focus on Ruth's trajectory. Turning towards Naomi allows her to be seen as a wise elder and grandmother. Her grief at the loss of home, husband, and sons might be honored and seen as a bridge between this character and the many who mourn. Her anger need not be minimized as an opportunity for her to learn about God's providence but explored as an appropriate and good response to unfair, unjust circumstances.

In turning towards Naomi's grief, I hear resonance of ugly rhetoric that simmers in Australia in the commentary that passes over her experience. While not wishing to suggest any easy equivalence between characters in the book of Ruth and contemporary understandings of Indigenous and Settler identity, I note that dominant and dominating Settler rhetoric often works to minimize the multiple griefs experienced by Indigenous peoples in this place, from stolen land to ongoing material disadvantage seen in decreased life expectancy as compared to other Australians, high rates of chronic health issues, and the highest proportion of incarceration worldwide, all the while packaging this disadvantage as a deficit of Indigenous peoples rather than as colonial legacy (see Brigg and Murphy 2011, 23; Kowal 2015, 40–42; Leane 2010, 32–39; Strakosch 2021, 342; Watego 2021, 109). To this is asked the question of why Aboriginal and Torres Strait Islander peoples cannot just "get over it" and "move on." The "it" here stands in for the whole process of colonization and the impact of ongoing colonial legacies on Indigenous land, lifeways, and culture. Reflecting on presiding at funeral after funeral after funeral, Kabi Kabi and Gurang Gurang theologian Uncle Ray Minniecon notes the exhaustion that comes from grief at too much death (Minniecon and Broughton, 2022).

Why can Naomi not just get over her grief? After all, Ruth has vowed herself to Naomi (1:16–17) and made the journey with her from Moab to Bethlehem, accompanied only by Naomi's silence (vv. 18–21). I am not suggesting that Naomi's experience is equivalent to that of Aboriginal and Torres Strait Islander peoples in Australia or other minoritized peoples elsewhere. I am arguing that the process of turning away from Naomi's grief can work to frame out the experiences of real people in material situations. To refuse Naomi's anger and grief is to push aside the anger and grief that calls dominating and dominant common sense into question. To turn toward her anger is to enter its unsettling accusations against Naomi's assumed status quo, including against God. It is, perhaps, to listen to Watego indict hope as disabling for Indigenous sovereignty (2021, 189–218). Watego writes:

> I have been in countless meetings with colonisers who hold positions of power where they perform care or interest or helpfulness, but fail to actually offer anything. Rather than allow them to impose a sense of disorienting or dispossessing hope or helplessness upon my body, I find joy in dealing with the truth of things and act accordingly – it really confuses them. (2021, 217)

Naomi's defiance resonates with Watego's strategy. I am *not* Naomi, she says, call me Mara (v. 20).

Amidst celebrating strong women and eventual resolution of its story, the book of Ruth points towards violent possibility in assault, displacement, and grief. To sit in the tension between these possibilities is to open my gaze toward the communities in which I live and work where violence is also routinely passed over. Whose experiences of violence have I been taught to overlook because my body moves with ease? If I acknowledge Naomi as Mara and hear her pain, who else might disrupt my status quo? This first "but" stirs up questions about the setting of the book and its assumptions. In the next section, I turn to relationships between characters and the tension between love and exploitation.

4. The Second "But": Loving Family and Self-Serving Exploitation

In the previous section I highlighted the invisibility of Naomi's grief and anger in much interpretation. Focus on Naomi's character, however, foregrounds the second interpretive tension between loving and exploitative relationships. The book of Ruth is often celebrated for its depiction of family, highlighting a positive and reciprocal relationship between Ruth and Naomi in contrast to the rivalry between other pairs of biblical women such as Sarah and Hagar or Rachel and Leah. Saul Olyan, for example, names Ruth and Naomi as "peers" in a mutually reciprocal relationship of chosen friendship (2021, 33–35). Yet, if the relationship between Naomi and Ruth is one of chosen friendship, Naomi's engagement seems more akin to "frenemies" than "bffs." Naomi, on the one hand, moves between praising (1:8), ignoring (v. 18), manipulating (3:1-4), and displacing (4:16) her daughter-in-law. Ruth, on the other hand, offers a vow of allegiance to Naomi without response from her mother-in-law (1:16-17), takes responsibility to provide for Naomi's needs (2:2; 3:5; 4:13), and acts a surrogate mother on her behalf (4:17), seeming both to comply with and counter Naomi's expectations of her. Interpretation that turns away from the complications of this relationship misses the uneven power dynamics between the two women, whose relationship is critical to understanding the story.

Ruth's ambiguous relationship with Naomi is seen as Naomi responds to Ruth's vow of commitment (1:16-17) with silence (v. 18). The ambiguity held in the women's relationship comes into focus as Ruth goes to glean (2:2-17) and in the circumstances that lead to her presence on the threshing floor (3:1-5). These scenes are discomforting, given the question as to what extent the characters are motivated by mutual love or to manipulate circumstances for their own gain. Tension also arises within these possibilities as there is no reason these must be set against each other. Rather, love and self-preservation or loyalty and manipulation could be concurrent motivational factors for the characters.

On arrival in Bethlehem, Ruth takes the initiative to seek out the food that she and Naomi require (2:2-3). Ruth is noticed as an outsider (vv. 5-6), a body out-of-place in Boaz's field, dependent on the harvesters to leave something on the edges. While the Torah laws offer provisions for gleaners (Lev 19:9-10; 23:22; Deut 24:19-22), it is ambiguous as to whether Ruth, as a Moabite, is included within their provisions. As a Bethlehemite widow, however, Naomi would be included within the provision of these laws. The question arises as to why she does not accompany Ruth or direct her to a welcoming field, given the text has already named her kinsman as Boaz (Ruth 2:1) and will go on to name the existence of another, closer, relative (3:12). These omissions suggest a lack of care about Ruth on Naomi's part. Naomi is perhaps too old to glean or too wounded by grief to care for food. Ruth may then be understood as "brave, never-complaining, hard-working and sacrificing" (Saxegaard 2010, 105). She takes up the care of her mother-in-law in a time of Naomi's frailty. Ruth's provision is often celebrated as is seen in Edward Campbell, for example, who argues that

> Ruth in relation to Naomi is a diligent younger companion, strong enough to do the gleaning, considerate in bringing home not only the fruit of her work but also the leftovers of her meal at the field, and exuberant in reporting her adventures and accepting Naomi's reaction and advice. (Campbell, Ruth, 111)

Ruth undertakes what is necessary to survive, but she does this willingly for Naomi's sake.

There is a shadow side, however, to Ruth's determined labor in the fields seen in interpretations that compare Ruth to modern workers with few rights and choices (Brenner 1999, 2010; Lim 2020). Drawing on the culture of Christian, middle-class families in his Singaporean location, Chin Ming Stephen Lim, for example, parallels Ruth with the foreign domestic workers such families employ. He observes that "what makes Ruth exceptional is that the needs of Naomi (as a woman of the host culture) will always supersede her own (as a foreign woman)" (Lim, 2020 132). This shifts the relationship of Naomi and Ruth, highlighting the subservience of the younger Moabite woman to Naomi, who waits to receive grain and food. Lim goes on to note the stereotyping of foreign domestic workers in Singapore as a social contaminant – poor, sexualized, and imagined as petty thieves – who are thus subject to high levels of surveillance (Lim 2020, 126). The text alludes to surveillance of Ruth in the fields, by the supervisor (2:6–7) and by Boaz, who asks to whom she belongs (v. 5) and who gives explicit directions regarding her to his workers (15–16). The disjunction in Naomi and Ruth's relationship intensifies when Naomi sets out a plan for her daughter-in-law to surprise Boaz on the threshing floor (3:1–4). Ruth is instructed to beautify herself (wash, anoint, dress) and secretly approach a sleeping Boaz after he has satisfied himself with food and drink (vv. 3–4). Naomi tells Ruth that Boaz will then direct her actions (v. 4). Ruth agrees to do what Naomi has asked of her (v. 5) and the scene unfolds, full of sexual double entendre (Schipper 2016, 156–57) and ambiguity as to Naomi's expectations (Fewell and Gunn 1990, 78).

While the sexual ambiguity of what takes place between Ruth and Boaz has been noted since the earliest interpretations, the argument that this ambiguity is present to exemplify the good character of Boaz and Ruth for *not* engaging in sex can be found from the Targum to Ruth and *Ruth Rabbah* to more contemporary scholars including Campbell and Block. This position is difficult to hold, with a gap between scholars and other interpreters. Sakenfeld's experience teaching the book of Ruth among teenage girls in India is illuminating. Her students' response caused her to rethink her earlier commentary on the threshing floor scene:

> I recall vividly telling this part of the story to a group of twelfth year high school girls in a Christian hostel in a boarding school in northern India. The girls were nearly all from small villages where the tradition of threshing the rice and guarding the harvest against thieves was part of their own context. I had been asked to teach them an Old Testament story, and was summarizing the plot of Ruth with one of the girls serving as translator for the others. When I reached this part about Naomi's

instructions, the girls with one accord began tittering. I didn't need any translation help to understand their reaction. The girls imagined Ruth fixing herself up to entice Boaz in a situation that they had been taught should be avoided at all costs by any self-respecting woman. Boys and girls should not meet in the dark. They were sure Ruth ought not to be putting herself forward to a man in the night in this way, even though their teenage hormones made them quite interested in observing the boys' hostel from afar. It is fair to say that the reaction of those Indian teenagers set me on the road to this paper. I began to realize that I had subconsciously protected a traditional version of Ruth's 'morality' that excused on various scholarly pretexts her approach to Boaz. I had not faced up sufficiently to the reality of what Ruth was doing. (Sakenfeld 2002, 165)

This account suggests a domestication of the text when scholars turn away from the possibility of sex because it does not match their assumptions of appropriate relationships between unmarried men and women or behavior befitting characters in Scripture. Furthermore, turning toward the possibility of sex creates a conundrum for the relationship between Naomi and Ruth.

In traditional interpretations, Naomi's motivation in sending Ruth to the threshing floor is marriage to Boaz, drawing upon the Levirate tradition (Deut 25:5–10). Bush, for example, argues that Naomi is unconcerned with Elimelech's legacy and acts out of concern for the security and wellbeing of Ruth herself (1996, 142). Again, there is a disjunction between scholarly and other interpretations, such as observed by Rhiannon Graybill among her undergraduate students:

When I teach Ruth, my students often argue that Naomi pimps Ruth out to Boaz. When I read the first student paper reading Naomi as a sex trafficker, I was surprised. Now, I read at least one such paper nearly every time I teach the text. (Graybill 2021, 321; and Chapter 13 in this volume)

Naomi exploits Ruth, seeking to entrap Boaz sexually, to force his ongoing provision for her and perhaps to reclaim the land belonging to Elimelech. She knows the consequences for Ruth could be severe, given the association of the threshing floor with prostitution (Hos 9:1) and the possibility that a Moabite might easily be assumed acting outside accepted sexual mores. The multiple allusions to the story of Tamar and Judah (Gen 38) within the threshing floor scene (see Lindsay 2022; Van Wolde 1997) point to the potential consequences for Ruth if she is identified as sleeping around. When Judah discovers Tamar's pregnancy, he calls for her to be put to death (v. 24), only to relinquish when she offers evidence that he is the father (vv. 25–26). Naomi risks Ruth's life for the sake of her own future.

Naomi's sexual manipulation of Ruth leads some scholars to identify her as a pimp (Graybill 2021, 321; Koosed 2011, 89). Fulata Lusungu Moyo (2016) goes further, drawing on her experience of sexual abuse to identify Naomi as a sex trafficker. She argues that Ruth's body is objectified and used for the sake of Naomi's survival, with Ruth's survival entangled within this exploitation (Moyo 2016, 87). While both women are vulnerable, Moyo points to their uneven power and different standing within Bethlehem, where "Naomi uses Ruth's beauty and youth as potential for reclaiming her property and decent livelihood" (2016, 90). Ruth as foreigner is reliant upon Naomi, who is considered to belong to the community.

Some interpretations highlight Naomi and Ruth's relationship as one of reciprocal care. Others point to the exploitative ways that Naomi uses Ruth. Discomfort emerges in trying to hold these characterizations together, smoothing out the tension between them into an either/or. Yet, stepping into the uncomfortable contradictions of the relationship between Naomi and Ruth enables readers to see the complicated entanglement of these women with each other and with their circumstances. Naomi may be taking advantage of her younger daughter-in-law to do the hard work of gleaning. Ruth may also be taking advantage of Naomi's community connections. Naomi may be exploiting Ruth sexually to manipulate Boaz. Ruth's ability to consent may be limited, but in instructing Boaz (3:9), rather than waiting for him to instruct her in their encounter, she also demonstrates agency in moving beyond Naomi's directions (v.5). Naomi's end goal may be selfish, but it may also reflect the desperation of both women, who have limited options if they want to survive. This may all be true alongside genuine affection and care between the women ... or not.

The discomfort in this possibility turns Settler readers towards a similar discomfort in uncovering their complicity in systems of colonial exploitation and control. I am reminded of a story recounted by Marda Marda writer Stephen Kinnane (2020) as he traces the story of his Aboriginal grandmother Jessie and English grandfather Edward. Jessie spent her childhood in a mission home for Aboriginal children who had been removed (stolen) from their families. Kinnane recounts visiting with Baby Jones, the daughter of mission managers remembered fondly by his grandmother, as he sought to learn more about his grandmother's early life (2020, 86). In their conversation, he is struck that Baby Jones cannot see the difference between her childhood and that of Jessie and the other Indigenous children living in the mission home. Kinnane observes that, despite her privilege and freedom as compared to the other children, Baby Jones sees her childhood as equivalent to theirs. Jessie and Baby Jones grew up eating, playing, washing, praying together, their lives entangled in a shared "home." Genuine affection is named by both. Yet,

> Baby Jones does not seem to realise that she was not one of them. Simply by having her parents, she was not one of them. She got to keep the name her parents had given her and live the choices in life they would make for her. When she turned sixteen she would not be sent out as a domestic servant. (Kinnane 2020, 87)

The opportunities and dreams available to Jessie and Baby Jones were not the same, even if Baby Jones was unable to articulate this. Similarly, no matter the affection or commitments that may be present, Naomi and Ruth's relationship is one of imbalanced power.

5. The Third "But": Model Israelite or Suspicious Moabite?

The relationship between Ruth and Naomi is ambiguous in its entanglement of care and exploitation. A similar tension is held within the characterization of Ruth herself, when she is celebrated as a foreigner integrated into the story of Israel and ancestor of leaders (Block 2015, 51–55; Hubbard 1988, 72–74; Lau and Goswell 2016, Ch 9). Such celebration of Ruth requires her character to be molded into something unified, almost shedding her Moabiteness to embrace her acceptance into the Bethlehemite community. Ruth is seen as exemplary in loyal lovingkindness through her dedication to Naomi and Naomi's God (Campbell 1975, 80–82; Lau and Goswell 2016, Ch 3), through her hard work and provision for her mother-in-law (Block 2015, 116–18), and through the "plenty" enabled by her eventual remarriage and motherhood (Trible 1976, 277). Praise of Ruth's character is explicit within the text: the field overseer observes her tireless determination (2:7), Boaz states that the people of Bethlehem recognize her to be a woman of valor (3:13), and she is lauded by the townswomen as worth more to Naomi than seven sons (4:15). There is also implicit blessing by God who is credited with Ruth's conceiving Obed (4:13). Ruth, "the daughter-in-law faithful beyond death," resolves Naomi's emptiness, mediating Naomi's "transformation to life" (Trible 1976, 277). Completing the story is the double genealogy of King David, who represents a golden era of Israelite history, of which Ruth, while unnamed, is a key part (4:17–22).

Eschewing Ruth's Moabiteness, however, turns away from her complex and complicated identity. Much is written to explain whether and how Ruth the Moabite finds belonging in Bethlehem, querying whether she moves, assimilates, integrates, translates, and/or is absorbed between

Moabite and Israelite identity (Honig 1997; Southwood 2014). Gale Yee also draws on the categorization of Asian Americans by White society as both "model minority" and "perpetual foreigner" to argue that Ruth is also caught between conflicting identities placed upon her by the Israelite community (Yee 2018, 2009). She is a *gēr* akin to Abraham (Gen 12:1–4; see Ruth 2:11) and, simultaneously, a *nokrîyâ* akin to the women sent away by Ezra (Ezra 10; see Ruth 2:10). Caution is required in not assuming that ancient Near Eastern conceptions of identity map onto modern ones or the modern concept of ethnicity (see Thambyrajah 2021; and Chapter 6 in this volume). The likely postexilic dating of a book that recounts a story set in pre-monarchic time further complicates how its writers, editors, and characters might understand their belonging to and with land and nation (Brenner 2013, 308–10; Yee 2018, 64–66). Turning toward Ruth's belonging as complicated, however, might enable nuanced discussion of identity among complex interpretive communities.

Identity is a slippery thing. As I turn toward Ruth's complex and complicated belongings, a sleight of hand becomes clearer in the text. The story, of course, begins with Elimelech and his family (1:1). Later, after the death of Elimelech and his sons, when Boaz negotiates for Naomi's land before the elders at the city gate (4:1–12), he equates his purpose in marrying Ruth as desire to ensure Elimelech's legacy is not lost (vv. 5, 9–10). Yet Obed is never named for Elimelech or for Mahlon, nor really for Ruth, whose name disappears from the story immediately after his birth (v. 13). Obed is instead named as Naomi's child (v. 17), taken to Naomi's breast (v. 16), and described as joy in her gray-haired days (v. 15). He is then embedded into Boaz's genealogy, which leads to David (vv. 18–22), extinguishing the names he was meant to bear. I wonder how Obed would reflect on this and tell the story of his parentage and belonging: complex, complicated, multiple, messy.

The possibility of Obed knowing his Moabite heritage is also imagined by Musa Dube in the letters that Orpah might have sent Ruth after returning to Moab (Dube 1999). In Orpah's voice Dube writes: "when you have borne children, you should tell them these stories of the Moabites: of their origins, of their kindness, of their hospitality and of their struggles for survival" (Dube 1999, 150). Here, Moab does not exist to symbolize what is opposite to Israel but evokes its own way of thinking and being in the world. A similar movement is seen as Cherokee scholar Laura Donaldson turns toward the often neglected character of Orpah as "the one who does not reject her traditions or her sacred ancestors" (1999, 143).

As Dube undercuts assumptions about Moab in biblical narratives, Euayelai and Gamillaroi scholar Larissa Behrendt (2016) critiques pejorative stereotypes and tropes of Indigenous people, particularly Indigenous women, that occur in Australian colonial storytelling. She takes as a prime example the story of Eliza Fraser, a white woman shipwrecked on K'gari in 1836, who subsequently spent time among the Butchulla people, the island's traditional owners. Eliza's story is retold many times by Settlers, usually naming her as in danger among the Indigenous peoples: the men pose a threat and danger to her while the women are jealous of her civility (Behrendt 2016, 37–55). Depicted as vulnerable, innocent, and chaste, Eliza must survive the threat of violation until such time as she is rescued by other white people and returned to safety. The Butchulla, however, have their own oral histories of encountering Eliza. These highlight their care of a severely sunburnt woman who was offered protection and kindness (Behrendt 2016, 57–59). The characterizations of the Butchulla people in the colonial telling of this story are used to justify their dispossession, as they are cast as uncivilized and unlawful, and thus unworthy of land (Behrendt 2016, 9). This characterization simultaneously pushes aside the more common experience of Aboriginal women abused by settler men to portray a sole white woman's "captivity" (Behrendt 2016, 64). As Behrendt observes, from her Indigenous standpoint, "Eliza Fraser's story says: 'they' are the barbarians, not 'us'" (2016, 55).

The way Fraser's story is told presents a problematic caricature of Indigenous peoples that lingers in ongoing stereotypes (see, for example, Grant 2019; Healy 2008; Langton 2003; Leane 2010). How to understand and name identity is a tension present within settler colonial contexts. Avril Bell critiques the "us and them" colonizer/colonized binary that is foundational to colonization:

> the problem with binaries is not the existence of difference per se, but the hierarchical valuation of difference and the either/or assumptions involved ... Overcoming colonial binaries requires overcoming the problematic demand for unity/singularity, the demand that there is only one way to be modern and only one way to belong to these settler nation-states. (Bell 2014, 17)

The assumed binary that pits settler vs indigene, male vs female, civilized vs savage is similar to the sense of hierarchy that seeks to play Moabites off against Israelites in the book of Ruth. It is a binary that sidelines curiosity, turning away from engaging difference.

Behrendt ends her book on Fraser by introducing another character from Australia's colonial history: William Dawes, an English engineer and surveyor who arrived with the British First Fleet. She contrasts the curiosity Dawes displayed about the First Nations peoples he encountered and about the land that he had come to inhabit (Behrendt 2016, 194–202). While acknowledging that colonization would still have been a reality impacting Indigenous peoples and land, Behrendt wonders what might have been different if Dawes's curiosity had been at its forefront rather than Fraser's fear (Behrendt 2016, 199). Following Behrendt, I wonder how a posture of curiosity rather than antagonism might read Ruth's character differently. Much interpretation focuses on the extent to which Ruth is or is not Moabite and/or Israelite at various points of the narrative. Perhaps Ruth, like Dawes, is curious about the language and culture of her mother-in-law. Perhaps Bethlehem and those within it might also be curious about how to engage with the difference that Ruth brings among them. In raising these questions, the book of Ruth and Behrendt combine in eschewing binaries that dehumanize those who are different. They invite conversation about how to hold difference in tension in communities where it is weaponized or linked to injustice. This invitation is not to a simplistic and naïve romanticism but a wrestling for life against a violent backdrop in which options may be limited and structures may be suffocating.

6. Turning Away and Turning Towards

Remaining within interpretive tension is hard for those trained to read within Western, Settler frameworks. Such thinking includes a tendency towards universalized experience which synthesizes disparate ideas into a whole. This synthesis is comfortable and comforting over and against the ambiguity of in-betweens. Traditional biblical interpretation tends to turn away from ambiguity, precluding the discomfort that comes when readings cannot be easily resolved into positive, happy, and "good" interpretations. Such reading is unstable, however, because there is something else to turn toward, the tension held, for example, in the three "buts" explored in this chapter. The positive readings of Ruth as charming and liberative are good readings and beautiful ones. They are worth celebrating. They are not, however, the only good readings, and perhaps not the only beautiful ones. Rather, it is important for interpreters to avoid minimizing the aspects of biblical text that cause discomfort within cultural settings distant and different from those ancient Hebrew cultures that created them. Reflecting on Australian history, Indigenous scholar Mary Spiers Williams also cautions against feeling too comfortable. She urges readers to "stay with the paradoxes, recognise the gaps in the account, become conscious of positioning. I encourage you not to stabilise the uncertainties, especially the uncomfortable ones. The past is not yet over" (Nugent et al. 2022, 11). Readings of Ruth that focus on what is violent, exploitative, or problematic in the text invite us into these gaps and uncertainties.

I find reading with new conversation partners helpful in turning towards what I have learned not to see in the book of Ruth. Reading contrapuntally by placing the narrative alongside texts authored by Indigenous scholars helps to change the positions of the switch described by Ahmed (2017, 32). In a similar way, bringing the Ruth narrative into conversation with Australian settler colonial legacies brings different learnings to this context, at times puncturing (my) settler common sense and highlighting the limitations of (my) knowing. It is hard to unsee the violence, assimilation, and exploitation present in the book of Ruth. It is similarly difficult to unsee these elements within settler colonial Australia. Both cause (me) discomfort. Williams asks me to remain uncomfortable, rather than moving quickly to resolve tension. Ahmed points out that the switch, once turned on, is difficult to switch back off, although the tenacity of colonizing legacies suggests that this possibility always remains.

Why can we not just leave Ruth alone and let the book be idyllic? Or why can we not let it just be all violence and oppression? Graybill (2021, 330–31) notes her own wistful desire for the narrative to be simple, rather than entangled between positive and negative behaviors and attributes. Noticing these entanglements and sitting in the tension they create is both uncomfortable and potentially transformative. As I turn from what traditional interpretation obscures in biblical texts to embrace the messy, complex, complicated shadows of characters and settings, I might learn to similarly turn my attention to what I am taught to ignore in the "real world." This is Ahmed's political labor of noticing and turning toward. When I leave Ruth alone, unwilling to acknowledge violence, exploitation, or flattened identity, my reading teaches me to bracket out violence, exploitation, and assimilative practices in my context. Turning toward these elements within the biblical text might help to turn my attention toward what my settler common sense seeks to erase.

Works Cited

Ahmed, Sara. 2017. *Living a Feminist Life*. Durham NC: Duke University Press.

Alpert, Rebecca. 1994. "Finding Our Past: A Lesbian Interpretation of the Book of Ruth." Pages 91–96 in *Reading Ruth: Contemporary Women Reclaim A Sacred Story*, edited by Judith A. Kates and Gail Twersky Reimer. New York: Ballantine.

Anderson, Matthew R. 2019. "'Aware-Settler' Biblical Studies: Breaking Claims of Textual Ownership." *Journal for Interdisciplinary Biblical Studies* 1 (1): 42–68.

Arthur, Jay. 1999. "The Eighth Day of Creation." *Journal of Australian Studies* 23 (61): 65–74. https://doi.org/10.1080/14443059909387475.

Bailey, Randall C., Tat-siong Benny Liew, and Fernando F. Segovia. 2009. *They Were All Together in One Place? Toward Minority Biblical Criticism.* Semeia Studies 57. Atlanta: SBL.

Battell Lowman, Emma, and Adam J. Barker. 2015. *Settler: Identity and Colonialism in 21st Century Canada.* Halifax and Winnipeg: Fernwood.

Bauman, Zygmunt. 1993. *Modernity and Ambivalence.* Cambridge: Polity.

Behrendt, Larissa. 2010a. "Asserting the Doctrine of Discovery in Australia." Pages 187–206 in *Discovering Indigenous Lands,* edited by Robert Miller, Jacinta Ruru, Larissa Behrendt, and Tracey Lindberg. Oxford: Oxford University Press.

–––––. 2010b. "The Doctrine of Discovery in Australia." Pages 171–86 In *Discovering Indigenous Lands.* edited by Robert Miller, Jacinta Ruru, Larissa Behrendt, and Tracey Lindberg. Oxford: Oxford University Press.

–––––. 2016. *Finding Eliza: Power and Colonial Storytelling.* St Lucia, Qld: University of Queensland Press.

Bell, Avril. 2014. *Relating Indigenous and Settler Identities Beyond Domination.* London: Palgrave Macmillan.

Bledstein, Adrien J. 1993. "Female Companionships: If the Book of Ruth Were Written by a Woman...." Pages 116–33 in *A Feminist Companion to Ruth,* edited by Athalya Brenner. London: Bloomsbury.

Block, Daniel I. 2015. *Ruth: The King Is Coming.* Zondervan Exegetical Commentary on the Old Testament 8. Grand Rapids: Zondervan.

Brenner, Athalya. 1999. "Ruth as Foreign Worker and the Politics of Exogamy." Pages 158–62 in *Ruth and Esther: A Feminist Companion to the Bible* (Second Series), edited by Athalya Brenner. Sheffield: Sheffield Academic.

–––––. 2010. "From Ruth to the 'Global Woman': Social and Legal Aspects." *Interpretation* 64 (2): 162–68. https://doi.org/10.1177/002096431006400204.

–––––. 2013. "Ruth: The Art of Memorizing Past Enemies, Ambiguously." Pages 306–10 in *Remembering Biblical Figures in the Late Persian and Early Hellenistic Periods: Social Memory and Imagination,* edited by Diana V. Edelman and Ehud Ben Zvi. Oxford: Oxford University Press.

Brett, Mark G. 2009. *Decolonizing God: The Bible in the Tides of Empire.* Sheffield: Sheffield Phoenix.

–––––., and Naomi Wolfe. 2020. "Sovereignty: Indigenous Counter-Examples." *International Journal of Public Theology* 14 (1): 24–40. https://doi.org/10.1163/15697320-12341599.

Brigg, Morgan, and Lyndon Murphy. 2011. "Beyond Captives and Captors: Settler-Indigenous Governance for the 21st Century." Pages 16–31 in *Unsettling the Settler State Creativity and Resistance in Indigenous Settler-State Governance,* edited by Sarah Maddison and Morgan Brigg. Annandale, NSW: Federation Press.

Bush, Frederic. 1996. *Ruth, Esther.* WBC 9. Dallas: Word.

Campbell, Edward F. Jr. 1975. *Ruth: A New Translation with Introduction, Notes, and Commentary*. Anchor Bible Commentary 7. Garden City NY: Doubleday.

Caspi, Mishael, and Rachel Havrelock. 1996. *Women on the Biblical Road: Ruth, Naomi and the Female Journey*. Lanham MD: University Press of America.

Chapman, Cynthia R. 2023. "The Field Belonging to Boaz: Creating Kinship through Land, Labor, Food, and Feeding." *Journal of Biblical Literature* 142 (3): 431–50. https://doi.org/10.15699/jbl.1423.2023.4.

Cottrill, Amy. 2021. *Uncovering Violence: Reading Biblical Narratives as an Ethical Project*. Louisville: Presbyterian Publishing Corporation.

Curthoys, Ann. 1999. "Expulsion, Exodus and Exile in White Australian Historical Mythology." *Journal of Australian Studies* 23 (61): 1–19. https://doi.org/10.1080/14443059909387469.

Dijk-Hemmes, Fokkelien van. 1993. "Ruth: The Product of a Woman's Culture?" Pages 134–39 in *A Feminist Companion to Ruth*, edited by Athalya Brenner. Sheffield: Sheffield Academic.

Donaldson, Laura E. 1999. "The Sign of Orpah." Pages 130–44 in *Ruth and Esther: A Feminist Companion to the Bible*, edited by Athalya Brenner. Sheffield: Sheffield Academic.

Dube, Musa W. 1999. "The Unpublished Letters of Orpah to Ruth." Pages 145–50 in *Ruth and Esther: A Feminist Companion to the Bible*, edited by Athalya Brenner. Sheffield: Sheffield Academic.

Eskenazi, Tamara Cohn, and Tikva Simone Frymer-Kensky. 2011. *The JPS Bible Commentary: Ruth: The Traditional Hebrew Text with the New JPS Translation*. Philadelphia: Jewish Publication Society.

Fewell, Danna Nolan, and David M. Gunn. 1990. *Compromising Redemption: Relating Characters in the Book of Ruth*. Literary Currents in Biblical Interpretation. Louisville: Westminster John Knox.

Fischer, Irmtraud. 1999. "The Book of Ruth: a 'Feminist' Commentary to the Torah." Pages 24–49 in *Ruth and Esther: A Feminist Companion to the Bible 2/3*, edited by Athalya Brenner. Sheffield: Sheffield Academic.

Grant, Stan. 2019. *On Identity*. Melbourne: Melbourne University Press.

Graybill, Rhiannon. 2021. "'Even unto This Bitter Loving': Unhappiness and Backward Feelings in Ruth." *Biblical Interpretation* 29 (3): 308–31. https://doi.org/10.1163/15685152-00284P11.

------. 2023. "Conquest's Compulsion: Against the Promise of the Promised Land in the Hebrew Bible." Pages 45–64 in *Lee Edelman and the Queer Study of Religion*, edited by Kent L. Brintnall, Rhiannon Graybill, and Linn Marie Tonstad. New York: Routledge.

Griffin, Laura. 2021. "Terrorizing Indigenous Women in the Contact Zone: Placing Cozbi and the Midianites in Colonial Australia." Pages 17–36 in *Terror in the Bible: Rhetoric, Gender, and Violence*, edited by Monica Jyostna Melanchthon and Robyn J. Whitaker. Atlanta: SBL.

Havea, Jione. 2011. "The Cons of Contextuality... Kontextuality." Pages 38–52 in *Contextual Theology for the Twenty-First Century*, edited by Stephen B. Bevans and Katalina Tahaafe-Williams. Eugene, OR: Pickwick.

———. 2021. *Losing Ground: Reading Ruth in the Pacific*. London: SCM.

Havrelock, Rachel. 2020. *The Joshua Generation: Israeli Occupation and the Bible*. Princeton NJ: Princeton University Press.

Hawk, L. Daniel. 2012. "The Truth about Conquest: Joshua as History, Narrative, and Scripture." *Interpretation* 66 (2): 129–40. https://doi.org/10.1177/0020964311434872.

Healy, Chris. 2008. *Forgetting Aborigines*. Sydney: UNSW Press.

Honig, Bonnie. 1997. "Ruth, the Model Émigrée: Mourning and the Symbolic Politics of Immigration." *Political Theory* 25 (1): 112–36. https://doi.org/10.1177/0090591797025001006.

Hubbard Jr., Robert L. 1988. *The Book of Ruth*. New International Commentary on the Old Testament. Grand Rapids: Eerdmans.

Kinnane, Stephen. 2020. *Shadow Lines*. Corrected edition. Fremantle, WA: Fremantle Press.

Koosed, Jennifer. 2011. *Gleaning Ruth: A Biblical Heroine and Her Afterlives*. Studies on Personalities of the Old Testament. Columbia: University of South Carolina Press.

Kowal, Emma. 2015. *Trapped in the Gap: Doing Good in Indigenous Australia*. New York: Berghahn.

Kwok, Pui-Lan. 2021. *Postcolonial Politics and Theology: Unveiling Empire for a Global World*. Louisville: Westminster John Knox.

Langton, Marcia. 2003. "Aboriginal Art and Film: The Politics of Representation." Pages 109–24 in *Blacklines: Contemporary Critical Writing by Indigenous Australians*, edited by Michele Grossman,. Carlton, Vic: Melbourne University Press.

Lau, Peter. 2010. *Identity and Ethics in the Book of Ruth: A Social Identity Approach*. Beihefte zur Zeitschrift für die Alttestamentliche Wissenschaft 416. Berlin: De Gruyter.

Lau, Peter, and Gregory Goswell. 2016. *Unceasing Kindness: A Biblical Theology of Ruth*. New Studies in Biblical Theology. Downers Grove IL: Apollos.

Leane, Jeanine. 2010. "Aboriginal Representation: Conflict or Dialogue in the Academy." *Australian Journal of Indigenous Education* 39 (Supplementary): 32–39.

Liew, Tat-siong Benny, and Fernando F. Segovia. 2022. *Reading Biblical Texts Together: Pursuing Minoritized Biblical Criticism*. Semeia Studies 98. Atlanta: SBL Press.

Lim, Chin Ming Stephen. 2019. *Contextual Biblical Hermeneutics as Multicentric Dialogue: Towards a Singaporean Reading of Daniel*. Biblical Interpretation 175. Leiden: Brill.

———. 2020. "Ruth as Esperanza? A Trans-Textual Reading of Ruth with Foreign Domestic Workers in Singapore." Pages 122–39 in *Faith, Class, and*

Labor: Intersectional Approaches in a Global Context, edited by Jin Young Choi and Joerg Rieger. Eugene OR: Pickwick.

Linafelt, Tod. 1999. "Ruth." In *Ruth & Esther*, by Tod Linafelt and Timothy K. Beal. Berit Olam. Collegeville MN: Liturgical Press.

Lindsay, Rebecca. 2022. "Threshing out Grandmother Stories: Reflecting on Ruth 3 in Colonial Australia." Pages 79–98 in *Feminist Interpretations of Biblical Literature*, edited by Lilly Nortjé-Meyer. Newcastle-upon-Tyne: Cambridge Scholars.

Matheny, Jennifer M. 2022. *Judges 19-21 and Ruth: Canon as a Voice of Answerability*. Biblical Interpretation 200. Leiden: Brill.

Meyers, Carol. 1993. "Returning Home: Ruth 1.8 and the Gendering of the Book of Ruth." Pages 85–119 in *A Feminist Companion to Ruth*, edited by Athalya Brenner. Sheffield: Sheffield Academic.

Miller, Robert J., Jacinta Ruru, Larissa Behrendt, and Tracey Lindberg. 2010. *Discovering Indigenous Lands: The Doctrine of Discovery in the English Colonies*. Oxford: Oxford University Press.

Minniecon, Ray, and Geoff Broughton. 2022. "Re-locating Theology to Aboriginal Places of Deep Connection," July 4, 2022, Parramatta: ANZATS Conference.

Moreton-Robinson, Aileen. 2015. *The White Possessive: Property, Power, and Indigenous Sovereignty*. Minneapolis: University of Minnesota Press.

Moyo, Fulata Lusungu. 2016. "'Traffic Violations': Hospitality, Foreignness, and Exploitation: A Contextual Biblical Study of Ruth." *Journal of Feminist Studies in Religion* 32 (2): 83–94.

Nugent, Maria, Ben Silverstein, Mary Spiers Williams, and Mark McKenna. 2022. "Review Forum: Mark McKenna's Return to Uluru." *Journal of Australian Studies* April: 1–16. https://doi.org/10.1080/14443058.2022.2051262.

Olyan, Saul M. 2021. "'She and Her Friends': On Women's Friendship in Biblical Narrative." Pages 79–88 in *Friendship in Jewish History, Religion, and Culture*, edited by Lawrence Fine. University Park: Penn State University Press.

Ostriker, Alicia Suskin. 2002. "The Book of Ruth and the Love of the Land." *Biblical Interpretation* 10 (4): 343–59. https://doi.org/10.1163/15685150260340734.

Pascoe, Bruce. 2014. *Dark Emu: Black Seeds Agriculture or Accident?* Broome: Magabala Books.

Pattel-Gray, Anne. 2023. "Freedom from Colonial Bondage: Decolonizing Biblical Narratives and Theological Education." *International Review of Mission* 112 (2): 240–56. https://doi.org/10.1111/irom.12478.

Paulson, Graham, and Mark G. Brett. 2013. "Five Smooth Stones: Reading the Bible through Aboriginal Eyes." *Colloquium* 45 (2): 199–214.

Pitkänen, Pekka. 2017. "Ancient Israelite Population Economy: Ger, Toshav, Nakhri and Karat as Settler Colonial Categories."

Journal for the Study of the Old Testament 42 (2): 139–53. https://doi.org/10.1177/0309089216677665.

Powell, Stephanie Day. 2018. *Narrative Desire and the Book of Ruth*. Library of Hebrew Bible/Old Testament Studies 662. London: Bloomsbury.

Prentis, Brooke. 2021. "What Can the Birds of the Land Tell Us?" Pages 19–30 in *Grounded in the Body, in Time and Place, in Scripture: Papers by Australian Women Scholars in the Evangelical Tradition*, edited by Jill Firth and Denise Cooper-Clarke. Eugene OR: Wipf & Stock.

Rifkin, Mark. 2013. "Settler Common Sense." *Settler Colonial Studies* 3 (3–4): 322–40. https://doi.org/10.1080/2201473X.2013.810702.

Said, Edward W. 1993. *Culture and Imperialism*. London: Chatto & Windus.

Sakenfeld, Katharine Doob. 1999. *Ruth*. International Bible Commentary. Louisville: John Knox.

-----. 2002. "At the Threshing Floor: Sex, Reader Response, and a Hermeneutic of Survival." *Old Testament Essays* 15 (1): 164–78.

Saxegaard, Kristin Moen. 2010. *Character Complexity in the Book of Ruth*. Forschungen zum Alten Testament 2/47. Tübingen: Mohr Siebeck.

Schipper, Jeremy. 2016. *Ruth: A New Translation with Introduction and Commentary*. Anchor Yale Bible Commentary. New Haven: Yale University Press.

Shepherd, David. 2001. "Violence in the Fields? Translating, Reading, and Revising in Ruth 2." *Catholic Biblical Quarterly* 63 (3): 444–63.

-----. 2018. "Ruth in the Days of the Judges: Women, Foreignness and Violence." *Biblical Interpretation* 26 (4–5): 528–43. https://doi.org/10.1163/15685152-02645P07.

Southwood, Katherine. 2014. "Will Naomi's Nation Be Ruth's Nation?: Ethnic Translation as a Metaphor for Ruth's Assimilation within Judah." *Humanities* 3 (2): 102–31.

Strakosch, Elizabeth. 2021. "Indigenous–Settler Relationships: Policy, Rights, Reconciliation, and Sovereignty." Pages 336–55 in *The Oxford Handbook of Australian Politics*, edited by Jenny M. Lewis and Anne Tiernan. Oxford: Oxford University Press.

Taute, Hermanus, and Raymond Potgieter. 2020. "The Message of the Book Ruth: A Reflection on Naomi's Traumatic Journey to Mara and Back." *In die Skriflig* 54 (1): 1–10.

Thambyrajah, Jonathan A. 2021. "Israelite or Moabite? Ethnicity in the Book of Ruth." *Journal for the Study of the Old Testament* 46 (1): 44–63.

Trible, Phyllis. 1976. "Two Women in a Man's World: A Reading of the Book of Ruth." *Soundings: An Interdisciplinary Journal* 59 (3): 251–79.

-----. 1978. *God and the Rhetoric of Sexuality*. Overtures to Biblical Theology 2. Philadelphia: Fortress Press.

Veracini, Lorenzo. 2022. *Colonialism: A Global History*. Abingdon: Routledge.

Warrior, Robert Allen. 1989. "Canaanites, Cowboys, and Indians: Deliverance, Conquest, and Liberation Theology Today." *Christianity and Crisis* 49 (12): 261–65.

Watego, Chelsea. 2021. *Another Day in the Colony*. St Lucia, Qld: University of Queensland Press.

West, Mona. 2019. "The Book of Ruth: An Example of Procreative Strategies for Queers." Pages 51–60 in *Our Families, Our Values*, edited by Robert Goss and Amy Adams Squire Strongheart. New York: Routledge.

–––––. 2022. "Ruth." Pages 190–94 in *The Queer Bible Commentary*, edited by Robert E. Shore-Goss and Mona West, 2nd ed. London: SCM.

Westwood, Sue. 2023. "'It's the Not Being Seen That Is Most Tiresome': Older Women, Invisibility and Social (in)Justice." *Journal of Women & Aging* 35 (6): 557–72. https://doi.org/10.1080/08952841.2023.2197658.

Wolde, Ellen J. van. 1997. "Texts in Dialogue with Texts: Intertextuality in the Ruth and Tamar Narratives." *Biblical Interpretation* 5 (1): 1–28. https://doi.org/10.1163/156851597X00012.

Wolfe, Patrick. 1999. *Settler Colonisation and the Transformation of Anthropology*. London: Cassell.

Yee, Gale. 2009. "'She Stood in Tears amid the Alien Corn': Ruth, the Perpetual Foreigner and Model Minority." Pages 119–40 in *They Were All Together in One Place? Toward Minority Biblical Criticism.*, edited by Randall C. Bailey, Tat-siong Benny Liew, and Fernando F. Segovia. Semeia Studies 57. Atlanta: SBL Press.

–––––. 2018. "Racial Melancholia and the Book of Ruth." Pages 61–70 in *The Five Scrolls: Texts @ Contexts*, edited by Athalya Brenner-Idan, Gale Yee, and Archie C. C. Lee. London: Bloomsbury T&T Clark.

About the Author

Rebecca Lindsay lives on Gadigal and Bidjigal land (the south-east of Sydney). She teaches Hebrew Bible/Old Testament at United Theological College, part of the Charles Sturt University School of Theology. Rebecca's research explores the entanglements of settler colonialism and biblical interpretation in the lands now called Australia. Her Orcid ID is 0000-0002-3569-8686.

Chapter 9
Wisdom in a Time of Prose: Form, Function, and the Book of Ruth

Laura Quick

Abstract

The genre of the book of Ruth has been much debated. Variously described as a novel, novella, folktale, or short story, the book is often connected to the Israelite "wisdom" tradition as an example of "narrative wisdom." Typically, scholars who make this connection suggest that the book was written to affirm and demonstrate some of the ideals of the book of Proverbs. Recently, I turned this idea on its head by arguing that far from affirming these ideals, the book of Ruth can instead be understood as an extended problematization of the limits of "wisdom" as espoused in books such as Proverbs (Quick 2020). Rather than Proverbs, therefore, the book of Ruth might in fact be closer to two of the other so-called canonical texts of the biblical wisdom genre: Qoheleth and Job, which also reflect on and complicate conventional wisdom. In this chapter, I reflect upon these suggestions by further developing the connections between Ruth and the wisdom tradition. By focusing on the thematic and formal characteristics of wisdom literature, I argue that Ruth can be understood as a wisdom text – but one which destabilizes traditional wisdom tenets. And this is inherent to the adoption of prose discourse in the book of Ruth, as a discursive and aesthetic strategy for complicating wisdom conventions.

Keywords: Book of Ruth, Book of Proverbs, wisdom literature, genre, prose, proverb, parable

The genre of the book of Ruth has been much debated. The narrative develops over four well-plotted chapters and builds to an apparently happy ending. Consequently, the story has variously been described as a novel, novella, folktale, or short story (Matheny 2020, 13–14). In particular, Ruth has been connected to the biblical "wisdom" tradition as an example of "narrative wisdom." According to this reading strategy, the book of Ruth was written to affirm and demonstrate some of the ideals of the wisdom tradition, in particular as are found in the book of Proverbs. But in a recent article I turned this idea on its head by arguing that far from affirming these ideals, the book of Ruth can instead be understood as an extended problematization of the limits of conventional wisdom as espoused in books such as Proverbs (Quick 2020). Rather than Proverbs, therefore, the book of Ruth might in fact be closer to two of the other so-called canonical texts of the biblical wisdom genre: Qoheleth and Job, which also reflect on and complicate conventional wisdom.

In this chapter, I further develop the connections between Ruth and the wisdom tradition. By focusing on the thematic and formal characteristics of wisdom literature, I reconsider the boundaries of that genre. Emphasizing the gaps, fissures, and divergencies within the book of Ruth muddles our understanding of this novella text. Consequently, I argue that Ruth can be understood as a wisdom text – but one which destabilizes traditional wisdom tenets. And this is inherent to the adoption of prose discourse in the book of Ruth, as a discursive and aesthetic strategy for complicating wisdom conventions. Interrogating this complex entanglement between discourse genre and wisdom critique should therefore be at the forefront of our engagement with the biblical wisdom tradition, which can be understood according to this meeting of form and function.

1. What is Wisdom Literature?

Wisdom literature is a somewhat amorphous category within biblical scholarship. Traditionally, the books of Proverbs, Job, and Qoheleth constitute the three canonical texts of biblical wisdom literature. On the other hand, scholars such as Stuart Weeks (2010), Mark Sneed (2011), and Will Kynes (2019) have problematized the existence of a well-defined genre that we can call "wisdom literature" after all. A brief consideration of the genre is therefore helpful.

By labeling a particular biblical text as "wisdom literature," scholars are making claims about that text's genre: namely, the expectations and conventions that governed the production of the text. The Hebrew Bible is comprised of multiple genres. Some of these are emic genres, which is to say, they are explicitly labeled as such within the text. For example, the Hebrew term קינה, usually translated as "lament," is used to describe certain pericopes, for example David's "lament" for Saul and Jonathan, which appears as a heading for the poetic discourse that follows (2 Sam 1:17–27). Even here, however, there is a difficulty with precisely describing the discourse labeled as a "lament": the Hebrew Bible provides no native literary criticism or theory which reflects upon or describes the boundaries of a particular genre (Najman 2012). Instead, scholars must derive these conventions themselves by searching for interconnections among texts. We can therefore widen the pool of literature associated with a particular genre on the basis of thematic and formal similarities shared between texts. Consequently, texts which are not explicitly designated as "laments" may be associated with this genre, including multiple examples from the books of Psalms.

This is the same rhetorical move made by scholars of wisdom literature: certain texts are associated with the genre "wisdom" on the basis of their shared thematic and formal similarities. Nevertheless, as Kynes (2019) has emphasized, this is an etic category: no biblical text self-consciously describes itself in these terms, but rather scholars have argued for the genre's existence on the basis of those perceived thematic and formal similarities.

Thematically, the books of Proverbs, Qoheleth, and Job are all engaged, to a greater or lesser degree, with metaphysical questions about life and learning. Proverbs explicitly claims itself to be concerned with wisdom and teaching (1:1–7). The speaker of Qoheleth is self-styled as a teacher concerned with wisdom (1:12–13), while Job is concerned with the location of wisdom (28:12). To a broad degree, therefore, there is a thematic overlap in the content of each of these texts in terms of their focus on metaphysical issues which we might characterize as concerning wisdom.

Formally, the book of Proverbs is an anthological collection of sayings and instructions. In particular, Proverbs utilizes the משל, often translated as "proverb" or "parable," in order to develop its particular pedagogically inflected content: these sayings seek to instruct the addressee in particular courses of action, or to develop the addressee's moral character. We might describe this as the *functional* purpose of a proverb. But the proverb also has distinct *formal* characteristics: namely, parallelism. Each verse is composed in pairs, or sometimes triplets, of parallel lines. In a recent study, Jacqueline Vayntrub has shown that in a proverb, form and function are linked. The strict prosodic demands of parallelism mean that each proverb develops its content in pairs or categories and makes claims about the relationship between those categories (Vayntrub 2019a, 117). For example, a fundamental distinction developed in Proverbs is between the wise and the foolish:

For the waywardness of the simpletons will kill them,
and the careless ease of fools will destroy them.
But the one who listens to me will live in security,
and will be at ease from the dread of harm. (Prov 1:32-33; NET)

Here the "simpletons" and "fools" are contrasted with "the one who listens" – namely, the one who listens to wisdom teachings, which is to say, the wise. This is part of a larger contrast which is developed across the book of Proverbs between those who demonstrate correct behavior, and those who do not. The implication is that the latter category has failed to heed wisdom's teachings.

The book of Proverbs therefore provides a demonstration of categories of right and wrong behavior, in all aspects of life. And by answering metaphysical questions about the world and its actors in categories, the wisdom developed in the book of Proverbs is straightforward and unambiguous. The world of Proverbs is general, bifurcated, and austere (Ansberry 2011, 99). As such, the book of Proverbs makes a claim that its wisdom is conventional: it provides the authoritative perspective on any given topic (Vayntrub 2019a).

If we turn to the books of Qoheleth and Job, these too make use of traditional proverbial sayings. The proverb is therefore one formal characteristic which is shared between the three biblical books traditionally grouped together as "wisdom literature." However, even a brief glance at the book of Job shows that other genres are just as if not more important than the proverbial saying to Job's discourse. Job certainly cites some traditional proverbial sayings (1:21; 2:10; 18:5) as well as more extended parables which are explicitly characterized as משל (27:1; 29:1). But there are also clear connections to other genres too, in particular the lament (Dell 1991). Poetic dialogue allows for different speakers to express their viewpoints via argumentation and rhetoric, while the prologue and epilogue set up and conclude the story in prose.

Similarly, while Qoheleth does utilize proverbial sayings, here they are employed "subversively and sceptically," in so doing undermining conventional wisdom. Suzanna Millar (2022, 37–38) gives the example of Qoh 7:1–12, which purport to express what is "good." But the pericope, as she demonstrates, "sits in the shadow" of the pronouncements immediately preceding it: namely, that no-one can know what is good, after all.

In order to account for this discrepancy, scholars have proposed evolutionary schemas whereby the "traditional" or "conventional" wisdom of the book of Proverbs is criticized by the later books of Job and Qoheleth (Schmid 1966, 173–96). The critique of conventional wisdom expressed in Job and Qoheleth has seen these texts described as "wisdom in revolt" (Von Rad 1970, 306–8; Scott 1971, 136; Perdue 1991, 260–73). These alternative voices engage in a corrective dialogue with the traditional wisdom tenets expressed by the book of Proverbs.

We might say, therefore, that the three canonical texts of biblical wisdom literature are all thematically engaged, to a greater or lesser degree, with metaphysical questions to do with wisdom. However, their answers to these questions are in fact incredibly diverse and may even be said to disagree with each other. Similarly, there are formal commonalities via the use of the proverbial saying. Yet in Qoheleth the adoption of this form is clearly subversive, while in the book of Job the critique of traditional wisdom is expressed via diverse literary forms including the proverb but also the lament, poetic dialogue, and even prose. As a genre, "wisdom literature" is therefore one which is seemingly rather fuzzy and open to diversity.

2. What is Narrative Wisdom?

A consequence to the openness of "wisdom literature" as a heuristic category has meant that other texts from across the Hebrew Bible and ancient Jewish literature have come to be associated with it. In the Second Temple period, a number of prose texts arose that can be characterized by their brevity, narrative consistency, and literary artistry: from the Hebrew Bible we might include the Joseph story (Genesis 37–50), the books of Esther and Ruth, and the stories about Daniel (Daniel 1–6). And one reading strategy for understanding these prose "novella" texts is to refer them to the genre "wisdom literature," understanding these stories as demonstrating wisdom values within a narrative setting.

An early proponent for reading the novella as wisdom literature was Gerhard von Rad (1958), who based his analysis on the Joseph story. According to von Rad, the Joseph story embodies the educational ideals of early wisdom as are elsewhere expressed in the book of Proverbs. For von Rad, rather than a text which had been *influenced by* this wisdom tradition, the Joseph story should be understood as an *example of* wisdom literature. He therefore broadened the category of biblical wisdom literature from comprising merely the books of Proverbs, Qoheleth, and Job, to include other texts, too. Hans-Peter Müller argued that alongside the Joseph story, the stories of Daniel and Esther have a pedagogical intent (1977). We might understand all three texts as belonging to a genre of "narrative wisdom," developing the theme of wisdom in a prose setting.

The stories of Joseph, Daniel, and Esther are all set in the royal court, and it is therefore easy to see how they might be interpreted as enacting a theme of wisdom literature as found in the book of Proverbs: the wisdom of scribes or courtiers (Talmon 1963, 426–27; Ansberry 2011). But this is actually quite a different setting from the book of Ruth. Nevertheless, the book of Ruth has also been connected to this genre of "narrative wisdom" on the basis of apparent connections which exist between Ruth with the acrostic poem in praise of the ideal wife, which is found in Prov 31:10–31. The crux of the comparison rests on the description of both Ruth and the ideal wife as אשת חיל, "capable wife." This phrase describes both Ruth (3:11) and the woman described in the acrostic poem of Proverbs (31:10); otherwise it is found elsewhere only in the book of Proverbs, where it once again describes the ideal bride (12:4). Ruth is then argued to demonstrate some of the characteristics of the "capable wife" as outlined in Prov 31:10–21, such as loyalty to family, resourcefulness, or in the praise which each receives from others (Campbell 1975, 29–30; McCreesh 1985; Hubbard 1988, 65–66, 72–74; Hamlin 1996, 16, 78; Sakenfeld 1999, 11–13, 47–48, 61–64; Zenger 2004: 333; Fischer 2013; Goh 2014; Goh 2015; Goswell 2016; Zakovitch 2018, 95–98; Tooman and Kelsey 2022, 110–12).

Katharine Dell (2019) has extended the comparison between Ruth with Prov 31:10–31 to include the proverbial maxims developed in the wider book of Proverbs, namely Proverbs 10–30, arguing that these chapters share with the book of Ruth a concern for friendship, family loyalty, hard work, obedience, and redemption. Kandy Queen-Sutherland (2016) and Jennifer Matheny (2022) have separately argued that the book of Ruth as a whole should be understood as a type of extended משל, a parable to do with ethical content according to the wisdom tradition. Queen-Sutherland explicitly contrasts this wisdom tradition to the counter-wisdom of Qoheleth, arguing that in the book of Ruth "traditional wisdom prevails" (Queen-Sutherland 2016, 237). According to these readings, then, the book of Ruth is related to the book of Proverbs as a narrative demonstration of some of the ideas and ideals of conventional wisdom that are developed in that text.

3. Ruth and the Limits of Proverbial Wisdom

Earlier, we recalled Vayntrub's characterization of the wisdom of the book of Proverbs as "categorising discourse" (Vayntrub 2019a). Proverbs develops categories of right and wrong behavior, in all aspects of life. Though this is primarily aimed at Israelite and Judahite men, we find categories of right and wrong behavior aimed at women, too. We have already seen this in our discussion of the capable wife, who provides a paradigm of ideal behavior for women (albeit this, too is ultimately aimed at men, in so far as it purports to give guidance on qualities to look out for in a potential bride). On the other hand, the "strange woman" is a paradigm of immorality. This woman is variously described as רע, "evil," or זרה or נכריה. While the meaning of the latter two lexemes primarily indicates foreignness, the descriptions of this character more often conjure up images of illicit sexual activity rather than an ethnic, legal, or social status (Camp 2000, 29). The strange woman is sexually active outside of the bonds of marriage. The sexuality of the capable wife, on the other hand, is exclusively restricted to marriage. These two women therefore function as paradigmatic examples of ideal and non-ideal female roles.

In the case of the capable wife and the strange woman, the categorizing themes are fairly obvious, but some others require more drawing out. For example, the book of Proverbs provides a paradigm of behavior towards one's parents:

> My child, guard the commands of your father,
> And do not forsake the instruction of your mother. (Prov 6:20; NET)

This is related to the larger instructional context developed in the book of Proverbs, in which knowledge is passed on, father-to-son (1:8; 2:1; 3:1, 21; 4:1, 10, 20; 5:1; 6:20; 7:1). Typically, this focus on transgenerational transmission has meant that the book of Proverbs is often understood in the context of ancient Israelite education (Vayntrub 2016, 97). Vayntrub, on the other hand, has incisively linked the importance of transgenerational succession to a larger theme found throughout biblical literature: the necessity of lineage with regard to a filial obligation to the dead, as a strategy for transcending individual death (2019b, 501). For example:

> When I was a son to my father,
> a tender, only child before my mother,
> he taught me, and he said to me:
> "Let your heart lay hold of my words;
> keep my commandments so that you will live." (Prov 4:3-4; NET)

Here, transgenerational succession in the form of passed-on teachings is explicitly related to a strategy for surviving death. In fact, knowledge transmitted across generational lines in the context of mortal anxiety is a key theme of biblical wisdom literature more generally (Crenshaw 1998, 7). It is consequently very important in the biblical wisdom tradition that one "builds a house" (Van Leeuwen 2007). In Biblical Hebrew, the verb בנה can be used to denote the "building" of a dwelling or monument, but also a family, people, dynasty, or individual. In fact, the word בן, "son," has been explained as a derivative of "build" (Wagner 1974, 166–68). To have a son is therefore to build a house, a lasting monument which will ensure post-mortem existence: therefore in Proverbs it is wise to build up one's house (Prov 9:1; 14:1); while the requirement for transgenerational succession is explicit in a father's advice regarding his own son's fecundity (Prov 5:15–19). But this strategy for post-mortem survival is a gendered one: only a son can guarantee the survival of the family name (Wright 2011).

And it is precisely this issue which dominates the narrative of the book of Ruth. The book tells the story of an Israelite woman named Naomi, and her Moabite daughter-in-law, Ruth. Naomi and her family sojourn in the foreign land of Moab, where Naomi's sons take Moabite wives: Ruth and Orpah. In quick succession, first Naomi's husband Elimelech, and then her two sons, Mahlon and Kilyon, die, without leaving any heirs. Naomi returns to Bethlehem with Ruth, and the plot is resolved via the imperfect application of two biblical legal practices: land redemption and levirate law (Lev 25; Deut 25:5–10; but see Chapter 3 in this volume). According to the obligations of the levirate law, the brother of a man who dies childless is required to marry the widow of the deceased, with the first-born child named for and treated as the son of the dead man. In the book of Ruth, Boaz is set up as a figure through which the levirate obligation might be fulfilled, although there is a closer kinsman available. Ruth and Boaz marry, and the story concludes with the birth of their child. The transgenerational survival of the house of Elimelech seems secured, after all.

At first glance, then, all this would seem to provide a functional demonstration of some of the values of wisdom as developed in the book of Proverbs: namely, the issue of transgenerational succession. Additionally, as we have seen, the description of Ruth as an אשת חיל has seen the character compared to the "capable wife" of Prov 31:10–31, as a demonstration of that ideal. There are, therefore, clear connections to the book of Proverbs that might suggest interpreting the book of Ruth as an example of "narrative wisdom." Yet as I have previously argued (Quick 2020), the workings of all of this are not quite as clear cut as we might suppose (see also Chapter 5 in this volume).

In this context, the characterization of Ruth is particularly intriguing. The categorical distinction between native and foreign is challenged by Ruth, a Moabitess who is nevertheless equal to the ancestors of Israel (4:11–12). Crucially, the author of the book of Ruth explicitly draws upon the language of Proverbs in order to develop this challenge (Quick 2020, 61). As we have seen, a typical reading strategy for understanding the book of Ruth has been to refer Ruth to the "capable wife" of Prov 31:10–31, arguing that these two women share various characteristics. But while many have noted that Ruth ends her story as an אשת חיל, a "capable wife," few have recognized that Ruth begins as a נכריה (Ruth 2:10). Though this is literally the case with Ruth, as a woman from Moab, it also recalls the other נכריה of the book of Proverbs, the strange woman. In fact, some of Ruth's actions are reminiscent of this strange woman. Like the strange woman, Ruth heightens her seductive powers through the application of cosmetic oil (Ruth 3:3; see Prov 7:16–17), before visiting a man alone, at night. She lies down upon the threshing room floor, and either uncovers a part of his body or undresses herself (Ruth 3:4, 7), and many scholars have noted the potential sexual implications of her actions (LaCocque 1990, 2; Klein 2003, 4).

Cynthia Chapman has also proposed a reading of Ruth in light of the strange woman of Proverbs. She focuses on Proverbs 5, where the male teacher commands his student to keep away from the strange woman, highlighting the woman's "smooth speech" (Prov 5:3–6). "Smooth" here describes not the modality of this woman's voice, but rather characterizes her speech as persuasive: her words are slippery, "smoother than olive oil," and will ultimately lead the man astray (Dahood 1973). Ruth is not only foreign like this strange woman, but as Chapman notes, she speaks to Boaz "with utmost politeness and deference." We might understand her deferential address as being an example of rhetorically affective speech, designed to appeal to Boaz and so to solicit his attention and aid. Consequently, Chapman concludes that Boaz "could easily have judged her to be precisely the kind of foreign woman with smooth speech that his elders had warned him against" (Chapman 2023, 440).

There is little in the book itself, then, that would actually suggest that Ruth is behaving in any ways characteristic of the woman described in the acrostic poem of Prov 31:10-31 – and in fact, some of her actions are more in line with those of the strange woman. The paradigmatic figurations of femininity from the book of Proverbs, the נכריה and the אשת חיל, are therefore mediated via Ruth, who models characteristics of both binary figures.

Gender itself is subverted. Ruth takes on various roles that conform more to masculine than to feminine expectations (Purcell 2022). She gleans in the fields, the danger of which is made apparent by Boaz's request that she stay near to his servants (2:8). Ruth's activities are precarious and put her in the publicly visible sphere. Accordingly, there are a number of instances in which Ruth, as well as Naomi and Orpah, are described using grammatically masculine forms (1:8, 9, 11, 13, 19, 22; 4:11). On the other hand, males are twice described using a feminine plural pronoun (1:13). Naomi's sons, both actual and potential, have been as beneficial to her as daughters would have been. They have left her just as bereft of offspring as if she had had daughters who had married and moved away to the houses of their husbands. Ruth, on the other hand, is praised as more valuable to Naomi than seven sons (4:14). The categories of correct behavior for men and women are therefore explored and destabilized throughout the narrative (Quick 2020, 63–64).

But most importantly, central to the book of Ruth is a mediation – even an abortion – of an essential idea voiced in wisdom literature more generally: the desire to "build up one's house" as a strategy for postmortem remembrance. Many scholars interpret the law of levirate marriage to do with the supposed benefit which it would have for the widow. But Boaz's speech concerning his claim to Ruth appeals instead to male interests. "His proposition is not worded in terms of meeting the physical needs of impoverished widows; rather, he focuses on the incorporeal male needs – the sacred male name and lineage" (Fewell and Gunn 1989, 59 n. 33). Levirate marriage therefore promised the Israelite male a kind of generational immortality: the preservation of the male name (and property, hence the necessity of linking the levirate law with the law of land redemption in the book of Ruth) throughout the generations. It relates, therefore, to the importance of the endurance of the family as an entity with "name" – one of the key issues of biblical wisdom literature.

Elimelech's post-mortem survival seemed ensured by the birth of his two sons. With their death, the central conflict of the plot is established: who will ensure the post-mortem survival of the house of Elimelech? It seems at first that, through the practice of the levirate law and the law of redemption, both Elimelech's family name and property have been given a second chance at survival. Indeed, Ruth is praised that she become like "Rachel and Leah, who together built up the house of Israel" (4:11): the focus is clearly on building up ancestry (Quick 2020, 64).

Yet the outcome of the narrative is not quite what we would expect. Boaz is *not* the closest kinsman of the house of Elimelech. The child born of Ruth and Boaz is *not* named for the dead house of Elimelech. In fact, there are a number of subversions or even reversals of our expectations in the story. Though the story has been couched as a problem in the survival of the male house of Elimelech, it is actually the women who name the child (4:17). Boaz as redeemer is brought in to secure the transgenerational line and yet is strangely divorced from the procreative process. The elders bless Boaz and his household: "May your house become like the house of Perez, whom Tamar bore to Judah, *from the seed whom the Lord gives to you from this young woman*" (4:13). Grammatically, the "seed" comes not from Boaz, but from both God and Ruth (Quick 2021, 49–51). Ruth is praised as more precious to her mother-in-law than seven sons (4:15). Yet thereafter she disappears from the narrative. The focus switches from Ruth to her mother-in-law, and the narrative concludes with the declaration that "a son has been born to Naomi" (4:17). In fact, it is *not* the father's house which is the locus of social organization, but the house of the mother (1:8). At every juncture, our expectations for the successful continuity of the house of Elimelech are subverted (Quick 2020, 64–65).

Consequently, it is difficult to conclude that the book of Ruth provides a narrative demonstration of some of the tenets of conventional wisdom as found in the book of Proverbs. Instead, we might understand the book as providing an extended problematization of the limits of conventional wisdom expressed in categorizing discourse. It draws upon the language of the book of Proverbs, only to explore and destabilize various wisdom conventions and categories: native and foreign, insider and outsider, male and female, the capable wife and the strange woman, even life and death. Ruth doesn't necessarily offer any answers to the metaphysical dimensions posed by these categories, but rather demonstrates the limitations of binary ethics.

Does this mean that the book of Ruth should no longer be understood according to the category of narrative wisdom? Certainly, this reading problematizes the interpretation of the book of Ruth as a form of "narrative wisdom" meant to demonstrate or emulate some of the ideas and ideals found in the book of Proverbs. On the other hand, this brings the book much closer to the other two texts which make up the conventional corpus of biblical wisdom literature: the book of Job and Qoheleth. Like Job and Qoheleth, Ruth engages in a corrective dialogue with the traditional tenets expressed by the book of Proverbs, demonstrating some of the limitations of Proverbial wisdom. In the same way that the wisdom of Qoheleth and Job is revolutionary when compared to the conventionalized wisdom developed in the book of Proverbs, Ruth, too, provides a revolutionary exploration of the wisdom genre.

4. When Form Meets Function

Of course, from a formal perspective these three texts are diverse, encompassing proverb, parable, poetic dialogue, lament, and prose. Yet we began by noting that, for many biblical scholars, the proverbial sayings of the book of Proverbs have often been taken to be the most characteristic form of Israelite and Judahite wisdom. Norbert Lohfink (2003, 13), for example, calls Proverbs the "first-level" of biblical wisdom literature. This is then taken up and elaborated upon by the later books of Qoheleth and Job, texts which develop their wisdom "in revolt" of the conventions of Proverbs.

In part, this prioritization of the book of Proverbs as the prototypical form of the biblical wisdom tradition relates to the prioritization of another ancient literary tradition to serve as comparanda to the biblical texts: the wisdom literature of the wider ancient Near East, in particular from Egypt and Mesopotamia. As many scholars have noted, here, too, existed a tradition of didactic wisdom. Like Proverbs, this literature aimed at educating young men and focused upon the intergenerational transmission of this knowledge, and there are significant similarities and overlap between some of these texts with the book of Proverbs (Fox 2009, 753–67).

In fact, the appellation "wisdom literature" as a genre designation for the ancient Near Eastern traditions is itself derivative from biblical literature, and like biblical literature, can be applied to diverse categories of texts: to proverbs, sayings, and instructions, but also to theodicy and lament more akin to the book of Job. And while biblical literature is inarguably indebted to the literary traditions of the wider ancient Near East, it is also a part of the ancient eastern Mediterranean, where Greco-Roman texts also develop and reflect on wisdom themes. This includes in texts akin to the biblical and ancient Near Eastern wisdom developed as sayings and proverbs – what can be called gnomic instruction (Martin 2010). But philosophical treatise (Nightingale 2000), epic poetry (Legaspi 2018, 17–45), and prose tales (Kurke 2010; Morgan 2007) have also been interpreted according to their themes of pedagogy and ethics.

What I am arguing against, therefore, is the existence of any single literary genre such as the proverbial saying under which a genre "wisdom literature" might be subsumed. Instead, wisdom is addressed across diverse literary contexts, and this is consistent across the ancient literary record. Scholars have prioritized proverbial sayings and instruction as paradigms of a tradition of ancient wisdom and shared across a biblical and ancient Near Eastern horizon. But if instead of the ancient Near Eastern texts we prioritized Greco-Roman ones, we might widen the pool of wisdom to include not only sayings and instruction but diverse genres including philosophy, poetry, and prose.

Considering the ancient Greek tradition of wisdom, Gaston Basile interprets this not as a "genre-specific category" but rather one which "signals a composite body of communal, oral lore (dealing with theodicy, the Gods/human relations along with morality and codes of conduct within a culture) which becomes partially entwined and encoded into different discourse genres" (Basile 2022, 172). This allows Basile to consider early Greek prose writers according to a tradition of wisdom, showing how these often adopted a critical or polemical stance towards traditional written authority. Basile's definition of wisdom might also be levelled at the biblical tradition (as well as the Egyptian and Mesopotamian ones), allowing us to seek wisdom across diverse literary contexts, including prose texts like the book of Ruth. The question then becomes how wisdom is "entwined and encoded" within the different discourse genre of prose, when compared to the other texts which are typically understood to be wisdom. In the book of Ruth, the prose format allows the author to emphasize the gaps, fissures, and divergencies of their story, and in so doing craft a narrative which subverts our expectations at every juncture.

Like Basile's early Greek prose writers, in the book of Ruth prose allows for a discursive exploration of traditional authority.

Earlier, we noted Vayntrub's observation that in a proverb, form and function are linked: the strict prosodic demands of parallelism mean that each proverb develops its content in pairs or categories. Wisdom developed in this way is straightforward and unambiguous, and by articulating metaphysical questions in this way, the book of Proverbs makes a claim to provide the authoritative treatment of these issues (Vayntrub 2019a, 117). In the book of Ruth, the narrative genre allows for a discursive exploration of the constraints of this type of categorizing discourse. Form and function are therefore linked here too – the discourse genre prose is inherent to the specifics of Ruth's critique of proverbial wisdom.

In the case of Qoheleth, the proverbial saying is employed subversively and as such, is also essential to this book's critique of conventional wisdom. In the book of Job, the critique is expressed as a poetic dialogue between different speakers, set within a prose framework. Through poetic dialogue, the wisdom of Job develops across rhetorically affective argumentation, in so doing attempting to persuade not only its characters but also the audience of the text. At the same time, Job's critique of conventional wisdom would hardly be comprehensible without the prose framework that introduces and concludes the dialogue: without it, we would not know that Job was blameless after all (1:8).

We might argue that in both Qoheleth and Job, then, form and function are also inherently related: it is through these formal conventions that the authors of these texts are able to develop their functional critique of wisdom. While formally diverse, there is a remarkable equivalence between form and function that characterizes these texts concerned with ideas and ideals about wisdom. In seeking to characterize wisdom as a heuristic category of biblical aesthetics, it is this equivalence which we might therefore seek. Rather than a codified genre comprised of specific formal features, wisdom can be expressed across diverse discourse genres, to include proverbs, parables, poetic dialogues, laments, and prose texts. But each of these modes of discourse encodes their own particular philosophical, ethical, or pedagogical intent which can be characterized under the broad designation of wisdom.

5. Conclusions

In this chapter, I have revisited some of my earlier considerations of the genre of the book of Ruth and its relation to the biblical wisdom tradition. In contrast to most other commentators on Ruth, I have disconnected the text from the conventional wisdom of the book of Proverbs. Instead,

I suggest that Ruth be understood as an extended problematization of the limits of conventional wisdom expressed in categorizing discourse. Ruth draws upon the language of Proverbs, only to explore and destabilize various wisdom conventions and categories, demonstrating the limitations of binary ethics. In this way, Ruth can be understood in relation to the wisdom tradition – but rather than the conventional wisdom of Proverbs, Ruth's wisdom is revolutionary. Like the books of Job and Qoheleth, Ruth reflects upon and complicates conventional wisdom, entering into a corrective dialogue with the traditional wisdom tenets expressed by the book of Proverbs. Thematically, there is a link between these three texts and their brand of revolutionary wisdom.

To be sure, Job, Qoheleth, and Ruth develop their critique of conventional wisdom using diverse literary forms. In Qoheleth, traditional wisdom forms are subversively reused. In Job, the critique is expressed via a personal account of the underserving sufferer, expressed in poetic dialogue, and bookended by prose. And in the book of Ruth, Ruth's revolutionary wisdom is expressed as a prose narrative. At the same time, as I have attempted to show, form is inherent to each of these texts' specific critique. Incorporating Ruth into the tradition of wisdom literature might mean widening the formal characteristics of the wisdom genre to include prose narrative. Yet at the same time, this diversity of formal features is nevertheless coupled with a congruence between form and function, particular to each text and its thematic concerns. This congruence may therefore be forwarded as a characteristic of wisdom in and of itself, suggesting that a complex and nuanced dialogue between form and function is negotiated within these texts.

Works Cited

Ansberry, C. B. 2011. *Be Wise, My Son, and Make My Heart Glad: An Exploration of the Courtly Nature of the Book of Proverbs*. Beihefte zur Zeitschrift für die alttestamentliche Wissenschaft 422. Berlin: de Gruyter.

Basile, Gaston J. 2022. "In the Wake of Wisdom: The Early Greek Prose Inquiries from a Comparative Perspective." Pages 171–220 in *After Wisdom: Sapiential Traditions and Ancient Scholarship in Comparative Perspective*. Edited by Glenn W. Most and Michael Puett. Philological Encounters Monographs 4. Leiden: Brill.

Camp, Claudia V. 2000. *Wise, Strange and Holy: The Strange Woman and the Making of the Bible*. Journal for the Study of the Old Testament Supplement Series 320. Sheffield: Sheffield Academic Press.

Campbell, Edward F. 1975. *Ruth: A New Translation with Introduction, Notes, and Commentary*. Anchor Bible 7. New York NY: Doubleday.

Chapman, Cynthia R. 2023. "The Field Belonging to Boaz: Creating Kinship through Land, Labor, Food, and Feeding." *Journal of Biblical Literature* 142: 431–50.

Crenshaw, James L. 1998. *Old Testament Wisdom: An Introduction.* Louisville KY: Westminster John Knox.

Dahood, Mitchell. 1973. "Honey That Drips: Notes on Proverbs 5:2–3." *Biblica* 54: 65–66.

Dell, Katharine J. 1991. *The Book of Job as Sceptical Literature.* Beihefte zur Zeitschrift für die alttestamentliche Wissenschaft 197. Berlin: de Gruyter.

-----. 2019. "Didactic Intertextuality: Proverbial Wisdom as Illustrated in Ruth." Pages 103–14, in *Reading Proverbs Intertextually.* Edited by Katharine J. Dell and Will Kynes. The Library of Hebrew Bible/Old Testament Studies 629. London: Bloomsbury T. & T. Clark.

Fewell, Danna Nolan and David M. Gunn. 1989. "Boaz, Pillar of Society: Measures of Worth in the Book of Ruth." *Journal for the Study of the Old Testament* 45: 45–59.

Fischer, Irmtraud. 2013. "Von der *Vorgeshichte* zur *Nachgeschichte*: Schriftauslegung in der Schrift – Intertextualität – Rezeption." *Zeitschrift für die Alttestamentliche Wissenschaft* 125: 143–60.

Fox, Michael V. 2009. *Proverbs 10–31: A New Translation with Introduction and Commentary.* Anchor Bible 18A. New York: Doubleday.

Goh, Samuel T. S. 2014. "Ruth as a Superior Woman of חיל? A Comparison between Ruth and the 'Capable' Woman in Proverbs 31.10–31." *Journal for the Study of the Old Testament* 38: 487–500.

Goh, Elaine W. F. 2015. "An Intertextual Reading of Ruth and Proverbs 31:10–31, with a Chinese Woman's Perspective." Pages 73–88 in *Reading Ruth in Asia.* Edited by Jione Havea and Peter H. W. Lau. International Voices in Biblical Studies 7. Atlanta, GA: Society of Biblical Literature Press.

Goswell, Gregory. 2016. "Is Ruth Also Among the Wise?" Pages 115–33 in *Exploring Old Testament Wisdom: Literature and Themes.* Edited by David G. Firth and Lindsay Wilson. London: Apollos.

Hamlin, E. John. 1996. *Surely There is a Future: A Commentary on the Book of Ruth.* International Theological Commentary. Grand Rapids MI: Eerdmans.

Hubbard, Robert L. 1988. *The Book of Ruth.* The New International Commentary of the Old Testament. Grand Rapids MI: Eerdmans.

Klein, Lilliam. 2003. *From Deborah to Esther: Sexual Politics in the Hebrew Bible.* Minneapolis MN: Fortress.

Kurke, Leslie. 2010. *Aesopic Conversations: Popular Tradition, Cultural Dialogue, and the Invention of Greek Prose.* Princeton NJ: Princeton University Press.

Kynes, Will. 2019. *An Obituary for "Wisdom Literature:" The Birth, Death, and Intertextual Reintegration of a Biblical Corpus.* Oxford: Oxford University Press.

LaCocque, André. 1990. *The Feminine Unconventional: Four Subversive Figures in Israel's Tradition*. Overtures to Biblical Theology. Minneapolis MN: Fortress.
Legaspi, Michael C. 2019. *Wisdom in Classical and Biblical Tradition*. Oxford: Oxford University Press.
Lohfink, Norbert. 2003. *Qoheleth: A Continental Commentary*, trans. Sean McEvenue. Minneapolis MN: Fortress.
Martin, Richard P. 2010 "Gnomic Literature and Wisdom." Pages 305–6, in *The Oxford Encyclopedia of Ancient Greece and Rome*, Vol. 3. Edited by Michael Gagarin. Oxford: Oxford University Press.
Matheny, Jennifer M. 2020. "Ruth in Recent Research." *Currents in Biblical Research* 19: 8–35.
———. 2022. *Judges 19-21 and Ruth: Canon as a Voice of Answerability*. Biblical Interpretations Series 200. Leiden: Brill.
McCreesh, Thomas P. 1985. "Wisdom as Wife: Proverbs 31:10–31." *Revue Biblique* 92: 25–46.
Millar, Suzanna R. 2022. "The Multiple Genres of Wisdom Literature." Pages 34–56 in *The Cambridge Companion to Wisdom Literature*. Edited by Katharine J. Dell, Suzanna R. Millar, and Arthur Jan Keefer. Cambridge: Cambridge University Press.
Morgan, Theresa. 2007. *Popular Morality in the Early Roman Empire*. Cambridge: Cambridge University Press.
Müller, Hans-Peter. 1977. "Die weisheitliche Lehrerzählung im Alten Testament und seiner Umwelt." *Die Welt Des Orients* 9: 77–98.
Najman, Hindy. 2012. "The Idea of Biblical Genre: From Discourse to Constellation." Pages 307–21 in *Prayer and Poetry in the Dead Sea Scrolls and Related Literature: Essays in Honor of Eileen Schuller on the Occasion of Her 65th Birthday*. Edited by Jeremy Penner, Ken M. Penner, and Cecilia Wassen. Studies on the Texts of the Desert of Judah. 98 Leiden: Brill.
Nightingale, Andrea Wilson. 2000. "Sages, Sophists, and Philosophers: Greek Wisdom Literature." Pages 156–91 in *Literature in the Greek and Roman Worlds: A New Perspective*. Edited by Oliver Taplin. Oxford: Oxford University Press.
Perdue, Leo G. 1991. *Wisdom in Revolt: Metaphorical Theology in the Book of Job*. Bible and Literature Series 29. Sheffield: Sheffield Academic Press.
Purcell, Richard Anthony. 2022. "Playing the Man in the Book of Ruth: Reshaping the Masculine Ideal." *Biblical Interpretation* 30: 486–508.
Queen-Sutherland, Kandy. 2016. "Ruth, Qoheleth, and Esther: Counter Voices from the Megilloth." *Perspectives in Religious Studies* 43: 227–42.
Quick, Laura 2020. "The Book of Ruth and the Limits of Proverbial Wisdom." *Journal of Biblical Literature* 139: 47–66.
———. 2021. "Bitenosh's Orgasm, Galen's Two Seeds, and Conception Theory in the Hebrew Bible." *Dead Sea Discoveries* 28: 38–63.

Sakenfeld, Katherine Doob. 1999. *Ruth: A Bible Commentary for Teaching and Preaching*. Interpretation. Louisville KY: John Knox.

Schmid, Hans Heinrich 1966. *Wesen und Geschichte der Weisheit: Eine Untersuchung zue altorientalischen und israelitischen Weisheitsliteratur*. Beihefte zur Zeitschrift für die alttestamentliche Wissenschaft 10. Berlin: Töpelmann.

Scott, R. B. Y. 1971. *The Way of Wisdom in the Old Testament*. New York: Macmillan.

Sneed, Mark. 2011. "Is the 'Wisdom Tradition' a Tradition?" *Catholic Biblical Quarterly* 73: 50–71.

Talmon, Shemaryahu. 1963. "'Wisdom' in the Book of Esther." *Vetus Testametum* 13: 419–455.

Tooman, William A. with Marian Kelsey. 2022. *(Re)reading Ruth*. Eugene, OR: Wipf and Stock.

Van Leeuwen, Raymond C. 2007. "Cosmos, Temple, House: Building and Wisdom in Mesopotamia and Israel." Pages 67–90, in *Wisdom Literature in Mesopotamia and Israel*. Edited by Richard J. Clifford. Atlanta: Society of Biblical Literature.

Vayntrub, Jacqueline. 2016. "The Book of Proverbs and the Idea of Ancient Israelite Education." *Zeitschrift für die Alttestamentliche Wissenschaft* 128: 96–114.

Vayntrub, Jacqueline. 2019a. *Beyond Orality: Biblical Poetry in its Own Terms*. The Ancient Word. London and New York: Routledge.

-----. 2019b. "Like Father, Like Son: Theorizing Transmission in Biblical Literature." *Hebrew Bible and Ancient Israel* 7: 500–26.

Von Rad, Gerhard. 1958. "Josephsgeschichte und ältere Chokma." Pages 272–80, in *Gesammelte Studien zum Alten Testament*. Munich: C. Kaiser.

-----. 1970. *Wiesheit in Israel*. Neukirchen-Vluyn: Neukirchener Verlag.

Wagner, Siegfried. 1974. "banah." Pages 166–68 in *Theological Dictionary of the Old Testament*, Vol. 2. Edited by G. Johannes Botterweck, Helmer Ringgren, and Heinz-Josef Fabry. Winona Lake IN: Eerdmans.

Weeks, Stuart. 2010. *An Introduction to the Study of Wisdom Literature*. New York: T. & T. Clark.

Wright, Jacob. 2011. "Making a Name for Oneself: Martial Valor, Heroic Death, and Procreation in the Hebrew Bible." *Journal for the Study of the Old Testament* 36: 131–255.

Zakovitch, Yair. 2018. *The Song of Songs: Riddle of Riddles*. Library of Hebrew Bible/Old Testament Studies 673. London: Bloomsbury T. & T. Clark.

Zenger, Erich. 2004. *Einleitung in das Alte Testament*. Kohlhammer-Studienbücher Theologie. Stuttgart: Kohlhammer.

About the Author

Laura Quick is an Associate Professor of the Hebrew Bible/Old Testament at the University of Oxford. She specializes in the Hebrew Bible and the study of gender, sex, and the body in antiquity. Laura has published monographs on *Deuteronomy and the Aramaic Curse Tradition* (Oxford University Press, 2017) and *Dress, Adornment and the Body in the Hebrew Bible* (Oxford University Press, 2021). She has published articles and chapters in edited volumes on issues such as cursing and ritual, dress and adornment, and gender and sexuality, and also enjoys teaching on these subjects.

Chapter 10
Ruth and Moab: Abjection and Intimacy

Peter Sabo and Francis Landy

Abstract

The chapter is a dialogue between its two authors. In the first section, Sabo discusses the significance of Moab in the Hebrew Bible and its relation to the book of Ruth, in which the lines of Moab and Judah converge. In the second section, Landy analyses the first five verses of the book, in which the family of Elimelech travels to Moab, in the context of the origin story of Moab, concluding with the crucial encounter on the threshing floor. In the third section, Sabo shows how both Ruth and Boaz subvert the stereotypes associated with their ethnicities; Boaz is an anti-Judahite as much as Ruth is an anti-Moabite. In the fourth section, Landy discusses the relation of Ruth to the story of the Levite's concubine in Judges 19; its role as metahistory in foregrounding the question of whether love survives death; and its evocation of the death of Moses in the plains of Moab and Balaam's blessing of Israel, which Ruth fulfills.

Keywords: Moab, abjection, Lot, Lot's daughters, incest, intermarriage

Moab in the Hebrew Bible is strange and subversive – a place of mystery, temptation, and danger – but it is also strangely familiar, oddly similar. On the one hand, Moab is presented as a contrast to Israel by a number of structural dichotomies: family/other, full/empty, life/death, proper/taboo, domestic/foreign, and male/female. On the other hand, Moab complicates and deconstructs all these dichotomies. Moab is the abject (Kristeva 1982). It is that which must be cast out and distinguished as other in order for the self to develop. Accordingly, it is precisely that which complicates self-identity, threatening the distinction between subject and object. Moab is alternatively kin and other, a place of nourishment and death, an entryway and barrier into the Cisjordan, a mirror and distorted parallel of Israel's settlement into the land, a place of incest and exogamy.

The connecting thread of this chapter is the significance of Moab in Ruth. For us, Moab in Ruth is a *mise-en-abîme* of Moab in the Hebrew Bible. The term *mise-en-abîme* refers to a formal technique in art in which a copy of an image is placed within itself; in literary terms, it refers to a story within a story. As a *mise-en-abîme* of the overarching story of Moab in the Hebrew Bible, Moab in the book of Ruth encapsulates the ambiguity of Moab . From its incestuous origin between Lot and his elder daughter (Gen 19:30–38), Moab is cast as Israel's uncanny double. That is, Moab is at once a mirror of Israel and a distinct other. Part of Israelite identity is established by differentiating itself from Moab, but there are distinct similarities and kinship ties as well. In tracing Moab's uncanny doubleness, we examine how Ruth interacts with certain biblical texts about Moab (e.g. the Balak/Balaam story in Num 22–24, the Baal-Peor episode in Num 25:1–5, the condemnation against Moabites entering the assembly in Deut 23:4–7, the Eglon story in Judg 3:12–20) as well as other biblical texts related by theme and/or other intertextual connections (e.g. the wife-sister episodes of Abraham and Sarah in Gen 12 and 20, Rachel's death, the Levite stories in Judges). In Ruth, the criss-crossing from Israel to Moab back to Israel reflects and distorts other biblical journeys between Moab and Israel. Ruth's story, moreover, reveals the intimacy between abject Moab and Israel.

The chapter is a dialogue between its two authors. In the first section, Peter Sabo discusses the significance of Moab in the Hebrew Bible and its relation to the book of Ruth, in which the lines of Moab and Judah converge. In the second section, Francis Landy analyzes the first five verses of the book, in which the family of Elimelech travels to Moab, in the context of the origin story of Moab, concluding with the crucial encounter on the threshing floor. In the third section, Peter Sabo shows how both Ruth and Boaz subvert the stereotypes associated with their ethnicities; Boaz is an anti-Judahite as much as Ruth is an anti-Moabite. In the fourth section, Francis Landy discusses the relation of Ruth to the story of the Levite's concubine in Judges 19; its role as metahistory in foregrounding the question of whether love survives death; and its evocation of the death of Moses in the plains of Moab and Balaam's blessing of Israel, which Ruth fulfills.

1. From Moab's Origins to Ruth

In line with its selective and subtle style, Ruth never describes Moab in an explicitly negative or positive way and offers no direct elaboration of its significance (Koosed 2011, 106). Thus, many scholars read Ruth in combination with other biblical texts about Moab. It is common, for instance, to read Ruth as a contrast to, or polemic against, biblical texts that view Moab negatively and condemn relations with Moabites (Num 22–24; Num 25:1–3; Deut 23:4–7; Judg 3:12–30; 1 Kgs 11:1–2; 2 Kgs 3:4–27; Ezra 9:1–2; Neh 13:1–2). Strands of this reading include the interpretation that Ruth is a defense of David's Moabite ancestry (Gow 1992; Nielsen 1997); an opposition to post-exilic bans on intermarriage (LaCocque 2004; Matthews 2004; Hawk 2015), or an intertextual commentary on other biblical texts about Moab (Fewell and Gunn 1990). Similarly, Ruth may be read as a redeeming of negative texts about Moab, particularly in how the marriage of Ruth and Boaz brings together the descendants of Lot and Abraham (Fisch 1982; Kaniel 2015). It is also possible, however, to read Ruth in line with biblical texts that do not present Moab negatively and/or recount relations between Israelites and Moabites without condemnation (Deut 2:9; 2:19; 1 Sam 22:3–4; 1 Chron 4:22; Schipper 2016). Because the Hebrew Bible contains conflicting attitudes toward Moab, all these readings are possible. Furthermore, these readings are not mutually exclusive, since Moab in Ruth carries with it the ambiguities that accompany Moab throughout the Hebrew Bible.

The origin story for the Moabites in the Hebrew Bible reads like a xenophobic joke from an Israelite perspective (Gen 19:30–38). The founding figure of the Moabites, Lot, is characterized by his greed (Gen 13:10–11), ineffectiveness (Gen 19:14), and cowardice (Gen 19:18–22). From a literary perspective, he is a foil to Abraham, and indeed the entire Lot story is a distorted parallel to the Abraham story (see below). The incestuous begetting of Lot's son Moab serves as a metaphor for the problematic existence of the nation of Moab. It suggests, as Robert Alter comments, that the Moabites "will be somehow trapped in their own inward circuit, a curse and not a blessing to the nations of the earth, in consonance with their first begetting" (1990, 154). Indeed, passage suggests a folk etymology of Moab meaning "from a father," referring to the incestuous act between Lot and his older daughter. This etymology is suggested by the repetition of the phrases "from our father" (*mē'ābînû*) (19:32, 34) and "from their father" (*mē'ăbîhen*) (19:36) that play with the name Moab (*mō'āb*). This wordplay then colors Moab's naming scene: "The firstborn gave birth to a son, and she called his name Moab [from a father]; he is the father of Moab [from a father] to this day" (Gen 19:37, this translation and all that follow are our own). This emphasis on Moab's incestuous origins, highlights its divergence from the typical biblical progression of family lineages (Sabo 2020, 95). And yet, this difference between Moab and Israel is complicated by their kinship, since Lot is Abraham's nephew. To be sure, Moab is one of many close others to Israel in a genealogical sense (e.g. Edom and Ishmael), but Lot's separation (Gen 13) marks the first division within Abraham's family and, therefore, serves a paradigmatic role in Israel's relation to its close others. In short, if the origin story for Moab is a xenophobic joke, then Israel is part of the punchline.

The shared ancestry of Lot and Abraham is mirrored by the territory shared by their descendants elsewhere in the Hebrew Bible. The boundaries and borders between Moab and Israel are fluid and unstable (Matheny 2022, 155). For example, the tribe of Gad builds the city of Dibon in Num 32:34, but elsewhere this city is attributed to Moab (Isa 15:2; Jer 48:18, 22). The city of Aroer, which the Gadites also build in Num 32:34, is likewise categorized elsewhere as Moabite (Jer 48:19) or as Ammonite territory (Josh 13:24-25). It is also assumed that the city is part of Moabite/Ammonite territory in the Jephthah story (Judg 11:33).

Broadly, the border issue between Israel and Moab revolves around the Transjordanian territory north of the Arnon river; certain parts of the Hebrew Bible present this territory as Moabite while other parts explicitly deny it. Examples for the northern placement of Moab include the repeated phrase "the plains of Moab" for such territory in Numbers, Deuteronomy, and Joshua, and the Oracle against Moab in Isa 15-16 in which the majority, if not all, of the Moabite cities listed are north of the Arnon. There are, however, several biblical stories that explicitly draw the northern border of Moab at the river Arnon. This is particularly the case in Num 21:13 and Judg 11:18, which recount how Israel conquered Sihon, king of the Amorites. Sihon himself had formerly conquered the Moabites, taking all the Moabite land until the river Arnon (Num 21:26; Judg 11:18-19), and thus these texts reason that Israel did not (at least directly) take over any Moabite territory. In addition to Num 21 and Judg 11, there are numerous references to the Sihon story in the Hebrew Bible (Deut 2:24-37; Jos 1:2; 13:9-10; Ps 135:11-12; 136:19-22; Neh 9:22) that emphasize the importance of this claim. This very emphasis, though, is perhaps evidence of protesting too much, betraying a knowledge that this territory was, or could be, associated with Moab (Jobling 1986, 114; Havrelock 2011, 121-23). Indeed, the Moabite cities listed in the Mesha Inscription, including Mesha's capital city of Dibon, all lie north of the Arnon river (Routledge 2004, 41-57).

Deuteronomy explicitly links the Israelite avoidance of taking over Moabite territory with the divine command not to take territory from the descendants of Lot (Deut 2:9). In addition to highlighting this familial connection between Israel and Moab, Deuteronomy also imagines the Moabites as emerging in their land in a similar way to that of Israel – namely, by displacing an indigenous population of giants. The Moabites displace the Emim, which the text likens to Anakim (giants), and then asserts that Emim is the Moabite name for Rephaim (also giants) (Deut

2:10–11). This parallels Israel's settlement in the Transjordan with its victory over Sihon and King Og of Bashan, who is the last remnant of the Rephaim (Deut 3:11). These Transjordanian conquests of giants echo the Cisjordanian Anakim (also called Nephilim in Num 13:25–33) and subscribe to a fairy-tale like idea in which a nation comes to adulthood by slaying the giants who stand in their way (Pardes 2000, 114–15).

Indeed, Moab plays a central role in Israel's birth and emergence, as it is the last stop from the exodus out of Egypt to Canaan. It is thus a transitionary space – from the nomadic to the sedentary, from the Transjordan to the Cisjordan. However, it also functions as a primary barrier to Israel's crossing of the Jordan. The most obvious example of this is the Moabite king Balak's hiring of the prophet Balaam to curse the Israelites so that they might be easily defeated in battle (Num 22–24; Deut 23:4–5; Jos 24:9–10; Neh 13:2; Mic 6:5). Added to this is the repeated claim that the Moabites did not provide food and water for the Israelites in their desert wandering (Deut 23:4–5; Neh 13:2). The Balak/Balaam story thus presents Moab as a place of (attempted) cursing against Israel, death, and lack of nourishment. Of course, Deut 2:28–29 states just the opposite – namely, that Moab *did* offer/sell food and water to Israel, and therefore is a place of nourishment.

The ambiguity of Moab that we have highlighted so far in terms of kinship and territory relates to matters of deviancy and gender. Moab is generally associated with the improper and taboo. It is, for example, a place of incest (Gen 19:30–38), idolatry (Num 25:1–3), and child sacrifice (2 Kgs 3:27). More specifically, Moab is a place of gender deviancy, according to the patriarchal gender ideology of the Hebrew Bible (Havrelock 2011; Sabo 2020). Lot and his daughters, for instance, can be seen as archetypal figures of Moabite men and women. This is the case not just because of their incestuousness, but by the way that Lot is feminized and his daughters are masculinized. In the cave-scene, Lot is an entirely passive character, exploited by his daughters as a mere vessel for procreation. Both times Lot and his daughters have sex, the narrator comments: "and he did not know (*yāda'*) when she lay down and when she arose" (Gen 19:33, 35). The wordplay underlines that Lot carnally "knows" his daughters but does not cognitively "know" what is happening. So, while the text does not say outright that Lot's daughters "know" their father, it is clear that they are the active subjects who hold both purpose and knowledge, the conventional features of power in the sexual act in the Hebrew Bible, while Lot is deprived of them.

In Judg 3:12–30, the Moabite king Eglon, like Lot, is also penetrated by deceit. His defining feature is that he is an "exceedingly fat man" (*'iš barî' me'od* Judg 3:17), which connects to the text's presentation of him as an animal who will be slaughtered (Amit 1989, 110). His very name is derived from the word for "calf," *'egel*. The fatness and beastly features of Eglon relate to his murder by Ehud. In contrast to the Lot story, this deceptive penetration in the form of a dagger Ehud thrusts into Eglon's gut that is concealed by his rolls of fat does not lead to birth but to death. Nevertheless, the penetration of Eglon carries sexual undertones. As Susan Niditch observes, "the short sword worn on the thigh, a male erogenous zone, begins the play, for one hitches a sword at the thigh… but the thigh (or loins) is also the seat of male fertility… the short blade a phallic image" – additionally, "the term used for Ehud's ample belly is the same as the term for womb, while the image of fat closing around the blade is strongly vaginal" (2008, 58).

This motif of penetration in stories about Moabites reflects the anxiety over the porous boundaries between Israel and Moab. In this case, Eglon's initial conquest results in foreign Transjordanian penetration into Israel's borders and body (Judg 3:12–14). The disturbing logic appears to be that Ehud's violent penetration of Eglon "reverses" this, as it leads to, and is a symbol of, Israel reclaiming its lost territory and forcing Moab to retreat. The scatological elements of the story (Judg 3:24–26), moreover, relate to this theme of penetration, for both relate to the proper boundaries of the body. In associating the Moabites themselves with excrement (see also Isa 25:10–11), the story requires that the Moabite presence in Israelite territory be "flushed" out. And indeed, Ehud rallies together the people from the hill country of Ephraim and leads them to victory over the Moabites (Judg 3:28–29). By the end of the story, not a single Moabite is left within Israel. The abject element within the Israelite body – the excess, the extraneous, the wasteful – has been removed.

The passiveness of Moabite men contrasts with the activeness of Moabite women, and thus interaction between Israelite men and Moabite women produces rather different results. In Num 25:1–5, for example, Moabite women follow the archetype set by their foremother, the firstborn daughter of Lot, by "inviting" (feminine plural verb) Israelite men to follow "their" (feminine plural pronoun) god(s) (Num 25:2). The text describes the Israelite men as "fornicating" (*zānâ*) (Bird 1989 and 2006) with the daughters of Moab (Num 25:1). Jacob Milgrom (1989, 212) notes that this is the only place in the Hebrew Bible where *zānâ* takes a masculine subject and is meant in its literal (sexual) sense, thereby emphasizing gender deviancy and Israelite anxiety. For, from the patriarchal and Israelite perspective of the Hebrew Bible, the beckoning of these daughters of Moab has resulted in the worst possible outcome for the Israelite men who fall prey to it – the erasure of their masculine and Israelite identity.

Interaction with Moabite women also relates to the dynamic by which Moab becomes associated with both incest (Gen 19:30–38) and exogamy (1 Kgs 11:1–2; Ezra 9:1–2; Neh 13:1–2). The incest taboo and the prohibition against exogamy reflect fears of lost identity from opposite sides of the spectrum. The incest taboo reflects fear of losing identity in the familial, the same. The prohibition against exogamy reflects the fear of losing identity in the foreign, the other. Israel creates its identity by prizing endogamy, and it does so by navigating between incest and exogamy, especially in comparison to Moab, its primary close other.

This is a good point to return to Ruth and the idea that Moab in Ruth is a *mise-en-abîme* of Moab in the Hebrew Bible. Leaving Bethlehem for Moab (Ruth 1:1) is a reversal of the direction of the desert wandering and Abraham and Sarah's journey to Canaan. André LaCocque states that it is "a regression toward the prenatal, toward the unconscious" (2004, 3). And yet, the purpose of the journey is for food, for nourishment that apparently cannot be provided anywhere in the Cisjordan. This aligns with Deut 2:28–29 and, as is often noted, David sending his parents to dwell in Moab for safety (1 Sam 22:3–4). To be sure, Elimelech and his sons die in Moab, but this is in tension with Moab as an initial place of nourishment. If not for Moab, there might not be any more story to tell after the famine in Bethlehem. This association with both life/nourishment and death exists for Bethlehem, too. It is, of course, the initial place of famine, but less noted is the repetition of sounds – *kaph* (k/ch), *ḥet* (guttural h), *lamed* (l), and, to a lesser extent, *mem* (m) – between Bethlehem and the names Elimelech, Machlon, and Chilion (Hawk 2015, 51). That is, sound-play links all the men who die in the opening verses not with Moab but with Bethlehem.

The journey back to Judah (Ruth 1:6) is another beginning, echoing Israel's initial entrance into the Cisjordan, which itself echoes Abraham's journey there. The story of Lot and Abraham's separation in Gen13 thus lurks in the background of this scene. In contrast to her ancestor Lot – who "separates" (*pārad*) from Abraham (Gen 13:9, 11, 14) and moves from the Cisjordan to settle in the Transjordan – Ruth refuses to let anything "separate" her from Naomi (Ruth 1:17) and moves from the Transjordan to settle in the Cisjordan. This then connects to Ruth's marriage to Boaz at the end of the book, which brings together descendants from the line of Lot and Abraham. For the moment, though, nothing is certain. The text implies, for instance, that the dialogue between Ruth and her daughters-in-law occurs in the Transjordan, between Moab and Judah. It is an appropriate in-between setting in which Ruth, the Moabite, is not yet in Judah and Naomi, the Judahite, has not yet left the Transjordan.

This chapter also recalls the Baal-Peor episode in Num 25:1–5. A predominately male, solely Israelite family goes to Moab, but a female family, split between Moabite and Israelite identity, departs from the land. Thus, Israelite men who cross over into Moab do not go back to Israel. This foregrounds the thread of biblical tradition that associates

Moab with the loss and erasure of both masculine and Israelite identity. On the one hand, then, the threat of Moabite women is intensified, as a Moabite woman enters Cisjordan. On the other hand, the outcome in terms of cultural/religious assimilation appears to have already been avoided, as Ruth has expressed her loyalty to Naomi's people and God (Ruth 1:16). In Num 25:1–5, Israelite men adopt the traditions of Moab; in Ruth, a Moabite woman adopts the traditions of Israel. In line with the ambiguity of Moab, though, Ruth's assimilation is not a straightforward matter. She is continually referred to as a Moabite even after her initial marriage to Mahlon, her adherence to Naomi's people and deity, her migration to Bethlehem, and her marriage to Boaz. Though she appears to lose this qualification after the birth of Obed in 4:13, there is still an ongoing debate as to whether Ruth is adopted by the Bethlehemite community, and, correspondingly, whether ethnic identity is constructed or innate (Glover 2009 represents the former position; Thambyrajah 2021 and Chapter 6 in this volume).

Ruth is a "foreigner-kinswoman" (Lee 2006, 92–93). This refers, on the one hand, to the fact that Moab and Israel are foreign to each other – and indeed, Ruth refers to herself as a foreigner (Ruth 2:10). But the allusions to the Lot story throughout the book evoke the distant kinship between Moabites and Israelites and thereby recall that Ruth is kin who has *become foreign* since the generations of separation from the time of Lot. The intermingling of identities is reflected in the fusing of incest and exogamy in the book. The marriage between Ruth and Boaz is, on the surface, an exogamous one – but it is tinged with incestuous links. This is most obvious in Ruth's seduction of Boaz in ch.3, since it characterizes Ruth as a typical Moabite woman (an active subject who holds both awareness and knowledge) by echoing the rape of Lot by his daughters. The genealogy at the end of the book, however, connects Boaz to the line of Perez, the son of Tamar (4:18–22, see also 4:12). Both Ruth and Boaz, therefore, are descendants of ancestors from incestuous unions (Fisch 1982; Kaniel 2015). Ruth descends from the line of Moab, a son born from the seduction of Lot by his firstborn daughter (Gen 19:30–38). Boaz descends from the line of Perez, a son born from the seduction of Judah (the great grandson of Abraham) by his daughter-in-law Tamar (Gen 38). Their union blurs the lines between Moab and Israel, kin and other, incest and exogamy.

2. Caves and Threshing Floors

Ruth does have a saving grace. She is not a Canaanite. There is no specific interdict of marriage with a Moabite in the Torah. William Tooman

(2022b) has traced the process whereby the prohibition of intermarriage gradually expanded so as to include not only Moabites, but all gentiles. Nonetheless, a certain ambiguity about Ruth's status remains.

> And it was in the days of the judging of the judges, that there was a famine in the land, and a man went from Bethlehem of Judah to sojourn in the field of Moab, he and his wife, and his two sons. And the name of the man was Elimelech, and the name of his wife, Naomi, and the name of his two sons, Mahlon and Chilion, Ephrathites of Bethlehem of Judah, and they came to the fields of Moab, and they were there. (Ruth 1:1-2)

There are so many questions, but let us first imagine the scene. A man looks over from Bethlehem of Judah to the field of Moab, across the giant caesura of the Jordan Valley. The mountains of Moab, red, formidable, look back. Jennifer Koosed (2011, 44) has well intimated the difficulty of the return journey: "Ruth and Naomi had to descend 4,329 feet to cross the Dead Sea and then ascend 3,679 feet into the Judean hill country." The journey to Moab, steeper and higher than Bethlehem, would be correspondingly more taxing. And what would await them there? Commentators wax prolix on the Israelite abhorrence of Moabites, but, judging from the Mesha Inscription, the feeling was reciprocated, at least at certain times. As strangers they would be entering into uncertain terrain, without family connections or an obvious basis of subsistence. The transition is evident, for instance, in the move from a "house," Bethlehem, to a "field," between the Mediterranean littoral and the desert (Koosed 2011, 42; Grossman 2015, 78-79; Tooman 2022a, 29). Daniel Hawk (2015, 24) thinks that "field" is a "mediating metaphor," associated with death and loss in the case of Moab, and fullness and life in the case of Bethlehem.

But they settle somehow. The text circles back on itself: "and they came to the field of Moab, and they were there." Elimelech may have intended to reside temporarily, as the word *gur*, "sojourn," suggests, but "they were there", in a kind of limbo. Elimelech dies, and the two sons marry Moabite women, Orpah and Ruth. Marrying into a country is a sure means of integrating into it, then as now; it implies, moreover, a certain social status. If the *ger*, the stranger, is emblematic of marginality, these are immigrants who have made it.

Of course, everything goes wrong. Mahlon and Chilion die, their names "sickness" and "destruction," respectively, are indicative of their fate. The names, however, are not entirely unrealistic. A daughter of Ishmael is called Mahlat (Gen 28:9), and one of Zelophehad's daughters is Mahlah (Num 27:1; 36:11). A Levite clan is Mahli (Exod 6:19). The name Kilion is found in Ugaritic (Zakovitch 1990, 47, but Bush (1996, 64) is skeptical of etymological interpretations).

There is another beginning, which, together with "the judging of the judges," introduces the motif of repetition in the first five words (Koosed 2011, 36): "and there was a famine in the land." It takes us back to the wife-sister stories in Genesis (Gen 12; 20; 26), when the patriarch leaves the Promised Land because of a famine and pretends his wife is his sister; she is then taken by the foreign king, only to be restored after divine intervention. In each case, the return is accompanied by an access to fertility (Sonnet 2021, 48). The famine is a sign of sterility, which affects not only the land but the patriarchal family; both Sarah and Rebecca are barren. The fundamental problem for the patriarchal family is how to reconcile the conflicting demands of endogamy, entailing real or imagined incest, and exogamy, marrying into the land while remaining separate from it. The wife/sister symbolically marries the foreign king, while actually retaining her husband/brother. She then becomes fertile, either in herself or through a surrogate, such as Hagar.

Here none of the expectations are met. Elimelech does not pass off Naomi as his sister; she is not procured by the Moabite king; instead, he dies, and his Moabite daughter-in-law becomes the progenitress of Israelite kings. If intermarriage, especially with daughters, is the principal temptation in Judges, for example, in Judges 3.6 and the Samson stories, threatening Israelite identity and fealty to Yhwh, in Ruth it is generative. The famine at the beginning of the book is indicative of infertility, both human and agricultural, since the land is always responsive to the human condition. It is the dead end of Judges. Through Ruth the land, and Bethlehem in particular, is transformed from emptiness to fullness. Bethlehem lives up to its name, *beth lehem*, "house of bread."

Bethlehem is not an innocent signifier. Both the last stories in Judges concern Bethlehem, from opposite points of view. In the one a Levite from Bethlehem goes to Ephraim and eventually helps establish the apostate shrine of Dan, outside the prescribed Israelite borders (Judg 17–18). In the other, a Levite from Ephraim acquires a concubine from Bethlehem, who is raped and murdered at Gibeah (Judg 19). Both stories concern the abortive union of Ephraim and Judah, under the aegis of the sacred but landless tribe, Levi (Landy 2016; 2024). In both cases, Bethlehem represents the Davidic future, which is both anticipated, for example through the refrain "In those days there was no king in Israel," and deferred (Goitein 1959, 50).

There is another sign of the hidden presence of Ephraim. Elimelech and his sons are Ephrathites, recalling Rachel's death in Gen 35:17, 19–20 at Ephrath, which is specified as Bethlehem. Similarly, in 1 Sam 1:1, Elkanah is an Ephrathite. Ruth has several correlates with the beginning of Samuel, notably that in each a woman is worth many sons (Grossman 2015, 20; Hawk 2015, 55; Tooman 2022a, 48). Ephrath in 1 Sam 1:1 clearly means Ephraimite; that Elimelech and his sons are Ephrathites suggests a dual identity, that the two halves of Israel are not so distinct after all. Ephraim and Judah meet through Ruth. Ilana Pardes (1992, 107) has argued persuasively that Ruth is an avatar of both Rachel and Leah, in whom the sisters are reconciled.

"And they died, also the two of them, Mahlon and Chilion" (1:5a). Both are presumably buried in Moab, as is Elimelech, far from their ancestral tomb; being buried in exile is an ultimate alienation, since it means one can never return. Mahlon has an afterlife, thanks to Ruth and Boaz and the quasi-Levirate marriage; Boaz acts "to raise up the name of the dead over his inheritance" (4:5, 10). The name has a future separated from the corpse, though it seems to be forgotten, both in the genealogy and in all subsequent history. Chilion has no heir, it seems; his grave in Moab, with his wife Orpah, perhaps, makes him part of a different adoptive family. All that was his is bought by Boaz, "from the hand of Naomi" (4:9), except perhaps for her memories, of a mother who has lost her child, far away in a foreign land. If Mahlon's name is not "cut off from his brothers and from the gate of his place" (4:11), Chilion's assuredly is. As Zakovitch (1990, 48) points out, there is a progression from Mahlon, "sickness," to Chilion, "destruction." The fates of Mahlon and Chilion correspond to those of Ruth and Orpah, one absorbed into the Judean polity, the other left outside it. Orpah turns her back, literally her neck (Orpah puns on the word *'oref*, "neck") on Ruth; she is Ruth's other side, the one left behind in Moab. This does not mean they do not remain in touch (see Dube 1999 for an imaginative reconstruction of Orpah's letters to Ruth). There is thus a complex set of mediations:

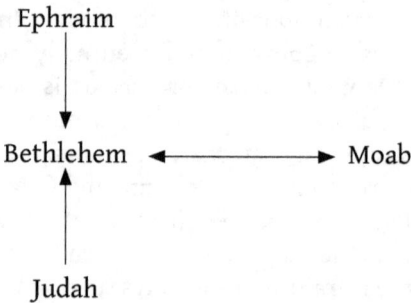

Ephraim and Judah meet in Bethlehem; Bethlehem intermarries with Moab; reciprocally Moab marries into Bethlehem.

Alongside these mediations, whereby the two halves of Israel are united in the house of David, and the lines of Lot and Abraham converge, there are insistent splittings, between Ruth and Orpah, Mahlon and

Chilion, Boaz and Mr. So-and-So, Perez and Zerah, Rachel and Leah, Moab and Ammon. For everyone who is brought into the equation, someone is left out. In other words, integration is never complete; it is always a system of exclusions.

Moab is the land of death (Hawk 2015, 23), "and the woman was left without her two sons and her husband" (1:5b), but it is also the land of rebirth. From there Ruth comes to revitalize Israel, to resolve the problem of its disunity, to incubate the sacred dynasty. It is as if Israel needs Moab, its constitutive other, to become itself.

The problem, as ever, is that of intermarriage. On the one hand, there is the imperative of endogamy, whose extreme form is incest. Only thus will Israel remain distinct from the nations and not be corrupted by them. On the other hand, there is the temptation of exogamy; in other words, Israel should be part of the nations, in particular the land of Canaan. With Ruth, the problem of intermarriage *in* the land is projected *outside* it, at one remove. Moreover, as already noted, Moab is ambiguous, both kin and alien. It holds an intermediate position between Israel and its others.

Moab is a displacement of the problems of Genesis and Judges; across the caesura of the Rift Valley, Moab is a split off part of the self, a haunting double, in which Genesis and Judges are reflected and distorted. In literature, a "double" is a figure who resembles one of the other characters, and which can work out possibilities otherwise left unexplored. In the wife-sister stories, incest is either fictitious – the patriarch pretends his wife is his sister – or defused by the claim, true or not, that Sarah is Abraham's half-sister, and thus it is not truly incest. The story of Lot inverts the patriarchal narrative. Instead of the symbolic or vicarious fulfillment of the fantasy of incest, whether through deception or by proxy, it is drastically consummated. Father-daughter incest is notoriously excluded from the incest code in Lev 18. Here the lacuna, and the desire it represents, is filled in the abhorred land of Moab, which is itself a displacement of Sodom. It is as if the sex that dare not speak its name is spoken, but only in the Medusa-like gaze of the Lot story. It is a point of traumatic fixation outside the main narrative, which reflects on it. The subplot works out possibilities, ways not taken, inflected and reversed in the main narrative. If the culminating trauma in the Abrahamic cycle is that of the father who almost kills his son, here it is the daughters who sleep with the father. It is a primal scene, which fascinates and induces recoil. The temptation, and the anxiety, is the exposure of nakedness, which is both sacrilege against the dignity of the father, and hence the deity, and threatens with the fragility of being, without our habitual disguises and protections. On the one hand, the child imagines intercourse with the father and, hence, the foreclosure of the Oedipal drama; on the other, the father rapes the child (Herman 2000, 60–61).

The cave is the site of sex; the daughters return to the scene of their own conception, to be impregnated in their turn. As such, the cave is a womb-like space, in which both father and daughters are contained (Sabo 2017, 70–74; Graybill and Sabo 2018). But the mother is dead, petrified at the moment of turning back, horrified perhaps by what she saw, preserved forever as a witness to catastrophe. The father and daughters take refuge from a death imagined to be universal, but the womb is that of the dead mother; it, too, is pervaded by death. Hence, it is paradoxical. It is a story of castration as well as insemination, since the daughters steal the father's seed, and thus evokes the fantasy of sex as death, as emasculation. The father both "knows" and does not "know" his daughters (Gen 19:33, 35).

Ruth comes to redeem the story, as well as her husband's memory (Fisch 1982, 385); she salvages Moab's reputation, as well as bringing new life to Judah. But Ruth only tells half the story of the Moabite, and thus incestuous, origins of the Davidic dynasty. There is still Ammon, which seems to be left out of the picture. Only with Rehoboam, whose mother is Na'amah the Ammonite (1 Kings 14:21), is the line of Ammon reintegrated into that of the Davidic kingdom, for better or for worse.

Ruth and Boaz reenact the story of Lot and his daughters, but at a safe distance. Boaz is not really Ruth's father, even though he calls her "my daughter"; though he is drunk, he awakens to his responsibility; thereby seed is preserved for the future. The displacements continue; he is not truly a *levir* – a brother of a husband who died childless and is obligated to father a son with his widow (Deut 25:5). Boaz thus does not commit the mandatory incestuous act of sleeping with his brother's wife, and he isn't even the proper redeemer. The text is very careful to project the dynamics of the family story outwards.

The scene takes place on the threshing floor. Boaz comes at night to winnow the barley; he eats, drinks, his heart is merry, and he falls asleep next to the heap of grain. Naomi, and presumably everyone else, knows that this is what he does on that night, and advises Ruth accordingly. We do not know why he acts in this way, why he winnows at night, why this solitary celebration, why he does not sleep at home. It may be a folk ritual, an incubation scene (Sasson 1979, 65; Landy 2001). In Hos 9:1–2, threshing floors are the site of cultic or sexual prostitution, drunkenness, and infidelity to Yhwh. One can imagine harvest festivals, such as Shavuot, as complex symbolic affairs. The story is related intertextually to others about threshing floors, notably that of David's purchase of Araunah/Arnon's threshing floor as a sacred site in 2 Sam 24 = 1 Chr 21 (Landy 2014). Threshing floors are sites of judgment, separating the grain from the chaff, and of divine blessing. Accordingly, they may be associated with testing, both of God and humans, as when Gideon tests Yhwh on a threshing floor in Judg 6:37-40 and is actually tested himself.

Boaz goes down to the threshing floor; the nocturnal setting, the solitude, inebriation, even his heart being "good" – either from drink or satisfaction in his labor – make it a psychic as well as topographical space apart from the everyday world. The grain of the house of bread is processed here; it is a sign of its prosperity and, thus, its state of blessing and its hope for the future. The ritual, if such it is, announces Boaz's presence and communicates, presumably, with Yhwh in thanksgiving, but also with whatever other powers there be. In an incubation ritual, the postulant solicits a significant dream in a sacred site. Ruth may be the answer to Boaz's quest. That the ritual takes place outside a temple suggests continuity with the Canaanite past, a transfer from the gods of the land to Yhwh. In the night who knows what specters might come, Ruth certainly, but also Mahlon, since Ruth evokes his presence. Jack Sasson (1979, 76-79) suggests that Boaz might fear the intrusion of some night demon, like Lilith. Here Moabite and Israelite meet, and the living and the dead. Here the dead can be reintegrated into the human community, the sickness signified by Mahlon's name cured.

Threshing floors have a liminal quality. Enclosed from the rest of the world, cleared and demarcated, the threshing floor may be the focus of community tensions and anxieties, a place for public performance, like the threshing floor at the gates of Samaria in 1 Kgs 22. Threshing floors are particularly associated with the intersection of life and death, such as the oxymoronic "thorn threshing floor" in Gen 50:10, where Jacob is mourned, or the outburst of Yhwh against Uzzah at the "threshing floor of Nakon" in 2 Sam 6:6. In particular, David's purchase of the threshing floor of Araunah the Jebusite in 2 Sam 24:16-25 marks the point where the destroying angel relents at the divine command (2 Sam 24:16) and is the foundation story of the Temple, according to 2 Chr 3:1. In 1 Kgs 22, similarly, the threshing floor exposes the weakness of Ahab and his dynasty and leads directly to his doom (Landy 2014).

Threshing floors are associated also with hybridity. David builds his altar on the site of a Jebusite threshing floor. Boaz encounters Ruth on his threshing floor, resulting in their marriage. There is a trajectory from the threshing floor, where Ruth awakens Boaz to his responsibility and thus initiates the Davidic dynasty, to the culminating moment of the purchase of the land for the temple, in 2 Sam 24. The hybridity suggests an instability in the sacred foundations.

3. Anti-Moabite and Anti-Judahite

LaCocque writes that "Ruth the Moabite is the anti-Moabite" (2004, 3). For LaCocque, this means that Ruth is not only different from other Moabites but, also, that she is like Judahites. Indeed, "her 'heroism' is to become more of a Judean than those who are Judean by birth" (LaCocque 2004, 24–25). There are, however, layers to consider with these distinctions between Ruth's Moabite-ness and her Judahite-ness. Considering these layers, moreover, takes us back to the complex network of difference and similarity between the descendants of Lot and Abraham. We have seen, for example, that Ruth's actions in ch.3 strongly echo those of Lot's daughters. It is precisely at the moment of Ruth's greatest connection to her Moabite ancestors, though, that Ruth consummates her connection to Boaz. In other words, Ruth establishes her Judahite-ness by acting like an archetypal Moabite woman.

Similarly, Boaz, a "pillar" of the Judahite community, is likened to Lot, the archetypal Moabite man, in ch.3. The similarity reveals the Moabite-ness that lies within Judahite identity. Indeed, the very features of the text that link Boaz to Lot also link Boaz to Judah. And so, there is a web of connections between Lot, Judah, and Boaz of which one result is that the eponymous ancestor of Judah is also likened to the archetypal Moabite man. The biblical origins of the Judahites are not so different from the origins of the Moabites. On the other hand, these similarities emphasize difference. The series of displacements between Boaz and Lot is mirrored by the series of displacements between Boaz and Judah. Unlike Judah, for example, Boaz does not marry a Canaanite and does not have sex with his daughter-in-law (compare Gen 38 with Ruth 3–4). Whereas Judah does have his moment of self-awareness (unlike Lot) by acknowledging Tamar's righteousness over his own (Gen 38:26), Boaz makes his responsibility public and seeks approval from the elders (Ruth 4:1–12). From this perspective, Boaz the Judahite is the anti-Judah. If Ruth "redeems" her ancestors by way of connections that emphasize difference, then Boaz "redeems" his in the same way.

Whatever redemption that Ruth and Boaz offer to their ancestors, however, is mediated by multiple other threads and directions in the book. As noted above, the doublings in the book of Ruth result in acts of unity and acts of separation paralleling each other. Ruth's adoption and inclusion into Judah is paralleled by Orpah's return to Moab; Boaz's marriage to Ruth is paralleled by Mr. So-and-So's rejection of it; and he raising up of the name of Mahlon is paralleled by both Chilion's name not being raised up and the effacement of Mahlon's name in the concluding genealogy.

All of these doublings are linked to the doubling between Moab and Judah/Israel. When Bethlehem experiences a famine, Moab is a place of nourishment and refuge. When death overtakes Judahites in Moab, fertility returns to Bethlehem. These seeming dichotomies betray a deeper connection, as in the fact, noted above, that Elimelech, Mahlon, and Chilion die in Moab but are linked through sound-play with Bethlehem. The pivotal divide between Orpah's return to Moab and Ruth's to Judah occurs in Transjordan, a symbol of unity and separation between Moab and Israel *and* between the different parts of Israel itself. Thus, the way Ruth both confirms and traverses the boundaries between Moab and Israel parallels Israel's internal issues of separation and unity. The perpetuation of Mahlon's name differentiates his fate from Chilion, but the effacement of his name from the genealogy differentiates his fate from Boaz. The patrilineal genealogy also effaces Ruth and Naomi. After focusing primarily on the actions of women, the book reverts back to archetypal patriarchal mystification, the subsuming of the female into the male.

4. Love and Death

Ruth is an antidote to Judges. The murder of Eglon is reversed in the intercourse of Ruth and Boaz; disjunction becomes conjunction. Ehud's sword penetrates Eglon's belly, and presumably his bowels, in a parody of anal sex; it is as if he has raped, certainly humiliated, as well as killed, Eglon. Ehud is left-handed, deviating from the right-handed norm, as well as from the significance of the tribal name, itself a distortion, a euphemism, for Benjamin's real name, *ben 'oni*, "son of my affliction," and the trauma it represents (Gen 35:18). Benjamin is the son who kills his mother, leaving a vacancy where maternal presence should be. Ilana Pardes proposes that Ruth reenacts, and reclaims, the story of Rachel (1992, 115). Ehud is an initiatory emblem of the queerness of Judges. The story of Ehud is echoed and amplified in that of the Levite's concubine (Judg 19) and its ramifications in Judg 20–21. Here Ehud's left-handedness characterizes the entire right-handed tribe of Benjamin, infecting them with his perversity; they become literally sinister. In Judg 19 the Gibeahites demand to "know" the travelling Levite, whose sacrality makes him a surrogate for the deity; in wishing to rape him they threaten to violate Yhwh, too. Their desire is deflected onto the concubine, who becomes a symbol, as Alice A. Keefe (1993) argues, for the murdered and butchered maternal body of Israel. Judges 19 replays the story of Sodom as tragedy rather than farce; there is no divine intervention, and the woman is not saved. The Moabite origin story is transferred to the heart of Israel. Cisjordan and Transjordan mirror each other. If Moab, in the story of Eglon and Lot's daughters, is abjected, in Judges 19 the abject is reincorporated into the body politic of Israel, the repressed returns.

Jennifer Matheny (2022, 143–49) argues that Ruth is a *mashal*, a parable, which answers the silence, violence, and victimization of women in Judg 19–21. In particular, Ruth responds to the story of the Levite's concubine (Judg 19) in the context of a subversive intertextual canon (Matheny 2022, 226). In the story of the Levite's concubine, a woman goes from her father's house in the nutritive matrix of Bethlehem, to become a victim of exogamy, fair game for anonymous strangers. Her body is dispersed through the land of Israel. She is a figure both for the dying parturient, Rachel, and for the recalcitrant indigeneity of Canaan, persistent under the Israelite veneer. Ruth comes from outside, to bring life to the sterile womb of the bereaved mother, Naomi, a bride for the patriarch, Boaz, posterity and a name to the dead husband, Mahlon. The two stories present opposite trajectories: from inside to outside, and from outside in. It is not that Ruth "redeems" the story of the Levite's concubine in any sense, for it is irredeemable (for unhappy readings of the story, see Graybill 2021 and Landy 2024), but it answers for it, acknowledges it.

Let us go back to the beginning of the story. "In the days of the judging of the judges." The irony, emphasized by the doubling of the term, is that in the book of Judges there was no justice, only travesties of justice, as in the absurdly legalistic attempts to put right the genocide of the Benjaminites in Judg 21. Ruth, however, is obsessed with legality, notably the laws of gleaning, the levirate, and redemption (but see ch.3 in this volume). In each case, the law is interpreted in the interests of generosity, of *ḥesed*. It becomes the basis of a benevolent society. However, there is one implacable exception, discreetly passed over, yet, as Avivah Zornberg says (2009, 244), looming over the book: "No Ammonite or Moabite may enter the congregation of Yhwh; until the tenth generation, none of them may enter the congregation of Yhwh, for ever" (Deut 23:4). The rabbis circumvented the problem by claiming that the prohibition only applied to Moabites, not Moabitesses (Baba Bathra 15b). But did Ruth ever enter "the congregation of Yhwh"? Right until the end she is called "Ruth the Moabitess," unassimilable, perhaps retaining her accent, her difference. Only at the very end, finally, is she just "Ruth," at the moment when Boaz consummates their marriage. "And Boaz took Ruth, and she became his wife, and he went in unto her…" (4:13). Boaz may recognize her, as in 2:10, but no longer as a foreigner. At that very moment, Ruth disappears from the narrative. The women of Bethlehem praise her to Naomi as her "daughter-in-law"; Naomi suckles the child; we pass on to the concluding genealogy and back into history.

Zornberg (2009, 354) adduces D. A. Miller's *Narrative and Its Discontents* to highlight how there is tension in every novel between the desire for closure, the solution to all its problems, and the need for complication, which makes the story interesting. Ruth is the agent of complication and transformation. Once the story ends, there is no need for her. She disappears into a cloud of approbation, which marks her communal acceptance: she is like the arch-mothers Rachel and Leah, "who built between them the house of Israel"; like the Judahite foremother Tamar, whose scandalous story is interwoven with Ruth's; and, finally and most dramatically, Yhwh grants her pregnancy and birth. Yet she is also the site of resistance to closure, and thus the happy ending. Her life is one of choice, contingency, and risk, with even a whiff of satire. When she creeps to Boaz on the threshing floor, she acts the part of a typical Moabite woman, but of course "everyone knows" that she is virtuous (3:11). We are drawn back into the story even as we end it. Nowhere is this clearer than in her first speech:

> Do not press me to forsake you, to turn back from you, for wherever you go, I will go; wherever you lodge, I will lodge; your people shall be my people, your God my God. Where you die, I shall die, and there I will be buried; so may Yhwh do to me, and more so, if death should separate us. (Ruth 1:16–17)

What is Ruth's imagined life here? Certainly not Boaz and the threshing floor or the redemption of Mahlon's field and name. All this happens, as life goes on. It is a full life story, with the woman she loves, according to the women of Bethlehem (4:15). It is ḥesed, and perhaps more than ḥesed. It is a life that ends with death. But there is also an ambiguity. The last clause could read either "For (ky) only death will separate us" or "If death will separate us." It may be positive or negative.

Ruth is a sidetrack, an interlude. In the LXX/Christian Bibles, Ruth is part of the narrative history between Judges and Samuel. On the other hand, in the Masoretic tradition, it is part of the Ketuvim, the third section of the Hebrew Bible, and thus has a metahistorical function. While great and terrible events were going on, this, too, was happening; ordinary people living out their lives. As the Lot story functions as a comment on and a reflex of the tensions of the patriarchal narratives, Ruth presents an image of what life in the Promised Land could be, before there were kings, in an idealized imagined past. Ruth crosses the boundary between Moab and Israel; the history of Moab is imprinted on that of Israel. The abjectness of Moab, its being cast out, its excremental and promiscuous associations, is reclaimed as part of the self, the future of Israel. According to Kristeva's classic theory, the abject is threatening, regarded as loathsome, because it is so intimate, evoking primary bodily experiences and substances. These experiences can readily be transformed into the sublime, into the beautiful (Kristeva 1982, 12). Ruth "sticks" (*dabaq*) to Naomi, as to the reapers (2:18–23); she is something that cannot be shaken off. Stickiness, which Graybill (2021, 52–54) sees as contagious, as indicating an inability to discard uncomfortable feelings, is a sign of love. Zornberg (2009, 364) writes of Ruth's "viscosity." Similarly, the loathsomeness of Moab's promiscuity, and the impurity of sexual fluids generally, is reversed in the threshing floor scene, in which every detail of Ruth's preparations – her scent, her dress – evinces sexual attractiveness (Landy 2001, 224–25).

In the Jewish Bible, Ruth follows the Song of Songs, as it does in the liturgical year: Song of Songs is recited on Passover, Ruth on Shavuot (Weeks). In the Song of Songs, the wager is that "love is as strong as death" (8:6). Ruth exemplifies, in narrative form, the question intrinsic to the Hebrew Bible of whether love is as strong as death, whether it survives the catastrophes that befall us. Ruth asserts that only death will divide her from Naomi, or, contrariwise, not even death will do so. Survival happens in various ways; through the book that is named after her, through the act of intercourse in which the dead vicariously participates, in our imaginative reliving of the story.

There is another ghost: Moses, who is buried in the land of Moab, and "no one knows his grave until this very day" (Deut 34:6). Moses, as Francesca Stavrakopoulou (2010, 55–80) argues, is a liminal figure, between this world and the world of the dead, in the abhorred land of Moab, unvisited, houseless, in contrast to Ruth, who finds a home in the family vault in Bethlehem. Ruth can be a biological ancestor; Moses will be the forefather of a scribal guild (Rossi 2024). Moses, through his speech on the plains of Moab, encodes the future, of which he cannot be part. His shadow pervades the entire history, from Joshua to Kings. Moses is buried opposite Peor, the site of Israel's cultic and sexual transgression with the daughters of Moab. Moab is both the abject – the object of disgust – and the place from which Deuteronomic Torah comes forth, in which intercourse with Moab is forbidden: "You shall not inquire after their well-being or fortune" (Deut 23:7). It is untouchable in both senses. The past is buried with the past. But from there Ruth comes to claim a future.

A similar transformation attends Balaam. From the heights of Moab, he is hired to curse Israel but blesses it instead. His blessing, on the eve of the entrance into the Promised Land, recalls Yhwh's commission to Abraham: "I will bless those who bless you, and those who execrate you I will curse" (Gen 12:3a). Balaam presages ideal harmony between Israel and the nations, in which "through you will all the families of the earth be blessed" (Gen 12:3b). His twin fates, to return safely home (Num 24:5) and to die with the Midianites (Num 31:8), adumbrates his ambivalence.

Ruth, similarly, leaves the land of Moab to bring blessing and fertility to Israel. Ruth is a book of blessing, from Boaz's initial greeting to his reapers to the women's celebration of Obed's birth. Blessing circulates, as a sign of the affective ties within the community and between them and Yhwh. It also suggests the possibility of reconciliation, when all who are cast out, beginning with the line of Lot, are welcomed home, and of an ideal world, in which Abraham's promise is fulfilled.

Works Cited

Alter, Robert. 1990. "Sodom as Nexus: The Web of Design in Biblical Narrative." Pages 146-60 in *The Book and the Text: The Bible and Literary Theory*. Edited by Regina Schwartz. Oxford: Blackwell.

Amit, Yairah. 1989. "The Story of Ehud (Judges 3:12-30): The Form and the Message." Pages 97-112 in *Signs and Wonders*. Edited by J. Cheryl Exum. Atlanta: Society of Biblical Literature.

Bird, Phyllis. 1989. "'To Play the Harlot': An Inquiry into an Old Testament Metaphor." Pages 75-94 in *Gender and Difference in Ancient Israel*. Edited by Peggy L. Day. Minneapolis: Fortress.

-----. 2006. "Prostitution in the Social World and the Religious Rhetoric of Ancient Israel." Pages 40-58 in *Prostitutes and Courtesans in the Ancient World*. Edited by Christopher A. Faraone and Laura K. McClure. Madison: University of Wisconsin Press.

Bush, Frederic. 1996. *Ruth-Esther*. Word Bible Commentaries. Waco, TX: Word.

Dube, Musa W. 1999. "The Unpublished Letters of Orpah and Ruth." Pages 145-50 in *A Feminist Companion to the Bible. 2nd series. Ruth and Esther*. Edited by Athalya Brenner. London: Bloomsbury.

Fewell, Danna and David Gunn. 1990. *Compromising Redemption: Relating Characters in the Book of Ruth*. Louisville: Westminster John Knox.

Fisch, Harold. 1982. "Ruth and the Structure of Covenant History." *Vetus Testamentum* 32: 425-37.

Glover, Neil. 2009. "Your People, My People. An Exploration of Ethnicity in Ruth." *Journal for the Study of the Old Testament* 33: 293-313.

Goitein, Shlomo D. 1959. "Megillat Rut." Pages 49-58 in *'Iyyunim BaMikra*. Tel Aviv: Yavneh.

Gow, Murray D. 1992. *The Book of Ruth: Its Structure, Theme and Purpose*. Leicester: Apollos.

Graybill, Rhiannon. 2021. *Texts After Terror: Rape, Sexual Violence, and the Hebrew Bible*. Oxford: Oxford University Press.

-----. and Peter J. Sabo. 2018. "Caves of the Hebrew Bible: A Speleology." *Biblical Interpretation* 20: 1-22.

Grossman, Jonathan. 2015. *Ruth: Bridges and Boundaries*. Bern: Peter Lang.

Havrelock, Rachel. 2011. *River Jordan: The Mythology of a Dividing Line*. Chicago: University of Chicago Press.
Hawk, Daniel L. 2015. *Ruth*. Downers Grove: InterVarsity.
Herman, Judith L. 2000. *Father-Daughter Incest*. Cambridge, MA: Harvard University Press.
Jobling, David. 1986. *The Sense of Biblical Narrative: Structural Studies in the Hebrew Bible, II*. Sheffield: JSOT.
Kaniel, Ruth Kara-Ivanov. 2015. "The Myth of the Messianic Mother in Jewish and Christian Traditions: Psychoanalytic and Gender Perspectives." *Journal of the American Academy of Religion* 83: 72–119.
Keefe, Alice A. 1993. "Rapes of Women/Wars of Men." *Semeia* 61: 79–97.
Koosed, Jennifer. 2011. *Gleaning Ruth: A Biblical Heroine and Her Afterlives*. Columbia: University of South Carolina Press.
Kristeva, Julia. 1982. *Powers of Horror: An Essay on Abjection*. Translated by L. S. Roudiez. New York: Columbia University Press.
LaCocque, André. 2004. *Ruth: A Continental Commentary*. Translated by K. C. Hanson. Minneapolis: Fortress.
Landy, Francis. 2001. "Ruth and the Romance of Realism, Or Deconstructing History." Pages 285–317 in *Beauty and the Enigma: And Other Essays on the Hebrew Bible*. Sheffield: Sheffield Academic.
–––––. 2014 "Threshing Floors and Cities." Pages 79–98 in *Memory and the City in Ancient Israel*. Edited by Diana V. Edelman and Ehud Ben Zvi. Winona Lake: Eisenbrauns.
–––––. 2016. "Between Centre and Periphery: Space and Gender in the Book of Judges in the Early Second Temple Period." Pages 133–162 in *Centres and Peripheries in the Early Second Temple Period*. Edited by Ehud Ben Zvi and Christoph Levin. Tübingen: Mohr Siebeck.
–––––. 2024. "'Of all the Characters in Scripture, She is the Least': The Levite's Concubine and the Discourse of Silence." Pages 221–38 in *Characters and Characterization in the Book of Judges*. Edited by Keith Bodner and Benjamin J. M. Johnson. London: T & T Clark.
Lee, Eunny P. 2006. "Ruth the Moabite: Identity, Kinship, and Otherness." Pages 89–101 in *Engaging the Bible in a Gendered World: An Introduction to Feminist Biblical Interpretation in Honor of Katherine Doob Sakenfeld*. Edited by Linda Day and Carolyn Pressler. Louisville: Westminster John Knox.
Matheny, Jennifer M. 2022. *Judges 19–21 and Ruth: Canon as a Voice of Answerability*. Leiden: Brill.
Matthews, Victor. 2004. *Judges and Ruth*. Cambridge: Cambridge University Press.
Milgrom, Jacob. 1989. *Numbers*. New York: The Jewish Publication Society.
Miller, D. A. 1982. *Narrative and Its Discontents: Problems of Closure in the Traditional Novel*. Princeton: Princeton University Press.

Niditch, Susan. 2008. *Judges: A Commentary*. Louisville: Westminster John Knox.

Nielsen, Kirsten. 1997. *Ruth: A Commentary*. Louisville: Westminster John Knox.

Pardes, Ilana. 1992. "The Book of Ruth: Idyllic Revisionism." Pages 98–117 in *Countertraditions in the Bible: A Feminist Approach*. Cambridge, MA: Harvard University Press.

-----. 2000. *The Biography of Ancient Israel*. Berkeley: University of California Press.

Routledge, Bruce. 2004. *Moab in the Iron Age: Hegemony, Polity, Archaeology*. Philadelphia: University of Pennsylvania Press.

Rossi, Benedetta. 2024. Pages 247–277 in "Master Scribe and Forefather of a Scribal Guild: Moses in Deuteronomy," in *Deuteronomy: Beside the Ark*, ed. Diana V. Edelman and Philippe Guillaume. Themes and Issues in Biblical Studies. Sheffield: Equinox.

Sabo, Peter. 2017. *The Lot Complex: The Use and Abuse of Daughters in the Hebrew Bible*. PhD thesis. University of Alberta.

-----. 2020. "Moabite Women, Transjordanian Women, and Incest and Exogamy: The Gendered Dimensions of Boundaries in the Hebrew Bible." *Journal for the Study of the Old Testament* 45: 93–110.

Sasson, Jack, 1979. *Ruth: A New Translation with Philological Commentary and a Formalist-folklorist Interpretation*. Baltimore: The Johns Hopkins University Press.

Schipper, Jeremy. 2016. *Ruth*. New Haven: Yale University Press.

Sonnet, Jean-Pierre. 2021. *A l'ombre de ses ailes: Le livre de Ruth. Une lecture narrative*. Brussels: Lessius.

Stavrakopoulou, Francesca. 2010. *Land of Our Fathers: The Role of Ancestor Veneration in Biblical Land Claims*. London: Bloomsbury.

Thambyrajah, Jonathan A. 2021. "Israelite or Moabite? Ethnicity in the Book of Ruth." *Journal for the Study of the Old Testament* 46: 44–63.

Tooman, William A. 2022a. *(Re)reading Ruth*. Eugene: Cascade.

-----. 2022b. *The Torah Unabridged: The Evolution of Intermarriage Law in the Hebrew Bible*. University Park: Penn State University Press.

Zakovitch, Yair. 1990. *Ruth, with Introduction and Commentary* (Hebrew). Tel Aviv: Am Oved.

Zornberg, Avivah Gottlieb. 2009. "Law and Narrative in the Book of Ruth." Pages 344–78 in *The Murmuring Deep: Reflections on the Biblical Unconscious*. New York: Schocken.

About the Authors

Peter Sabo is an assistant professor of Jewish Studies and Global Great Books at Huron University College.

Francis Landy is Professor Emeritus of Religious Studies at the University of Alberta. His most recent publication is *Poetry, Catastrophe, and Hope in the Vision of Isaiah* (Oxford: Oxford University Press, 2023).

Chapter 11
The Moral Content of Caring for Oneself (First)

Jennifer J. Williams

Abstract

Interpretations of Ruth's character present her as a model of self-sacrifice, supporting a Western and Christian technology of the self and claiming self-sacrifice as an admirable moral principle. Similarly, there exists a modern tendency to view self-care as selfishness. This creates an unhelpful dichotomy. This chapter challenges such ideas, considers Michel Foucault's concept of the "technology of the self," and generates a new claim for the ethical content of Ruth's actions. Ruth's contracts with Naomi in ch. 1 and then Boaz in ch. 3 demonstrate profound resourcefulness and care of oneself rather than self-sacrifice. She repeatedly exhibits an ethic that benefits and transforms her self and others. Thus, Ruth reveals the importance of and inherent virtues in self-care, especially in the face of various difficulties.

Keywords: care of oneself, technology of self, Michel Foucault, Ruth, self-sacrifice, contracts, oath, self-care

My aim is to offer a new direction and an alternative way of thinking about Ruth and her actions as ethical. Thus, readers might interpret Ruth differently and emulate her for new reasons. Also, perhaps this project will help the reader to similarly consider "self-care" in a different way. Some have read Ruth's actions as self-sacrifice. However, when viewed through the lens of Michel Foucault's *technology of the self*, Ruth's actions in chs 1 and 3 demonstrate resourcefulness and *care of oneself* instead. Her self-interested actions are also ethical and socially interested; good for her and good for others.

1. Self-Sacrifice or Self-Care?

Interpreters of the book of Ruth tended to focus on the self-sacrificing nature of the protagonist's speech and actions, especially in Ruth's pledge to Naomi in 1:16–17. Forsaking everything she has, Ruth pledges complete devotion to Naomi. Her act of going with her mother-in-law appears to some as an act of self-effacement and total relinquishing of her self (LaCocque 2004, 99; 1990, 106). This is not just self-sacrifice but also a submission to Naomi's will; Ruth gives up her freedom of movement and choice (Sasson 1995, 124). One way of interpreting Ruth's clinging to Naomi in ch. 1 is to read it as the self-sacrificial action that defines her *ḥesed*, or "loving-kindness." Her actions provide a clear moral prescription for readers regarding how to behave and demonstrate God's loving-kindness. She is also lauded as the *'ēšet ḥāyil*, a "woman of valor." Thus, generations of interpreters "have held up the character of Ruth as a model of morality" (Farmer 1998, 892). This perspective sets Ruth as a model of morality because she is self-sacrificial. In turn, because she is a biblical character worthy of emulation, self-sacrifice becomes always and inherently moral. I am primarily focusing on Christian interpretations that have applauded Ruth's actions as self-sacrificial. And as I consider Foucault, it is similarly important to mention that he, also, is primarily focused on Greco-Roman and Christian contexts (for Jewish contexts, see Boyarin 1995).

Other commentators recognize the pitfalls of this uncritical support of Ruth's "self-sacrifice" as a universal moral exemplar (Lee 2012, 145; Farmer 1998, 906 and 946; Sakenfeld 1995, 257; Greifenhagen 2015, 239; Fuchs 1982, 149–160; Fewell and Gunn 1989, 40; Haug 2008, 167). If self-sacrificial behavior is considered prescribed, then "the book of Ruth becomes an oppressive instrument" (Farmer 1998, 906). This perspective explicitly warns against claims to the absolute moral superiority of self-sacrifice, and it also brings to light a dichotomy between self-sacrifice and self-care. Emulating self-sacrifice, selflessness or self-emptying leads to view self-care as selfish. Caring for self and caring for others become mutually exclusive.

Furthermore, "self-care" carries its own ambiguity. In popular sense, self-care is synonymous with getting a massage, practicing yoga, eating chocolate, taking a bubble bath, resting, eating healthier food, or doing any number of things to care for one's body, typically when deprived or overworked. Typically, self-care arises as a form of calming oneself down or even indulging oneself. This popular notion of pacifying oneself, relaxing, and treating oneself gently typically implies taking care of oneself so that the person can put their nose back to the proverbial grindstone. This view of self-care promotes care of oneself so that a person can return to being more productive; a version of self-care that lacks moral content.

In contrast, Audre Lorde and others understand self-care as a radical feminist praxis: "Caring for myself is not self-indulgence. It is self-preservation, and that is an act of political warfare" (Lorde 1988, 130). This quote comes at the end of an essay wherein Lorde, living with a terrible cancer diagnosis, contemplates parallels between her fight for her life and her fight against anti-black racism. Such self-care is an act of survival, understood as a political, even revolutionary move. Building on Lorde, Sara Ahmed (2014) identifies self-care as warfare.

I focus on Foucault's understanding of care of the self, mostly because it is decidedly neither self-sacrificial nor self-indulgent, but also because it contains an essential principle of morality and ethical conduct. Lorde's radical feminist perspective of self-care gets close to the idea of the Foucauldian care of the self, or at least closer than the idea of pacifying oneself. Both Lorde and Foucault argue that care of the self is political and can be good for others. But the feminist perspective includes a more revolutionary component lacking in Foucault's ethic of the care of the self.

2. Technologies of the Self

Before examining the biblical story, it is first necessary to consider Michel Foucault's project that both provides an account of antiquity's technologies of the self and frames his ideas about care of oneself. Relevant to this discussion is his assessment of the transition from Greek philosophy's technologies of self to Christian ethics and asceticism. Foucault focuses on the Hellenistic world's technologies of self and its transition into a Christian ethic of self-care. Foucault is also interested in looking cross-culturally at other technologies of self, yet he admits the limits of his own project (see Collins 2018, 28). The tension between these two technologies of the self is a useful place to begin when considering tensions between self-sacrifice, self-care and the character of Ruth.

It should be noted at this point that the book of Ruth is commonly considered to be Persian in date, thus earlier than the Hellenistic era. If so, the concept of individualism, which arose in the Hellenistic period under the influence of Greek philosophy, would seem to be irrelevant for the study of Ruth, where only the concept of corporate identity would apply. Common as it used to be, the dates scholars ascribe to the first production of biblical texts appears now as arbitrary given the lack of precise enough criteria. Moreover, any strict delimitation between the Persian (or Achaemenid) era and the Hellenistic era is artificial as Greek influences in the Levant (and vice-versa) did not wait until 333 BCE, the year of the passage of the armies of Alexander the Great there. For this reason, some scholars do not exclude a Hellenistic date for the book of Ruth (Zenger 1992, 28).

To further emphasize the blending and influence of one culture upon another, Foucault notes a very early Greek reference to care of the self in Xenophon's idealized Cyrus, who, even though his conquests are ended, still does not consider his existence to be complete (Foucault 1986, 44). Thus, it is important to bear in mind that Foucault's idea of care of oneself is likely not intrinsic to the Ruth text. But Foucault was interested in looking cross-culturally at other technologies of self. In directions suggested by him, I am looking comparatively and historically at a "non-Western" context. Although Foucault insisted that one has to recognize and stay within historical and cultural settings, he did advocate for following past practices and techniques of self. In this way, the character of Ruth might exemplify practices and techniques of the self, though the book of Ruth does not operate in the Hellenistic setting that is Foucault's focus.

Foucault's examination of the ethic of the care of oneself in antiquity constitutes the culmination of his professional work and appears in both his 1981–1982 lectures at the Collège de France and in Volume 3 of the *History of Sexuality* (Foucault 1986). The care of oneself represents a shift in focus from his first volume of the *History of Sexuality*, which concentrated on politics and power. Moving into the second and third volumes, Foucault faced a choice: to continue with a survey of the theme of desire or reorganize the project around antiquity's slow development of a hermeneutics of the self (Foucault 1990b, 6). He chose the latter.

In Greco-Roman philosophy, Foucault found a particular way of understanding the subject: as a subject "no longer constituted but constituting itself through well-ordered practices" (Gros 2001, 513). Thus, while his project focused on the history of sexuality and specifically the emergence and demands of sexual austerity that have occurred in our current era, Foucault noted that the *context* of this sexual austerity needed exploration. He found that the context has a "long historical range," but at one point reached a pivotal moment: "I am referring to the development of what might be called a 'cultivation of the self,' wherein the relations of oneself to oneself were intensified and valorized" (Foucault 1986, 43). It is this concept, the cultivation of the self, that Foucault focused on until his death.

2.1 The Genealogy of the Subject

Foucault found that "moral conceptions in Greek and Greco-Roman antiquity were much more oriented toward practices of the self and questions of *'askēsis'* ('self-formation') than toward codifications of conducts and the strict definition of what is permitted and what is forbidden" (Foucault 1990a, 30). In the philosophies of antiquity, Foucault observed an interest in the personal subject rather than social or religious laws and prohibitions. This idea that one should attend to oneself and care for oneself "was actually a very ancient theme in Greek culture" and it represents a widespread imperative (Foucault 1986, 43–44). However, the idea did not remain static and was adopted and transformed over many centuries.

Foucault tracks the development of the idea and its various permutations and implementations through Greek and Roman philosophy, starting primarily in the early fourth century BCE (Gros 2001, 526; Foucault 1988b, 27). According to Foucault, *Alcibiadies*, ca. 390 BCE, is the place to start, as the care of oneself is the basic theme of the dialogue between Socrates and Alcibiades:

> Socrates shows the ambitious young man that it is quite presumptuous of him to want to take charge of the city, manage its affairs, and enter into competition with the kings of Sparta or the rulers of Persia, if he has not first learned that which it is necessary to know in order to govern; he must first attend to himself – and right away, while he is young, for "at the age of fifty, it would be too late." (Foucault 2001, 494; 1986, 44)

In the *Apology*, Socrates presents himself to his judges as the master of the care of oneself, for "the gods sent him to remind men that they need to concern themselves not with their riches, not with their honor, but with themselves and with their souls" (Foucault 1986, 44).

Later philosophers took up the idea and placed it at the center of the "art of existence"; the idea eventually became known as the "cultivation of the self." It was placed in several doctrines, and it comprised more than an attitude but also modes of behavior and a social practice. Foucault claims that the "first two centuries of the imperial epoch can be seen as the summit of a curve – a kind of golden age in the cultivation of the self (Foucault 1986, 44–45). The turning point is Roman Stoicism, in which Foucault discovers "the moment when the excess, the concentration of imperial power, the assumption of powers of domination by a single person, enable the techniques of the self to be isolated as it were, and to burst forth in their urgency" (Gros 2001, 526).

2.2 Foucault's Care of Oneself: Immanence and Distance

Through the modifications of preexisting themes regarding the care of oneself, Foucault notes how this ethic is "a development of an art of existence dominated by self-preoccupation" (Foucault 1986, 238). Cultivation of the self in antiquity was dominated by the idea that one must take care of oneself. To take care of yourself or apply yourself operated in conjunction with know yourself, but eventually "know yourself" superseded the others. According to Foucault, the two imperatives could not be separated, and "apply yourself" was arguably more important in Greek thought than "know yourself." Thus, the care of oneself started with the focus on the self and privileged the practices, technologies, or techniques of the self. Foucault defines "technology of the self" as

> techniques which permit individuals *to effect, by their own means, a certain number of operations on their own bodies,* on their own souls, on their own thoughts, on their own conduct, and *this in a manner so as to transform themselves,* modify themselves, and to attain a certain state of perfection, of happiness, of purity, of supernatural power, and so on. (Foucault 1993, 203, emphasis mine)

Frédéric Gros outlines three components of the ethic that Foucault observes in antiquity: immanence, vigilant introspection and distance. For the purposes of this essay and to examine Ruth's actions as ethical, the elements of immanence and distance will be the methodological lens by which I examine Ruth's ethical actions (Gros 2001, 530–37–66).

Immanence, as an element of the care of self, focuses on incorporating an inherent order into one's self. Foucault characterizes the Hellenistic technology of the self as a set of occupations or "acts of freedom" over time. First, care of oneself is active and creative. These are actions that are not necessarily prescribed but are intended, over time, to generate a form of life that is an "establishment of a complete, perfect and adequate relationship of self to self" (Foucault 2001, 210). In this way, care of oneself is an activity, not a preoccupation, but a set of occupations over time (Foucault 1986, 50). It is not "just a brief preparation for life; it is a form of life" (Foucault 2001, 494). Personal choice is central; laws, rules, religious doctrines, and social customs hold little influence (Gros 2001, 530–32).

While these actions might be unconventional, they neither denote anarchy nor revolution. "Although the necessity of respecting the law and the customs – the *nomoi* – was very often underscored, more important than the content of the law and its conditions of application was the attitude that caused one to respect them" (Foucault 1990a, 31). In this way, one was not ruled by the law itself, but was responsible for one's relationship to the law.

While care of oneself requires an intense concern with one's self and actions, it is not a self-serving ethic. Care of the self includes the component of distance and seeks to find the proper relationship one has to the world. Care of oneself is an intrinsically social practice. The care of oneself takes place within social frameworks and relations and is concerned with how one operates within the world (Gros 2001, 536–37; Foucault 1986, 51–53). Thus, care of oneself is at the same time personal and socially aware and relational.

2.3 Sacrificing Self: Christian Ascetism

The Hellenistic notion of technology of the self was adopted and modified over many centuries, shifting from the imperative to take care of oneself to knowing oneself and eventually, to confessing (Foucault 1993, 204 and 211). These movements away from ancient ideas of self-care are evident in Platonic and Christian ethics, both of which emphasize a distancing from the self. Hellenistic and Roman philosophical notions of a conversion to the self argue that "the subject [through the care of oneself] is not tied to his truth according to a transcendental necessity or inevitable destiny" (Gros 2001, 526). No external locus of authority is necessary. Foucault emphasizes that the judge or administrator against the self is the self, not God, the Law, or even a mentor (Foucault 1993, 204). In contrast, Platonic ideas support the "passage to a higher reality through recollection" and Christian ethics "install a sacrificial style of break with the self" (Gros 2001, 532).

It is important at this point to compare Christian and Hellenistic technologies of the self. Foucault's account of the Hellenistic technologies of the self identifies the techniques and actions for the sake of the self. In other words, this technology of the self is twofold. It is both the means, techniques, and operations that an individual performs to reach a certain goal for the self, and it is the end that constitutes the final goal or transformation of self (Williams 2020, 21). The aim for the Christian technology of the self is to find what is hidden, "to discover the truth about oneself." One does this by confessing sins, renouncing oneself, and sacrificing oneself. Truth about oneself is the end, and a sacrifice of self is the means. These are inseparable in the Christian technology of the self (Foucault 1993, 222).

In Hellenistic and Roman philosophy, care of self and individual liberty were ethical principles that were eventually viewed with suspicion and became known as self-love or egoism (Foucault 1988b, 18). With Christianity's emergence, self-love and self-care "came to clash with a more rigorous morality and principles of austerity" (Shields 1992, 4). Because of Christian tendencies to celebrate self-sacrifice and denigrate self-care, both Hellenistic care of oneself and Foucault's proposal to return to this ethic have been widely misunderstood (Shield 1992, 4; Gros 2001, 530). In general, an ethic where the self receives primary attention has been largely rejected. Foucault has been wrongly denounced as promoting "contemporary individualism" and giving into "narcissistic temptation," calling individuals to "systematic transgression" or the "cult of cherished marginality" (Gros 2001, 530). But is the care of oneself narcissistic?

2.4 Reclaiming Care of Oneself: Care of Oneself Concerns Self and Others

Contrary to emerging Christian assumptions, "the Greek *ethos* of freedom is also a way of caring for others" (Shield 1992, 4). There was no antipathy between self and other, no necessary correlation between self and selfishness (McNay 1992, 90; Shield 1992, 7). Care of oneself does not imply selfishness but the active and creative self involves the other and the world and aims at the common good (Shield 1992, 6–7; Foucault 1988a, 4). It was good to concern oneself with oneself because the gods say one should do it and because it is useful for the city. Thus, the idea of the care of oneself was intensely concerned with caring for others, but first by caring for self (Foucault 2001, 494).

Rather than reinforcing forms of ascetic morality that denounce self, it is possible that biblical texts, like the book of Ruth, more closely reflect another ethos found in antiquity. It is possible that the book of Ruth and its private contract scenes reflect a concept of selfhood and a hermeneutics of the self that more closely suggests a positive and practical emergence of the self than the hermeneutics of sacrifice of the self. In Ruth, this ethos of self-care is pragmatic and creative, not based on moral obligations but rather on who Ruth might be and what is possible for her to become (McNay 1992, 90).

3. Modern Individualism and Ancient Collectives

The primary question of this chapter concerns what constitutes Ruth's actions and why she is a model to be emulated. Is it because she sacrifices herself for the sake of others or because she demonstrates some other ethic? If this first question seeks to answer what constitutes the ethical value in Ruth's actions and the reason to emulate her, we might also examine the impetus for and origin of the question itself. Why are modern readers concerned with finding ethical value in a biblical character's action? Why are modern readers interested in emulating those characters? These are questions rooted in individualism.

The emphasis on the self-care of individual characters must be examined with a critical awareness of the impact of modern individualism on the modern Western reader. Whether we read Ruth's actions as self-care or as self-sacrifice, either option reeks of individualism. It is individualism that keeps the modern reader asking, "How can Ruth be a model for *me*?"

Walter Wink deems this individualism a "snag" that modern readers cannot help but experience when reading the Bible (Wink 1975, 818). When leading a Bible study "with the most politically aware and intellectually astute of all our students," he claims,

> No matter how much I wanted discussion to verge on the social, it generally tended to remain privatized individual, personal ... Later they would become social activists, I hoped. Finally, I had to concede that it was not going to happen... It would not happen because it *could not happen*. There has been erected an invisible glass wall between ourselves and the social system. (Wink 1975, 818)

Wink (1975, 818) argues that this glass wall is the ideology of individualism from which the modern reader cannot escape. This individualism is especially problematic given that such an ideology is not fundamental to the Hebrew Bible. Joel Kaminsky (1995, 182) argues that "this individualistic bias not only distorts the past, but in so doing it obscures our ability to imagine new and different philosophical and theological options that might be made available for the future." For example, ideas of corporate personhood are extremely prevalent in the Hebrew Bible and Israelite theology (Kaminsky 1995, 179 and 188; Kaminsky 2000, 286).

The contrast between modern individualistic ideologies and the collective reality and ideology of ancient Israel becomes most evident in scholarly disagreements on corporate and individual concepts of retribution in the Hebrew Bible. Recent scholarship criticizes older theories that argue for a linear progression of Israelite ideology from an emphasis on collectivism and corporate retribution to a more "evolved" individualistic ideology; in fact, Israel, like other neighboring religions, did not separate the individual from the group (Kaminsky 2000, 286).

To argue that the Hebrew Bible reveals an ideological movement away from a more "primitive" type of collectivism to an emerging individualism is historically and theologically problematic. A linear progression from collectivism to individualism is not accurate as the corporate body of Israel and God's relationship to this community remains the emphasis of the Hebrew Bible all of the way through (Kaminsky 2000, 287). In fact, the biblical writers had a very acute and dynamic understanding of the complementary relationship between the individual and the group. Thus,

> biblical writers were aware that our individuality can only be understood in relation to the various collectivities in which we participate and that being human means that the individual is linked to other people through the consequences that flow from each person's actions. (Kaminsky 2000, 287; 1995, 187)

When ideas of corporate personhood in the Hebrew Bible are denigrated by scholars, this denigration reveals the interpreters' prejudices and "stems from a larger Enlightenment bias that places greater value upon moral systems that emphasize the individual over against those that value the community" (Kaminsky 1995, 179).

Let's return to Ruth. While Ruth's care of oneself and private contracts between individual characters dominate the narrative, Ruth's well-being and future as an individual is hardly the narrator's interest. The construction and advancement of the group, namely the future of the Israelites and a Davidic lineage, remains the chief concern in the tale. This concern is frequently repeated in the emphases on Ruth's foreignness and familial connections, references to Israel's past, and the story's final focus on Naomi and David's lineage.

If we might view Ruth's actions through the lens of Foucault's care of oneself, the modern reader might see that Ruth exhibits care of herself rather than self-sacrifice, and her actions are good for herself and good for others. Ruth demonstrates that self-interested actions need not be selfish, and these self-interested actions are also socially interested actions (Haug 2008, 174).

On the one hand, as a model of self-care, Ruth perpetuates an individualism that a modern reader recognizes. On the other hand, the lens of Foucault's care of oneself enables a more thorough understanding of the social systems at work. Self-sacrifice requires the creation of a binary system and decision: one must choose between the good of the self or the good of the other person (or group) – the self vs. another. Care of oneself supports the self *and* the group. This creates a new way of acknowledging *both* the individualism that is Wink's "glass wall" into which modern readers inevitably run head first *and* the ancient context that lacks the same kind of central focus on the individual. Kaminsky suggests that a reading that consciously considers both the individual and the collective is necessary.

> Inasmuch as the biblical view of the relationship between the individual and the community takes account of both poles, but places more emphasis upon the community and the individual's responsibility to

that community, it can provide a much needed corrective to current ethical thinking that seems to treat society as nothing more than a collection of unrelated individuals who just happen to live together. (Kaminsky 1995, 188)

Foucault's concept of care of oneself and its recognition of both self-care of the individual and care of the group arguably complements a biblical perspective while acknowledging the reality of the ideology of individualism to which modern readers are confined.

4. Contracts in the Book of Ruth

Ruth's care of herself is demonstrated through contracts sealed with formal oaths she makes with two other characters in the narrative, Naomi and Boaz. These private moments drive the story's plot and alter the futures of the three characters. They have important repercussions for all of Israel.

The contract scenes also demonstrate the ethical components of immanence and distance for understanding Foucault's care of oneself. Related to the element of immanence, Ruth routinely refuses to abide by a set of established expectations. Instead, she engages in a set of recurring occupations over time, at one point on a road with Naomi and at another point on a threshing floor with Boaz, that demonstrate personal motivation and choice. The element of distance appears in the book of Ruth through the negotiation of her foreignness, while the way characters navigate social practices and their relationship to the world is illustrated in the book's final chapter. I will treat the elements of immanence and distance separately and in more detail below; even so, let me briefly highlight these elements of care of the self in the contract scenes.

4.1 Ruth 1:16–17

The first contract in the book of Ruth establishes the background for the plot of the entire narrative. After Naomi and her Moabite daughters-in-law, Ruth and Orpah, lose their husbands, the women find themselves at a crossroads. Naomi begs the women to return to their maternal homes. Her words focus primarily on the welfare of the daughters-in-law, but Naomi correctly realizes that she has a better chance to integrate in Judah with no additional widow. At first, both Ruth and Orpah refuse to leave Naomi. The daughters-in-law may have a better chance of survival if they return to their homeland and seek new husbands. Orpah kisses her mother-in-law goodbye. In a remarkable act, Ruth pledges her life to Naomi, Naomi's people, and Naomi's god.

In the first contract of the novellette, Ruth begs her mother-in-law Naomi, "Do not urge me to leave you, to turn from following you," and swears "For wherever you go, I will go. And where you lodge, I will lodge. Your people, my people. And your god, my god. Wherever you die, I will die. And there I will be buried" (Ruth 1:16–17). With the oath "May Yhwh do to me and thus may he add, that only death divides me from you," Ruth employs public and political language in a very private moment. The reader can find similar contractual language elsewhere in the biblical material, especially in contracts between kings (2 Kgs 3:7, 2 Chr 18:3). In 1 Kgs 22:4, King Jehoshaphat pledges his resources to the King of Israel. A literal translation emphasizes the parallel phrasing, "Like me, like you. Like my people, like your people. Like my horses, like your horses." And a more fluid translation might contain, "I am as you are. My people are your people, my horses are your horses" (NRSV). King Jehoshaphat pledges to share his possessions with his ally, and it is understood that his ally's possessions are available to Jehoshaphat. In other words, "What's mine is yours and what's yours is mine."

Ruth's language sounds similar to King Jehoshaphat's contract, but her words contain important differences. Rather than pledge to give what is hers to Naomi, Ruth's pledge of allegiance begins with Naomi's people and god: "Your people, my people. And your god, my god." Ruth does not expect to take Naomi's resources; this is not a sharing of resources (see Smith 2007, 256 and Schipper 2016, 105). And unlike King Jehoshaphat, Ruth has no resources to share, except herself. Because she is pledging total dedication, one might argue that the laws and customs in Exod 21 or Deut 15 might be more relevant to Ruth's story than Jehoshaphat's pledge to another king in Kings (see ch. 2 in this volume). But the contractual language is intentional and should not be overlooked. In this way, Ruth utilizes and pushes the boundaries of several customs, including contractual language, slavery laws, levirate marriage, and the *gō'ēl* (but see ch. 3 in this volume).

Ruth's oath also digresses from Jehoshaphat's contract in another important way. When she says, "where you die, I will die," she pledges a never-ending contract (Smith 2007, 257), contrary to Jehoshaphat's treaty in 1 Kgs, which constitutes a limited alliance with Israel's king during the period they shared the goal of defeating a common enemy.

Ruth seals her declaration with the oath formula that finalizes the contract (Smith 2007, 256). This is the only instance when Ruth invokes the name of Naomi's God, Yhwh stands here as the witness who enforces the agreement between the parties. No longer married to a man, Ruth indefinitely pledges her life to a woman and is now devoted to Naomi.

Ruth embarks on a journey that privileges individual choice, thus demonstrating the element of immanence. Ruth uses customs and political treaty language and turns the expected evaluation of her as a Moabite on its head. This opening contract also highlights broader implications and the element of distance as Ruth the Moabite becomes the model of self-care for the other main characters and secures Israel's future.

4.2 Ruth 3

Naomi sets into motion the narrative's second contract as she sends Ruth to Boaz's threshing floor. In this scene, Naomi recognizes how her servant Ruth might be useful to both of them. She orders Ruth to bathe, anoint herself, dress up, secretly go to Boaz's threshing floor, wait for him, uncover his feet, lie down beside him, and obediently wait until he tells her what to do (3:3–4). The verbs that include to bathe, anoint one's self, and dress up are part of an "ancient Near Eastern literary trope that foreshadows a major change in an individual's life" (Eskenazi and Frymer-Kensy 2011, 51). Ruth, indeed, engages in transformational self-care as she seeks in Boaz a particular kind of security for both Naomi and herself.

Ruth follows Naomi's instructions until she gets to the threshing floor, but then Ruth deviates from the plan. "Ruth does not wait for Boaz to tell *her* what *she* has to do (as Naomi instructed), instead *she* tells *him*" (Fischer 1999, 30). When he discovers the woman, Boaz asks, "Who are you?!" Ruth answers, "I am Ruth, your servant." Instead of waiting for Boaz to respond, Ruth takes matters into her own hands and quickly reveals her intentions through an imperative, "Spread out your robe upon your handmaid, for you are a redeeming kinsman" (3:9).

Ruth's imperative to Boaz reveals the two issues at stake. Ruth needs a husband to marry, and Naomi needs a redeemer (*gō'ēl*) to purchase Elimelech's share of land (see ch. 2 in this volume). Her first request aims to secure Boaz as her husband in the phrase "spread your robe upon your handmaid." Then the declaration, "You are a redeeming kinsman," urges Boaz to take Naomi under his care.

Remarkably, Boaz praises the foreign Moabite with two significant compliments. He references her as a "worthy woman" and uses the term *ḥayil*. Importantly, the narrator uses this same term to describe Boaz in 2:1. He is a "strong" or "worthy" man, a "man of standing" (NIV) Boaz commends Ruth's hard work to improve her life and Naomi's. Boaz equates Ruth with himself, putting her on his level (Levine 1998, 88). Boaz reverses her status and "accepts the socially weak, alien widow as a 'strong woman'" (Fischer 1999, 30). Ruth becomes a woman to be desired (Schipper 2016, 154; Eskenazi and Frymer-Kensky 2011, xxxviii).

Boaz's accolades of Ruth also include the assertion that her acts are acts of ḥesed. This term is also intentional. Both ḥayil and ḥesed describe God's work. Ḥesed is often translated as "steadfast love, loving-kindness, fidelity or dedication." In 1:8, Naomi wishes that Yhwh will deal kindly with Orpah and Ruth; Naomi again references Yhwh's ḥesed in 2:20. In the intimate scene of ch. 3, Boaz praises Ruth's ḥesed in v. 10, stating that Ruth's latest ḥesed is greater than the first. Although he does not explicitly identify what are her "first" and "latest" acts of ḥesed, it is likely that the latest refers to Ruth's presence on the threshing floor while the first is her oath to Naomi in 1:16–17. To emphasize the value of Ruth's actions, it is important to note that the entire Hebrew Bible ascribes the term ḥesed more often to God than to humans. In a story where God is noticeably absent as an actor, it is even more striking that a foreign woman demonstrates this divine quality.

Boaz neither chastises nor banishes the foreign woman. Although he is startled, he hears Ruth's plea, applauds her, and promises to care for her and Naomi. Boaz seals the contract between Ruth and himself in a final oath (3:12–13). Because oath language typically precedes the content of the promise, and the verb "lie down" (šākab) bears a sexual undertone, it is "most suitable" to understand Boaz's words not only as a promise of marriage but as the consecration of the marriage before Yhwh (Sasson 1995, 92). By the same oath, Boaz commits himself to deal with the matter of Elimelech's share of a field and thus links the story's three protagonists.

The connection between the two contracts accentuates Ruth's inherent ordering of herself in her actions and the form of life she is developing. This *modus operandi* of care of oneself contains the element of immanence. Ruth has not only defied the expectations for a widow and daughter-in-law in ch. 1, but she has also now traversed a man's threshing floor. She begins pushing the boundaries of gō'ēl and levirate marriage practices. Ruth's actions will situate her in a new place in the world.

5. Care of Self in the Book of Ruth: Immanence

If the element of immanence in care of oneself reflects a set of occupations that are not prescribed, then Ruth makes this a habit. The inherent order that constitutes Ruth's self is a practice of following internal endeavors and personal choice, given whatever the situation might hold. Specifically, immanence of self-care in the book of Ruth is concerned with actions and the work and time that it takes for Ruth and Naomi to find the security they seek. Ruth's actions demonstrate awareness of social and political laws and customs, yet she is not bound by these transcendent values or social norms.

Whereas Orpah acts in typical fashion in ch. 1, Ruth chooses a different course. There exists no law requiring the widow Ruth to remain linked to her mother-in-law. Thus, Orpah is not considered aberrant, and the story places no judgment on her (Farmer 1998, 905–906; Lee 2012, 145). Instead, the emphasis rests on Ruth's remarkable decision. Her oath exhibits care of herself and the choosing of a path that best fits her needs; it is a strategy of survival and self-preservation (Haug 2008, 172–3).

Naomi's instructions to Ruth and Ruth's actions in ch. 3 demonstrate creative maneuvers. The threshing floor is "set apart from daily activity, a liminal and transitional space. It could be the site of transgressions since it was also associated with freedom from ordinary constraints" (Eskenazi and Frymer-Kensky 2011, 51). And sexual innuendo dominates the threshing floor scene. "Threshing floors" are known as places for sexual behavior and can be euphemism for female genitalia; "feet" is a euphemism for male genitalia, and "lie down" is a euphemism for intercourse. It is impossible to know if Ruth and Boaz actually engage in sexual acts on his threshing floor, but the sexual act is not the point. The narrator is most interested in highlighting the privacy and vulnerability of the scene. Should Ruth be discovered, securing a husband would be impossible or at least it would become more difficult to secure a better party than Boaz. But she seems to have little concern for adhering to a morality that follows a strict adherence to a set of external, codified rules (Stone 1997, 146, Shields 1992, 7). Her actions of self-care are risky. Ruth addresses her struggle head on; on the threshing floor, she is proactive and takes initiative, engaging in real activity, for the "concern for self always refers to an active political and erotic state" (Foucault 1988b, 24).

The circumstances in this contract scene are secretive, and efforts are made to keep the meeting confidential. The furtiveness in the scene is palpable. Ruth's shrewd actions on Boaz's threshing floor move her closer to the realization of her new status. She is on a quest to transform her situation, and she courageously engages in a daring maneuver. The story in no way vilifies Ruth's actions.

Nor does the story vilify her because of her questionable identity. Ruth is no innocuous character; she is a *Moabite*. "The book goes to pains to show Ruth as a foreigner" (LaCocque 1990, 85; 2004, 84); the stranger theme reverberates throughout the story (Rauber 1970, 31). The opening scene and the first oath take place in the country of Moab. Numerous scholars note that Ruth's association as a Moabite portrays her negatively and links her to perversion and destruction; others disagree (LaCocque

1990, 85; Fewell and Gunn 1990, 87; Berlin 1982, 88; Frymer-Kensky 2002, 257). However, even with her Moabite associations, the text repeatedly portrays Ruth positively. The story contrasts her in every way with the Moabite women at Shittim in Num 25. They brought death and incited faithlessness; but Ruth the Moabite brings new life and is the model of fidelity (Frymer-Kensky 2002, 257).

This highlights Foucault's care of the self and the element of immanence, namely the primacy of an individual and their relationship to a group. The repeated designation of Ruth *as a Moabite* insists on looking at the relationship between the self and the group and thus creates a striking contrast. An Israelite wouldn't expect a Moabite to perform this way! And, why should an Israelite emulate a foreigner's behavior?! "Ruth the Moabite, the deviant par excellence, reverses the norm. She turns things on their head: Ruth herself becomes the prototype of the ḥasid" (LaCocque 2004, 153). And thus, the relationship between the self (i.e. Ruth, the foreigner and Moabite) and the group or audience (i.e. the Israelites) divulges preexisting frameworks, prejudices, and social relations (but see ch. 6 in this volume). If the elements of relationship between self and group and the preexisting understanding of Moabites were not meant to be foregrounded, the often-repeated reminder that Ruth is a Moabite would seem repetitive, tedious, and irrelevant.

6. Ruth Demonstrates Awareness of Customs but Is Not Bound by Them

Ruth's words and actions reflect an awareness of social conventions, but Ruth finds creative ways to utilize these customs. Importantly, the behavior of the characters, and especially Ruth, are not revolutionary. Laws and customs are not challenged, changed, or abolished in the book, but Ruth uses these systems to her advantage.

The oath language that is employed in 1:16–17 and ch. 3 also illuminates the element of immanence; these oaths hearken back to the known social conventions and language of political treaties and marriage contracts. Social conventions are represented, even employed, yet are changed by the particular circumstances in the words of the characters making personal choices.

For example, the language used in ch. 1 not only belongs in the language of kings and royal contracts, it is also familial language. Paul Kalluveettil argues that the declarations of Ruth and Jehoshaphat are commitments to behave as if the two parties belong to the same family (Kalluveettil 1982, 102). Just as kings enter into contracts with each other (calling one another brothers), Ruth creates "an artificial brotherhood/

sisterhood" and a "fictitious extension of kinship" with Naomi (Kalluveettil 1982, 205). Ruth demonstrates awareness of social and political laws and customs, but she alters them for her purposes.

On the threshing floor, Ruth admits what she needs: marriage and a gō'ēl, that is, a relative who redeems through "the restoration of the status quo" (Milgrom 2001, 2189; Schipper 2016, 135). Rather than acts of liberation or revolution against customary laws, Ruth's relationship to these customs are individual acts of freedom (Foucault 1988a, 3). She neither overthrows the system nor seeks to establish a new one. In Foucault's terms, Ruth operates with the goals of "refusal, curiosity, and innovation" (Bess 1988, 1–2).

In fact, the precise content of the social institutions Ruth references are debated. Many scholars question whether levirate marriage is really operative in this scene and what it is that Ruth is asking Boaz to do for her. Schipper notes how the legal situation in Ruth differs from other representations of levirate marriage, even as the text employs terminology and legal idioms related to the levirate custom (Schipper 2016, 9). Ruth might not be speaking about a levirate marriage in a proper sense, but she is alluding to something like it, and she uses the institution to her advantage. The narrator in Ruth is less concerned about demonstrating the upholding of proper customs (or even describing the proper customs); he is more interested in demonstrating how characters respond to and creatively navigate through the situations at hand.

Ruth engages in decisive social and political action as she chooses to cling to Naomi and seeks Boaz as a redeemer and husband. She binds herself to a woman by oath and, therefore, rejects a morality that insists on strict loyalty to pre-established rules (Foucault 1988b, 24; Stone 1997, 146). Thus, the order by which she chooses her acts of care of self are not primarily conditioned by social norms, at least. Ruth demonstrates awareness of social conventions and navigates through them.

7. Care of Self: Distance

Foucault's ethic of the care of oneself includes the component of distance. Its intention is to help one find the proper relationship one has to the world. Foucault understands the care of oneself as an inherently social practice and describes it as an "intensifier of social relations" (Gros 2001, 536–37). Not in opposition to or antithetical to social norms, care of oneself takes place *within* "organized institutional frameworks" and "preexisting social relations" (Gros 2001, 536–536; Shields, 1992, 3; 2007, 3; Foucault 1986, 51–53). Thus, in its distance, care of oneself is socially aware and relational.

The book of Ruth shows that self-care neither requires solitude nor invites inaction. Quite the opposite. Ruth's actions help her carve out her political and social space; this self-care "is what enables us to situate ourselves within it (the world) correctly" (Gros 2001, 537–38). While Ruth focuses on herself first, her actions are always socially oriented and demonstrate the component of distance (Foucault 1988b, 18; 1985, 367). Ruth not only attains a better state for herself but also for Naomi and Boaz and for all of Bethlehem. Ruth's actions solidify the possibility of social and familial relations and larger communal interests. The contract scenes move the plot forward but also connect individuals to each other and to greater purposes. A reader witnesses the element of distance in Ruth's designation as the Moabite and in the story's final chapter.

8. Ruth the Moabite

"Ruth the Moabite" not only emphasizes Ruth's foreignness but also reminds the reader that individuals belong to larger groups. Ruth is not simply an individual with her own self-interests in mind. Ruth's actions benefit Naomi and her life, yes, but her actions ultimately benefit the Israelites. Yet, she remains associated with her people of origin (Ruth 1:22; 2:2, 21; 4:5, 10), even when she is once designated as a "Moabite woman" in 2:6. And to emphasize Ruth's connection to others, the tale twice identifies Ruth with some other relational marker: she is "Ruth her daughter-in-law" (2:22) and to Boaz, she identifies herself as "Ruth your servant" (3:9). In two cases, Ruth and Boaz are paired (2:8 and 4:13). In the narrator's first mention of Ruth, she is paired with Orpah to describe the two Moabite wives of Mahlon and Chilion.

Only three times does Ruth's name occur on its own and without an identity marker. Thus, in typical biblical fashion, Ruth is most often identified with an identity marker that connects her to another person or group. Like other biblical women, Ruth is rarely identified as an individual, alone. Even if the reader observes the actions of this singular woman, the implicit concern is ultimately communal. The story always centers on how this one foreign woman will be connected to other people in general and the Israelites specifically.

9. The End of Ruth

By the end of the story, Ruth vanishes. Her acts of self-care and private interactions with the other main characters control most of the narrative. But in the end, Ruth's departure is indicative of her complete integration into Boaz's household. The narrator is concerned with the future of the collective group. The final contract scene in ch. 4 involves the (male) elders at the gate and Bethlehem's council of women and emphasizes Israel's future.

When Boaz announces to the witnesses that he will acquire all that belonged to Elimelech, to Mahlon, and to Chilion and will take Ruth as his wife (4:9-10), all the people at the gate and the elders bless them (4:11-12). But this blessing does not name Ruth. Instead, Ruth has been subsumed into the larger group. The narrator repeatedly emphasizes the collective group (at least eleven times in one chapter!), the members of this Israelite community, who witness this final agreement. This sudden stress on the assembly of people in ch. 4 contrasts with the oft-repeated motif of Ruth as the Moabite throughout the rest of the book. The narrator ultimately shifts attention to what has been the underlying motivation all along: bolstering the Bethlehem village commune. Similarly, genealogical focus at the end of ch. 4 and the matriarchs who "built the house of Israel" (4:11) shifts the focus away from Ruth. Such genealogical emphasis suggests that Ruth's acts of self-care were not merely for her own benefit but for securing the Davidic line.

One might argue that because of her absence in the final scene, the story completely sacrifices Ruth. Amy-Jill Levine claims that because of ch. 4, this book cannot really be "a celebration of Ruth's abilities" but instead, is a "pernicious, exploitative tract" (Levine 1998, 85). This reading misses the important point that she is enacting care of herself and doing so in a way that benefits herself *and* the greater community.

It is Ruth's oath to Naomi that reveals her initiative as she begins engaging in acts that redefine her self. "In her unswerving devotion to Naomi, and in her initiative, as a Moabitess, in forging an identity for herself within the confines of an alien society, Ruth acts as an exemplary figure of solidarity" (Rutledge 1996, 24). In changing herself, she begins the path of securing Israel's future.

10. The Reward for Ruth's Ethical Behavior

Ultimately, the story not only advocates for but also rewards Ruth's behavior. This reward manifests itself in an act by Yhwh. That Yhwh as an actor has been absent does not mean that the deity has not been operative throughout the story. Ruth's ḥesed performs the work of Yhwh. As Ruth *disappears* in ch. 4, Yhwh appears and directly acts. In the final commendation of Ruth's acts of self-care, "Yhwh gave to her a pregnancy, and she bore a son" (4:13). From famine and death, the lack of a man and lack of protection, Yhwh gives Ruth the new life she needs. Is the story's "happy ending" problematic (see ch. 8 in this volume)? Yhwh blesses Ruth by initiating her into the only truly "worthy" institution for women of the time: the institution of motherhood. This reminds the reader of the limitations that Ruth faces, and that her actions were not – and could not – be revolutionary.

Conclusion

Reading the book of Ruth through the lens of Foucault's concept of care of the self enables a new way of reading Ruth and her actions as ethical. Ruth's contracts in chs 1 and 3 demonstrate resourcefulness and attention to both herself and the other person. Rather than reading Ruth as a model of self-sacrifice, and rather than understanding self-care as selfishness, Foucault's concept of the care of the self allows a more thorough understanding of the connection between individuals and social systems at work in antiquity. Self-care supports the self and the group. They interact with one another to enhance preexisting relations and intensify social relations.

Ruth is an exemplary figure as she demonstrates the ethical value of care of oneself despite systems that hardly make room for the experiences of individuals. She demonstrates how one might carve a way for personal thriving and for the benefit of the larger group. Revolution is not the sole option to freedom.

Works Cited

Ahmed, Sarah. 2014. "Selfcare as Warfare." *Feminist Killjoys*. https://feministkilljoys.com/2014/08/25/self-care-as-warfare.

Berlin, Adele. 1982. *Poetics of Interpretation of Biblical Narrative*. Sheffield: Almond Press.

Bess, Michael. 1988. "An Interview with Michel Foucault." San Francisco: 3 November, https://michaelbess.net/foucault-interview/

Boyarin, Daniel. 1995. "Are There Any Jews in 'The History of Sexuality'?" *Journal of the History of Sexuality* 5:333–55.

Campbell, Edward F. 1975. *Ruth: A New Translation with Introduction and Commentary*. Anchor Bible 7. Garden City NY: Doubleday.

Collins, Steven. 2018. "Some Remarks on Hadot, Foucault, and Comparisons with Buddhism." Pages 21–70 in *Buddhist Spiritual Practices: Thinking with Pierre Hadot on Buddhism, Philosophy and the Path*. Edited by David V. Fiordalis. Berkeley: Mangalam.

Eskenazi, Tamara Cohn and Tikva Simone Frymer-Kensky. 2011. *Ruth: The Traditional Hebrew Text with the New JPS Translation*. Philadelphia: Jewish Publication Society.

Farmer, Kathleen A. Robertson. 1998. "The Book of Ruth." Pages 889–946 in *New Interpreter's Bible*. Edited by Leander E. Keck. Nashville: Abingdon.

Fewell, Danna Nolan and David Miller Gunn. 1989. "Is Coxon a Scold? On Responding to the Book of Ruth." *Journal for the Study of the Old Testament* 45:39–43.

–––––. 1990. *Compromising Redemption: Relating Characters in the Book of Ruth*. Louisville: Westminster/John Knox Press.

Fischer, Irmtraud. 1999. "The Book of Ruth: A 'Feminist' Commentary to the Torah?" Pages 24–29 in *Ruth and Esther*. Edited by Athalya Brenner. Feminist Companion to the Bible 3. Sheffield: Sheffield Academic.

Foucault, Michel. 1985. "Sexuality and Solitude." Pages 365–72 in *On Signs*. Edited by Marshal Blonsky. Baltimore: Johns Hopkins University Press.

–––––. 1986. *The Care of Self*. Volume 3 of *The History of Sexuality*. Translated by Robert Hurley. New York: Vintage Books Edition.

–––––. 1988a. "The Ethic of Care for the Self as a Practice of Freedom." Pages 1–20 in *The Final Foucault*. Edited by J. Bernauer and D. Rasmussen. Translated by J.D. Gauthier, S.J. Cambridge, MA: MIT.

–––––. 1988b. "Technologies of the Self." Pages 16–49, in *Technologies of the Self: A Seminar with Michel Foucault*. Edited by Luther H. Martin. Amherst: University of Massachusetts Press.

–––––. 1990a. The Use of Pleasure: Volume 2 of *The History of Sexuality*. Translated by Robert Hurley. New York: Vintage Books.

–––––. 1990b. "An Introduction: Volume 1 of *The History of Sexuality* Volume 1. Translated by Robert Hurley. New York: Vintage.

–––––. 1993. "About the Beginning of the Hermeneutics of the Self: Two Lectures at Dartmouth." *Political Theory* 21:198–227.

–––––. 2001. *The Hermeneutics of the Subject: Lectures at the Collège de France, 1981-1982*. Edited by Frédéric Gros, François Ewald, and Alessandro Fontana. Translated by Graham Burchell. New York: Palgrave Macmillan.

Frymer-Kensky, Tikva Simone. 2002. *Reading the Women of the Bible*. New York: Schocken.

Fuchs, Esther. 1982. "The Status and Roles of Female Heroines in the Biblical Narrative." *The Mankind Quarterly* 23:149–60.

Greifenhagen, Franz Volker. 2015. "Bargaining with Patriarchy in the Book of Ruth." Pages 239–270 in *Celebrate Her for the Fruit of Her Hands: Essays in Honor of Carol L. Meyers*. Edited by Susan Ackerman, Charles E. Carter, and Beth Alpert Nakhai. Winona Lake, IN: Eisenbrauns.

Gros, Frédéric. 2001. "Course Context." Pages 507–50 in *Michel Foucault. The Hermeneutics of the Subject: Lectures at the Collège de France, 1981-1982*.

Edited by Frédéric Gros, François Ewald, and Alessandro Fontana. Translated by Graham Burchell. New York: Palgrave Macmillan.

Haug. Jon. 2008. "Self-interest as Holy in Ruth." *Journal of Religious Thought* 14: 167–74.

Kallutveettil, Paul. 1982. *Declaration and Covenant: A Comprehensive Review of Covenant Formulae from the Old Testament and the Ancient Near East.* Analecta Biblica 88. Rome: Pontifical Biblical Institute.

Kaminsky, Joel S. 1995. *Corporate Responsibility in the Hebrew Bible.* Library of Hebrew/Old Testament Studies 196. Sheffield: Sheffield Academic.

Kaminsky, Joel S. 2000. "Corporate Personality." Pages 285–86 in *Eerdman's Dictionary of the Bible.* Edited by David Noel Freedman. Grand Rapids, Michigan: W. B. Eerdmans.

LaCocque, André. 1990. *The Feminine Unconventional: Four Subversive Figures in Israel's Tradition.* Philadelphia: Fortress.

—————. 2004. *Ruth: A Continental Commentary.* Translated by K. C. Hanson. Continental Commentaries. Minneapolis: Fortress.

Lee, Eunny. 2012. "Ruth." Pages 142–94 in *Women's Bible Commentary.* Edited by Carol A. Newsom, Sharon H. Ringe, and Jacqueline E. Lapsley. Louisville: Westminster John Knox.

Levine, Amy-Jill. 1998. "Ruth." Pages 84–91 in *Women's Bible Commentary.* Edited by Carole A. Newsom and Sharon H. Ringe. Louisville: Westminster John Knox.

Lorde, Audre. 1988. *Burst of Light and Other Essays.* Garden City, NY: Ixia.

McNay, Lois. 1992. *Foucault and Feminism: Power, Gender and the Self.* Cambridge: Polity.

Milgrom, Jacob. 2001. *Leviticus 23–27: A New Translation with Introduction and Commentary.* Anchor Bible 3b. New York: Doubleday.

Rauber, D. F. 1970. "Literary Values in the Bible: The Book of Ruth." *Journal of Biblical Literature* 89: 27–37.

Rutledge, David. 1996. *Reading Marginally: Feminism, Deconstruction, and the Bible.* Leiden: Brill.

Sakenfeld, Katherine Doob. 1995. "'Feminist' Theology and Biblical Interpretation." Pages 247–249 in *Biblical Theology: Problems and Perspectives in Honor of J. Christiaan Baker.* Edited by Steven J. Kraftchick, Charles D. Meyers, Jr., and Ben C. Ollenburger. Nashville: Abingdon.

Sasson, Jack M. 1995. *Ruth: A New Translation with a Philological Commentary and a Formalist-Folklorist Interpretation.* Sheffield: Sheffield Academic.

Schipper, Jeremy. 2016. *Ruth: A New Translation with Introduction and Commentary.* New Haven, CT: Yale University Press.

Shields, James Mark. 1992, Revised 2007. "Foucault's Dandy: Constructive Selfhood in the Last Writings of Michel Foucault." https://jamesshields.blogs.bucknell.edu/files/2012/12/Foucaults-Dandy.pdf

Smith, Mark S. 2007. "'Your People Shall Be My People': Family and Covenant in Ruth 1:16–17." *Catholic Biblical Quarterly* 69:242–58.

Stone, Ken. 1997. "Biblical Interpretation as a Technology of the Self: Gay Men and the Ethics of Reading." *Semeia* 77:139–155.

Williams, Jennifer J. 2020. "Contracts and Care of Oneself in the Book of Ruth." *Horizons in Biblical Theology* 46–42:14.

Wink, Walter. 1975. "How I Have Been Snagged by the Seat of My Pants While Reading the Bible." *The Christian Century* 92/30: 816–819.

Zenger, Erich. 1992. Das Buch Ruth. *Zücher Bibelkommentare* 8. 2nd edition. Zürich: Theologischer Verlag.

About the Author

Jennifer J. Williams is an associate professor in the religious studies department at Linfield University. Her research focuses on women and gender studies, and feminist and queer interpretations of the Bible. She holds a PhD from Vanderbilt University, and has published on the books of Ruth, Job, and Judges, and on Hosea in 2024: "A Queer Reading of the Book of Hosea." Pages 364–379 in *The Oxford Handbook of the Book of Hosea*. Edited by Brad Kelle. Oxford: Oxford University Press.

Chapter 12
Who is the Central Character in the Book of Ruth?

Anthony H. Dekker and John T. Dekker

Abstract

This book is entitled "Ruth," but who is actually the central character of the book? Mathematical methods for analyzing narrative can shed light on this. In a previous work we applied the mathematics of social network analysis to the book. This analysis suggested that Boaz was the most central character. Here we apply more sophisticated social network analysis techniques, which identify either Ruth, Naomi, or Boaz as the most central character. Exploring this conflict, we use the mathematics of sentiment analysis to show that the narrative divides naturally into four acts, which correspond to the existing chapters. These acts are: 1. *Naomi's Tragedy*, 2. *Ruth's Dilemma*, 3. *Ruth Obeys*, and 4. *Boaz Acts*, with central characters Naomi, Ruth, Ruth, and Boaz respectively. As the spotlight of the narrative shifts, so does the central character: the book is not a simple story about one person.

Keywords: social network analysis, sentiment analysis, narrative analysis, centrality, Ruth

1. Introduction

Who is the central character in the book of Ruth? The name of the book suggests the obvious conclusion that it is Ruth herself. Digging deeper, however, there are other candidates. Wesley Fuerst points out that, although Ruth is the central character, Naomi and Boaz are also "principal characters" (Fuerst 1975, 8). Adele Berlin goes further, arguing that, although Ruth is the "main point of interest," it is Naomi who is the central character (Berlin 1994, 83–84). Indeed, one key thread in the book is Naomi's journey from emptiness (1:21) to fullness (4:14–17). Our previous network study of Ruth (Dekker and Dekker 2018), using a less sophisticated analysis than presented here, suggested that Boaz could be seen as the most central character. On the other hand, although Boaz does indeed perform most of the action after his introduction in 2:1, these actions largely relate to Ruth and Naomi.

Here we provide a more detailed exploration of the centrality of the characters in Ruth using the mathematical tools of social network analysis (Wasserman and Faust 1994) and sentiment analysis (Hu and Liu 2004). Of necessity, these mathematical tools imply a literary approach (Alter 1981). As Berlin (1994, 21) states, "biblical narrative is a literary art-form." We assume that the story is the one which the author wished to write, and analyze the relationships and interactions which the author chose to highlight, and the specific words which the author chose to use. These tools thus provide a kind of mechanized "close reading" of the text, highlighting points that may have been under-appreciated. These tools cannot take into account theological frameworks, historical records, archaeological findings, or other material external to the text itself. However, these tools may prompt questions that require exploration by other means.

The tool of social network analysis in particular focuses attention on "*relationships* among social entities, and on the patterns and implications of these relationships" (Wasserman and Faust 1994, 3). Social network analysis has been applied successfully to anthropology, sociology, economics, and other social sciences (Borgatti et al. 2009) as well as in the analysis of literature (Rydberg-Cox 2011), where it goes beyond the quantitative approach to literature advocated by Moretti (2005). The application of social network analysis to biblical studies is relatively recent (e.g. Czachesz 2016; Massey 2016; McClure 2016, 2020).

A *network* is a collection of *nodes* (represented by circles in Figure 1) connected by *links* (represented by lines, or sometimes arrows). One example is an airline flight network, where the nodes are airports and the links are direct flights between them. For example, the network for Australian airline Qantas has a link from Sydney to LAX. Network diagrams are familiar to students of the documentary hypothesis (see e.g. Baden 2012), which is often communicated using a diagram in which the nodes are documents and the links indicate transfer of material from one document to another. In our work, the nodes are people or groups of people and the links are connections between them.

One aspect of social network analysis ideal for exploring our question is the calculation of *centrality scores*, which identify nodes in a network that are, in some sense, the most important. For example, classic mathematical anthropology work by Hage and Harary (1995) identified the "politically and symbolically most important islands" in the Ratak (sunrise) and the Ralik (sunset) island chains of what is now the Republic of the Marshall Islands. This was done using a network where the nodes were islands and the links were feasible canoe voyages between islands. Using their mathematical definition of centrality, Hage and Harary identified the islands of Aur, Maloelap, and Wotje in the Ratak chain and Namu in the Ralik chain as most central. Two of these (Aur and Namu) were the traditional capitals and "mother of all the clans" in their respective island chains.

Social network analysis has also been widely used for identifying the most important members of organized crime or terrorist networks (Sparrow 1991; Morselli 2008). These central individuals are obvious targets for law enforcement activity.

2. The Network

Our network for Ruth has 15 nodes. These nodes in the network include the ten named individuals in the story: Boaz, Ruth, Naomi, Elimelech, Obed, Mahlon, Chilion, Orpah, Jesse, and David. In addition, there are the *men* (2:3–21) and the *women* (2:8–23, 3:2) who work for Boaz, the alternate *redeemer* (3:12–13, 4:1–8), the city *elders* (4:2–11), and the *townswomen* who interact with Naomi in 1:19, 4:14, and 4:17. The latter are variously named tōʾmrᵉnâ, hannāšîm, and haššᵉkēnôt in the Hebrew text, but are the same women in each case (Hubbard 1988, 270). The network is shown in Figure 1.

The genealogy in 4:18–22 is not included, since the genealogy is distinct from the four chapters of narrative which form the bulk of the book. However, unlike our previous network study (Dekker and Dekker 2018), we include the references to Jesse and David in 4:17. We are guided here by the fact that the only paragraph break in the Tiberian manuscript tradition of the book occurs at the end of 4:17 (Goswell 2023). Kristin Moen Saxegaard notes that "Tamar, Judah, Rachel, Leah, and David, on the other hand, are not present as characters in this narrative but only occur as references lent from other narratives" (Saxegaard 2010, 57). However, Tamar, Judah, Rachel, and Leah occur only in reported speech, while Jesse and David are specifically mentioned by the narrator, prior to the genealogy in 4:18–22.

A link is drawn between characters in Figure 1 if the narrator describes the characters as *interacting* or *being in a relationship* – such as marriage (e.g. Naomi with Elimelech, Ruth with Mahlon), parent/child (e.g. Elimelech with Mahlon, Boaz with Obed), or other kinship (e.g. Boaz with

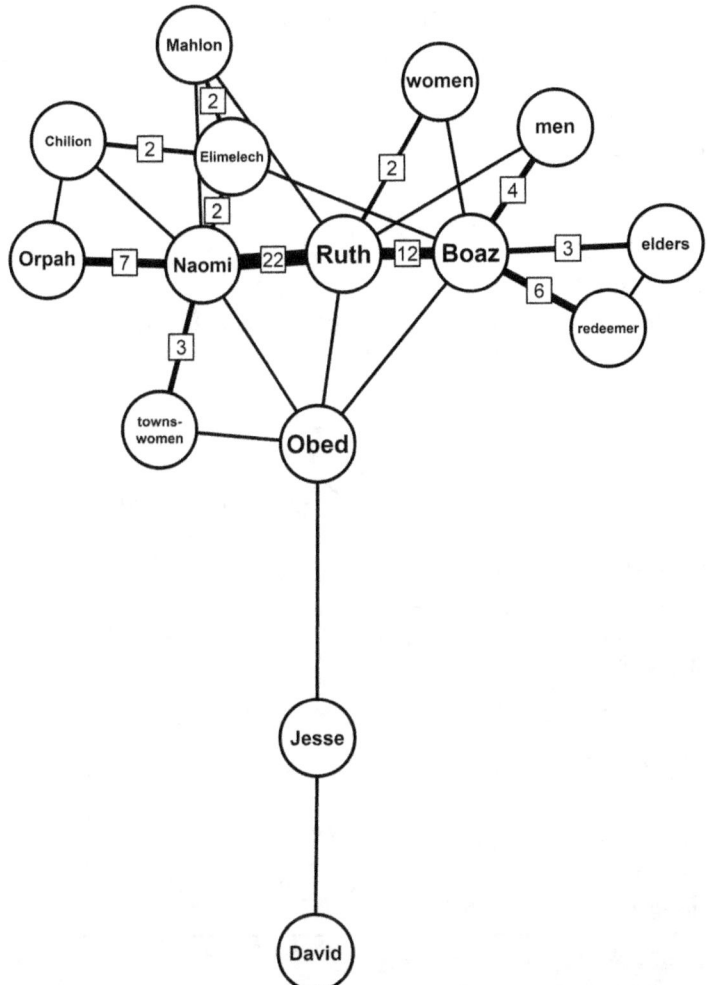

Figure 1: Full network for Ruth, showing weights. Unmarked links have a weight of 1. Physical distances between nodes correspond approximately to the calculated distances.

Elimelech). We do not include interactions described by characters in the story, such as Ruth's interaction with the men in 2:7 as described by their foreman. Such reported speech may, in general, be unreliable (differing from the narrator's story) or redundant (repeating interactions described by the narrator).

Unlike our previous network study of Ruth in (Dekker and Dekker 2018), we add *weights* to the network links. These weights reflect the *number of verses* in which an interaction occurs or a relationship is stated. Our analysis is based on a digital version of the Hebrew text: Biblia Hebraica

258 *Ruth*

Table 1: Network link weightings for Ruth, with corresponding verses.

Elimelech–Naomi (2)	1:1–2
Elimelech–Mahlon (2)	1:1–2
Chilion–Elimelech (2)	1:1–2
Mahlon–Naomi (1)	1:2
Chilion–Naomi (1)	1:2
Chilion–Orpah (1)	1:4
Mahlon–Ruth (1)	1:4
Naomi–Ruth (22)	1:6–11, 1:14–16, 1:19, 2:2, 2:18–23, 3:1, 3:5, 3:16–18
Naomi–Orpah (7)	1:6–11, 1:14
Naomi–townswomen (3)	1:19–20, 4:14
Boaz–Elimelech (1)	2:1
men–Ruth (1)	2:3
Boaz–Ruth (12)	2:3, 2:8, 2:10–11, 2:13–14, 3:7, 3:9–10, 3:14–15, 4:13
Boaz–men (4)	2:4–6, 2:15
Boaz–women (1)	2:8
Ruth–women (2)	2:14, 2:23
Boaz–redeemer (6)	4:1, 4:3–6, 4:8
Boaz–elders (3)	4:2, 4:9, 4:11
elders–redeemer (1)	4:2
Boaz–Obed (1)	4:13
Obed–Ruth (1)	4:13
Naomi–Obed (1)	4:16
Obed–townswomen (1)	4:17
Jesse–Obed (1)	4:17
David–Jesse (1)	4:17

Stuttgartensia (Amstelodamensis) from the Eep Talstra Centre for Bible and Computer at the Vrije Universiteit Amsterdam. Analyzing at a verse-by-verse level means that the same results would be obtained by analysis of English translations such as the ESV or NRSV (i.e. the analysis is not sensitive to the details of translation). The weights and corresponding verses are shown in Table 1.

Even without further analysis, we can use Figure 1 as a framework for examining the text. For example, it is readily apparent that there is no direct connection between Naomi and Boaz: they never interact directly in the story, and Boaz is a relative of Naomi's husband (2:1) rather than directly of her. However, additional analysis of the network, calculating *centrality* scores, gives us greater insight.

3. Network Centrality Analysis

Having defined the network, we now calculate *distances* between every pair of entities. The weights on the links range from 1 to 22 (for Naomi-Ruth), but 80% of these weights are at most 3. Given this highly skewed distribution, we first take the square root of the weights, reducing the range to be from 1 to $\sqrt{22}$ = 4.69. This is a standard statistical approach for handling skewness (for its use in social network analysis, see e.g. Kostic et al. 2020). We then define the *distance along each link* to be the reciprocal of that square root, ranging from 1 for a weak connection (such as Mahlon-Naomi) to $1/\sqrt{22}$ = 0.213 for the strong connection between Naomi and Ruth. That is, Naomi and Ruth are very close together in the network, since the distance between them is the small value 0.213.

We extend this concept of distance to every pair of entities by calculating the length of shortest paths in the network. For example, the shortest path from Orpah to Boaz has three links, for a total distance of $1/\sqrt{7}$ + $1/\sqrt{22}$ + $1/\sqrt{12}$ = 0.378 + 0.213 + 0.289 = 0.880. The resulting shortest-path distances may involve indirect paths. For example, there is a link with weight 1 between Ruth and the men who work for Boaz, but the shortest distance between Ruth and these men is the indirect path via Boaz, with distance $1/\sqrt{12}$ + $1/\sqrt{4}$ = 0.289 + 0.5 = 0.789. These calculated distances between nodes are approximately represented by the physical distances in Figure 1.

We then calculate the *centrality* of each entity by looking at the distances between that entity and every other entity. For example, for Ruth, these distances are 0.213, 0.289, 0.591, 0.697, 0.707, 0.789, 0.791, 0.866, 0.920, 1.000, 1.000, 1.213, 2.000, and 3.000. The raw centrality is the sum of the reciprocals of these distances, e.g. 4.69 + 3.46 + 1.69 + 1.43 + 1.41 + 1.27 + 1.26 + 1.15 + 1.09 + 1.00 + 1.00 + 0.82 + 0.50 + 0.33 = 21.1 for Ruth. We then divide all the centralities by 21.1 so that the largest value will be 1.00 (for Ruth). The resulting values are shown in the fourth column of Table 2. This definition of centrality was called "harmonic centrality" in Marchiori and Latora (2000) and "valued centrality" in Dekker (2005). All computations were performed using the R statistical toolkit (R Core Team 2013) and its "igraph" package (Csárdi and Nepusz 2006).

We see from Table 2 that Ruth has the highest centrality (1.00), Naomi the second highest (0.97), Boaz the third highest (0.90), and Orpah the fourth highest (0.64).

For comparison, the second column of Table 2 shows the count of names in the Hebrew text (for named characters only). This is not a reliable measure of importance, because it ignores references to the characters by pronouns. However, it highlights the fact that Naomi, Boaz,

Table 2: Centralities and other measures for the book of Ruth. Each column represents a specific kind of analysis. As well as the centralities in column 4, the table also shows name counts in the Hebrew text (column 2), node degrees (column 3), flow centralities (column 5) and centrality scores for the individual chapters, as discussed later (columns 6 through 9). In each column, ★ marks the highest value and ☆ the second highest value.

Name	Count	Degree	Centrality	Flow	Chap. 1	Chap. 2	Chap. 3	Chap. 4
Ruth	12	★39	★1.00	0.84	☆0.78	★1.00	★1.00	0.65
Naomi	★21	☆37	☆0.97	☆0.95	★1.00	0.74	☆0.75	0.58
Boaz	☆18	28	0.90	★1.00		☆0.93	☆0.75	★1.00
Orpah	2	8	0.64	0.09	0.72			
redeemer		7	0.59	0.07				0.80
Elimelech	6	7	0.56	0.29	0.64	0.41		
townswomen		4	0.54	0.07	0.49			0.58
men		5	0.54	0.01		0.63		
elders		4	0.50	0.03				0.68
Obed	1	5	0.49	0.26				☆0.85
women		3	0.47	0.01		0.54		
Mahlon	4	4	0.45	0.07	0.51			
Chilion	3	4	0.44	0.09	0.51			
Jesse	1	2	0.33	0.09				0.60
David	1	1	0.24	0.00				0.42

and Ruth (with counts 21, 18, and 12 respectively) are significantly more important than other named characters (with counts from 1 to 6).

The third column of the table shows the *node degrees*, which are simply the sum of the raw link weights for all the links connected to a character. For the four most central characters (Ruth, Naomi, Boaz, and Orpah), the ordering of node degrees is the same as the ordering of centrality scores. Ruth has the highest degree (39), Naomi the second highest (37), Boaz the third highest (28), and Orpah the fourth highest (8).

The fifth column of Table 2 shows *flow centralities*, calculated according to the method of Freeman et al. (1991). This method identifies Boaz as most central, followed by Naomi and Ruth. Although flow centralities are not particularly appropriate for social networks of this kind, this column highlights the fact that different definitions of network centrality can give different results. Indeed, our previous (unweighted) network analysis in Dekker and Dekker (2018) identified Boaz as most central, followed by Ruth and Naomi.

In Dekker and Dekker (2018), we noted that Boaz, Ruth, and Naomi could all be considered the "most central character" in different senses.

Boaz is in fact the most *active* character, intervening personally to address the problems experienced by Ruth and Naomi (2:9, 3:18), providing food (2:14–18), negotiating to redeem Elimelech's property (4:1–12), becoming Ruth's husband (4:13), and providing a son for Naomi (4:14–17).

Brady (2013, 133) writes that "Ruth is a central figure and a key character in the book that bears her name. There is little debate about that fact. Over the millennia, however, her role and that of Naomi have been minimized, in some cases inadvertently and in others deliberately, through the aggrandizement of Boaz, himself a marginal figure in the book of Ruth." The numbers in Table 2, however, suggest that Boaz can hardly be called "marginal." He is at least one of the top three characters. Still, there are good reasons why the book is called "Ruth." As Berlin (1994, 84) points out, "Ruth appears or is assumed to be in every scene except the meeting between Boaz and the nameless *goel*, where she is the topic of conversation."

Naomi is also very significant. She is directly named (as "Naomi") most often (21 times in the Hebrew text). As a general, but not invariable, rule "the more often a name is repeated, the more central is the character to the plot" (Saxegaard 2010, 5). Naomi is named eight times in the first chapter, six in the second, only once in the third, but six times in the fourth. This variation points out the importance of a *temporal* element. The central character may be different in different chapters, as the narrative switches from emphasizing one character to emphasizing another. Indeed, to speak of a single "most central character" for the book as a whole may be misguided. We therefore repeat our network analysis for the four chapters individually (columns 6 through 9 of Table 2).

This chapter-by-chapter analysis is required because, although Ruth is only four chapters in length, it has quite a complex structure. The action shifts from Bethlehem to Moab and back; then back and forth between Ruth and Naomi at home and Ruth in Boaz's fields; then to the town gate; then to the new family of Ruth and Boaz; and finally back to the townswomen of Bethlehem. New characters are introduced in both Chapter 2 and Chapter 4.

It is interesting to compare Ruth to Jonah which also has only four chapters. In contrast to Ruth, the book of Jonah, though complex in a literary sense, has a much simpler network structure. The action primarily takes place on a ship at sea, inside a large fish, and in the city of Nineveh and its surrounds. Much of the book consists of interactions between Yhwh and Jonah, who are the main characters (Person 1996, 78), although there are also interactions involving the crew of the ship, the fish, and the people of Nineveh. For that book, there is no doubt that Jonah is the central character.

4. Sentiment Analysis

To shed further light on the network analysis, before we examine the chapters individually, we explore the temporal structure of the book using sentiment analysis (Hu and Liu 2004). Sentiment analysis assesses the *polarity* of text based on the presence of words with positive or negative connotations.

For example, in the famous opening sentence of *A Tale of Two Cities* by Charles Dickens, we see an alternation between words with positive sentiment and words with negative sentiment, giving a zero average: "It was the best (+) of times, it was the worst (-) of times, it was the age of wisdom (+), it was the age of foolishness (-), it was the epoch of belief (+), it was the epoch of incredulity (-), it was the season of Light (+), it was the season of Darkness (-), it was the spring (+) of hope (+), it was the winter (-) of despair (-) ..."

This kind of analysis is best done on the original text, since translation may insert or remove words, or blur the connotations of a word. There is also some subjectivity in the choice of positive and negative words, and therefore the method should only be seen as showing general trends, not precise numerical values.

For English, standard lexicons of positive and negative words exist (Hu and Liu 2004; Jockers 2017), but for this work we constructed a Hebrew lexicon specific to Ruth. Table 3 shows the positive and negative Hebrew words used in our analysis (which include proper names that have a positive connotation). For some of these words, the context inverts the sentiment, usually through one of the Hebrew words meaning "not" (e.g. biltî, lo', or 'al). In the case of Yhwh (Lord), the inverted context may involve Yhwh inflicting punishment or hardship, rather than blessing.

To qualify for inclusion in Table 3, a word should be consistently used either positively (negatively in an inverted context) or negatively (positively in an inverted context). This excludes, for example, words like gā'al (kinsman-redeemer), which is used with strong positive sentiment in 4:14, 3:9, and perhaps 2:20, but only neutrally for its 18 other uses in the book.

We calculate the total sentiment of each verse (positive or negative) up to 4:17. The chart in Figure 2 shows the resulting sentiment values.

Chapter 1 is broadly negative in character, with verses having an average sentiment of -0.27. There are some positive verses, such as 1:6: "the **Lord** (Yhwh) had **visited** (pāqad) his people, giving them **bread** (leḥem)" (our translation, here and following). Also positive are 1:9, where Naomi blesses Ruth and Orpah, and 1:16, where Ruth promises to stay with Naomi.

Table 3: Positive and negative words used in sentiment analysis for Ruth. Brackets mark verses where the context inverts the sentiment of the word.

Positive Hebrew Words	
bāraḵ (bless)	2:4, 2:19, 2:20, 3:10, 4:14
dāviḏ (David)	4:17
ḥayil (prosper/worthy)	2:1, 3:11, 4:11
ḥēn (favor)	2:2, 2:10, 2:13
ḥeseḏ (mercy)	1:8, 2:20, 3:10
ḥāsâ (refuge)	2:12
ṭôḇ (good)	2:22, 3:13, 4:15
Yhwh (Lord)	1:8, 1:9, (1:13), 1:17, (1:21×2), 2:4×2, 2:12×2, 2:20, 3:13, 4:11, 4:12, 4:13, 4:14
yāṯar (left over)	2:14, 2:18
lē'â (Leah)	4:11
lēḇ (kindly)	2:13, 3:7
leḥem (bread/food)	1:6, 2:14
mānôaḥ (rest/security)	3:1
mᵉnûḥâ (rest/security)	1:9
nāḥam (comfort)	2:13
nāšaq (kiss)	1:9, 1:14
nāṯan (give)	1:6, 1:9, 2:18, 3:17, 4:7, 4:11, 4:12, 4:13
pāqaḏ (visit, consider)	1:6
rāḥēl (Rachel)	4:11
śāḇaʿ (be satisfied)	2:14
šālam (reward/repay)	2:12
šālēm (full/complete)	2:12

Negative Hebrew Words	
bāḵâ (weep)	1:9, 1:14
gāʿar (rebuke)	(2:16)
zāqēn (be old)	1:12
yārē' (fear)	(3:11)
kālam (reproach/humiliate)	(2:15)
kāraṯ (cut off)	(4:10)
mûṯ (die/dead)	1:3, 1:5, 1:8, 1:17×2, (2:20), 4:5×2, 4:10×2
mārar (bitter)	1:13, 1:20
nāḡaʿ (touch/strike)	(2:9)
pāḡaʿ (urge/assault)	(1:16), (2:22)
rêqām (empty)	1:21, (3:17)
rāʿāḇ (famine)	1:1
rāʿaʿ (afflict)	1:21
šā'ar (survive)	1:3, 1:5
šāḇaṯ (left without)	(4:14)

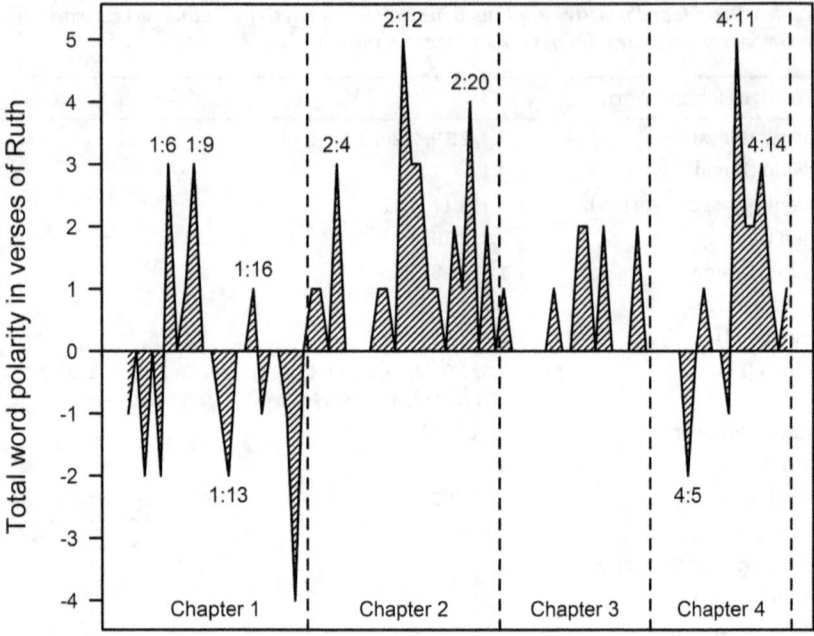

Figure 2: Sentiment analysis for Ruth up to 4:17.

On the whole, however, Chapter 1 is a tale of woe after woe experienced by Naomi, climaxing in 1:21: "I went away full, and the LORD (Yhwh, negative context) has brought me back **empty** (rêqām). Why call me Naomi, seeing that the LORD (Yhwh, negative context) has opposed me, and the Almighty has **brought calamity upon** (rāʿaʿ) me?" This negativity justifies interpreting the chapter as a tragedy.

Chapter 2 is far more positive in character, with verses having an average sentiment of +1.26. In fact, none of the verses in Chapter 2 or Chapter 3 has negative sentiment. Early on, in 2:4, Boaz is introduced very positively, blessing and being blessed by his workers: "And behold, Boaz came from Bethlehem and said to the reapers, 'The LORD (Yhwh) be with you,' and they said to him, 'The LORD (Yhwh) **bless** (bārak) you.'"

In 2:12, there is a very positive blessing of Ruth by Boaz: "May the LORD (Yhwh) **repay** (šālam) your work and a **full** (šālēm) reward be given you by the LORD (Yhwh), the God of Israel, under whose wings you have come to take **refuge** (ḥāsâ)!" A few verses later, in 2:20, Naomi gives a very positive characterization of Boaz: "And Naomi said to her daughter-in-law, 'May he be **blessed** (bārak) by the LORD (Yhwh), because he has not forsaken his **kindness** (ḥesed) to the living and to the **dead** (mût, inverted context)!' And Naomi said to her, 'The man is a relative of ours, one of our kinsman-redeemers.'" Although there is some question as to whether "he has not forsaken" refers to Boaz or to Yhwh (Rebera 1985;

Hubbard 1988, 186), this does not affect our sentiment analysis, nor the fact that Boaz is being praised.

Chapter 3 describes a series of interactions between Ruth and Naomi and between Ruth and Boaz. The average sentiment of the verses is +0.56. These interactions are described fairly subtly, and sentiment analysis does not fully recognize their significance.

Finally, Chapter 4 (up to 4:17) has an average sentiment of +0.71, with some verses using negative words, and other verses being intensely positive. The two negative verses are 4:5 and 4:10, both referring back to the death of Mahlon and its implications. Among the positive verses is the blessing of Ruth in 4:11: "And all the people who were at the gate and the elders said, 'We are witnesses. May the LORD (Yhwh) **make** (nātan) the woman who is coming into your house like **Rachel** (rāḥēl) and **Leah** (lē'â), who together built the house of Israel, and may you **prosper** (ḥayil) in Ephrathah and be famous in Bethlehem.'"

Also of note is the thanks to God in 4:14: "Then the women said to Naomi, '**Blessed** (bārak) be the LORD (Yhwh), who has **not** (lo') left you this day **without** (šābat, inverted context) a kinsman-redeemer, and may his name be famous in Israel!'"

Generally speaking, sentiment analysis supports the traditional chapter divisions of the book. Goswell (2023) notes that these divisions "convincingly divide the book into four episodes." Sentiment in the four chapters trends from generally negative (in Chapter 1), to strongly positive (in Chapter 2), to weakly positive (in Chapter 3), to mixed (in Chapter 4). In addition, some chapters are marked by the introduction of new characters. For example, Chapter 2 sees the introduction of Boaz to the story, and Chapter 4 introduces the city elders.

5. Four Acts

Our sentiment analysis has justified us in seeing the story of Ruth taking place in four acts, corresponding to the traditional chapters. We therefore repeat our social network analysis on a chapter-by-chapter basis.

Chapter 1: Naomi's Tragedy

The first chapter of the book establishes the major characters of the book (other than Boaz and the alternate redeemer) and the relationships between them, but the focus is very much on Naomi. With her family (her husband Elimelech and their two sons, Mahlon and Chilion) she leaves Bethlehem to go to Moab because of a famine. The sons marry Moabite women. Tragedy strikes, and the deaths of Elimelech in 1:3 and of Mahlon and Chilion in 1:5 are described entirely from Naomi's point of view. In 1:5, we are told that Naomi is bereft of her two sons (as well as her husband), but we are not told anything about the perspective of the widows Ruth and Orpah.

In keeping with this, Naomi has the highest centrality score in this chapter, by a considerable margin (a score of 1.00).

Ruth is second in centrality, primarily because of her interactions with Naomi, giving her a centrality score of 0.78 (the network connects Ruth and Orpah to their respective husbands, although the question of which brother marries which woman is not answered until 4:10). Orpah is third in centrality, interacting less with Naomi than Ruth does, and leaving the story at 1:14, giving her a score of 0.72. Saxegaard (2010, 69) notes that Orpah, as a minor character, is in the narrative primarily as "a model to which Ruth might be compared."

Elimelech, who is the focus of the first two verses, dies in 1:3, and thus comes fourth in centrality for the chapter as a whole (a score of 0.64). Chapter 1 is very much told as Naomi's story, and the overall negative sentiment noted in Figure 2 underlines the fact that this story is a tragedy.

This chapter, in 1:19–21, also introduces the townswomen of Bethlehem, with whom Naomi has a very negative conversation (in 1:21, Naomi describes herself as having moved from fullness to emptiness). The townswomen reappear in a more positive light in 4:14.

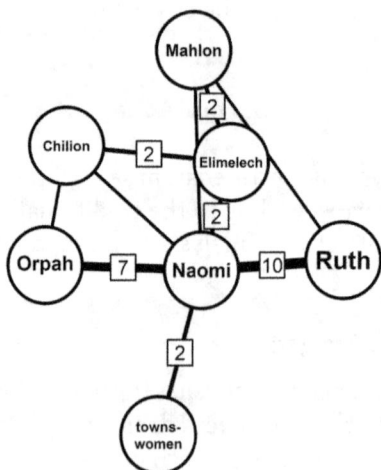

Figure 3: Network for Chapter 1: Naomi's Tragedy. Naomi is the most central character here.

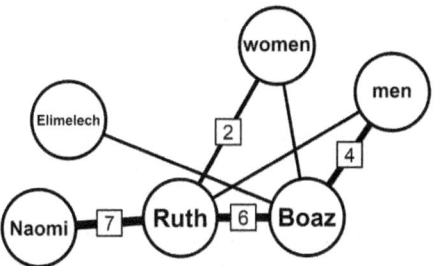

Figure 4: Network for Chapter 2: Ruth's Dilemma. Here Ruth is the most central character.

Chapter 2: Ruth's Dilemma

In Chapter 2, Ruth has the highest centrality score (1.00), followed closely by Boaz (0.93). Naomi is third in centrality (0.74), and the men working for Boaz are fourth in centrality (0.63). Ruth, having volunteered to glean in the barley fields, follows these men as they reap in 2:3, but primarily these men interact with Boaz (2:4–6,15). The women who work for Boaz are fifth in centrality (0.54), interacting with Ruth more directly in 2:14,23. The network is shown in Figure 4.

In this chapter, the focus lies on Ruth's multifaceted dilemma. How is Ruth to feed herself and her mother-in-law? Without crops of their own, the barley harvest (1:22) is of no immediate help, and so gleaning in the fields (a form of charity established in Lev 23:22) seems to be the only option. How is Ruth to avoid sexual assault (2:22)? Specific action by Boaz seems necessary to prevent this (2:9), perhaps because of Ruth's status as a foreigner. The chapter leaves unresolved the longer-term dilemma: how is Ruth to have a future in a land where she is a widow and a foreigner?

Ruth interacts extensively with Boaz in this chapter (2:3,8,10–11,13–14), setting the scene for the events of Chapter 3. Naomi remains at home, advising Ruth and commenting on the events of the day (2:2,18–23). As noted in the section on sentiment analysis above, both Ruth and Boaz are praised in very positive terms.

Chapter 3: Ruth Obeys

In Chapter 3, Ruth approaches Boaz in the famous night scene described in 3:6–9. She does so following Naomi's instructions in 3:1–5. Boaz responds to Ruth's action in 3:10–15, and Ruth reports back to Naomi in 3:16–18. Ruth's reference to a "redeemer" (haggōʼēl) in 3:9 implies a request for marriage, which runs into the problem of the alternate redeemer mentioned in 3:12. This problem requires Boaz to take the leading role in the next chapter.

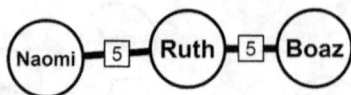

Figure 5: Network for Chapter 3: Ruth obeys. Here Ruth acts as a bridge between Naomi and Boaz.

Since the only interactions are Ruth with Naomi, on the one hand, and Ruth with Boaz, on the other, we have the very simple network shown in Figure 5. Acting as the bridge between Naomi and Boaz, Ruth has the highest centrality (1.00), with Boaz and Naomi equal second (0.75). Berlin (1994, 84) notes that Naomi "participates vicariously in the encounters between Ruth and Boaz." However, this vicarious participation is indirect: Boaz and Ruth do not actually meet.

Chapter 4: Boaz Acts

The network for Chapter 4 (Figure 6) introduces several new characters: the alternate redeemer (previously mentioned by Boaz in 3:12–13), the city elders (4:2–11), and Obed (plus his descendants Jesse and David). Boaz interacts with the alternate redeemer in the presence of the city elders, in a process similar to, but not identical with, Lev 25:25 and Deut 25:5–10 (Leggett 1974). This enables Boaz to marry Ruth (4:13), leading to the birth of their son Obed. In addition, the resolution of Naomi's tragedy is celebrated with the reintroduction of the townswomen from Chapter 1 (although Naomi has only a moderate centrality value in this chapter: 0.58).

The names Elimelech, Chilion, and Mahlon occur in 4:9–10, but only in reported speech, and so are not included in the network in Figure 6. Having died in Chapter 1, these men are no longer participants in the story.

Boaz has the highest centrality score in this chapter (1.00), reflecting his multiple interactions with people as he resolves Ruth's dilemma of impoverished widowhood. Obed comes second (0.85) because he provides the connection to his famous grandson David. Third and fourth are the alternate redeemer (0.80) and the city elders (0.68) with whom Boaz interacts. Ruth herself comes only fifth in this chapter (0.65), marrying Boaz and giving birth to Obed in 4:13. However, the emphasis is on Obed being a son for Naomi (4:17) rather than for Ruth (and the narrator does not give us Ruth's perspective on this arrangement). As the story concludes (4:14–17), the townswomen celebrate Naomi's return to fullness after the emptiness of 1:21, and thus the resolution of Naomi's tragedy.

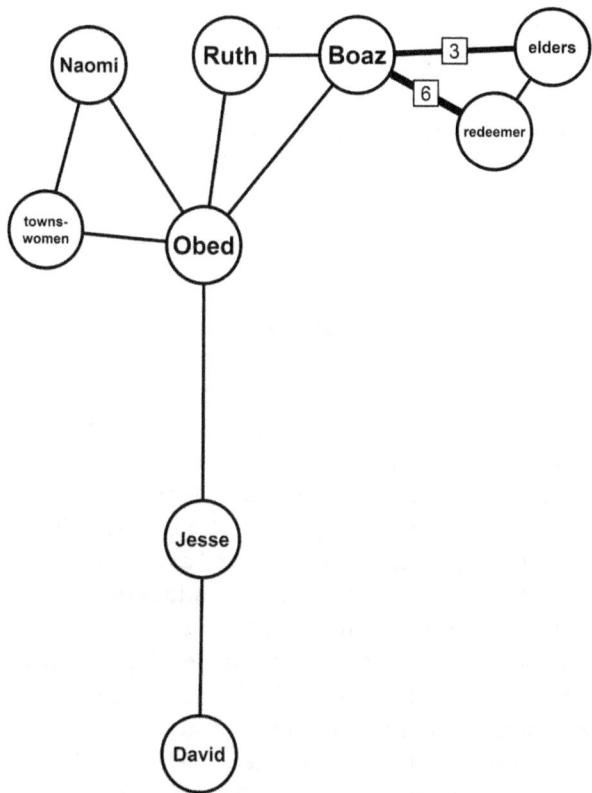

Figure 6: Network for Chapter 4: Boaz Acts. Here Boaz is the most central character. Note the triangle Boaz/elders/redeemer resolving the legal issues, the triangle Boaz/Ruth/Obed of marriage and childbirth, and the triangle Naomi/Obed/townswomen celebrating Naomi's return to fullness.

Summary

Our chapter-by-chapter analysis of Ruth has simplified the question of centrality. For the book as a whole, the highest centrality scores were very close together (Ruth 1.00, Naomi 0.97, Boaz 0.90), making the "most central" character dependent on the details of how the analysis was done. Indeed, the results of the analysis presented here for the book as a whole differ from those of Dekker and Dekker (2018).

However, for individual chapters, the most central character is more evident. In Chapter 1 it is Naomi (followed by Ruth, 1.00 vs 0.78), with the events of the chapter being described from Naomi's point of view. In Chapter 2, the most central character is Ruth (closely followed by Boaz,

1.00 vs 0.93), with both Ruth and Boaz being praised in very positive terms. In Chapter 3, the most central character is Ruth (followed equally by Naomi and Boaz, 1.00 vs 0.75), with Ruth acting as a bridge between Naomi and Boaz. Finally, in Chapter 4 it is Boaz (followed by Obed, 1.00 vs 0.85), with Boaz being the primary actor, and Obed providing the connection to his famous grandson David as well as being "a son" for the previously bereft Naomi.

6. Conclusion

We have used sentiment analysis to support the traditional division of Ruth into chapters. Analyzing centrality on a chapter-by-chapter basis illuminates the book of Ruth as a story in four acts.

Chapter 1 is a tale of woe, full of negativity, and largely from Naomi's point of view. The most central character is Naomi, with Ruth second and Orpah third. This chapter can be interpreted as *Naomi's Tragedy*.

Chapter 2 introduces Boaz as a character, and is full of positivity. Both Boaz and Ruth are described in very positive terms. The most central character is Ruth, with Boaz second and Naomi third. Given the issues of food (2:2), sexual assault (2:9,22) and Ruth's uncertain long-term future, we can interpret this chapter as *Ruth's Dilemma*.

Chapter 3 is more neutral in sentiment. Acting on Naomi's instructions, Ruth approaches Boaz. This makes Ruth the most central character, with Boaz and Naomi equal second. This chapter can therefore be interpreted as *Ruth Obeys*.

Finally, Chapter 4 (up to 4:17) is mostly positive in sentiment. Boaz is the most central character, as he acts to solve Ruth's dilemma and fathers the child (Obed) who resolves Naomi's tragedy. Partly because our network analysis has included the references to Jesse and David in 4:17, this child is the second-most central character. The alternate redeemer with whom Boaz interacts is third in centrality. This chapter can therefore be interpreted as *Boaz Acts*.

As in our previous network study (Dekker and Dekker 2018), Boaz, Ruth, and Naomi can all be considered to be central characters in different senses. However, a chapter-by-chapter analysis highlights the shifting focus of the book: from Naomi in the first chapter, to Ruth in the middle chapters, and to Boaz in the final chapter. The book of Ruth is a complex and multifaceted story. To interpret it as a narrative about a single central character is to oversimplify it.

Works Cited

Alter, Robert. 1981. *The Art of Biblical Narrative*. New York: Basic Books.
Baden, Joel S. 2012. *The Composition of the Pentateuch: Renewing the Documentary Hypothesis*. New Haven, CT: Yale University Press.
Berlin, Adele. 1994. *Poetics and Interpretation of Biblical Narrative*. Winona Lake, IN: Eisenbrauns.
Borgatti, Stephen P., Ajay Mehra, Daniel J. Brass, and Giuseppe Labianca. 2009. "Network Analysis in the Social Sciences." *Science* 323 (5916): 892–95. doi:10.1126/science.1165821.
Brady, Christian M. M. 2013. "The Conversion of Ruth in Targum Ruth." *Review of Rabbinic Judaism* 16: 133–46. http://dx.doi.org/10.1163/15700704-12341252.
Csárdi, Gabor, and Tamas Nepusz. 2006. "The Igraph Software Package for Complex Network Research." *InterJournal* (Complex Systems), 1695. See also igraph.org.
Czachesz, Istvan. 2016. "Network Analysis of Biblical Texts." *Journal of Cognitive Historiography* 3: 43–67. doi:10.1558/jch.31682.
Dekker, Anthony H. 2005. "Conceptual Distance in Social Network Analysis." *Journal of Social Structure*. www.cmu.edu/joss/content/articles/volume6/dekker.
Dekker, John T., and Anthony H. Dekker. 2018. "Centrality in the Book of Ruth." *Vetus Testamentum* 68 (1): 41–50. http://dx.doi.org/10.1163/15685330-12341310.
Freeman, Linton C., Stephen P. Borgatti, and Douglas R. White. 1991. "Centrality in Valued Graphs: A Measure of Betweenness Based on Network Flow." *Social Networks* 13: 141–154. http://dx.doi.org/10.1016/0378-8733(91)90017-n.
Fuerst, Wesley J. 1975. *The Books of Ruth, Esther, Ecclesiastes, The Song of Songs, Lamentations* (Cambridge Bible Commentary). Cambridge: Cambridge University Press.
Goswell, Gregory. 2023. *Text and Paratext: Book Order, Title, and Division as Keys to Biblical Interpretation*. Bellingham, WA: Bellingham, WA: Lexham Academic.
Hage, Per, and Frank Harary. 1995. "Eccentricity and centrality in networks." *Social Networks* 17 (1): 57–63. doi:10.1016/0378-8733(94)00248-9.
Hu, Minqing, and Bing Liu. 2004. "Mining Opinion Features in Customer Reviews." Pages 755–60 in *Proceedings of the 19th National Conference on Artificial Intelligence*. Washington, DC: AAAI Press.
Hubbard, Robert L. 1988. *The Book of Ruth*. New International Commentary on the Old Testament. Grand Rapids, MI: Eerdmans.
Jockers, Matthew L. 2017. "Syuzhet: Extracts Sentiment and Sentiment-derived Plot Arcs from Text." R software package, see github.com/mjockers/syuzhet.

Kostic, Stefan M., Mirjana I. Simic, and Miroljub V. Kostic. 2020. "Social Network Analysis and Churn Prediction in Telecommunications Using Graph Theory." *Entropy* 22: 753. http://dx.doi.org/10.3390/e22070753.

Leggett, Donald A. 1974. *The Levirate and Goel Institutions in the Old Testament: With special attention to the book of Ruth*. Cherry Hill, NJ: Mack.

Marchiori, Massimo, and Vito Latora. 2000. "Harmony in the Small-world." *Physica A: Statistical Mechanics and Its Applications* 285: 539–46. http://dx.doi.org/10.1016/s0378-4371(00)00311-3.

Massey, Steven E. 2016. "Social Network Analysis of the Biblical Moses." *Applied Network Science* 1.

McClure, Jennifer M. 2016. "Introducing Jesus's Social Network: Support, Conflict, and Compassion." *Interdisciplinary Journal of Research on Religion* 12. www.religjournal.com/articles/article_view.php?id=110.

──────. 2020. "Jesus's Social Network and the Four Gospels: Exploring the Relational Dynamics of the Gospels Using Social Network Analysis." *Biblical Theology Bulletin: Journal of Bible and Culture* 50. http://dx.doi.org/10.1177/0146107919892841.

Moretti, Franco. 2005. *Graphs, Maps, Trees: Abstract Models for a Literary History*. London: Verso.

Morselli, Carlo. 2008. *Inside Criminal Networks*. New York: Springer Science & Business Media.

Person, Raymond F., Jr. 1996. *In Conversation with Jonah: Conversation Analysis, Literary Criticism and the Book of Jonah*. Sheffield: Sheffield Academic Press.

R Core Team. 2013. *R: A Language and Environment for Statistical Computing*, Vienna: R Foundation for Statistical Computing. See also www.R-project.org.

Rebera, Basil A. 1985. "Yahweh or Boaz? Ruth 2.20 Reconsidered." *The Bible Translator* 36: 317–27. http://dx.doi.org/10.1177/026009358503600302.

Rydberg-Cox, Jeff. 2011. "Social Networks and the Language of Greek Tragedy." *Journal of the Chicago Colloquium on Digital Humanities and Computer Science* 1.

Saxegaard, Kristin Moen. 2010. *Character Complexity in the Book of Ruth*. Forschungen zum Alten Testament, Volume 47. Tübingen: Mohr Siebeck.

Sparrow, Malcolm K. 1991. "The Application of Network Analysis to Criminal Intelligence: An Assessment of the Prospects." *Social Networks* 13: 251–74. http://dx.doi.org/10.1016/0378-8733(91)90008-h.

Wasserman, Stanley, and Katherine Faust. 1994. *Social Network Analysis: Methods and Applications*. Cambridge: Cambridge University Press.

About the Authors

Anthony H. Dekker earned his PhD in computer science and mathematics from the University of Tasmania in 1991. After a number of years as an academic in Australia and Singapore, he joined the Defence Science and Technology Organisation (Australia), where his interested included social network analysis, human behavior, agent-based simulation, and computerized text analysis. Following this, he worked as an independent consultant. His current interests include theology and the *Chronicles of Narnia*. He is a fellow of the Modelling and Simulation Society of Australia and New Zealand.

John T. Dekker earned his PhD in Old Testament from Christ College, Sydney in 2017. From 2015 to 2019 he taught at the Talua Theological Training Institute in the island nation of Vanuatu. He is pastor of Christ the King Church in Oregon, and Adjunct Professor at Reformed Evangelical Seminary.

Chapter 13
Is Ruth a Rapist? The Sexual Victimization of Boaz

Jennifer Lehmann

Abstract

The threat of sexual violence looms over the book of Ruth, for Ruth herself, but also for Boaz whose consent over whatever happened on the threshing floor is conspicuously missing from the conversation. This chapter fills this lacuna by examining the sexual ambiguities and the possibility of Boaz's consent in the narration of the scene on the threshing floor in Ruth 3. Coupled with Ruth and Naomi's deliberate subterfuge, this shows Boaz to be a victim of sexual violence, and Ruth his assailant.

Keywords: Ruth 3, sexual violence, consent, threshing floor, subterfuge, bed-trick

1. Introduction

The threat of sexual violence looms over the book of Ruth. When Boaz warns Ruth to stay with the women and orders his men to stay away from her, the implied threat to Ruth is likely one of sexual violence (2:8–9). David J. Shepherd (2018, 528–43) takes the explicit setting of the book in "the days when the judges ruled" (1:1) as another indication that the threat to Ruth is one of sexual violence, specifically because of the theme of sexual violence against women and foreigners throughout Judges. While several scholars have noticed Ruth's sexual vulnerability, as both a woman and a foreigner, as she travels with Naomi and gleans in the field (for an overview, see, Matheny 2020, 16–17), Boaz's sexual vulnerability as he sleeps on the threshing floor after a night of harvest activities has received much less scrutiny. This will be the focus of this contribution. Tikva Frymer-Kensky (2002, 248) argues that Ruth is vulnerable to sexual assault from Boaz when she goes to find him on the threshing floor at night, but as the scene unfolds, it is Boaz's sexual agency that seems to be in question.

In Ruth 3, Naomi concocts a plan to secure both her future and Ruth's. Naomi sees Boaz, a "mighty man of valor" (2:1) whose kindness has already helped both Naomi and her daughter-in-law and who also is a relative of her late husband, as their ticket to financial security. So Naomi instructs Ruth to wait until Boaz is drunk, find where he sleeps, uncover his *margelot* מרגלתיו ("legs" or perhaps something else), and lie down, adding that Boaz will then "tell you what to do" (3:4). Ruth immediately agrees and tells her mother-in-law, "all that you say I will do" (3:5). She waits until Boaz

> ate, drank, and was merry, and he went to lie down at the edge of the heap of grain. She approached him stealthily, uncovered his legs (מרגלת) and lay down. And then, at midnight, the man trembled, he turned, and behold, lying by his feet (מרגלת) was a woman! (Ruth 3:7–8)

Ruth then broaches the subject of marriage and redemption, and Boaz agrees (as long as the other man who is a closer relative refuses to fulfill this duty). When this business is concluded, he invites her to lie until morning and sends her home with a cloak full of barley.

There are many elements in the story that make it unclear exactly what is meant to have happened on the threshing floor. However, the repetition of sexual euphemisms in the surrounding narrative suggest strongly that there is some sexual valence to the events in Ruth 3, even though there is no explicit narration of sex between Ruth and Boaz.

Seeing hints of a sexual encounter in the text is not unique to modern readers. Both Josephus and Ruth Rabbah specify that Boaz did "not touch her [Ruth]" (*Ruth Rabbah* 6:4; *Ant.* 5.9.3), indicating they felt it was possible for a reader to read their encounter on the threshing floor as sexual, though they disagree with this reading. My question is not whether Boaz touched Ruth, but whether Ruth touched Boaz, and whether Boaz consented to this act. Though Kandy Queen-Sutherland contends that "what happens on the threshing floor is between adults, consenting adults" (2016, 124), the narrative is not clear about that. In fact, the strong hints of a sexual encounter, paired with a theme of deception and Boaz's intoxication, suggest that what happens on the threshing floor is not consensual, in which case Boaz would be a victim of sexual assault.

The investigation has three sections. In the first, I will explore the textual ambiguities and sexual innuendos in Ruth 3 in order to understand the narrative possibilities for us to evaluate through the lens of sexual violence. Most important of these textual ambiguities are the meanings of גלה ("uncover"), מרגלת (usually translated as "legs" or "feet"), and שכב ("lie"), each of which can have sexual implications. The second section will examine the possibility of Boaz's consent (or lack thereof), whether it is appropriate to assume that he was interested in Ruth, and whether that matters in our assessment of the narrative from the perspective of sexual violence. Not only is Boaz likely drunk, but Ruth and Naomi intentionally wait until he has "finished eating and drinking" before Ruth uncovers him (or herself) while he sleeps on the threshing floor. Boaz's judgment and ability to fully consent to sexual activity would certainly be affected by his alcohol consumption, and Ruth and Naomi count on that. In the final section, with the help of some intertextual clues, I will argue that the narrative in Ruth 3 is one of sexual violence. Ruth is linked with three other narratives (Gen 19; 29; 38) where men are sexually violated, which also supports reading the ambiguities in Ruth as sexually violent. As we will see, the evidence, both intertextual and intratextual, presents Boaz as a victim of sexual assault and Ruth as his assailant.

2. Textual Ambiguity in Ruth 3

Before discussing the possibility of sexual violence in this scene, it is important to address some of the textual ambiguities present in the narrative. There are many elements that infuse the scene with sexual tension. To begin, the theme of fertility/barrenness of both the land and the women is a repeated cause of tension and movement throughout the book (for an overview see Sutskover 2010). The fertility of the land is a major issue in the story, moving the plot and literally moving people. The book begins with a "famine in the land" (1:1) that prompts the move to Moab. After the death of Naomi's husband and sons, she hears of the end of that famine and a return of fertility to the land, which prompts her return (Ruth 1:6–7). Naomi also draws attention to her own barrenness, in contrast to the potential fertility of her daughters-in-law (1:11–13). And finally, the problem of Naomi's inability to produce more sons is linked to the problem of Ruth and Orpah's lack of husbands. Though Orpah's problem is solved by her returning to her family, Ruth decides to remain with Naomi, leaving the problem of Ruth's lack of a husband, established explicitly by Naomi, unresolved.

When Naomi and Ruth arrive in Bethlehem, we are introduced to Boaz, "a mighty man of valor from the family of Elimelech" (2:1). Ruth, a childless widow in need of the security a husband could provide, and Boaz, a relative of Ruth's late father-in-law, meet in the field after Ruth goes out to find someone "in whose eyes I may find favor" (אשר אמצא חן 2:2) (בעיניו, see Esth 2:17). This primes us to see Boaz as a potential sexual and marital partner for Ruth. Edward F. Campbell (1975, 124–25) also notices the use of the same epithet ("man of valor" איש... חיל and "woman of valor" אשת חיל) for both Boaz and Ruth (2:1; 3:11), which reinforces their potential match. To this we add a man and a woman meeting in a secluded area after dark. This is highlighted by the narrator by referring to the two simply as "the man" (3:3, 8, 16, 18) and "the woman" (3:8, 14) multiple times in the chapter. The specific setting and timing of this meeting heightens the erotic energy as well; the threshing floor is elsewhere referred to as a place of illicit sexual activity (Hos 9:1), and the time of the harvest reinforces the return of fertility to the land. Further, the repetition of "know" (yd'), "come" (bw') and "lie" (škb), which often accompany (or are euphemisms for) sexual activity, serves as a strong *wink* from the narrator.

But all we have is winks and innuendos. The narrative is cleverly formed using multiple double *entendres* and ambiguous grammar, making it impossible to pin down exactly what happens between Boaz and Ruth on the threshing floor. The most interesting ambiguities and difficulties in interpretation come from three words: גלה, מרגלת, and שכב.

2.1 Legs?

The word מרגלת (*margelot*) is the most troubling because it only appears in one place other than Ruth 3 and because of its ambiguous grammatical position in the verses where it appears in Chapter 3. While it is clear it contains the root *r-g-l* and so is related to "feet" or "legs," it is not the usual way of referring to "feet" or "legs" and could, therefore, be designating something else. In Dan 10:6, it is used in parallel with "his arms": "His body was like beryl, his face like lightning, his eyes like flaming torches, his arms and his legs (מרגלתיו *marglotāyw*) like the gleam of burnished bronze, and the sound of his words like the roar of a multitude." In this context, *margelot*, seems to have the same function as "arms" and therefore should be translated simply as feet or legs.

However, our example in Ruth is complicated by the fact that in two instances (3:4, 7) *margelot* seems to be the direct object of a verb, while in the other two instances (3:8, 14), it seems to indicate the location the verb occurs:

> 3:4 And you will uncover his *margelot*
> 3:7 And she uncovered his *margelot*
> 3:8 And behold, lying [at] his margelot, a woman!
> 3:14 And she laid [at] his מרגלת (ketiv) or מרגלית (qere)

To make the text even more confusing, though *margelot* in question are Boaz's in particular, not just any *margelot*, it lacks the definite direct object marker ('et את), which is usually used to indicate the definite direct object of a transitive verb. Ellen van Wolde (1997, 19) argues that this missing *'et*, along with its usage in Ruth 3:8 and 3:14, indicates that *margelot* cannot be the direct object of the verb "uncover" but must instead be the place where the uncovering occurs, thus indicating that Ruth uncovers *herself* at Boaz's feet. However, such a strong stance is not warranted, as there are many cases in the Hebrew Bible where *'et* is not used alongside a definite direct object (Muraoka 1985, 150–51). Rather than eliminating the possibility of *margelot* being the direct object of "uncover," the missing *'et* opens up the possibility of a double meaning of the phrase "uncover his legs." Frymer-Kensky argues that the ambiguity is likely intentional: "she is uncovering him, or herself, and the narrator may be playing with the reader by not making the scene absolutely clear" (2002, 248).

Adding to the ambiguity, feet and hands are often used as a euphemism for genitals, or more specifically, the penis (Linafelt and Beal 1999, 49). Considering the other sexual imagery already discussed, this should not be ignored. Though the text does not make it clear, there is certainly a hint that *margelot* refers to Boaz's genitals. For Ruth to surreptitiously uncover Boaz's genitals while he slept would certainly constitute sexual assault. Additionally, it is also possible she did more than simply "uncover."

2.2 Uncover?

The verb *gālah* ("to uncover") is repeated twice in Ruth 3, first in Naomi's instructions to Ruth (3:4), and then in the narration of Ruth's actions (3:7). This is the same verb used in many laws in Leviticus and Deuteronomy dealing with illicit sexual activity. In most cases, the verb is paired with nakedness (ערוה *'erwah*) as the object (Lev 18; 20; Deut 22:30; 27:20). These passages prohibit "uncovering the nakedness" of various familial relations and are widely interpreted to be prohibitions against sexual intercourse.

Here, as was discussed above, the object of "uncover" seems to be *margelot*. Even simply uncovering his legs would be a violation of Boaz, not to mention exposing his genitals. But considering the sexual implications of the verb elsewhere, the use of language suggests that Ruth does more than simply "uncover" Boaz's "feet" by actually initiating sexual intercourse while Boaz is sleeping, and this is what rouses him from his sleep.

Another possibility is that Naomi instructs Ruth to uncover *herself*, as van Wolde suggests. In addition to the curious case of the missing *'et*, Jeremy Schipper also notes that the root *g-l-h* in *pi'el* (as it is here) is frequently used reflexively and is most often used to refer to the uncovering of female bodies (Lev 18:6–9; 20:11, 17–22; Deut. 23:1[22:30]; 27:20; Ezek 16:37; 22:10; 23:10, 18; Nah 3:5.). According to this interpretation, Boaz's feet/legs/genitals are the location at which Ruth undresses. This interpretation helps explain the *mem* at the beginning of *margelot*, as that prefix can indicate location (Schipper 2016, 143). Again, this does not rule out the possibility that Ruth uncovers Boaz, but further complicates the scene, making it unclear who (or what) is the object of the verb.

Whether Ruth uncovers Boaz or herself, it is also possible that nothing sexual occurs, but that Ruth means for Boaz to *assume* that something sexual has occurred. Waking up in the middle of the night, his mind and memory still clouded by alcohol, with a naked woman lying next to him, it would not be unreasonable for Boaz to assume that something had happened between him and the woman in the seclusion of the threshing floor. After all, the threshing floor is known as a place for illicit sexual activity (Hos 9:1). By making Boaz think something happened, Ruth could make Boaz feel obligated to her without actually committing a sexual act. Though this does not constitute sexual assault, it is surely sexual manipulation.

Once again, the language makes it impossible to give a static interpretation of the text. It leaves open two possibilities, both of which are sexually violent. Either Ruth approaches Boaz while he sleeps and sexually assaults him, or she undresses and positions herself next to him with the intention of making him believe that he had engaged in sexual acts with this woman while he was drunk.

2.3 Lie?

The verb *šākab* ("to lie") is repeated eight times in the chapter (thrice in 3:4; twice in 3:7, and in 3:8, 13, 14). This verb is very frequently used to unambiguously refer to sexual activity, but like many other words used to describe sexual activity in biblical Hebrew, *šākab* can also be literal and non-sexual. The repetition of the word certainly plays with the possibility of sexual activity but never actually "goes all the way." It is implied that Naomi intends for something more than "lying down" when she sends Ruth to a drunken Boaz after Ruth washes and anoints herself and puts on her best clothes (3:3), but it is not as clear if that actually occurs. The frequent use of the word teases the reader but always stops just short of describing sexual activity.

It is significant that Boaz asks Ruth to "lie down," not "lie *with me*" until the morning (3:13). In all other cases where *šākab* indicates sexual activity, it is accompanied by "with" (*'im* or *'et*). The presence of the preposition "with" would make the sexual meaning explicit, but there is still some suggestion that Ruth might be doing something more than just lying when she lies at Boaz's "feet."

With all of these ambiguities and double meanings, we can only see the scene slightly out of focus. Mirroring the darkness and confusion on the threshing floor that night, the scene is carefully constructed to hint at many things but show nothing clearly. It is as if we see the scene from Boaz's perspective. The reader is made to feel as confused as Boaz would have been, waking up suddenly and startled in the middle of the night. However, though each of these ambiguities have the potential to be read without a sexual valence, there are too many sexual innuendos to argue that there is nothing sexual implied in this chapter. Importantly, because of the emphasis on Ruth's deception and Boaz's lack of awareness, the sexual activity implied is missing a crucial element: Boaz's consent.

3. Boaz's Consent

In this essay, I frame my discussion of sexual violence around the notion of consent, rather than penetration. My understanding aligns with the definition offered by the Centers for Disease Control and Prevention as "a sexual act that is committed or attempted by another person without the freely given consent of the victim or against someone who is unable to consent or refuse" (Basile et al. 2017, 11). This definition is echoed (with very little difference) by many other organizations worldwide that deal with sexual violence. While there are of course important points of divergence between the ancient and modern worlds, contemporary definitions can be a helpful tool to focalize our understanding of sexual violation. Importantly, the sexual act need not include penetration or completion on the part of any involved parties and the central issue is the consent of the victim. The question of consent on the part of the victim is fundamental to assessing sexual violence, as a lack of consent is, in large part, what constitutes sexual violence and sexual assault. For our purposes, the integral question is whether Boaz consents to what happens on the threshing floor between him and Ruth. It is obvious that Boaz cannot consent to anything Ruth does while he is sleeping, but this is not the only evidence that he was sexually assaulted. There are other indications, such as his intoxication, the theme of knowledge and deception throughout the chapter, and his reaction to finding her upon waking that suggest that Boaz did not consent.

3.1 Sleep

It is important to note that Ruth approaches Boaz after "he went to lie down at the end of the heap of grain" (3:7), just as Naomi instructs her to do before she goes out (3:4). The phrase "he went to lie down" implies that Boaz is lying down in order to sleep. That he does not respond when Ruth approaches him and uncovers him (or herself) but, rather, turns with surprise and fear at midnight, confirms that he is indeed asleep and unconscious when Ruth comes to him on the threshing floor without waking him.

Once we establish that Boaz was sleeping when Ruth joins him on the threshing floor, it is clear that he is unable to consent to anything Ruth might do to him at this time. Further, there is a particular phenomenological harm in the sexual assault of an unconscious victim. Sleep is a time of particular vulnerability. As Cressida J. Heyes points out, "Sleep is a state of distinctive defenselessness for all humans that requires us to trust in the surrounding world as we fall (and stay) asleep" (2016, 378) As such, Heyes goes on to argue that the experience of sexual assault while sleeping, or being woken up by someone attempting sexual assault, "is to have the deepest place of anonymity, the part of one's life when one's existence is most dangerously yet crucially suspended, erased" (Heyes 2016, 378). Ruth waits until Boaz is asleep in order to take advantage of this vulnerability and, in doing so, deprives him of his agency, subjectivity, and the anonymity of sleep. Crucially, Boaz's consumption of alcohol also contributes to his sexual vulnerability.

3.2 Intoxication

The text makes a note multiple times of Boaz's intoxicated state. First, Naomi specifies to Ruth that she should wait "until he has finished eating and drinking" (3:3). An obvious explanation for this is that Naomi hopes that Boaz will be drunk when he has finished his meal. The phrase "eating and drinking" often implies "feasting, carousing, and celebration" and thus also hints at Boaz's potential intoxication (HALOT 3, 1668). Later, when Ruth is about to approach Boaz, the narrator confirms that Boaz has eaten and drunk and that "he was merry" (3:7). Though in Judg 18:20; 1 Kgs 8:66; and Prov 15:15 the expression "his heart was good" does not indicate intoxication, the phrase is often paired with alcohol consumption and the resulting intoxication (see Judg 19:6, 9, 22; 2 Sam 13:28; Esth 1:10). Coupled with the mention of Boaz drinking beforehand, it is certainly meant to be a euphemism for "drunk" or at least "tipsy" here. Boaz's drunkenness also indicates his vulnerability. In 2 Sam 13:28, Absalom specifically orders his men to attack Amnon when "he is merry with wine" (2 Sam 13:28). It is clear here that Amnon's drunkenness is intended to make him vulnerable to physical attack, but drunkenness is also often linked narratively with *sexual* vulnerability in particular throughout the Hebrew Bible, as can be seen in the following cases.

The clearest example comes from Habakkuk which specifically condemns making one's neighbor drink "in order to gaze (הביט *habiyṭ*) on their nakedness" (Hab 2:15). This unequivocally links alcohol with premeditated sexual violence and implies that it can facilitate sexual violence. We can see this in other stories in the Hebrew Bible.

In 2 Sam 11:13, David gets Uriah the Hittite drunk in the hopes that Uriah might forget his temporary vow of celibacy and sleep with his own wife, Bathsheba, in order to cover up David's affair with her. Though David's plan is unsuccessful (Uriah does not sleep with his wife and David has him killed), a clear connection is present between drunkenness and sexual manipulation. Lot's daughters, on the other hand, are successful in their plan to intoxicate their father and have sex with him. It is Lot's drunkenness that allows them to lie with him without him knowing "when she lay down or when she rose" (Gen 19:33, 35).

Alcohol also likely aids Laban in tricking Jacob into sleeping with Leah instead of Rachel (Gen 29:15–30). Jacob's drunkenness is implied by the word "feast" (*mišteh,* from the root š-t-h "to drink"), rendered as "bout of drinking" and "banquet" (HALOT 2, 653). The same root is found in Ruth 3:3 to describe Boaz's drinking.

Importantly, the fact that Naomi specifically emphasizes to Ruth that she should only approach Boaz once he is intoxicated suggests that she intends for Ruth to do something or ask for something Boaz might not normally consent to while sober. As Danna Nolan Fewell and David M. Gunn suggest, "entrapment is the goal" (1990, 78). Even though Naomi and Ruth do not personally get Boaz drunk as Lot's daughters do to their father (Gen 19:31–35), Naomi instructs Ruth to take advantage of Boaz's already drunken state, which suggests nefarious intent.

3.3 Knowledge

The root *y-d-ʻ* relating to knowing and knowledge is a keyword in this chapter of Ruth. It appears eight times in Ruth, the majority of which are in Chapter 3 (2:1, 11; 3:3, 4, 11, 14, 18; 4:4). The repetition of *y-d-ʻ* serves two functions: it introduces sexual innuendo that often accompanies the root, hinting at sexual activity without actually describing it (as with the repetition of the verb *šākab* discussed above) and simultaneously emphasizes who has knowledge and who does not. In this case, Ruth knows, while Boaz does not. Naomi instructs Ruth to "not make yourself known (*tiwādʿy* תּוֹדִעִי) to the man" (3:3) and to "know (*weyādaʿate* וְיָדַעַתְּ) the place where he lies" (3:4). Naomi thus orchestrates a situation where Ruth is in control because of her knowledge and Boaz's lack of awareness.

It is no coincidence that the same theme is prominent in Gen 19; 29; 38 as well. In the Hebrew Bible, the metaphor of sexual knowledge almost always refers to the man as the grammatical subject, the "knower," and the woman as the object, the known. Yet, the incidents in Gen 19; 29; 38 all reverse this assumption: the woman is aware of the reality of the situation while the man is left in the dark. In each of these cases, it is the woman who has the knowledge, (though not necessarily the power) while the man is reduced to "a blind creature of sense, a stumbler and a fumbler in the very act of procreation" (Jagendorf 1984, 192). In each case, the woman knows more than the man and the man is deceived into sleeping with her. Following the same thread of knowledge and deception, James Black goes farther and connects these three narratives with Ruth, noting that they each utilize the literary convention of the "bed-trick," which he defines as "the device of surprising a man with a bed-partner or of substituting one 'bride' for another" (Black 1991, 20; see also Adelman 2012; Fisch 1982, 431). In each story the male victim is unaware of the reality of the situation and is deceived into performing sexual acts. In light of this deception, each of these cases should be understood as nonconsensual, and thus as sexual assault.

The dichotomy of knowledge/deception is also strengthened by the adverb used to describe the way Ruth approaches Boaz while he is sleeping in the dark. Once Ruth is sure Boaz was asleep, "she came stealthily, uncovered his legs, and lay down" (Ruth 3:7). The more traditional translation as "softly" (KJV) does not convey the deception and danger that the word (*balāṭ*, בלט) implies elsewhere. The adverb is not particularly common in the Hebrew Bible (only seven occurrences). It is also found in Judg 4:21, when Jael approaches Sisera to assassinate him with a tent peg, and in 1 Sam 24:4, when David sneaks up behind Saul while he is "relieving himself" (literally "covering his feet") in a cave. All three instances involve men being attacked while in a vulnerable position.

Boaz's lack of knowledge, emphasized by the narrator and ensured by Ruth and Naomi, his intoxication, and most importantly, the fact that he is sleeping when Ruth approaches him, leave little room for his consent to any act on the threshing floor before he wakes up and Ruth allows him to recognize her. But because of his inebriation, we cannot assume he could fully consent to anything even after she makes herself known.

3.4 Fear and Confusion

When Boaz wakes up, he does not recognize Ruth right away. In fact, when he finds a woman lying next to him, his first reaction is fear: "the man trembled (*wayyeḥerad* ויחרד), he turned (*wayyillāpit* וילפת), and behold, lying at his feet, was a woman!" (3:8). The NRSV and NRSVUE downplay the presence of reactive fear and render the Hebrew verb instead with of sense of Boaz being "startled." However, most other instances of the verb *ḥārad* imply trembling in fear, not simply surprise (Gen 42:28; Exod 19:16; 1 Sam 28:5; 1 Kgs 1:49; Ezek 26:16, 32:10; Isa 10:29, 19:16, 32:11; Amos 3:6). It certainly does not imply that finding Ruth at his feet was a pleasant surprise. Rather, he seems to be afraid of what might be happening or what might have happened already.

Linafelt suggests a more euphemistic reading of *wayyeḥerad*, arguing it refers to the involuntary shudder that might accompany an orgasm. Linafelt's reading is supported by reading the *niphal wayyillāpit* in a standard passive rather than reflexive sense (he/it was "turned over"); "... it likely carries a metaphorical sense of 'being grasped/seized' by something involuntarily" (Linafelt and Beal 1999, 53). Linafelt suggests that Boaz, or more specifically Boaz's genitals, are being grasped by Ruth when he awakes in the middle of the night. For Ruth to surreptitiously approach Boaz while he is sleeping and manually stimulate him to ejaculation would certainly constitute rape. Being asleep, Boaz is unable to consent to Ruth's actions. Though, once again, the text is ambiguous, this is a potential intentionality in the text. Whether Boaz "he turned himself" or "he was grasped," he trembled as he awoke to find Ruth lying next to him. This is not a response that indicates consent but, rather, the opposite.

Then the narrator shows us what Boaz sees as he awakes trembling: "Behold! Lying at his feet was a woman!" (3:8). This phrasing recalls Jacob's experience finding Leah in his bed in the morning after his wedding to her sister Rachel: "Behold! It was Leah!" (Gen 29:25) Like Jacob, who immediately chastises Laban for tricking him, Boaz does not seem particularly pleased to find an unfamiliar woman next to him. He experiences fear rather than pleasure. Unlike Jacob, Boaz does not even know who is in his bed with him when he wakes up, and he asks, "Who are you?" (Ruth 3:9) Boaz is unable to recognize Ruth until she fully reveals herself by telling him her name, showing Ruth's full control over Boaz's knowledge.

The fact that he does not recognize Ruth when he wakes up emphasizes that Boaz was unaware of what was happening or even who was with him, meaning he was unable to give informed consent. His fearful reaction hints that Ruth's actions were unwelcome, even once he regained consciousness.

3.5 But He Wanted It?

It is often assumed that Boaz is attracted to Ruth. Anthony Phillips claims that "Boaz was clearly attracted to her [Ruth], treated her with favor, and ordered the young men not to molest her" (Phillips 1986, 1). Since when is it safe to assume that any act of kindness is a sign of sexual attraction? Fewell and Gunn (1990, 84–86) also suggest that Boaz was already interested in Ruth. Their argument relies primarily on Boaz's statement to Ruth in 3:10: "The last instance of your loyalty (ḥasdēk) is better than the first; you have not gone after young men, whether poor or rich." The implication here is that "the last instance of your loyalty" to which Boaz is referring to is that Ruth went after Boaz instead of a younger possibly more attractive man. This does seem to imply that Boaz thinks of himself as an old, less than attractive man, but does it imply that he is attracted to Ruth? To the contrary, the evidence suggesting that Boaz is attracted to Ruth is not entirely conclusive. Brett Krutzsch (2015) questions whether it is appropriate to assume that Boaz is even attracted to women at all. Krutzsch rightly points out that though the fact that Ruth marries two men does not deter scholars from seeing the potential of a romantic relationship between Ruth and Naomi, Boaz is assumed to be interested in Ruth partly because he agrees to marry her (Krutzsch 2015, 543–44). Even those who do not argue for a queer Boaz sometimes suggest that romantic feelings between Ruth and Boaz are read into the text. Cheryl Exum, for example, protests the tendency to "romanticize the bonds between Ruth and Boaz at the expense of the bond between Ruth and Naomi" (Exum 1996, 57). There are other hints that Boaz might not be interested in Ruth. Though he asks Ruth to lie near him, he never asks Ruth to lie *with* him. And when he finds a (possibly naked) woman lying next to him, he responds by uttering a blessing and discussing matters of business. Though Naomi tells Ruth that "he [Boaz] will tell you what to do," (3:4) it is Ruth who instructs Boaz to "spread your cloak over your servant" (3:9), another sexually charged suggestion. Even Queen-Sutherland, who assumes Boaz is attracted to Ruth, makes note of this frustrating anomaly: "The situation is maddening. Someone please scream, 'Wake up, man! This is not the time for God-talk'" (Queen-Sutherland 2016, 124). However, rather than a maddening and incongruous response, Boaz's failure to initiate sex with Ruth here is more likely an indication that he is simply not interested.

Indeed, we need not argue that Boaz is gay or even asexual in order to argue that it is possible that Boaz was not sexually attracted to Ruth. For a man, heterosexuality implies an attraction to women but does not include a desire to have sex with every woman. But even if we do assume that Boaz was interested in Ruth, it does not excuse Ruth's deliberate deception or her waiting until he was drunk to approach him.

4. Intertextual Links

The literary evidence in the chapter is enough to classify Ruth's actions as sexual assault; nevertheless, this reading is further supported by the stories that lie in the background of the narrative in the book of Ruth. Ruth's story is connected intertextually with the stories of five other biblical women: Lot's two daughters, Rachel and Leah, and Tamar. Incidentally, each of their stories contain elements of sexual violence, specifically against men.

From her introduction in the first chapter, Ruth is connected with the daughters of Lot through her characterization as a Moabite woman. When Lot's daughters rape him on successive nights, the products of these incestuous unions turn out to be the ancestors of the Moabites and the Ammonites (Gen 19:31–38). Ruth is not just a Moabite by implication; the narrator will not let us forget it. Her ethnic status is stated no less than seven times in the four chapters of the book (1:4, 22; 2:2, 6, 21; 4:5, 10). This repetition encourages the reader to see the story of Lot's daughters in the background of the present narrative.

Beyond the familial connection, as Peter Sabo (2020, 107) argues, "the seduction of Boaz on the threshing floor in Ruth 3 echoes the rape of Lot by his daughters." The theme of knowledge/deception and the presence of alcohol as a sexual stimulant are discussed above, but there are other ways in which Ruth's story is connected to the story of Lot's daughters. The threshing floor, like the cave, is a secluded yet not quite private space, and both have a slightly erotic valence (Graybill and Sabo 2018). Boaz, an older man, being approached by a younger sexually aggressive woman, recalls the age dynamics in Gen 19 (Boaz even refers to Ruth as "my daughter" in 2:8 and 3:10–11). Finally, though Naomi does not perform the act herself (at least not according to the second *qere* in 3:3, on which see below), the older woman's instructions to the younger Ruth are reminiscent of the older daughter's instructions to her younger sister. Each of these commonalities deepen the connection between these stories and encourage the reader to read them together.

In Chapter 4, Ruth is also explicitly linked with Rachel, Leah, and Tamar in the blessing given by the elders and the people at the gate:

> May the Lord make the woman who is coming into your house *like Rachel and Leah*, who together built up the house of Israel. May you produce children in Ephrathah and bestow a name in Bethlehem; and,

through the children that the Lord will give you by this young woman, may your house be like the house of Perez, *whom Tamar bore to Judah.* (Ruth 4:11-12, emphasis added)

In addition to the emphasis on Ruth's Moabite ancestry, this blessing encourages the reader to see these narratives together and strengthens the implications of sexual violence in Ruth 3.

Tamar's story, like Ruth's, is concerned with the perilous status of the widow in society and her attempts to secure her own future. After Tamar's first and second husbands (both sons of Judah) are killed, leaving her a childless widow, Judah sends her back to her father's house. Although Judah promises to send for her when his youngest son is of age, some time passes and Judah never does. Tamar takes matters into her own hands and tricks Judah into impregnating her by posing as a sex worker. Tamar's story, like Ruth's, includes a theme of knowledge and deception. Much like Ruth with Boaz, Tamar controls what Judah knows and when he knows it. Unlike in Ruth, it is entirely clear what happens between Tamar and Judah on the side of the road. The narrative is very clear that Judah "went in to her, and she conceived by him" (Gen 38:18). There can be no doubt that Tamar and Judah had sex. It is also clear that, while Judah consents to sex, he does not consent to sex with Tamar (see Fischel 2019, 94–116).

At first glance, Ruth's story might not seem connected to that of Rachel and Leah. However, like Lot's daughters, Tamar, and Ruth, Leah also gains a husband/children through deception. What sets her apart from Lot's daughters and Tamar is that Leah herself is not the mastermind behind the deception – her father Laban is. Through Laban's trickery, Jacob is deceived into sleeping with Leah instead of Rachel. Like Judah, Jacob does not consent to sleeping with the woman he ends up sleeping with.

The theme of deception and sexual violence is carried though each of these intertexts. We are explicitly encouraged to see Ruth in the role of the deceiver and, therefore, Boaz as the victim. Reading these texts together makes more explicit the sexual violence that is already hinted at in the chapter.

5. Synthesis and Conclusion

Ruth 3 is exceedingly vague about what exactly happens between Ruth and Boaz on the threshing floor. It includes euphemisms, words with double meanings, and verbs with unclear objects. None of these devices allows for clear explicit statements, but all point toward a sexual encounter. Further, we can sharpen our understanding of events when we consider conspicuous absences in and the details of Ruth and Naomi's plan. Importantly, Boaz's consent to this sexual encounter is conspicuously missing, by virtue of both his being asleep and drunk and the lack of evidence of interest after he awakes. Not only does Boaz seem uninterested when he awakes, Ruth and Naomi's plan intentionally and explicitly takes advantage of Boaz's unconscious and inebriated state.

To answer the question posed by the title of this article: the narrative, with its innuendos and ambiguities, certainly suggests that Ruth rapes, or at least sexually violates, Boaz while he sleeps on the threshing floor. Importantly, no matter how we interpret the ambiguities of the passage – even if Ruth only intends for Boaz to *think* something had happened – it is clear that Boaz does not consent to whatever Ruth is doing. As a result, we should identify Boaz as a victim of sexual assault. This assessment is also supported by the explicit intertextual links to other cases of premeditated sexual assault, specifically of women against men. Therefore, Ruth is a rapist or, at the very least, a sexual assailant.

Though Ruth is the one to commit the act, Naomi is not free of blame. As the one who instructs Ruth to catch Boaz in a vulnerable position and entrap him, she is culpable as well. In Chapter 7 in this volume, William Krisel makes a compelling argument that Naomi might have been even more culpable in an earlier version of the story. He argues there is evidence of an earlier text in which both Ruth and Naomi trick Boaz into sleeping with them on the threshing floor. With this in mind, it seems the newer version of the narrative not only makes Boaz monogamous, as Krisel emphasizes, but also reduces Naomi's involvement in his sexual assault.

Importantly, the sexual assault of Boaz is not an anomaly. The theme of sexual violence found throughout Judges is clearly carried through into Ruth, but the gendered expectations are reversed. Ruth's sexual vulnerability is emphasized in the first half of the story; nevertheless, much like her ancestors, the daughters of Lot, she defies gendered expectations by being the perpetrator of sexual violence rather than simply the victim of one. This does not mean that Ruth is not a victim. Her status as a widow and foreigner leave her with few avenues to support herself and her companion, Naomi. The line between victim and villain is not black and white. It is this nuance that makes the story interesting.

Much like Lot's daughters, Tamar, and Leah before them, Naomi and Ruth take their future into their own hands by maintaining control of knowledge and reproduction. Reading Ruth's actions on the threshing floor as sexual assault rather than romance further highlights Ruth's control of her future as well as that of her and her mother-in-law as she reduces Boaz to a means to, rather than the originator of, their deliverance. Ruth is not presented as a damsel in distress and Boaz is not her knight in shining armor. Ruth is able to secure her future and the future of her mother-in-law through her actions on the threshing floor. However, the method by which Ruth and Naomi secure their future is not a victimless crime; it violates Boaz's sexual agency and perpetuates the theme of sexual violence that runs through David's ancestry and is continued through his own reign.

Works Cited

Adelman, Rachel. 2012. "Seduction and Recognition in the Story of Judah and Tamar and the Book of Ruth." *Nashim: A Journal of Jewish Women's Studies & Gender Issues* 23: 87–109.

Basile, Kathleen C., Sharon G. Smith, Matthew J. Breiding, Michele C. Black, and Reshma Mahendra. n.d. "Sexual Violence Surveillance: Uniform Definitions and Recommended Data Elements. Version 2.0." Atlanta, GA: Centers for Disease Control and Prevention. Accessed December 27, 2023. https://stacks.cdc.gov/view/cdc/26326.

Black, James. 1991. "Ruth in the Dark: Folktale, Law and Creative Ambiguity in the Old Testament." *Literature and Theology* 5: 20–36.

Campbell, Edward F., ed. 1975. *Ruth: A New Translation with Introduction, Notes, and Commentary*. 1st ed. Anchor Bible 7. Garden City, NY: Doubleday.

Exum, J. Cheryl. 1996. *Plotted, Shot, and Painted: Cultural Representations of Biblical Women*. Journal for the Study of the Old Testament Supplements 215. Sheffield: Sheffield Academic.

Fewell, Danna Nolan, and D. M. Gunn. 1990. *Compromising Redemption: Relating Characters in the Book of Ruth*. 1st ed. Literary Currents in Biblical Interpretation. Louisville, KY: Westminster/John Knox Press.

Fisch, Harold. 1982. "Ruth and the Structure of Covenant History." *Vetus Testamentum* 32: 425–37.

Fischel, Joseph J. 2019. *Screw Consent: A Better Politics of Sexual Justice*. Oakland: University of California Press.

Frymer-Kensky, Tikva Simone. 2002. *Reading the Women of the Bible*. 1st ed. New York: Schocken Books.

Graybill, Rhiannon, and Peter J. Sabo. 2018. "Caves of the Hebrew Bible: A Speleology." *Biblical Interpretation* 26: 1–22. https://doi.org/10.1163/15685152-00261P01.

HALOT = Köhler, Ludwig, M. E. J. Richardson, Walter Baumgartner, and Johann Jakob Stamm. 1994–2000. *The Hebrew and Aramaic Lexicon of the Old Testament*. Leiden: E. J. Brill.

Heyes, Cressida J. 2016. "Dead to the World: Rape, Unconsciousness, and Social Media." *Signs: Journal of Women in Culture and Society* 41: 361–83. https://doi.org/10.1086/682964.

Jagendorf, Zvi. 1984. "'In the Morning, Behold, It Was Leah': Genesis and the Reversal of Sexual Knowledge." *Prooftexts* 4: 187–92.

Krutzsch, Brett. 2015. "Un-Straightening Boaz in Ruth Scholarship." *Biblical Interpretation* 23: 541–52. https://doi.org/10.1163/15685152-02345P04.

Linafelt, Tod, and Timothy K. Beal. 1999. *Ruth and Esther*. Edited by David W. Cotter, Jerome T. Walsh, and Chris Franke. Berit Olam. Collegeville, MN: Liturgical Press.

Matheny, Jennifer M. 2020. "Ruth in Recent Research." *Currents in Biblical Research* 19: 8–35. https://doi.org/10.1177/1476993X20930655.

Muraoka, Takamitsu. 1985. *Emphatic Words and Structures in Biblical Hebrew*. Jerusalem: Magnes.

Phillips, Anthony. 1986. "The Book of Ruth – Deception and Shame." *Journal of Jewish Studies* 37: 1–17. https://doi.org/10.18647/1245/JJS-1986.

Queen-Sutherland, Kandy. 2016. *Ruth and Esther*. Smyth & Helwys Bible Commentary. Macon, GA: Smyth & Helwys.

Sabo, Peter J. 2020. "Moabite Women, Transjordanian Women, and Incest and Exogamy: The Gendered Dimensions of Boundaries in the Hebrew Bible." *Journal for the Study of the Old Testament* 45: 93–110. https://doi.org/10.1177/0309089219862807.

Schipper, Jeremy, ed. 2016. *Ruth: A New Translation with Introduction and Commentary*. Anchor Yale Bible 7D. New Haven, CT: Yale University Press.

Shepherd, David J. 2018. "Ruth in the Days of the Judges: Women, Foreignness and Violence." *Biblical Interpretation* 26: 528–43. https://doi.org/10.1163/15685152-02645P07.

Sutskover, Talia. 2010. "The Themes of Land and Fertility in the Book of Ruth." *Journal for the Study of the Old Testament* 34: 283–94.

Wolde, Ellen van. 1997. "Texts in Dialogue with Texts: Intertextuality in the Ruth and Tamar Narratives." *Biblical Interpretation* 5: 1–28.

About the Author

Jennifer Lehmann is a lecturer in the Religious Studies department at Santa Clara University in Santa Clara, California. Her primary area of research is in gender and sexuality in the Hebrew Bible with a particular focus on men and masculinity.

CHAPTER 14
THE STORY OF RUTH ACCORDING TO PETER COMESTOR

Sara Moscone

Abstract

Peter Comestor's rewriting of Ruth in his *Scholastic History* (1160s) is original for its historical perspective and its use of Jewish sources like Flavius Josephus and rabbinical texts. Untainted by anti-Judaism and polemics, the *History* identifies the main questions arising from the story, without losing the immediacy of the narrative and the poetic nature of the tale. Some of these elements also survived in later vernacularizations and versifications of the story of Ruth, inspired by Comestor's work.

Keywords: Peter Comestor, Flavius Josephus, *Scholastic History*, twelfth century, Jewish and Christian relations

In the intellectual milieu of twelfth-century Paris, Petrus Comestor ("Peter the Eater", ca. 1100–1179) stands out for his famous biblical manual, the *Scholastic History* (ca. 1160). Comestor played a prominent role in the Renaissance of West European letters, covering both administrative and scholastic responsibilities as *magister* (teacher) of the cathedral school, as dean of St Peter in Troyes, and as chancellor of Notre Dame in Paris (Gandil 2013). The cultural development of the twelfth century paved the way for the soon-to-be European universities. The role of the *magister* became more and more important, together with the books linked to their teaching: the students chose one school or another to follow the most famous and prepared *magister* in a given field.

As these new cathedral schools began to have a more structured curriculum, aimed at preparing competent and qualified figures in a specific area, there was a new need to specialize in individual subjects. It is in this lively cultural context (on which see Southern 1999, 113–37; Mews 2019, 10–29) that the *Scholastic History* is written as a manual for biblical history, a compendium of different authorities on a specific subject.

The *History* is a biblical paraphrase and commentary in 20 books, based mainly on the Vulgate (Jerome's Latin translation of the Hebrew Bible and the New Testament) with additions and explanations from Christian, Jewish, and pagan sources (Clark 2015). The aim of this monumental work is to provide the students with a biblical manual that clarifies the historical and literal meaning of the Bible, to the exclusion of moral and allegorical exegesis.

For a long time, the *History* had a permanent place in the theological curriculum of European universities as a manual for sacred history. Its success, inside and outside academia, from the Middle Ages to Modern times, is proven by the 800 extant manuscripts, its many vernacular translations, citations, and adaptations (Sherwood-Smith 2000; Sylwan 2005, xxxi–xxxv; Clark 2013, 243–66; Delmas 2013, 267–88; Lobrichon 2013, 289–312; Salvador 2013, 313–28; Noblesse-Rocher 2013, 329–44)

1. Ruth in the History: Style and Sources

Ruth is the eighth book in the *History*, located after Judges and before 1 Samuel. It is sometimes titled *De Ruth* ("About Ruth") or *Historia Libri Ruth* ("Story of the Book of Ruth"). Dealing with biblical history, Comestor selects only the books that he thinks present historical content, leaving out most of the prophets and the poetic books.

Comestor's rewriting of the book of Ruth is about half the length of the text of the Vulgate, but it is richer in historical details. This results in a more condensed version of the story, told at a faster pace, lightened of some dialogues and repetitions compared to the original, in favor of the historiographical element. Nevertheless, unlike other biblical books he works on, Comestor chooses to maintain the theatrical element of Ruth by including some dialogues, very often quoted verbatim from the Vulgate, instead of reporting a briefer version as indirect speech.

The Parisian scholar crafts the composition as one long chapter, along the lines of the story written in the Vulgate. The modern division of the book of Ruth into four chapters is attributed to Stephen Langton, archbishop of Canterbury and Comestor's pupil. Before, Ruth was divided into different sections, depending on the manuscript. Comestor follows his own criteria to organize Ruth into self-contained scenes.

Comestor often inserts his own transitions from one scene to the other, or he provides the reader with more historical material and information to answer questions for which solutions are hard to find, even for modern readers. The main questions regard the exact time when the story takes place, who the protagonists are, what exactly is happening on the threshing floor, and how the sandal ceremony works precisely (Smith 1996, xi).

The array of sources employed by Comestor in the story of Ruth is similar to that of the other biblical books he deals with. He tends to amalgamate the plot with historical and exegetical information, without interrupting the narrative flow with interpretative questions. Instead, he offers the reader the answer directly, presenting it in a plain and apparently simple way. For this reason, he rarely cites his sources, with some remarkable exceptions. Though hidden within the text, it is possible to classify the sources of the *History* into three main traditions: Flavius Josephus, the Christian tradition, and the Jewish tradition (Karp 1978, 183–96).

Born of a Jewish priestly family and called to a high-rank military career, Flavius Josephus (37/38–105 CE) was one of the most fascinating personalities of the first century CE. A Jew by birth and a Roman by adoption, Josephus played a prominent role in the Judean War against Rome (66–70 CE). He was captured by Vespasian, to whom, according to the legend, he foretold a destiny as future Roman emperor. Siding with Titus and Vespasian himself, Josephus became protégé of the Flavian family.

During his new life in Rome, Josephus wrote important historical works, the *Jewish War* and the *Jewish Antiquities* (Mason 1999), both of which were a great success among Late Antique and Medieval Christians as sources of information about Palestine at the time of Jesus and about Jewish history and traditions (Schreckenberg 1972; Kletter 2016; Inowlocki 2016). Josephus was known also in the Latin West thanks to the fact that his work, originally written in Greek, was translated into Latin during Late Antiquity (ca. 400 CE) and thus reached Comestor's desk (for the critical edition of the Latin version of the *Jewish Antiquities*, see Blatt 1958).

The work of the Judean historian is the most important non-biblical source for Comestor's *History* (Moscone 2022, 1–19; 2023, 477–81; 2025; Clark 2023, 323–37). In fact, Comestor depends so much on Josephus that, in his retelling of Ruth, the Judean historian is the only author mentioned by name, together with Jerome. The *Jewish Antiquities* are an indispensable resource for Comestor because the work presents the history of the Jewish people against a broader background of "world history." As such, it solves many difficulties inherent to biblical narratives by reorganizing some episodes for better internal coherence, expanding the narrative to provide expository clarity, and explaining customs (Mason 1998, 67).

Comestor depends also on the long Christian tradition that preceded him, but he sticks to the litero-historical exegesis, leaving out moral and allegorical elements, due to the genre of his work. This is why, in the

History, we find no trace of the many Medieval commentaries on Ruth, such as the anonymous text from the abbey of St Victor in Paris (ca. 1160), the two commentaries by Peter of Celle, or those by Richard of Preaux and Irimbert of Preaux, all of them from the twelfth century (Barrau 2021). These works are more concerned with allegorical and Christological interpretations of the Book of Ruth than with its historical meaning, and thus are of minimal interest to Comestor.

Another source he used to draft his *History* is the so-called *Ordinary Gloss*, an edition of the Bible which was circulating during the twelfth century. Its innovative layout presents the biblical text in the middle of the page, supplemented in the margins and between the lines by commentaries excerpted from patristic authors and later scholars as well as from some non-Christian scholars like Josephus (Smith 2009; Clark 2015, 84–107).

The *Gloss on Ruth* presents a particularly interesting set of commentaries attributed to an anonymous Chaldaeus Paraphrastes ("Aramaic paraphrast"). Behind this unknown commentator are extracts from two Jewish texts: Ruth Rabbah and the Targum Ruth. Ruth Rabbah is a midrash, that is, a commentary on the book of Ruth with verse-by-verse interpretation composed in Israel around the sixth century CE, which expands the biblical story without adding new characters or supernatural elements. The Targum Ruth is the Aramaic translation and paraphrase of the Hebrew book, with exegetical elements embedded in it (Smith 1996, xvi).

This brings us to the third strand of Comestor's sources: Jewish traditions, including rabbinic interpretations and haggadic elements likely gathered from his contacts with the learned Jewish communities of Troyes and Paris (Moscone 2025, 169–174). The Haggadah ("lore") is the body of rabbinical text about folklore, historical anecdotes, moral exhortations, and more or less everything that is not Halakah, which is about the law itself. Comestor's interest in the Jewish exegesis is evident also in his treatment of the story of Ruth, as discussed below. His approach to Jewish interpretation is free from the prejudice and the controversy one would expect to find in a Medieval Christian text. But in the twelfth century we have extended proof of intellectual exchanges among Jewish and Christian communities, especially in Northern France and in Germany. Both shared a similar methodology in dealing with the literal interpretation of the biblical text, for example, by applying the philological and linguistic analysis to the sacred page (Cohen 2017, 39–86). That this interaction flowed both ways is demonstrated by the fact that Christians and Jews could communicate in Old French or even in Latin, as proven by the copies of the Talmud (a rabbinic compendium of the Pentateuch with related commentary) glossed in Old French or by the Hebrew translations of Latin texts (Liss 2011, 21–22; Fontaine and Freudenthal 2013). Hugh and Andrew of St. Victor in Paris, both colleagues of Comestor, often cite a Jewish source in their work without many reservations (see Smalley 1989, 149–72).

Not everyone agreed with the use of Jewish knowledge. A heartfelt concern appears in an anonymous commentary on Ruth, which probably belongs to the circle of St. Victor and may be written by the hand of Richard – also a contemporary of Comestor – who expressed his disagreement with citing Josephus and other Jewish texts. The anonymous author writes that "[Boaz] forbids her [Ruth] to go to another field, meaning to Judaism, to learn uneducated tales, treacherous discourses, and misleading follies" (Barrau 2021, 209–10; all the translations from Latin are my own, except where indicated). We cannot tell if this was an attack directed explicitly to Comestor, but his rewriting of Ruth is certainly rich in Jewish elements, without any trace of polemics or anti-Judaism.

As we do not have a modern edition of Comestor's treatment of Ruth, the best way to approach the text is to rely upon the two earliest manuscripts of the *History*, both of which date back to the 1180s: the Vienna manuscript (V) and the Paris manuscript (P). Both are available online (links at the end of the chapter). The text is also included in the *Patrologia Latina* (PL 198: 1293–1295), but this is a later version of the text, with errors and additions that distance it from the original. Nevertheless, it can be useful to consult, if one deals with a later reception of the *Scholastic History*.

2. A Historical Rewriting of the Book of Ruth, between Judaism and Christianity

The treatment of the book of Ruth begins in manuscript P (fol. 71 rb) with an interesting passage on the Hebrew canon that is absent in V and in PL. The text discusses the correct place of the book of Ruth inside the canon. The fact that Ruth belonged to the biblical canon was never doubted among Jews nor Christians, but the Hebrew canon places it among the Writings (see Chapter 4 in this volume). As the Talmud attributes Ruth to Samuel and the Psalms to David, who lived after Samuel, the Hebrew canon places the book of Ruth before Psalms, following chronological criteria. In the Septuagint (the Greek translation of the Old Testament) and in the Vulgate, Ruth is placed after Judges and before 1 Samuel (Smith 1996, xi). This is the sequence adopted by Comestor.

But before starting with the story of Ruth, he writes that "because the Hebrew Bible counts 22 volumes of books of the Old Testament, it does not divide this story of Ruth from the story of Judges. However, it is actually separated from the story of Judges." (P, fol. 71rb). This is a reference to a third tradition found in Josephus, *C. Apion* 1.8, where Ruth is considered a part of Judges and Lamentations a part of Jeremiah, thus counting 22 books instead of the standard 24 of the Hebrew Bible (see also Chapter 4 in this volume).

Comestor's chronological intent is evident from the very beginning. He introduces the story of Ruth by setting it in a precise time frame defined by the name of the judge of that period: "After Samson, Eli the priest, who was known not as much as a judge than as a priest from the worthier office, judged Israel. This first, among the sons of Ithamar, received the priesthood, after the priestly office was transferred [to them] from the sons of Eleazar. In his days, there was a famine in the land (Ruth 1:1)" (Paris ms, fol. 71rb-va; V, fol. 89ra, my translation).

Comestor's opening answers the first question regarding the book of Ruth: when does the story take place? It is much more precise than the general setting "in the days when the judges governed, there was a famine in the land" in Ruth 1:1, which is quoted at the end of the passage with few modifications. The historical information about the time and the genealogy of Eli the priest, who is a descendant of Ithamar, one of the sons of Aaron, stems from Josephus: from the beginning of the story of Ruth (*Ant.* 5.318), where Josephus informs us that after Samson it was Eli who led the people of Israel, and from the end of Book 5 (*Ant.* 5.361–362), where he explains the transition of the priestly office from the sons of Eleazar to the offspring of Ithamar. Eleazar and Ithamar were the sons of Aaron: only Aaron and his direct descendants could inherit the priestly office, but the role was taken by the descendant of one brother or the other in different times. At the time of Ruth, Eli was also the judge of Israel, that is the political leader before the foundation of the monarchy with Samuel, who anointed Saul king by the will of the people.

Then Comestor introduces Elimelech and his family. He notes the variations between the text of the Vulgate and that of Josephus; for example, regarding the fact that according to *Ant.* 5.319, it is Elimelech who chooses Moabite wives for his sons, while in the Vulgate they marry only after their father had already passed away. According to Josephus – as Comestor reports – Elimelech, his wife, and sons and their wives remained in the land of the Moabites for ten years. Then the three men died without heirs, and Naomi decided to go back to her homeland. Comestor neither provides an explanation for the differences between the two texts or a preference regarding which version is to be considered correct.

As he continues with the story, Comestor introduces the theme of levirate marriage to explain why Orpha chooses to go back to her people instead of following Naomi: Deut 25:7 grants to a brother-in-law the option to refuse to raise an heir for the deceased brother and have the sister-in-law perform the sandal ceremony against him.

While Orpha goes back to the Moabites, Ruth decides to stay with her mother-in-law. The dialogue staged between Naomi and Ruth is shorter than the Vulgate version but has some original elements, including Naomi's warning about her God being different from the gods of the Gentiles. Ruth's iconic answer is a direct quote from Ruth 1:16: "Your people shall be my people, and your God, my God."

When the two women arrive in Bethlehem, Comestor seizes the opportunity to explain the story behind the name of the town, which was originally called Ephrathah, from the name of Caleb's wife (1 Chr 2:19). Then he reports the haggadic interpretation, assigning it to "some" anonymous source, according to which Caleb's wife was Miriam, Moses's sister. Though there is no biblical evidence for Miriam's marriage, the Haggadah connects her with Caleb, making her his wife (ShemR 1:17). Since this information does not appear in the *Gloss* or in any other Christian text, we can assume that Comestor gathered it from his connections with the School of Rashi (Rabbi Shlomo Yitzhaqi, 1040–1105) in Troyes or with the rabbis of Paris.

The interpretation of Ephrathah as "she sees fury" – in the sense that Miriam experienced God's anger when she reproached Moses because of his Ethiopian wife (Num 12) – comes from the commentary of the Carolingian monk, Rabanus Maurus. It has no connection with the actual meaning of the Hebrew word, which is "fruitful" and is associated with Bethlehem, "the house of bread."

Perhaps influenced by Josephus, Comestor does not stage the dialogue between the two women in Ruth 2:2 but simply states that Ruth goes to Boaz's field to collect the ears of grain left behind by the harvesters with Naomi's consent (see *Ant*. 5.324). The reader is also informed that the Latin word *polenta* ("barley") is called *alphita* (which is Greek for "barley-meal") by Josephus (*Ant*. 5.326).

Another original addition to the story is the context of the feast in which Comestor sets the encounter of Ruth and Boaz in Ruth 3:6–15. What happens on the threshing floor? According to the *History*, Boaz organizes a banquet for his workers there because "it was the custom in Israel that the lord would prepare a great feast in the winnowing court for his servants and harvesters" (P, fol. 71vb; V, fol. 89va, my translation). This way the scene is connected to the feast of Shavuot, the harvest festival linked with the book of Ruth in Jewish tradition (Smith 1996, xi). He affirms that the same tradition applies to the sheep-shearing time, which is described as a kind of Spring festival (see Gen 31:19; 1 Sam 25:4-8; 2 Sam 13:23-29; 2 Kgs 3:4). Comestor adds that he has not read that a similar feast was associated with the grape harvest.

More crucial is Comestor's insistence that after the feast, Boaz abstained from women in a "quasi-religious" way, a pious commentary borrowed from Jewish texts. According to Ruth Rabbah 5:15, Boaz's "heart was merry" (Ruth 3:7) because he blessed the food or because he engaged in Torah study after the feast. Targum Ruth 3:8 praises Boaz for resisting the temptation to seduce Ruth when he sees her sleeping next to him, just like the righteous Joseph who refused to give in to the seductions of Potiphar's wife. A paraphrase of both of these texts appears in the *Ordinary Gloss* on Ruth as an addition attributed to Chaldaeus Paraphrastes ("Aramaic paraphrast"). This demonstrates that this Jewish interpretation of the story was known by twelfth-century Christians and likely by Comestor, too, as we know he made extensive use of the *Gloss*.

A further aspect of Comestor's work is his handling of the psychology of biblical characters. He likes to dive a little deeper to provide more insights into their motivations and thoughts than the biblical text. Very often the source of this psychological richness is Josephus. In fact, both Josephus and Comestor add that Boaz reassured Ruth that her chastity would be protected as he managed the situation, because Boaz knew there was a closer kinsman to Ruth who would have had priority to marry her (see *Ant.* 5.330 and P, fol. 71vb; V, fol. 89va). This is why he then told her to leave when it was still dark, so that even if someone saw her leaving, they would not be able to recognize her.

As mentioned above, the sandal ceremony is a clear allusion to Deut 25 in the book of Ruth. Contrary to other Christian commentators who are more interested in the moral aspects of the story, Comestor notes that in Ruth 4:7–8 it is the kinsman who takes off his sandal to signify that he passes his turn to another possible candidate, whereas in Deut 25:9 it is the wife of the deceased brother who removes the sandal of her unwilling brother-in-law to shame him publicly.

Comestor reverts to *Ant.* 5.335, where Josephus describes the ritual in line with Deut 25. Comestor also quotes the Gospel of John (1:27), where John the Baptist claims to be unworthy of untying the Messiah's sandal, to conclude that these texts confirm that the sandal ceremony could be performed differently according to the situation.

In concluding the story, Comestor quotes Josephus's explanation that the Hebrew name of Obed means "serving" (*Ant.* 5.336) as a transition to the Book of Samuel and the story of David from whom descends the Messiah.

3. The Book of Ruth beyond History: Poems and Vernacularizations

With the passing years, the success of the *Scholastic History* inspired many authors to produce adaptations based on Comestor's work that sometimes were addressed to a wider audience, not exclusively ecclesiastic ones. A first case is the Latin poem, "Aurora" (1200) by Pierre Riga (1140–1209), a canon from Reims based in Paris. "Aurora" is a versification of the *History*, which makes it easier to memorize, but it contains allegorical additions alien to the original (Lobrichon 2013, 292–293). The story of Ruth is rewritten as a 72-verse poem in PL 212: 24–25, with numerous Christological and allegorical interpolations that distance it from Comestor's original. A notable addition is the identification of Ruth with the Church. During the thirteenth century, "Aurora" was adapted and translated into Middle High German (1248) and into the Old French composition, *Bible de Macé*, produced in 1295 (see Lobrichon 2013, 296–297; Van der Krabben 1964). The latter poem cites "Aurora" and probably the *Scholastic History*, too. Here the story of Ruth is given more space than it gets in "Aurora" and covers some 200 verses (vv. 16,131–34).

The influence of Comestor's text may emerge from the reference to Eli's government as a time-reference for the setting of the story in verse 16,138. The sandal ceremony is interpreted allegorically as an allusion to Jesus and John the Baptist.

Towards the end of the fourteenth century, we find what is believed to be a metrical paraphrase of the Old Testament composed in Middle English around 1380 (Lobrichon 2013, 296). The so-called *Middle English Metrical Paraphrase of the Old Testament* (edited in Livingstone 2011) is, in fact, a very free translation and versification of the *Scholastic History*. The story of Ruth is developed along 191 verses (vv. 4,441–632) set between Judges and 1 Samuel. After having informed the reader that this is a story about a woman named Ruth, both beautiful and good, from whose family would descend Christ, the author offers an incipit quite similar to that of Comestor: after the death of Samson, Eli led the people of Israel (vv. 4,453–456). This specific information clearly comes from Comestor, as the Bible only gives a very vague time reference. The anonymous author of the poem seems to prefer Comestor's version (originally from Josephus's version) to the one in the Vulgate. The fact that Elimelech made the decision to marry his sons to Moabite wives and that they all lived together in the land of Moab for ten years are both citations from *Ant.* 5.318–19.

Another addition, perhaps from an unknown source, concerns Boaz's promise to Ruth to marry her to a younger man, a closer relative than him. The young man refuses Ruth, not because she is a Moabite but because he loves another woman. This romantic motif seems to be an original idea of the English author. The conclusion of the story presents the genealogy that links Ruth with David with an explanation that all of this happened because Jesus was meant to be born from both Israelites and Gentiles.

Conclusion

The adaptations prove the success of the *History* and its crucial role in introducing some Jewish traditions to a Christian non-scholastic audience. Comestor's work marks an important step for biblical studies on the path that leads to the culmination of thirteenth-century Scholasticism. His historical approach to the sacred page signals the rise of a new academic method widespread in twelfth-century France, influenced especially by the school of St. Victor in Paris. Equally relevant is Comestor's attitude toward his sources. We do not find reverential citations of past authors any more. Instead, there is an active and critical confrontation with them. The inclusion of Josephus and of rabbinical sources in the *History*, particularly evident in the story of Ruth, is a sign of the interaction between scholars of Christian and Jewish communities, an interaction that did not result in violence but in an exchange of opinions in the form of intellectual debate. This Jewish and Christian interaction in the Parisian milieu is even more relevant, if one considers that about sixty years after Comestor's death, precisely in Paris, copies of the Talmud were burned in Place de Grève in 1241 by order of King Louis IX.

Works Cited

Barrau, Julie. 2021. "Ruth in the Twelfth Century: The Multiple Identities of a Foreign Converted Widow from Scripture." Pages 203–26 in *Lives, Identities and Histories in the Central Middle Ages*. Edited by J. Barrau and David Bates. Cambridge: Cambridge University Press.

Blatt, Franz. 1958. *The Latin Josephus. Introduction and Text. The Antiquities: books I-V.* Aarhus: Universitetsforlaget.

Clark, Mark J. 2013. "Le cours d'Étienne Langton sur l'Histoire scolastique de Pierre le Mangeur: le fruit d'une tradition unifiée." Pages 243–66 in *Pierre le Mangeur ou Pierre de Troyes - maître du XIIe siècle*. Edited by Gilbert Dahan. Turnhout: Brepols.

------. 2015. *The Making of the Historia Scholastica, 1150-1200*. Mediaeval Law and Theology 7. Toronto: Pontifical Institute of Mediaeval Studies.

-----. 2023. "Peter Comestor: The Christian Josephus." Pages 323–37 in *"Abscondi eloquium tuum in corde meum". Mélanges en l'honneur de Gilbert Dahan*. Edited by Annie Noblesse-Rocher. Paris: Brépols.
Cohen, Mordechai Z. 2017. "A New Perspective on Rashi of Troyes in Light of Bruno the Carthusian: Exploring Jewish and Christian Bible Interpretation in Eleventh-Century Northern France." *Viator* 48: 39–86.
Delmas, Sophie. 2013. "La réception de l'Historia Scholastica chez quelques maîtres en théologie du XIII siècle." Pages 267–89 in *Pierre le Mangeur ou Pierre de Troyes – maître du XIIe siècle*. Edited by Gilbert Dahan. Turnhout: Brepols.
Fontaine, Resianne and Gad Freundenthal. 2013. *Latin-into-Hebrew: Texts and Studies*. Leiden: Brill.
Gandil, Pierre. 2013. "Pierre le Mangeur, doyen du chapitre cathédral de Troyes." Pages 17–25 in *Pierre le Mangeur ou Pierre de Troyes – maître du XIIe siècle*. Edited by Gilbert Dahan. Turnhout: Brepols.
Inowlocki, Sabrina. 2016. "Josephus and Patristic Literature." Pages 356–67 in *A Companion to Josephus*. Edited by Honora H. Chapman and Zuleika Rodgers. Malden, MA: Wiley Blackwell.
Karp, Sandra R. 1978. *Peter Comestor's Historia Scholastica a Study in the Development of Literal Scriptural Exegesis*. PhD Dissertation, Tulane University.
Kletter, Karen M. 2016. "The Christian Reception of Josephus in Late Antiquity and the Middle Ages." Pages 368–81 in *A Companion to Josephus*. Edited by Honora H. Chapman and Zuleika Rodgers. Malden, MA: Wiley-Blackwell.
Van der Krabben, Henry-C.-M. (editor). 1964. *La Bible de Macé de la Charité, volume 4, Ruth, Judith, Tobie, Esther, Daniel, Job*. Leiden: Brill.
Liss, Hanna. 2011. *Creating Fictional Worlds: Peshaṭ-Exegesis and Narrativity in Rashbam's Commentary on the Torah*. Leiden: Brill.
Livingstone, Michael (editor). 2011. *The Middle English Metrical Paraphrase of the Old Testament*. Kalamazoo, MI: Medieval Institute.
Lobrichon, G. 2013. "Le Mangeur au festin. L'*Historia scholastica* aux mains de ses lecteurs: Glose, Bible en images, Bibles historiales (fin xiiie-xive siècle)." Pages 289–312 in *Pierre le Mangeur ou Pierre de Troyes – maître du XIIe siècle*. Edited by Gilbert Dahan. Turnhout: Brepols.
Mason, Steve. 1998. "Should Any Wish to Enquire Further' (Ant. 1.25): The Aim and Audience of Josephus's Judean Antiquities/Life. Pages 60–100 in *Understanding Josephus: Seven Perspectives*. Edited by Steve Mason. Sheffield: Sheffield Academic.
-----. editor. 1999. *Flavius Josephus: Translation and Commentary*. Leiden: Brill.
Mews, Constant J. 2019. "The Schools and Intellectual Renewal in the Twelfth Century: A Social Approach." Pages 10–29 in *A Companion to Twelfth-Century Schools*. Edited by Cédric Giraud. Leiden: Brill.

Moscone, Sara. 2022. "Peter Comestor's *Historia Scholastica*: Pursuing the *veritas historiae* Through the Works of Josephus." *Judaica*: Neue digitale Folge 3: 1–19 https://doi.org/10.36950/jndf.2022.19.

———. 2023. "*Magis Iosephi sententiam sequimur*: The Compass of Comestor's Journey Through the *Historia*." Pages 477–81 in *IX Ciclo di Studi Medievali: Atti del Convegno 6–7 giugno 2023 Firenze*. Edited by NUME – Gruppo di Ricerca sul Medioevo Latino. Vibo Valentia: Libritalia.

———. 2025. *Pro Veritate Historiae. Flavio Giuseppe e le Fonti Ebraiche nell'Historia Scholastica di Pietro Comestore*. Basel: Schwabe.

Noblesse-Rocher, Annie. 2013. "Quelques observations sur la réception de l'Historia scholastica à l'époque moderne." Pages 329–34 in *Pierre le Mangeur ou Pierre de Troyes – maître du XIIe siècle*. Edited by Gilbert Dahan. Turnhout: Brepols.

Salvador, Xavier-Laurent. 2013. "Guyart des Moulins, traducteur de Pierre Comestor." Pages 313–28 in *Pierre le Mangeur ou Pierre de Troyes – maître du XIIe siècle*. Edited by Gilbert Dahan. Turnhout: Brepols.

Schreckenberg, Heinz. 1972. *Die Flavius-Josephus-Tradition in Antike und Mittelalter*. Leiden: Brill.

Sherwood-Smith, Maria. 2000. *Studies in the Reception of the 'Historia Scholastica' of Peter Comestor. The 'Schwalzwälder Predigten', the 'Weltchronik' of Rudolf von Ems, the 'Scolastica' of Jacob van Maerlant and the 'Historiebijbel van 1360'*. Oxford: Oxford University Press.

Smalley, Beryl. 1989. *The Study of the Bible in the Middle Ages*. Notre Dame, IN: Notre Dame University Press (3rd reprint).

Smith, Lesley M. 1996. *Medieval Exegesis in Translations. Commentaries on the Book of Ruth*. Kalamazoo, MI: Medieval Institute.

———. 2009. *The Glossa Ordinaria: The Making of a Medieval Bible Commentary*. Leiden: Brill.

Southern, Richard. W. 1999. "The School of Paris and the School of Chartres." Pages 113–37 in *Renaissance and Renewal in the Twelfth Century*. Edited by Robert L. Benson, Giles Constable and Carol D. Lanham. Toronto: Toronto University Press, 1982 (reprint Cambridge 1999).

Sylwan, Agneta. 2005. *Petri Comestori Scolastica Historia. Liber Genesis*. Turnhout: Brepols.

Manuscripts Cited

P = Paris, Bibliothèque nationale de France, lat. 16943 https://gallica.bnf.fr/ark:/12148/btv1b10543247v/f1.item.r=16943

PL = Patologia Latina. 1855. Edited by Jean-Paul Migne. Volume 1998. Paris https://books.google.ch/books?id=H_UQAAAAYAAJ&printsec=frontcover&hl=fr&source=gbs_ge_summary_r&cad=0#v=onepage&q&f=false

V = Vienna, Österreichische Nationalbibliothek, lat. 363 https://digital.onb.ac.at/RepViewer/viewer.faces?doc=DTL_4587063

About the Author

Sara Moscone earned a PhD from the University of Berne with a dissertation on the role of Flavius Josephus and rabbinical sources in Peter Comestor's *Historia Scholastica*. She is now working on the biblical figure of Samuel in Judeo-Hellenistic texts as a revealing example of interconnections and demarcations in Jewish and Christian imagery. Her dissertation thesis "*Pro veritate historiae*: Flavio Giuseppe e le fonti ebraiche nell'*Historia Scholastica* di Pietro Comestore" was published with Schwabe Verlag in 2024.

Author Index

Adams, S.L.   41, 70, 74, 76, 127
Adelman, R.   283
Ahmed, S.   109, 112, 113, 122, 163–168, 183, 233
Allen, J.S.   54
Alpert, R.   108, 113, 163
Alter, R.   90, 210, 255
Amit, Y.   212
Anderson, M.R.   167
Ansberry, C.B.   193, 194
Arthur, J.   166
Aschkenasy, N.   118
Auld, G.   104

Baden, J.S.   255
Bailey, R.C.   165
Baillet, M.,   20
Barker, A.J.   167
Barrau, J.   294, 295
Basile, G.J.   201
Basile, K.C.   280
Battell Lowman, E.   167
Bauman, Z.   168
Bay, C.   51
Beal, T.K.   278, 284
Beattie, D.   5, 45, 50, 74–76
Begg, C.   34, 51, 65
Behrendt, L.   166, 168, 180–182
Bell, A.   166, 167, 181
Benjamin, D.C.   44
Berlant, L.   109, 114, 115, 122
Berlin, A.   52, 246, 254, 255, 261, 268
Bertram, G.   15
Bess, M.   247
Black, F.   121
Black, J.   118, 283
Black, M.C.   280
Blatt, F.   293
Bledstein, A.J.   169
Block, D.I.   126, 127, 129, 142, 163, 170, 172, 176, 179

Bonano, B.   4, 6
Bons, E.   6, 17, 25, 27
Borgatti, S.P.   255
Boyarin, D.   232
Brady, C.M.M.   261
Braulik, G.   73, 127
Brenner, A.   32, 48, 109, 116, 170, 176, 180
Brett, M.   129, 167
Brigg, M.   173
Brintnall, K.L.   116
Broughton, G.   173
Brubaker, R.   134
Brueggemann, W.   130
Bush, F.W.   74, 142, 163, 164, 170, 172, 177, 216

Camp. C.V.   196
Campbell, E.F.   50, 69, 72, 74, 75, 87–90, 142, 170, 175, 176, 179, 195, 277
Caspi, M.   163, 169
Chandra, K.   133, 134
Chapman, C.R.   41, 170, 198
Christensen, D.   128
Christina, G.   118
Clark, M.J.   292–294
Coakley, J.   134
Cohen, M.Z.   294
Collins, J.J.   68
Collins, S.   218
Conczorowski, B.   131
Cottrill, A.   116, 121, 122, 170, 171
Craigie, P.   130
Crenshaw, J.L.   196
Csárdi, G.   259
Curthoys, A.   167
Czachesz, I.   255

Dahood, M.   198
Daniel-Hughes, C.   118
Davies, E.W.   76

De Pury, A.   85, 87
De Villiers, G.   55, 64, 65, 69, 132
de Waard, J.   1, 8, 12, 14, 23
Dekker, A.H.   255–257, 259, 260, 269, 270
Dekker, J.T.   255–257, 259, 260, 269, 270
Dell, K.J.   193, 195
Delmas, S.   292
Dempster, S.   88
Dijk-Hemmes, F. van   163, 169
Donaldson, L.E.   111, 119, 167, 180
Dube, M.W.   180, 218
Duncan, C.M.   76, 108, 114, 117, 120

Embry, B.   34, 71, 72
Eskenazi, T.C.   126, 129, 135, 163, 243–245
Exum, J.C.   285

Farmer, K.A.R.   232, 245
Faust, K.   255
Fensham, F.C.   131
Fentress-Williams, J.   126, 127
Fewell, D.N.   50, 52, 67, 74, 75, 109, 176, 199, 210, 232, 246, 282, 285
Fisch, H.
Fischel, J.J.   287
Fischer, I.   50, 74, 112, 163, 195, 243, 244
Fontaine, R.   295
Foucault, M.   234–238, 245, 247, 248
Fox, M.V.   201
Freeman, L.C.   260
Fresch, C.J.   20
Frymer-Kensky, T.   52, 74, 126, 129, 135, 163, 243, 244–246, 275, 278
Fuchs, E.   232
Fuerst, W.J.   254

Gallagher, E.L.   101
Gamoran, H.   48
Gandil, P.   291
Gerleman, G.   127
Gil-White, F.J.   115, 134
Glover, N.   127, 215
Gordis, R.   8, 39, 68
Goethe, J.W. von   112
Goh, E.W.F.   111, 195
Goh, S.T.S.   195
Goswell, G.   195, 256, 265, 179
Gow, M.D.   210
Grant, S.   181
Gray, J.   142
Graybill, R.   48, 73, 108, 110, 112–114, 167, 177, 178, 183, 220, 224, 226, 286

Green, B.   52, 75
Greifenhagen, F.V.   232
Griffin, L.   167
Gros, F.   234–238, 247–248
Grossman, J.   216, 217
Guillaume, P.   34, 35, 37, 41, 48, 68, 70, 72
Gunn, D.M.   50, 52, 67, 74, 75, 109, 176, 199, 210, 232, 246, 282, 285

Haddad, B.   48, 56
Hage, P.   256
Halberstam, J.   109, 117–119, 122
Halton, C.   111, 118
Hamlin, E.J.   195
Harary, F.   256
Haug, J.   232, 240, 245
Havea, J.   110, 164, 170
Havrelock, R.   163, 167, 169, 211, 212
Hawk, L.D.   126–129, 167, 210, 214–219
Healy, C.   181
Herman, J.L.   219
Heyes, C.J.   281
Honig, B.   180
Hu, M.   255, 262
Hubbard, R.L.   31, 40, 45, 46, 50, 70, 74, 76, 78, 172, 179, 195, 256, 265
Hunger, H.   37

Inowlocki, S.   293
Irwin, B.P.   156, 157

Jackson, B.S.   33, 39
Jagendorf, Z.   283
Jobling, D.   211
Jockers, M.L.   262
Jones, E.A.   52, 96, 152
Joüon, P.   26, 154

Kalla, G.   43
Kallutveettil, P.   246, 247
Kaminsky, J.S.   57, 239–241
Kaniel, R.K.-I.   210, 215
Karp, S.R.   293
Keefe, A.A.   223
Kinnane, S.   168, 178, 179
Klein, L.   198
Kletter, K.M.   293
Köhlmoos, M.   127, 132
Koosed, J.L.   69, 121, 163, 178, 210, 216, 217
Kostic, M.V.   259
Kostic, S.M.   259
Kotrosits, M.   121–123

Kowal, E. 173
Kwok, P.-L. 164
Kratz, R.G. 85, 87
Krisel, W. 89, 93, 100, 288
Kristeva, J. 208, 226
Krutzch, B. 49, 59, 285
Kurke, L. 201
Kynes, W. 191, 192

Lacocque, A. 50, 69, 74
Laffey, A.L. 52, 77
Landy, F. 217, 220, 221, 224, 226
Langlois, M. 4
Langton, M. 181, 292
Latora, V. 259
Lau, P.H.W. 38, 42, 74, 76, 77, 170, 179
Leane, J. 173, 181
Lee, E.P. 215, 232, 245
Lee, S. 5, 8
Legaspi, M.C. 201
Leggett, D.A. 268
Leonard Fleckman, M. 52, 77
Levin, C. 47
Levine, A.-J. 243, 249
Levine, B.A. 64, 74
Levine, E. 5, 12, 15, 27
Liew, T.-S. B. 165
Lightstone, J.N. 100
Lim, C.M.S. 164, 176
Lim, T.H. 101
Linafelt, T. 87–90, 104, 122, 127, 142, 163, 170, 278, 284
Lindsay, R. 177
Lindström, F. 56, 70
Lipiński, E. 72
Liss, H. 295
Liu, B. 255, 262
Livingstone, M. 299
Lobrichon, G. 292, 299
Lohfink, N. 200
Lorde, A. 233
Love, H. 110

Marchiori, M. 259
Martin, R.P. 201
Masenya, M.J. 108, 109
Mason, S. 293
Massey, S.E. 255
Matheny, J.M. 169, 191, 195, 211, 224, 274
Matthews, V.H. 98, 126, 127, 142, 210
Maxwell, A. 134
McClure, J.M. 255
McCreesh, T.P. 195

McKane, W. 75
McKenna, M. 182
McNay, L. 238
Meade, J.D. 101
Mews, C.J. 292
Meyers, C. 169
Milgrom, J. 131, 213, 247
Millar, S.R. 193
Miller, R.J. 167
Minniecon, R. 173
Mitchell, M.M. 52
Moretti, F. 255
Moreton-Robinson, A. 166
Morocho, M. 127, 128
Morgan, T. 201
Morselli, C. 256
Moscone, S. 293, 294
Moyo, F.L. 56, 109, 116, 178
Müller, H.-P. 194
Müller, R. 85, 87
Muraoka, T. 26, 278
Murphy, L. 173
Muscarella, O.W. 3
Myers, J.M. 154

Najman, H. 68, 192
Nepusz, T. 259
Niditch, S. 46, 142, 213
Nielsen, K. 50, 74, 80, 210
Nightingale, A.W. 201
Noblesse-Rocher, A. 292
Nu, R. 38
Nugent, M. 182

Olyan, S.M. 170, 174
Ostriker, A.S. 169, 170

Pardes, I. 212, 218, 223
Pascoe, B. 166
Pattel-Gray, A. 167
Paulson, G. 167
Perdue, L.G. 193
Phillips, A. 285
Pitkänen, P. 167, 169
Porten, B. 37
Potgieter, R. 172
Powell, S.D. 108, 163
Prentis, B. 166
Preser, R. 110
Purcell, R.A. 80, 198

Quast, U. 6
Queen-Sutherland, K. 195, 275, 285

Quick, L. 190, 191, 197–199

R Core Team 259
Rahlfs, A. 5
Rauber, D.F. 245
Rebera, B.A. 264
Rees, A. 33, 116
Renger, J. 43
Rifkin, M. 166, 168
Rollston, C. 129
Römer, T. 85, 87
Rosenberg, G. 115
Rossi, B. 226
Routledge, B. 211
Rowley, H.H. 50, 74
Ruberg, J. 109, 119–122
Rudolph, W. 50
Rutledge, D. 249
Rydberg-Cox, J. 255

Sabo, P. 210, 212, 220
Said, E.W. 168
Sakenfeld, K.D. 110, 163, 177, 195, 232
Salvador, X.L. 292
Sasson, J.M. 33, 39, 45, 48, 50, 67, 74, 142, 157, 159, 220, 221, 232, 244
Saxegaard, K.M. 46, 175, 256, 261, 266
Scheidel, W. 44
Schipper, J. 50, 73, 74, 77, 78, 128, 176, 210, 242, 244, 247, 278, 279
Schmid, H.H. 193
Schøyen, M. 3
Schreckenberg, H. 293
Scott, R.B. 193
Segovia, F.F. 165
Shemesh, Y. 108
Shepherd, D.J. 170, 171, 274
Sherwood-Smith, M. 292
Shields, J.M. 237, 245, 247
Silverstein, B. 182
Simic, M.I. 259
Sinnott, A.M. 44
Smalley, B. 295
Smith, L.M. 294, 295, 297
Smith, M.S. 242
Sneed, M. 191
Sonnet, J.-P. 43, 217
Southern, R.W. 292
Southwood, K. 129, 180
Sparrow, M.K. 256
Stavrakopoulou, F. 226
Steinberg, N.A. 91

Steinmetz, D. 79
Sternberg, M. 43
Stol, M. 44
Stone, K. 245, 247
Stone, T.J. 87, 89, 90
Strakosch, E. 173
Sutskover, T. 276
Sylwan, A. 292

Talmon, S. 194
Taute, H. 172
Thambyrajah, J. 133, 180, 215
Thomas Barnett, W. 35
Tong, S.-L. 48
Tooman, W.A. 195, 215–217
Torleif, E. 3, 4
Trible, P. 107, 108, 120, 170, 179

Van der Krabben, H.C.M. 299
Van Leeuwen, R.C. 196
Vayntrub, J. 196
Veracini, L. 166
Von Rad, G. 193, 194
Vriezen, T.C. 50, 74

Wagner, S. 196
Warrior, R.A. 167
Wasserman, S. 255
Watego, C. 168, 171–174
Weeks, S. 191
West, G.O. 48, 56
West, M. 108, 117, 163
Westwood, S. 173
White, D.R. 255
White Crawford, S. 4
Williams, J.J. 237
Williams, M.S. 182
Wink, W. 239
Wojcik, J. 69, 127
Wolde, E.J. van 177, 278
Wolfe, P. 166, 167
Woudhuizen, F.C. 37
Wright, J. 197

Yardeni, A. 37
Yee, G. 48, 108, 109, 111, 116, 119, 180

Zakovitch, Y. 195, 216, 218
Zenger, E. 195, 234
Zevit, Z. 42
Ziegler, Y. 88, 142
Zornberg, A.G. 224–226

Biblical Index

Genesis
1   112–113
2:24   65
7:7   11
7:13   11
11:31   97
12:1–4   180, 226
13:9–14   210, 214
16   40
17:1   15
19   118, 283
19:14   210
19:18   87, 210
19:30–38   169, 209, 210, 212, 215, 220, 282, 286
23   43
26:1   11
27:32–33   142
28:1–5   135
28:9 216
29   118, 283
29:15–30   282
29:23   96
29:25   284
30:4   96
30:43   18
31:11–30   79, 217
31:19   297
35:11   15
35:18   223
37–50   194
37   112, 118
38   65, 97, 170, 215, 283
38:2   96, 135
38:18   96, 287
38:24   177
38:26   222
42:28   284
43:4   15
48:3   15
48:5   134

49:25   15
50:10   221

Exodus
3:22   54
6:3   15
6:19   216
18:1–4   134
18:27   134
19:16   284
21:6   49
24:18   12
28:1   135
34:28   12

Leviticus
18   278, 279
19   70
20   278
20:11   158, 279
23   70
25   41, 70
25:23   37
25:36   47

Numbers
12   298
13:25–33   212
21:13   211
22–24   209, 210
22:1–4   170
24:5   226
25   73
25:1–5   209, 210, 212–215
26:20   153
27   51, 71–72
27:1   216
27:3   72
31:8   226
32:34   211
36   51, 71–72

310 Ruth

36:11 216

Deuteronomy
2:9–19 210–212
3:11 212
7:1–6 126, 127, 129–133, 136
14:28 71
14:29 32, 71
15:16 49
19:14 36
22:19–29 17
22:30 278
23 128–129
23:19(22:30) 279
23:2–9 15, 135, 209, 210
23:4[(3) 22, 73, 98, 126, 135–136, 224
23:7 226
23:20 47
24:17–21 71
24:19 70
25:5–10 68–70, 74, 78, 94, 220
25:7 51, 145–146, 296
25:9 65, 298
27:20 158, 278, 279

Joshua
13:24–25 211
24:9–10 212

Judges
3:12–30 170, 209, 213
3:24–26 158, 213
4:21 283
6:37–40 221
11:18 211
11:33 211
12:9 10
13–16 85
13:2 86
13:5 86
15:20 86
16:1 96
17–18 87, 217
17:4–12 11, 12
18:1 11
18:20 281
18:30 134
19–21 86–94
19:1–30 169
19:1 10, 11, 89
19:6 281
19:23 87
21:1 99

21:6–7 96–97, 99, 169
21:12–17 93–95, 97
21:19–21 90, 169
21:22–23 87, 89, 170
21:25 10, 100

Ruth
1:1–6 110
1:1 6, 10, 11, 100, 132, 168, 180, 274, 296
1:2 5–7, 12
1:3–4 12, 39, 87, 89, 110, 133, 170, 266
1:4 286
1:5 6, 12
1:6 214, 262, 276
1:8–22 198
1:8 9, 13, 113, 115, 169, 199, 244
1:9 5, 6, 8, 13, 14, 32, 262
1:11 32, 113, 115, 276
1:12 5, 7, 14, 69
1:13 87, 168, 172, 198
1:14 4, 6, 7, 14, 48
1:15 5, 15, 113
1:16–18 13, 15, 33, 91, 111, 113, 173, 175
1:16–17 241–244, 297
1:17 49, 79
1:18, 15, 115
1:19–21 33, 71, 116, 172, 173, 266
1:20–22 7, 11, 15, 26, 33, 111, 168
1:20 115
1:21 255, 264, 268
1:22 39, 97, 133, 248, 286
2:1 4, 9, 15, 16, 27, 34, 40, 46, 146, 258, 275, 277, 282
2:2–3:18 7, 15, 16, 92, 133
2:2–17 168
2:2 175, 248, 277, 286, 297
2:4 19, 264, 267
2:5–8 7, 15, 17, 18
2:5 49
2:6 71, 176, 286
2:7 179, 257
2:8 273, 286
2:9 170, 171, 261
2:10 197, 215, 267
2:11 49, 282
2:12 13, 264
2:13 7, 18, 49
2:14 4, 6, 7, 261
2:16 7, 19, 176
2:18 6
2:19 6
2:20–23 4, 6, 7, 17–20, 97, 171, 226

Biblical Index

2:20 33–34, 37, 38, 244, 264
2:21 248, 286
2:22 248
2:23 4, 5, 20
3 243–244, 267–268
3:1–15 141–145
3:1 49, 75, 176
3:2 16, 17, 18, 75
3:3 6, 7, 9, 14, 20–22, 27, 54, 153–154, 198, 278, 281, 282
3:4–14 153, 157–158, 282
3:4–5 9, 20, 23, 26, 175, 275
3:4 279, 281, 283, 285
3:6–16 297
3:7 4, 6, 7, 22, 275, 277, 279, 281, 283
3:8 277, 278, 284
3:9–12 33, 37, 45, 111, 277, 279
3:9 49, 248, 284
3:10 13, 16, 40, 49, 285, 286
3:11 7, 8, 22, 46, 79, 195, 225, 277
3:12 9, 19, 23, 38, 43, 74, 75, 145, 175
3:13 179, 244, 268
3:14 5, 6, 8, 9, 23
3:15 6, 23, 27
3:16 5, 16, 144
3:17 9, 23
3:18 16, 261, 277
4:1–12 26, 147, 180, 222
4:1 24, 37
4:3–16 33
4:3 7, 24, 33, 37, 39, 68, 70
4:4–10 39
4:4 7, 9, 24, 38, 282
4:5 9, 25, 32, 41–43, 50–52, 54, 66–68, 74, 77, 156, 248, 265
4:6 9, 37, 40, 42, 76
4:7–8 7, 8, 25, 37, 65, 68, 69, 298
4:9 40, 78, 218, 249, 268
4:10 22, 78, 92, 98, 133, 248, 265, 286
4:11–15 148–152, 180, 197
4:11 7, 13, 25, 41, 133, 144, 198, 199, 218, 265
4:12 13, 17, 25, 65, 95, 97, 98, 215, 249, 287
4:13 96, 111, 114, 175, 248, 249, 268
4:14–17 255
4:14 13, 41, 198, 265, 266, 268
4:15 49, 90, 97, 179, 225
4:16–22 152–153
4:16 41, 175
4:17 118, 128, 173, 199, 268, 270
4:18–22 88, 153, 179, 256
4:21–22 92, 128, 153

1 Samuel
1–7 85, 86, 90–93, 95–99
1:1 217
1:3–6 90, 95
1:8 90
1:11 86, 95
1:19 86, 96
1:22 95
2:18–21 96
2:20 95, 98
2:31 97
2:34 97
4:11 97
4:18–22 97
4:19 97
7:15 86
22:3–4 170, 210
24:3 158
24:4 283
25:4 297
28:5 284

2 Samuel
1:17–27 192
2:6 133 3:3 134
3:8 147
5:13–8:18 88
6:6 221
8:2 170
11:13 282
12:24 96
13:16 87
13:23–29 297
13:28 281, 282
24:16–25 221

1 Kings
1:1–4 17
1:49 284
8:66 281
11:1–8 127, 130–131
11:1–2 210, 213
14:21 135, 220
22 221

2 Kings
3:4–27 210, 212
3:4 297
3:7 242
3:13 87
4:16 87
5:20 23
10:11 16, 146

18:27 158

1 Chronicles
2:3–4 97, 153
2:19 297
4:22 210
11–20 104
23:14 134

2 Chronicles
18:3 242

Ezra
9–10 91, 131–132
9:1–2 73, 127, 210, 213
10 73, 98

Nehemiah
10:28–30 132
13 91
13:1–3 132, 210, 212, 213
13:23 73
13:25 93, 98, 99

Esther 103
1:10 281
2:17 277

Job 103
1:21 193
2:10 193
18:5 193
19:14 146
19:16 16
27:1 193
28:12 192
29:1 193

Psalms
31:12 16, 146
55:14 16, 146
68(67):15 15
88:9–19 16, 146
90(91) 15
109:13 94

Proverbs
1:1–7 192
1:32–33 193
4:3–4 196
5:3–6 198
5:15–19 196
6:20 196
7:1 196
7:4 16, 146–147
7:16–17 198
9:1 196
12:4 195
14:1 196
15:15 281
22:28 36
23:10 36
31 89
31:10–31 195, 197, 198

Qohelet/Ecclesiaste
1:12–13 192
7:1–12 193

Song of Songs 100
8:6 226

Isaiah
6:2 158
7:20 158
10:29 284
15–16 211
15:2 211
19:16 284
25:10–11 213
32:11 284

Jeremiah
2–46 156
2:33 154
3:4–5 154
4:19 154
22:23 154
31:21 154
32 53
46:11 154
48:18 211
51:13 154
51:14 23

Lamentations 100–103, 296

Ezekiel
1:24 15
10:5 15
16:13–51 154, 156
16:37 279
22:10 279
23:10–18 279
26:16 284
32:10 284

Daniel 103
1–6 194

Hosea 103
5:10 36
9:1 177, 220, 277, 279

Amos
3:6 284

Micah
6:5 212

Nahum
3:5

Malachi 100

Habakkuk
2:15 282

Sirach
48:20 102
49:7–9 102

Matthew
1:5 171
9:22 17

Mark
5:34 17

John
1:27 298

Rabbinic sources
Bava Batra 100–104, 224
Ruth Rabbah x, 27, 275, 294, 298

Targum Ruth 3:8 298

Haggada
ShemR 1:17 297

Talmud 295
m. Bik. 1:4–5 135
m. Qidd. 3:12–13 135
m. Yeb. 7:5 135

Dead Sea scrolls
2Q16Rutha 3–6, 20, 22
2Q17Ruthb 3–6, 23
4Q104Rutha 3–6, 10, 12, 13, 14
4Q105Ruthb 3–6, 14

Josephus
Ant. 293
5.318 296, 299
5.319 296
5.324 34, 297
5.326 297
5.329 27
5.333 34, 51, 65
5.335 298
5.336 298
5.361–362 296
5.9.3 275
Ag. Ap. 296

Ugarit
PRU IV 37

Assyria
SAA 8 37
SAA 13 37

Patristic sources
Eusebius
Ecclesiastical History 100
Jerome
Prologue Galeatus 101
Theodoret
Questiones in Ruth 52

Subject Index

Abigail 91
Abimelech 4, 7, 11, 24
acquaintance 9, 15–16, 24, 37–40, 146–147
antiquity trafficking 3
Aurora 299

barley 24, 36, 43, 53, 92, 220, 267, 275, 297
Bathsheba 91, 282
binary
  logic 168, 181, 240
  figures 198
  ethics 200, 203
bride price *see* dowry
brother
  associate 34, 37, 38, 47, 56, 147, 266
  sibling 143, 217, 296
  deceased 297, 298
  kinsman 16, 33, 73
  levir 46, 51, 65, 68, 69, 94, 146, 197, 220

chastity 298
consent 178, 276, 280–284, 287, 288, 297
crook 46

daughter
  father's 44, 93, 98, 178, 209–216
  -in-law 49, 90–97, 108, 109, 142–150, 165, 170–179, 197, 215, 217, 225, 244, 248, 275
  Lot's 209–215, 222
  mother's 33
  "my" 7, 16, 17 143, 144, 151, 220, 286
dowry 44, 52, 58, 79

Eleazar 296
Eli 296, 299
Elkanah 86, 90, 95, 96, 217

ethnicity 109, 127–129, 133–139, 180
euphemism 14, 143, 144, 158, 223, 245, 275–278, 281, 284, 287

feeling/s 2, 107–110, 120, 121, 183, 216, 226, 280, 285
fertility 32, 41, 45, 56, 71, 213, 217, 223, 276, 277

Hagar 25, 26, 40, 174, 217
Hannah 86, 90, 95–98
happy end 18, 43, 92, 94, 108–110, 141, 151, 160, 191, 225, 250

idyll/ic 46, 112–114, 122, 140, 160–165, 171, 183
incest 219
infertile 86, 90, 95–98, 152
Ithamar 296

Jerome (Bible translator) 71, 80, 84, 100–103, 293

ketiv-qere 2–27, 24, 31, 41, 50–58, 66–68, 74–77, 141–147, 153–159, 277, 286

land tenure 35–37
lectio difficilior 12, 26
levirate 19, 51, 68–70, 76–78, 92–94, 145–146, 197–199, 224, 244, 247, 296

midrash 8
mise-en-abîme 209–214

Potiphar 298

queer 108–122, 285

Rabanus Maurus, monk 297
Rashi, Shlomo Yitzhaqi, rabbbi 21, 155, 297

redeem/er
  Boaz   9, 10, 17, 45, 74, 75, 143, 147, 159, 220, 256
  other   34, 38, 65–75, 170, 258–262, 268, 270
  heir   7, 243
  husband   247
  must take Ruth   65, 267
  Obed   41, 149–153
  per Leviticus   145–159
Riga, Pierre   299

Samson   85–87, 99, 217, 296, 299
care
  and exploitation   179
  fatherly   170
  -less   111, 174, 175
  reciprocal   178
  self   231–244, 247–249
  survival   245
  widow-   67
self-indenture   49, 55
self-sacrifice   237–238
Shaddai   7, 15, 26
Shavuot   163, 220, 226, 297
silver   24, 47, 79

sterile   *see*, fertility
sugar-daddy   48, 56
swapping
  asset   39
  wife   54

terra nullius   166–167
trick
  bed-   26, 118, 283, 288
  reading-   78
  redeemer-   46, 52, 57–58, 76, 78
  trickster   22, 26, 46, 54, 58, 80, 143

usufruct   37–45, 51–52, 55, 58, 71, 75, 77, 147

violence
  and charm   168
  and integration, 183
  erased   171, 172, 174
  in Judges   121, 224
  in Ruth   163, 170
  sexual   116, 274, 276–282, 286–288
Vulgate   5, 51, 292, 295–299

Zelophehad   51, 71–72, 216

www.ingramcontent.com/pod-product-compliance
Lightning Source LLC
Chambersburg PA
CBHW050335230426
43663CB00010B/1868